LANDMARK ESSAYS IN
MISSION AND WORLD CHRISTIANITY

The American Society of Missiology Series, published in collaboration with Orbis Books, seeks to publish scholarly work of high merit and wide interest on numerous aspects of missiology—the study of Christian mission in its historical, social, and theological dimensions. Able proposals on new and creative approaches to the practice and understanding of mission will receive close attention from the ASM Series Committee.

American Society of Missiology Series, No. 43

LANDMARK ESSAYS IN MISSION AND WORLD CHRISTIANITY

Robert L. Gallagher
Paul Hertig

Editors

ORBIS BOOKS

Maryknoll, New York 10545

Library of Congress Cataloging in Publication Data

Landmark essays in mission and world Christianity / Robert L. Gallagher, Paul Hertig, editors.
    p. cm. — (The American Society of Missiology series ; no. 43)
    Includes bibliographical references and index.
    ISBN 978-1-57075-829-4 (pbk.)
    1. Missions—Theory. I. Gallagher, Robert L. II. Hertig, Paul, 1955-
    BV2063.C53   2009
    266—dc22
                            2008043917

Contents

Preface to the American Society of Missiology Series

The purpose of the American Society of Missiology Series is to publish—without regard for disciplinary, national, or denominational boundaries—scholarly works of high quality and wide interest on missiological themes from the entire spectrum of scholarly pursuits relevant to Christian mission, which is always the focus of books in the Series.

By *mission* is meant the effort to effect passage over the boundary between faith in Jesus Christ and its absence. In this understanding of mission, the basic functions of Christian proclamation, dialogue, witness, service, worship, liberation, and nurture are of special concern. And in that context questions arise, including, How does the transition from one cultural context to another influence the shape and interaction between these dynamic functions, especially in regard to the cultural and religious plurality that comprises the global context of Christian life and mission.

The promotion of scholarly dialogue among missiologists, and among missiologists and scholars in other fields of inquiry, may involve the publication of views that some missiologists cannot accept, and with which members of the Editorial Committee themselves do not agree. Manuscripts published in the Series, accordingly, reflect the opinions of their authors and are not understood to represent the position of the American Society of Missiology or of the Editorial Committee. Selection is guided by such criteria as intrinsic worth, readability, coherence, and accessibility to a range of intersted persons and not merely to experts or specialists.

The ASM Series, in collaboration with Orbis Books, seeks to publish scholarly works of high merit and wide interest on numerous aspects of missiology—the scholarly study of mission. Able presentations on new and creative approaches to the practice and understanding of mission will receive close attention.

THE ASM SERIES COMMITTEE
Jonathan J. Bonk
Angelyn Dries, O.S.F.
Scott W. Sunquist

Preface

Robert L. Gallagher and Paul Hertig

This volume collects fifteen of the most important essays on mission published over the past seventy years. We, the editors, hope it will serve the purpose we set out to achieve: making available the absolutely essential articles and papers that no person interested in the mission of the church can not have read. We hope we have succeeded. The reader deserves some indication of how we went about our work.

Many people love making lists: lists of the tasks for the day; jobs to do around the house; films to be viewed before forty years of age; books to be read in a lifetime. We all make lists at some time or another. The God of the Bible also loves making lists: items of the wilderness Tabernacle; people returning from the Babylonian captivity; the genealogical heritage of the Messiah. So it was during the American Society of Missiology annual meeting at Chicago in June 1999 that we began forming a list of the most influential missiologists since 1940 by asking Gerald Anderson, Samuel Escobar, Scott Moreau, Wilbert Shenk, and Charles van Engen their views. As the process proceeded over the next several years, we asked more people for their advice, consulted bibliographies, and eventually formulated our task of compiling an anthology of pieces that would comprise what we entitle *Landmark Essays in Mission and World Christianity* and be a resource for missionaries and students of mission.

This book covers a wide range of disciplines within the field of missiology, and each essay includes a brief biography of the missiologist's contribution to the field. We consulted widely in choosing the essays that comprise this book.

Why is it needed and by whom? The field of missiology is admittedly new in academia, and in many places not even recognized as a distinct theological discipline. As such, it needs continuing definition and direction. One way to achieve this is to look at the history of the discipline, since taking account of the past helps understand the present and propels us toward the future. This book, we believe, is an intelligent guide to missiology's recent past and can be a resource for reflection and propulsion into God's future.

In composing the anthology we were aware of the need to include men and women missiologists as well as Catholic, Protestant, and Orthodox scholars.

Within the Protestant arena a representation from Conciliar, Evangelical, and Pentecostal/Charismatic persons would be ideal. In addition, it would be important to include majority world missiologists from Latin America, Asia, and Africa. With this in mind we endeavored to bring a number of streams of thought together to choose the essays of influence.

The following scholars responded to our survey with suggestions regarding the prominent essays in missiology: Gerald H. Anderson, former editor of the *International Bulletin of Missionary Research* and emeritus executive director of the Overseas Ministries Study Center, New Haven, Connecticut; Stephen B. Bevans, SVD, Louis J. Luzbetak Professor of Theology and Culture, Catholic Theological Union, Chicago, Illinois; Jonathan J. Bonk, executive director, Overseas Ministries Study Center, New Haven, Connecticut, the editor of the *International Bulletin of Missionary Research,* and the project director of the *Dictionary of African Christian Biography*; François Bovon, the Divinity School, Harvard University, Cambridge, Massachusetts; William R. Burrows, managing editor, Orbis Books, Maryknoll, New York; Lindy Scott, professor of foreign languages, Whitworth College, Spokane, Washington; Cyril Hally, Columban Mission Institute, North Turramurra, NSW, Australia; A. Scott Moreau, professor of intercultural studies, Wheaton College Graduate School, Wheaton, Illinois; Robert L. Thomas, executive editor, *The Master's Seminary Journal,* Sun Valley, California; Dana L. Robert, Truman Collins Professor of World Mission, Center for Global Christianity and Mission Research, Boston University School of Theology, Boston, Massachusetts; Roger P. Schroeder, SVD, Bishop Francis X. Ford, M.M., Chair of Catholic Missiology, Catholic Theological Union, Chicago, Illinois; Choan-Seng Song, Distinguished Professor of Theology and Asian Cultures, Pacific School of Religion, Graduate Theological Union, Berkeley, California; Wilbert Shenk, emeritus professor of history and contemporary culture at the School of Intercultural Studies, Fuller Theological Seminary, Pasadena, California; Paul Vadakumpadan, SDB, the editor, *Mission Today,* Sacred Heart Theological College, Shillong, India; and D. J. Wyrtzen, managing editor, *Stulos Theological Journal,* Bandung Theological Seminary, Bandung, Indonesia.

We integrated our survey with the bibliographical reflections from the following works: G. H. Anderson, R. T. Coote, N. A. Horner, and J. M. Phillips, eds., *Mission Legacies: Biographical Studies of Leaders of the Modern Missionary Movement* (Maryknoll, NY: Orbis Books, 1994); G. H. Anderson, *Biographical Dictionary of Christian Mission* (Grand Rapids: Eerdmans, 1998); J. D. Douglas, ed., *Who's Who in Christian History* (Wheaton, IL: Tyndale House Publishers, 1992); J. D. Douglas, ed., *Twentieth-Century Dictionary of Christian Biography* (Grand Rapids: Baker Books, 1995); N. Lossky, J. M. Bonino, J. S. Pobee, T. F. Stransky, G. Wainwright, and P. Webb, eds., *Dictionary of the Ecumenical Movement* (Grand Rapids: Eerdmans, 1991); A. S. Moreau, ed., *Evangelical Dictionary of World Missions* (Grand Rapids: Baker Books, 2000); S. Neill,

G. H. Anderson, and J. Goodwin, eds., *Concise Dictionary of the Christian World Mission* (New York: Abingdon, 1971); and J. D. Woodbridge, ed., *Ambassadors for Christ* (Chicago, IL: Moody Press, 1994). In addition, the above streams of reflection were incorporated with bibliographies from "The Best of *International Bulletin of Missionary Research*" and Wilbert Shenk and Charles Van Engen's "MI 510 Thinking Missiologically." From these multiple sources it seemed that a number of articles and writers stood apart from the others.

It is no surprise that this collection of essays has contemporary relevance. Four writers deal with the southward shift of global Christianity. Dana Robert's essay, "Shifting Southward: Global Christianity since 1945," in fact preceded Philip Jenkins's landmark book, *The Next Christendom* (Maryknoll, NY: Orbis Books, 2002). Peter Phan in "A New Christianity, But What Kind?" critiques Jenkins's assumptions about Christianity in the South. Wilbert Shenk and Andrew Walls also discuss the ramifications of this southward shift.

Several writers discuss globalization. Robert Schreiter speaks of a "global capitalist order" that has "reconfigured the economic map of the world," creating new centers of wealth and large pockets of poverty. "The old economic system, which had inherited the center-periphery model of capital flow and production from the age of empire," he observes, "was replaced with a polycentric model that distinguishes between those who are inside and part of the process from those who are excluded and forgotten." Orlando Costas warns that "Christian mission has been joined to the world of free enterprise" and that it has utilized the "corporation model as a means of commercial expansion" from early on in its history. Wilbert Shenk speaks of "dehumanizing injustice and poverty as a consequence of forces controlled by the global economy and the powerful, rich nations." He then asks the crucial question, "Who do we say Jesus Christ is in relation to such conditions?"

Robert Schreiter gives his answer to the question by emphasizing that through God's reconciling love, in response to the brokenness in the world, we "discover a vocation, a calling from God to be the healers and reconcilers in the shattered world." C. René Padilla states, in a similar vein, that "with the coming of Jesus Christ all the barriers that divide humankind have been broken down and a new humanity is now taking shape *in* and *through* the church." Paul Hiebert speaks of hope, joy, and the surprising work of the Holy Spirit in the midst of suffering and death that brings glory to God.

The important topic of ecumenism is covered by Daisy Machado. She observes "a third world nation within the United States whose history is not European and whose tradition is not that of the 'fathers' of this country," stating that the United States includes "a third world nation of refugees from poor countries and dictatorial governments, of victims of wars in which the United States has played an active role; these people are the pilgrims of today whose roots lie in Latin America, Central America, the Caribbean, Africa, Asia, and the Middle East." Her prophetic voice awakens us to be "ecumenical in the barrio" in order to be faithful to "God's plan that the church be disestablished so that it can become that authentic expression of God's redemption, of God's diversity, of God's inclusiveness—not at the center of power, not in a position of dominance, but in the margins, outside the gate where Jesus came to serve, to redeem, and to empower."

The memory of women's work in mission is articulated by Dana Robert, who states, "the typical late twentieth-century Christian was no longer a European man, but a Latin American or African woman." Samuel Escobar illustrates the memory challenge by describing two mission history books in which the authors never mention the women's missionary movement. Yet, he states, "The women's missionary movement not only sponsored thousands of missionaries and Bible women and built schools and hospitals, but it also produced some of the greatest mission strategists and missiologists of the late nineteenth and early twentieth centuries."

The importance of the Bible and mission is found throughout this book, but especially in the exegetical work of David Bosch, Karl Barth, and René Padilla, who demonstrate the serious need for authentic biblical foundations in mission. David Bosch chases away the proof texters who isolate verses from the rest of scripture, mine for gold nuggets from isolated missionary texts, or seek to justify from the Bible the missionary enterprise in which they are already engaged. Karl Barth carefully interprets the "Great Commission" in Matthew 28:16-20 with the depth and breadth sorely lacking in the missionary use of the passage over the years. And René Padilla shakes the foundations of the homogeneous unit principle through careful, systematic, biblical work.

Concerning the deeply controverted topic of approaches to interreligious issues and religious pluralism, Lesslie Newbigin and Charles Van Engen focus on nonjudgmental, carefully considered, well-articulated, Christ-centered approaches. Kwame Bediako observes that Africa's Christian theologians have set the stage for a new, creative encounter of Christianity with the primal religions of the world, where "the opportunity for a serious *theological* encounter and cross-fertilization between the Christian religion and the primal religions, which was lost in the earlier evangelization of Europe, can be regained. In African Christianity, the peculiar historical connection between Christianity and primal religions can be studied on the basis of data which are both vital and contemporary, and on a scale that is probably unequalled in all Christian history."

Wilbert Shenk discusses the high value that Africans place on the environment and their respectful and caring roles in it. They take seriously the mandate for the liberation of creation in the midst of world industrialization and urbanization that have contributed to the destruction of the environment, and the church's need to provide clear guidance. Dana Robert recalls that in Zimbabwe in 1997, more than 150 indigenous churches expressed the metaphor of healing by partaking in a movement to heal the earth by planting 750,000 trees.

J. Samuel Escobar provides important summaries of the thought and writings of some of the finest missiologists over the years, and examines future ramifications.

ACKNOWLEDGMENTS

We cordially thank the missiologists mentioned above who took the time to dialogue with us as we sought to home in on particular essays from selected authors: Mark Lau Branson, Carlos Cordova, Jehu Hanciles, Young Lee Hertig, Wilbert Shenk, Richard Slimbach, Tite Tienou, and Darrell Whiteman.

We also express appreciation to those who laid the groundwork and did the legwork of scanning and formatting essays, and seeking permissions: Yu-Chin (Erica) Lin, Manar Metry, and Ami Osawa of Azusa Pacific University; and Michelle Asbill, Heather Davis, and Lori Miranda, Wheaton College Graduate School teaching assistants.

We are grateful for permissions to reprint these articles, which we received from authors, publishers, and copyright holoders. Bibliographic data for each article in the book is printed on the first page of that article.

Part I

BIBLICAL THEOLOGY

1

Reflections on Biblical
Models of Mission

David J. Bosch

David J. Bosch (1929-92), born in Cape Province, South Africa, served as a
missionary in the Transkei (1957-71) and became professor of missiology
at the University of South Africa in Pretoria in 1972. Bosch was general
secretary of the Southern African Missiological Society from 1968 and editor
of its journal *Missionalia* from 1973. Bosch wrote more than 150 journal
articles and six books, including his *magnum opus, Transforming Mission:
Paradigm Shifts in Theology of Mission* (Maryknoll, NY: Orbis Books, 1991),
which received wide acclaim as one of the finest and most comprehensive
books on mission.

THE NEED FOR A "BIBLICAL THEOLOGY OF MISSION"

There can be little doubt that what has traditionally been referred to as
the "biblical foundations of mission" will be as important in the twenty-
first century as it has been in the past. In fact, if we want the missionary
enterprise to be authentic and our reflections on mission to be relevant, we
will have to pay even more serious attention to this branch of missiology
than we used to do.

At least since the days of William Carey, two centuries ago, Protestant
missionary advocates have argued that they were defending and propagating
an enterprise that had its roots in Scripture. And indeed, much trouble
was taken to find biblical authorization for the missionary enterprise.
Unfortunately, this was frequently done by gleaning so-called "missionary
texts" from the Bible to undergird the contemporary missionary enterprise.
As far as the Old Testament was concerned, one accepted, even if only
implicitly, that it was "particularistic" and therefore hardly usable to support
mission. If, however, we looked carefully among the rocks and rubble, we
would detect small nuggets of pure "missionary" gold—stories of pagans

First published in *Toward the 21st Century in Christian Mission: Essays in Honor of
Gerald H. Anderson,* ed. James M. Phillips and Robert T. Coote (Grand Rapids: Eerdmans,
1992), 175-92. Reprinted with permission.

such as Ruth and Naaman who accepted the faith of Israel, "universalistic" expressions scattered throughout the Psalms and Second Isaiah, stories like Jonah's, a prophet of the God of Israel, who was sent as a missionary to Nineveh, and so on. Sometimes the "mine" would not readily yield such clearly identifiable gold nuggets. Then we would have to smelt the biblical ore, as it were, in order to extract our "missionary" gold from it.

The New Testament, of course, yielded its gold far more promptly. And yet advocates of mission tended to approach even the New Testament as a mine from which they might extract isolated missionary texts. This is, for instance, what Carey did in respect of the so-called Great Commission at the end of Matthew's Gospel (28:18-20). He isolated these verses from the rest of the Gospel, viewed them as a *verbatim* command of the risen Lord, and built his case for a worldwide mission in his own day on the argument that, if the promise of Jesus' *presence* (Matt. 28:20) remained valid, his *commission* (28:19) retained validity too.

Behind this entire approach lay the assumption that one already knew what "mission" was and now only had to prove that it was mandated by Scripture. And, of course, in the modern era mission meant (and by and large still means) the geographical movement from a Christian locality to a pagan locality for the purpose of winning converts and planting churches in that area. Please note that I am not—at least not at this stage—saying that mission does not mean this. What I do say is that, in looking for a biblical foundation for mission, missionary advocates as a matter of course took it for granted that it was *the enterprise they knew and were engaged in* that had to be justified biblically.

It may, in this respect, be salutary to remind ourselves that the very term "mission," used in the sense just outlined, is of fairly recent origin. It was introduced by the Jesuits in the sixteenth century to depict the ministry of those members of the society sent to distant places in order to reconvert Protestants or to convert pagans—the latter particularly in those territories recently colonized by the nations of "Christian" Europe. The origins of the term "mission" thus were intimately bound up with the colonial expansion of the West. Like colonization, it implied traveling to distant countries and "subjugating" pagans to the one and only true religion.

I do not draw attention to these origins of the concept "mission" out of a desire to participate in mission- and missionary-bashing, so popular a pastime in some circles today. Indeed, I am convinced that the missionaries were, by and large, a breed fundamentally different from their colonizing compatriots. Nevertheless, the sociohistorical context in which they found themselves could not but influence their theology, mission work, and day-to-day conduct. They carried the odor of the colonial enterprise with them— much the way the stale smell of cigarette smoke clings to the clothes of a nonsmoker coming out of a room full of smokers.

In spite of these exacerbating circumstances the terms "mission" and "missionary" can boast a respectable biblical pedigree. "Mission" means "sending," the idea expressed by the verbs *pempein* and *apostellein,* which together occur 206 times in the New Testament. The "missionary," that is, the one sent, is an *apostolos* (79 times), and the apostle's task or "mission" is *apostolē* (four times) (see Legrand 1990: xiv). This, however, suggests that if we wish to reflect on "biblical foundations for mission," our point of departure should not be the contemporary enterprise we seek to justify, but the biblical sense of what being sent into the world signifies. It also means that, however important single biblical texts may (seem to) be, the validity of mission should not be deduced from isolated sayings but from the thrust of the central message of Scripture. In other words, either mission—properly understood—lies at the heart of the biblical message or it is so peripheral to that message that we need not be overly concerned with it.

Fortunately, in more recent decades scholars have indeed begun to read the entire Bible missiologically. Even before the 1910 International Missionary Conference at Edinburgh, Martin Kähler suggested that mission was "the mother of theology" or of the New Testament: it was because of their involvement in mission that the early Christians began to theologize ([1908] 1971: 190). More recently, Martin Hengel said essentially the same: the history and the theology of early Christianity were, primarily, "mission history" and "mission theology" (1983: 53). Moreover, writes Heinrich Kasting, "Mission was, in the early stages, . . . a fundamental expression of the life of the church. The beginnings of a missionary theology are therefore also the beginnings of Christian theology as such" (1967: 127). Ben Meyer concurs: "Christianity had never been more itself, more consistent with Jesus and more evidently en route to its own future, than in the launching of the world mission" (1986: 206). And Donald Senior (1984) talks about mission as the "vantage point" for New Testament investigation. Rudolf Pesch (1976: 61) describes the Gospel of Mark as a *Missionsbuch;* and much the same could be said of the other three Gospels and of the letters of Paul (see Bosch 1991: 56-178; Legrand 1990: 107-45; Senior 1984: 71-81).

The advantage of reading the New Testament missiologically (I will return to the Old Testament) is that, instead of reflecting on isolated "missionary texts," we may look at them as a whole. And we may recognize that one of the main reasons for the existence of this body of literature is the missionary self-understanding and involvement of the people who gave birth to it.

The examples mentioned thus far are mostly from Protestant sources. Traditionally, the "biblical foundations of mission" received rather scant attention from Roman Catholics. In his 927-page handbook on missiology, Thomas Ohm (1962), for instance, refers only in passing to the biblical foundation of mission. Scripture indeed plays a role in his discussion of the rootedness of mission in God's, Jesus', and the church's "general salvific will" (Ohm 1962: 217-59), but all of this has merely an indirect bearing on the biblical *foundation* of mission. Still, in recent decades it has been Catholics rather than Protestants who are working to uncover the roots of mission in the Bible. In 1981, for instance, a number of German-speaking Roman Catholic New Testament scholars gathered in Würzburg to reflect on the "theology of mission in the New Testament." These outstanding papers were edited by

Karl Kertelge and published the following year (Kertelge 1982). In 1983 two biblical scholars from Catholic Theological Union in Chicago, Donald Senior and Carroll Stuhlmueller, published *The Biblical Foundations for Mission,* still the best study in the entire field. And in 1990 the English translation of Lucien Legrand's biblical theology of mission, first published in French in 1988, came out. One might even say that, by and large, Catholic biblical scholars are currently taking the missionary dimensions of Scripture more seriously than their Protestant counterparts. Even so, there are Protestant biblical scholars who are doing superb work in this respect—for instance, Ferdinand Hahn, Martin Hengel, and Ben F. Meyer.

Uncovering the "biblical foundations of mission" is, however—as Nicholas Lash has rightly pointed out—not a relay race in which the biblical scholar, after having identified the "original meaning" of the text, hands over the "baton" to the missiologist who now has to "apply" it (1985). What is necessary, rather, is for biblical scholars and missiologists to reflect *together* on this matter. It is this conviction that lies behind the decision of the International Association for Mission Studies (IAMS), in 1976, to launch a project called BISAM—an acronym for "Biblical Studies and Missiology." In spite of having had some ups and downs, the project is still on track and should remain on the agenda of IAMS; as a matter of fact, it is my firm conviction that it should also be on the agenda of the various societies for biblical studies.[1] We shall, after all, never reach the point where we will have established once and for all the "biblical foundations for mission."

Against this general background we may now proceed to draw the contours of a "biblical theology of mission." Such a project seeks answers (which of necessity will have to be preliminary and related to specific contexts) to three basic questions (see Spindler 1988: 139-40):

1. *Why mission?* Here we attempt to reflect, from the perspective of the witness of the Judeo-Christian Scriptures, on the fundamental charter of mission. Robert Schreiter (1982) refers to this as reflecting on "the Bible *for* mission." We are exploring the conviction that the church is sent *because* Jesus was sent, in terms of the words of the Johannine Jesus: "As the Father has sent me, so send I you" (John 20:21).

2. *How mission?* Here we examine the conviction that the church is sent as Jesus was sent. I refer once again to John 20:21: "*As* the Father has sent me, so send I you." There is an intimate relationship between the sending of Jesus and the sending of the church. I shall return to this theme in more detail.

3. *What is mission?* Here we explore what Schreiter (1982) refers to as "the Bible *in* mission." What is the content of our missionary involvement in the world? In reflecting on this it is important to realize that being faithful

---

1. Sadly, very little of this collaboration is evident at the moment. I mention one example: Some time ago the Department of Old Testament at my university invited the Department of Missiology for a seminar discussion on the question what missiologists expect of Old Testament studies. However, as I pointed out to my Old Testament colleagues, it never occurred to them to ask, "What do Old Testament scholars expect of missiology?"!

to the biblical models of mission does not mean copying them in minute detail. Neither did Jesus' disciples and the early church simply imitate Jesus. Rather, as Graham Stanton puts it, "the early Christian communities handled the traditions about the life and teaching of Jesus . . . with creative but responsible freedom. Traditions were retained carefully, but they were also modified to meet new circumstances" (1985: 72). Hugo Echegaray makes a similar point: Jesus has not left us a rigid model for action; rather, he "inspired his disciples to prolong the logic of his own action in a creative way amid the new and different historical circumstances in which the community would have to proclaim the gospel . . ." (1984: xv-xvi). In our missionary involvement today we must do the same.

In light of the exposition above it should be clear that it would not do to build a biblical theology of mission on isolated proof-texts. This is not to suggest that what we might refer to as the classical missionary texts are of no value for our quest. It does mean, however, that we should view them within their contexts and attempt to extrapolate our theology of mission from there. Hence in this chapter I will identify four cardinal missionary motifs in Scripture and discuss some of the classical missionary texts within the framework of these.

COMPASSION

A fundamental missionary motif in both the Old and the New Testament is that of God's compassion. God refuses to bypass humankind: he sends prophets, messengers, even his Son into the world. This divine compassion manifests itself already in the election of Israel. Israel had no claim to God's attention and yet God took compassion on Israel. Nowhere is this illustrated more dramatically than in Ezekiel 16:4-7a:

> On the day you were born your navel cord was not cut, nor were you washed with water to cleanse you, nor rubbed with salt, nor wrapped in cloths. No eye pitied you, to do any of these things for you out of compassion for you; but you were thrown out in the open field, for you were abhorred on the day you were born. I passed by you, and saw you flailing about in your blood. As you lay in your blood, I said to you, "Live!"

This is indeed one of the most powerful "mission statements" in the whole Bible, since it depicts God as the One who has compassion on the lost and the marginalized. This is also why the Exodus event ("I am the Lord your God, who brought you out of the land of Egypt, out of the house of slavery"—Exod. 20:2) became the cornerstone of Israel's confession of faith: God took compassion on a band of slaves in Egypt and saved them. "Father of orphans and protector of widows is God in his holy habitation. God gives the desolate a home to live in . . ." (Ps. 68:5-6).

In several periods of its history Israel understood its election either as an expression of favoritism or, especially in later Judaism, as something that it had *deserved* (it was sometimes even suggested that Yahweh *needed* Israel; without Israel he would have been a God without worshipers!). This does not, however, eclipse the fundamental conviction that Israel's election was unmerited and an expression of God's gratuitousness. In fact, precisely this is the point of the book of Jonah. We tend to view it in modern terms, as a story about a missionary who was sent to proclaim God's word to a pagan nation. It is nothing of the sort, however, since Jonah was not sent to preach a message of salvation but to announce judgment on Nineveh. The thrust of the story lies elsewhere. It ridicules the narrow ethnocentrism of Jonah (and Israel!), who "allowed" God to work only within Israel (see Verkuyl 1978: 97) and sulked about God treating those outside the covenant the same way he treats those inside (ibid., 99; Legrand 1990: 24-25). It is a story about God's *compassion,* which knows no boundaries and which, ironically, forms the basis of Jonah's complaint against God (4:2):

> O Lord! Is not this what I said while I was still in my own country? That is why I fled to Tarshish at the beginning; for I knew that you are a gracious God and merciful, slow to anger, and abounding in steadfast love, and ready to relent from punishing!

Jonah is the only "missionary" I know of who fervently hoped that his listeners would not heed his message! But God does not allow his compassion to be subverted. So the story of Jonah is a call to Israel to be converted to a compassion comparable to that of Yahweh.

It is, however, in the person and ministry of Jesus of Nazareth that the missionary dimensions of God's boundless compassion are expressed in an unequaled way. For instance, it is striking to note the way in which the people on whom Jesus has compassion are depicted; they are called the poor, the blind, the crippled, the leprous, the hungry, those who weep, the sick, the little ones, the widows, the captives, those who are weary and carrying heavy burdens, and the like (cf. Nolan 1976: 21).

As God has compassion on Israel and others, and as Jesus overthrows the codes of society in boundless compassion on the marginalized, so we too are called to show compassion. This is a fundamental thrust of the biblical picture of mission. Those who have experienced divine compassion are moved by the plight of others, whether or not their plight is "spiritual" or "material." When Jesus looks at the crowds, "harassed and helpless, like sheep without a shepherd" (Matt. 9:36), he is moved to compassion. His followers, too, should be compassionate; so he says to his disciples, "The harvest is plentiful, but the laborers are few; therefore ask the Lord of the harvest to send out laborers into his harvest" (9:37-38). The commission, "... teaching them to obey everything that I have commanded you" (28:19), thus includes compassion with those who suffer. To a significant extent it was because of Jesus' boundless compassion that the early church saw in him "the primal missionary" (cf. Hengel 1983: 63). A faith in which compassion occupies so central a position is indeed missionary.

MARTYRIA

Out of compassion flows passion—in the original sense of the word, which means suffering and martyrdom. Mission is not a triumphalist enterprise. It is by definition done in weakness.

We already see this in the Old Testament. The mightier Israel became, the less its existence revealed a missionary dimension: the nations moved into the background and remained at a distance. Conversely, the more Israel was stripped of earthly power and glory, the more the prophets recognized a missionary dimension to its life. Second Isaiah is a case in point. It reflects a period in Israel's history when Israel was, politically speaking, completely insignificant. And yet precisely these chapters represent a high point in Old Testament missionary thinking. In the case of the Servant of the Lord, being God's witness not only implies preaching but also silent suffering for the sake of others. Isaiah 53 thus reveals both the highest and the deepest dimensions of mission in the Old Testament: through his suffering many would find salvation. Small wonder that, since the beginning of the Christian movement, the Suffering Servant of Isaiah 53 was regarded as archetypal of Jesus of Nazareth: "the Son of Man came not to be served but to serve, and to give his life a ransom for many" (Mark 10:45). His mission was one of self-emptying (see Neely 1989).

What is true of the Master's mission is true of the disciples' also. After Paul's conversion the risen Lord says to Ananias, "I myself will show him how much he must suffer for the sake of my name" (Acts 9:16). And indeed, wherever Paul proclaims the gospel, opposition arises: in Pisidian Antioch, in Iconium, in Corinth, and finally in Rome. Nowhere is this more apparent than in Paul's second letter to the Corinthians (see Bosch 1979). Paul is not a "peddler of the gospel" (2 Cor. 2:17) like the "super-apostles," who define mission in the categories of triumphalism. Rather, he is a captive who glories in weakness (12:9). In fact, weakness, affliction, and suffering are key concepts in this letter in which Paul defends his ministry. Suffering and affliction are *normal* experiences in the apostle's life, but for those who can only think in success categories they remain a *skandalon*, a stumbling block. The difference between the Pauline mission and that of his opponents in Corinth lies in the cross—not only Christ's, but also the missionary's. So we read in Colossians 1:24, "in my flesh I am completing what is lacking in Christ's afflictions for the sake of his body, that is, the church." To the Corinthians Paul writes, "For while we live, we are always being given up to death for Jesus' sake, so that the life of Jesus may be made visible in our mortal flesh. So death is at work in us, but life in you" (2 Cor. 4:11-12). It is Paul the missionary who says, "I carry the marks of Jesus branded on my body" (Gal. 6:17).

In Greek, a witness is a *martys*. Almost imperceptibly, however, the noun *martys* acquired an added meaning in the early church, that of "martyr," the one who seals his witness (*martyria*) with suffering, even death. In Acts 22:20 Paul refers to the blood of Christ's "witness," Stephen. We could, however, also translate *martys* here as "martyr," for this is what Stephen became, because of his witness, his mission. William Frazier is correct when he says that Luke's writings, in particular, have a significance far beyond the first-century church. Referring to the Roman Catholic ritual that usually crowns the sending ceremony of missionary communities, where the new missionaries are equipped with cross or crucifix, he adds,

> Somewhere beneath the layers of meaning that have attached themselves to this practice from the days of Francis Xavier to our own is the simple truth enunciated by Justin and Tertullian: the way faithful Christians die is the most contagious aspect of what being a Christian means. The missionary cross or crucifix is no mere ornament depicting Christianity in general. Rather, it is a vigorous commentary on what gives the gospel its universal appeal. Those who receive it possess not only a symbol of their mission but a handbook on how to carry it out. (Frazier 1987: 46)

N. P. Moritzen (quoted in Triebel 1988: 9) expresses the same conviction: "It belongs to the essence (of the Christian faith) that it needs the weak witness, the powerless representative of the message. The people who are to be won and saved should, as it were, always have the possibility of crucifying the witness of the gospel." Hans von Campenhausen underscores this notion: "Martyrdom and mission—so experience teaches us—belong together. Martyrdom is especially at home on the mission field" (1974: 71). This is also the thrust of Tertullian's famous statement, at the end of the second century: *Semen est sanguis Christianorum*—freely translated: "The blood of the martyrs is the seed of the church" (see further Triebel 1988).

GOD'S MISSION

Inherent in the biblical understanding of mission is the conviction that the real author and sustainer of mission is God. This is particularly clear in the witness of the Old Testament. The Servant of the Lord in Second Isaiah, for instance, is a missionary figure, but by no means a prototype of the modern missionary who travels great distances to proclaim the gospel. The "proclamation" is not the spoken word but rather the events concerning the Servant. He is brought into court to witness in a lawsuit between Yahweh and the nations. He is, however, an extraordinary and, yes, a useless witness, for he can neither talk nor see (Isa. 42:18-20; 48:8-13)! Evidently the message of this dumb and blind witness does not consist in verbal preaching; rather, by his mere existence and experiences he is a witness for Yahweh. "Mission" is what God is doing *to* and *through* the Servant, not what the Servant does.

In other words, mission has two specific characteristics. It is a divine activity—God manifesting his glory in the sight of the nations by saving his people. It is an activity addressed primarily to the people of Israel, and to other nations only through them (see Legrand 1990: 20). Through Israel, God is busy with the nations. The emphasis is on what God does. This does not imply that Israel is excluded or passive. It is a perversion to suggest that if God is the primary "agent" of mission, people are inactive, or vice versa. That would be to argue that God's activity is the enemy of human freedom, that the more one emphasizes God's actions the less one can emphasize ours. Rather, the opposite is true: the more we recognize mission as God's work, the more we ourselves become involved in it. This is what Paul means when he says, "I worked harder than any of [the other apostles]—though it was not I, but the grace of God that is with me" (1 Cor. 15:10). If, however, we separate God's work from human activity, we soon land ourselves in one of two untenable positions: if we overemphasize the first, we become fatalists; if we stress only the second, we become fanatics and arrogant zealots.

In the early church, so it would seem, many Greek-speaking Jewish Christians appreciated this creative tension. They got involved in mission without viewing it as something they did in their own power. In the story Luke tells us in the book of Acts, mission is first and foremost the work of God; to be more precise, for Luke it is accomplished by the Spirit. Under no circumstances does this, however, exclude human mediation, and Luke recounts the unreserved commitment of many Christians to mission (see Legrand 1990: 105-6; Bosch 1991: 113-17). The same applies to the way Paul interpreted mission. Primarily, it is the *gospel* that is the power of God for everyone's salvation (Rom. 1:16). And yet, Paul does not allow himself a moment's rest as he traverses the Roman Empire, preaches ceaselessly, and establishes churches.

Many Aramaic-speaking Christians, by contrast, could not bring themselves to an active missionary involvement. They believed that the salvation of the Gentiles would take place by means of an eschatological pilgrimage of the nations to Jerusalem, as depicted in the Old Testament. God alone would bring them in, in his own time, and to attempt to precipitate their coming was blasphemy and human arrogance. Throughout the history of the church various Christian groups, because of a perverted understanding of predestination, would adopt a similar attitude: If God wished the heathen to be saved he would see to it himself! All of this, however, flows from a distorted interpretation of the biblical model of mission.

Others have tended to the opposite extreme. They were inclined to make the "success" of mission almost completely dependent on their own zeal and hard work. Perhaps this is, in part, what lies behind the tendency—

particularly in Protestant circles—to interpret the Matthean version of the Great Commission (Matt. 28:18-20) primarily as a *command* and, with that, to overemphasize the auxiliary verb "go" (Greek: *poreuthentes*). As I have argued elsewhere, this is based on a faulty exegesis (Bosch 1983a: 219-20, 229-30; see also Legrand 1990: 78-79). It is also, however, the product of a deficient theology: in semi-Pelagian manner, we tend to prioritize human intervention and relegate the power of God to secondary status. This happens particularly where the Great Commission is, for all intents and purposes, limited to verses 19 and 20a, that is, where we ignore the fact that the commission proper *follows on* the statement of authority given to Christ in verse 18 and *is dependent upon* the promise, in verse 20b, of the abiding presence of him who is the real missionary (Legrand 1990: 81).

HISTORY

The religion of Israel is a *historical* religion: God has a history with people and takes them into a new future. For the people of Israel, faith could never be a matter of embracing or acquiescing to the status quo. God is "the God who *acts*" (Wright 1952). The religions of Israel's neighbors, by contrast, were *nature* religions, caught up in the cycle of the seasons, where winter and summer follow each other in an eternal battle for supremacy. In Israel's faith the emphasis was on *salvation;* in the religions of its neighbors it was on *blessing.* Still, the God of Israel—the God who saves—is also the God who blesses, but in such a way that his blessing *flows from* his salvific (or historical) activities. This, too, has tremendous significance for our reflections on the biblical foundation of mission. We might even say that only a historical religion can be truly missionary. History means that nothing needs to remain unchanged. The Bible does not contain eternal, immutable truths—that would be Platonism. Neither is God an immutable God; the miracle of the story of Israel (and of the church) is that, again and again, God changes his mind and decides *not* to punish people as he intended to do!

History is, by nature, specific and concrete, or it is not history. God does not elect humankind in general or in the abstract; God elects a specific people. At first glance, the theme of election seems to run counter to that of universal mission (Legrand 1990: 8). In reality, however, election is for service—more particularly: for the sake of the nations. When Abraham, the father of the people of Israel, is called from Ur of the Chaldeans to go to the land of Canaan, the purpose of his calling is not just that God intends to make his name great, but also that he may be a blessing; indeed, that in him all the families of the earth shall be blessed (Gen. 12:1-3). Yahweh breaks the cycle of the eternal return and journeys with Israel into the future, for the sake of the nations. Israel, Jerusalem, and the temple remain at the center, however. The Lord of the universe has, as it were, a concrete, specific, historical address—in the famous words of Blaise Pascal:

He is not the God of the philosophers or the scholars, but of Abraham, Isaac, and Jacob.

The same historical specificity characterizes the New Testament. It is not true that, when we move from the Old Testament to the New, we suddenly move from the historical, mundane, and material to the eternal, celestial, and spiritual (*contra* Ohm 1962: 247). Salvation in the New Testament also is from the Jews (John 4:22). Jesus is born a Jew, at a specific locality and within a particular sociohistorical and political context. During his earthly ministry he is subject to human and historical constraints and limits his ministry almost completely to the people of Israel. It is from within Israel's experience that Jesus opens new horizons. This is confirmed in the Gospel stories, particularly in the Gospel of Luke, the only Gentile author of a New Testament book. The temple is, for Luke, more than an edifice; it is the center from which the word radiates forth to the ends of the earth (Legrand 1990: 88, 97). So we shall not understand Jesus' ministry or be able to reflect on it missiologically if we sever it from its historical moorings and simply universalize and spiritualize it.

The historical dimension of the faith also implies that things did not end with the life and ministry of the earthly Jesus. With his death on the cross and, even more particularly, his resurrection, a new era was inaugurated, an era with tremendous implications for mission. It is certainly no accident that all four Gospels link the beginning of the worldwide mission of the church explicitly with the resurrection. It is abundantly evident that the Easter experience determined the early Christian community's self-understanding and identity. This experience is both the springboard of mission and the main content of the missionary message: it is the risen Christ that is proclaimed by the early church. And intimately related to the resurrection, almost part of the Easter event itself, is the gift of the Spirit, which is likewise integrally linked to mission. It was Easter that gave those first Christians certainty, but it was Pentecost that gave them boldness; only through the power of the Spirit did they become witnesses (Acts 1:8). Easter is also the dawn of the end time. This introduces a fervent eschatological note to the church's mission. It looks forward to a real, historical *eschaton*. At the same time it knows that the end is not only still pending: it has already come. The church engages in mission on the basis of the already present eschaton and through its mission reaches out to the end that is still to come in fullness. Of that end the resurrection of Jesus is the "first fruits" (1 Cor. 15:20, 23), "first installment," "pledge," or "guarantee" (2 Cor. 1:22; 5:5; Eph. 1:14).

The four biblical "missionary motifs" discussed above are, of course, all intrinsically interrelated and interdependent. The God who has *compassion* on the stranger, the widow, the orphan, and the poor in Israel is also the God who turns human categories upside down: he uses the weak, the suffering, and those of no consequence as his *witnesses* (*martyres*) in the world. Ultimately, however, mission remains *God's mission, missio Dei*, since he retains the initiative, creates *history*, and guides it toward its fulfillment.

MISSION IN BIBLICAL PERSPECTIVE

Only now are we in a position to reflect on some of those passages that have traditionally been invoked in support of mission. Three observations may be made at this point. First, it is impossible to infer missionary principles or models in a direct manner from isolated texts or passages. This would be to disregard the fundamentally historical and contextual nature of Scripture. There are no simplistic or obvious moves from the Bible to contemporary missional practice (see Brueggemann 1982: 408). Second, and linked to the above, we may never utilize biblical sayings to undergird, in a one-to-one manner, the specific missionary projects in which we are involved. We would then be using those sayings not as texts, but as pretexts (see Schreiter 1982: 431). Third, at no stage—not even in the first stages of the missionary involvement of the early church—was there a uniform view of mission. The Bible, Old and New Testaments, reveals a variety of mission types. We may also not range the various forms of mission "along a linear evolutive trajectory that would begin with the Old Testament and finally come to the New" (Legrand 1990: 151).

Why would this be so? Basically, because of the four motifs outlined above: by its very nature, *compassion* takes concrete forms according to specific circumstances; *witness* depends on the situation in which one finds oneself; *God's actions in mission* are manifested in the contexts in which people live; *history* is, by nature, always contingent and never simply a rerun of what has been. And since the Christian faith is inherently *incarnational*, in the sense of God taking a concrete human form in a specific social context, the Christian mission—if it wishes to be incarnational—also has to be specific and contextual. In our reflections on the missionary dimensions of the biblical message, we must therefore be willing to be challenged by the rich variety of the biblical accounts. This variety corresponds to the diversity of what we actually see in mission today.

No two situations are exactly the same. Mission in Asia with its rich and ancient religious traditions will be very different from mission in Latin America, or in secularized Europe, or in those countries where for decades Marxism has been the official creed, or in Africa where people live in face-to-face communities. We will therefore—to cite Echegaray again—have to allow ourselves to be inspired by Jesus and the first missionaries to prolong the logic of their ministry in a creative way amid new and very different circumstances (1984: xv-xvi).

Studying the Scriptures in this spirit, we may indeed be enabled to draw on biblical sayings to validate but also to challenge, critique, and transform our missionary models and projects. We may, by all means, draw on the Great Commission, but we should do so in a way that does not violate the text's intentions. We will note, for instance, that each of our four Gospels contains its own version of the Commission.[2] All Gospels are unanimous that it is

---

2. Of course, the longer ending of Mark's Gospel (16:9-20), where the Markan Great

the resurrection of Jesus that generates mission. Put differently, mission is "the gospel confirmed and universalized by the power of the Resurrection" (Legrand 1990: 73). The four Gospels do this in different ways. *Matthew,* for instance, views mission as ministry done in the consciousness of the universal authority of Jesus and of his abiding presence (28:18-20). Mission is, primarily, making disciples, that is, turning others into what the disciples themselves are: those who practice justice-love and emulate "the works of Jesus" (Matt. 11:2) (see Bosch 1991: 56-83). In his Great Commission, *Luke* (24:46-49) understands mission as fulfillment of scriptural promises; becoming possible only after the death and resurrection of the Messiah of Israel; proclaiming the message of repentance and forgiveness; intended for all nations; beginning from Jerusalem; carried out by "witnesses"; and accomplished in the power of the Spirit (Bosch 1991: 84-122; Senior and Stuhlmueller 1983: 260-69). And *John's* version of the Commission (20:21) underscores the intimate relationship between Jesus' mission and that of his disciples: they have to emulate him. The Commission follows directly after he has shown them his hands and his side (20:20); this undeniably suggests that, as I have argued above, mission will take place in the context of suffering and opposition.

Each evangelist thus reports the Great Commission from within the context of that evangelist's particular orientation. The variations in the commissions reflect a variety of missionary experiences. This does not suggest arbitrariness, however, since the elements that the four Gospels share in their "definitions" of mission far outweigh those about which they differ. The mission of the church has continuity with that of the historical Jesus. For at least Matthew and Luke (and, of course, Paul) the church remains dependent on and committed to Israel. At the same time, all New Testament authors agree that the key to entering God's reign cannot be ethnic origin but faith in God through Jesus Christ. "Where faith appears, the Reign is present" (Legrand 1990: 61).

The mission of the church, then, has all the dimensions and scope of Jesus' own ministry and may never be reduced to church planting and the saving of souls. It consists in proclaiming and teaching, but also in healing and liberating, in compassion for the poor and the downtrodden. The mission of the church, as the mission of Jesus, involves being sent into the world—to love, to serve, to preach, to teach, to heal, to save, to free.

These reflections bring us in close proximity to another Lukan passage that has, for good reasons, been dubbed the *real* Great Commission of the Third Gospel: Luke 4:16-21. Indeed, within the overall structure of Luke, these verses are at least as important as the more explicit Great Commission

---

Commission appears (16:15-16), is not found in the best manuscripts and is regarded as inauthentic. Still, as more and more scholars are now recognizing, at least the two verses containing the Commission have a more Markan stamp than the rest and probably belong to the original but now lost ending of Mark (see also Legrand 1990: 75 and 173 n. 7, where additional references are given).

in 24:46-49. The words Jesus quotes from Isaiah (Luke 4:18-19) are set within the context of the dramatic story of Jesus' first public ministry in his hometown, Nazareth, and they introduce at least three crucial Lukan missionary motifs: the centrality of the poor and other marginalized and oppressed people in Jesus' (and the church's) ministry; overcoming vengeance by forgiveness and peace; and moving beyond the confines of Israel, first to the Samaritans and then to the Gentiles (Bosch 1991: 89-113). These motifs constitute a charter also for the church-in-mission today.

As the mission of the first apostles was, essentially, the resumption of the mission of Jesus, our mission is the continuation of theirs. Mission certainly involves human mediations, but always in total dependence on the initiative of God, particularly his initiative in the Christ-event. Mission is first and foremost the God who comes, in Jesus Christ (Legrand 1990: 152).[3] The gospel is the power of God for salvation (Rom. 1:16), and this power is more basic than the activities of the missionaries (Legrand 1990: 127). And yet, that power seeks to manifest itself in our missionary ministry. This is never performed in unbroken continuity with the biblical witness; it remains, always, an altogether ambivalent and flawed enterprise. Still we may, with due humility, look back on the witness of Jesus and our first forebears in the faith and seek to emulate them.

---

3. Note the original title of Legrand's book: *Le Dieu qui vient* (= the God who is coming) (Paris: Desclée, 1988).

2

An Exegetical Study of Matthew 28:16-20

Karl Barth

Karl Barth (1886-1968) was a pastor at Safenwil, Switzerland, from 1911 to 1921. The hardships of World War I caused him to question the liberal theology of his teachers, rooted in post-Enlightenment thought. With *The Epistle to the Romans* (1919), he inaugurated a radical shift in Protestant thought toward neoorthodoxy. In the second edition (1922) Barth argued that the God who is revealed in the cross of Jesus Christ challenges and defeats every attempt to associate God with human cultures, achievements, or possessions. This shift led to his appointments as professor of theology at Göttingen (1921), Münster (1925), and Bonn (1930). In Germany he founded the Confessing Church, which opposed the Nazi regime. His refusal to take the oath of allegiance to Adolf Hitler cost him his chair at Bonn. He returned to Basel and wrote his six-million-word *Church Dogmatics,* which was unfinished at his death. Barth was a forerunner in the use of the concept of *missio Dei* and linked the doctrine of the Trinity to the missionary character of God.

Now the eleven disciples went to Galilee, to the mountain to which Jesus had directed them. And when they saw him they worshiped him; but some doubted. And Jesus came and said to them, "All authority in heaven and on earth has been given to me. Go therefore and make disciples of all nations, baptizing them in the name of the Father and of the Son and of the Holy Spirit, teaching them to observe all that I have commanded you; and lo, I am with you always, to the close of the age." (Matt. 28:16-20)

Here we have part of the New Testament testimony about events that took place during the forty days after Easter.

Let us recall what happened in those days according to the New Testament record. It was during this period that the purpose of Jesus' life

Published in *The Theology of the Christian Mission,* ed. Gerald H. Anderson; trans. Thomas Wieser (New York: McGraw Hill, 1961), 55-71; originally published in German as "Auslegung von Matthäus 28,16-20" (Basel: Basler Missionsbuchhandlung). Reprinted here with permission.

and death, and with it the mission of his followers, could for the first time be seen, heard, and grasped by men. It was the time of the Son's coming in the glory of the Father, ushering in not more and not less than the approaching end of this world and the beginning of a new one. "To them he presented himself alive after his passion by many proofs, appearing to them during forty days, and speaking of the kingdom of God" (Acts 1:3). It became manifest in those forty days that neither the proclamation of God's kingdom at hand, as first heralded by John the Baptist and later by Jesus himself, nor the miracles and signs accomplished by Jesus were empty words. The petition "Thy kingdom come" had not been uttered in vain after all; "this generation," the generation of those alive at the time, was indeed not to pass away before "all these things" had taken place as foretold by Jesus according to Mark 13:30. It became manifest that some of the people who gathered around Jesus actually did not taste death before they had seen the kingdom of God come with power (Mark 9:1). The disciples truly were not to go through all the towns of Israel before the Son of man came (Matt. 10:23). Now he came, and now "all these things" happened. Peter's confession at Caesarea (Matt. 16:16), at the time premature, was now proven to be right and necessary. "You are the Christ, the Son of the living God." Right and necessary, therefore, was the name "Lord," *kyrios*, which the disciples had given to their master. It became manifest, in other words, that the *eschaton* had really begun. All these things were revealed when Jesus, after his death and burial, rose from the tomb and appeared to his followers anew, thereby "coming again" already then and there. He appeared to them not in order to continue his ministry of teaching and healing so to speak during the second part of his earthly life, but to disclose the hitherto hidden purpose of his life and death to his followers and to give them the charge of proclaiming his Lordship and the kingdom now manifest before their eyes. This is, very briefly, the content of the Easter stories at the end of the four Gospels, at the beginning of the book of Acts, and in 1 Corinthians 15. This is the *fact* of Easter.

Two preliminary observations about the form of these stories will facilitate our understanding.

1. We must be quite clear that these accounts relate a *real event* in space and time, and not just some thought or idea. They speak of an empty tomb (Matt. 27:62-66; 28:11-15), and of the newly visible, audible, and touchable body of Jesus (Luke 24:39f.; John 20:24f.; 1 John 1:1). These characteristics are all mentioned within the context of the story of Jesus and his followers, even of the history of the world (Pontius Pilate!). Christ's appearance is in itself a historical moment, marking the end of all preceding, and the antecedent and the turning point of all coming events. To speak here of a "myth" would be to confuse categories. Easter is an absolutely *unique* event. We must immediately specify that this unique event is the beginning of a new heaven and a new earth (Rev. 21:1; 2 Pet. 3:13), of the Last Day, of the glory of God in the flesh (John 1:14). It is the presence of the *eschaton*.

Such an event could only be described in incomplete and contradictory terms, such as are used in the Easter narratives. Think of the relationship between the reports of Matthew and Luke, or of the Synoptics and John, or of the Gospels and 1 Corinthians. It is impossible to construe from these reports a history in our understanding of the term. The topographical and chronological precision is lacking. There is no clear differentiation of the various scenes and no corroboration by impartial witnesses of the events described. These narratives are recounted not in the style of history but, like the story of creation, in the style of historical saga. The content bars any attempt at harmonizing. All these narratives deal no doubt with a common subject and are in basic agreement. Yet each of them needs to be read independently, as a unique testimony of God's decisive word and intervention at the turning point of the eons. Quite obviously each narrative needs to be consulted to clarify the others.

2. These texts speak of a "historically" inconceivable event, but do not mean that this event was subsequently interpreted or construed, much less invented by the faith and piety of the church. They unequivocally refer to an event that laid the foundation of, and gave shape to, the faith of the emerging Christian community. The crux of it was that Jesus' presence among his own revealed God to them. This revelation in Jesus' presence, placing the faithful in the center of time, disclosed to them the past and the future will and work of God. It is therefore both a recapitulation of the history of Israel, culminating in the earthly life of Jesus, and an anticipation of the history of Jesus' reign in the church and in the whole world. God's action, past and future, was present in those forty days as if it were still going on, or already going on.

One more preliminary remark about Matthew 28:16-20 as it relates to the other Easter stories. Two sets of narratives are to be distinguished among them.

1. The stories of Jesus and the women. These underscore the manifestation of the *fact* of the resurrection (the empty tomb) and the *identity* of the risen Lord with the crucified (28:1-6 and 9). Add to it the charge to the women to tell the disciples what they had seen (28:7-8 and 10). This charge is particularly significant because, according to Mark 16:8, the women "said nothing to any one for they were afraid" and, according to Luke 24:11, their words seemed to the disciples "an idle tale." Incidentally this particular role of the women in relation to the disciples may be interpreted as an analogy of the relationship between the historical community of Israel and the now-emerging Christian community of the end of time.

2. The stories of Jesus and the disciples. Here again the manifestation of the *fact* and of the *identity* (28:17-18; Luke 24:37f.; John 20:19f.) is important. However, it is overshadowed by the charge to the disciples to go and tell the world what they had seen (28:19; Luke 24:27; John 20:21). The passage about Jesus and the disciples is missing in Mark's original text. Mark 16:9-20 is a later addition. The charge to the disciples is validated

by the pouring out of the Holy Spirit. John 20:22 indicates that the fourth evangelist understood Easter and Pentecost as one and the same event. In content, they most certainly belong together. Easter together with Pentecost, Pentecost together with Easter, constitutes the gathering of God's people at the end of time.

Our text clearly belongs to this second set of narratives about Jesus and his disciples. Parallel texts are Luke 24:36-49 and John 20:19-29. In addition, Luke 24:13-35 relates the incident on the road to Emmaus; Luke 24:50-53 and Acts 1:4-12, the Ascension; John 21:1-23, the appearance at Lake Tiberias and the conversation with Peter. The Gospel according to Matthew, which offers the most coherent account, relates only the one appearance of Jesus before his disciples. To this we now turn our attention.

VERSE 16

"The eleven disciples" (also Luke 24:9, 33) are the first twelve of Jesus' followers, whose number is temporarily diminished by the loss of Judas. They embody and represent the Israel of the end of time. These "eleven"—according to biblical arithmetic!—equal "twelve," for even in their incompleteness they account for the totality of Israel. 1 Corinthians 15:5 explicitly mentions Jesus' appearance to the twelve. Judas could not impair the full number.

". . . went to Galilee . . ." Significantly, Matthew leads Jesus' history back to the place of its origin (Matt. 4:12-17), to the Galilee of the Gentiles, to the people who walked in darkness and have seen a great light. The history of the end stands in continuity with the previous events in the life of Jesus and the history of Israel, which in turn point to the end. (Luke transposes this scene to Jerusalem, to the life center of Israel, which is seen here—Luke 24:47—as the point of departure for the eschatological proclamation to all nations.) Note how the two narratives, topographically incompatible and with different theological emphases, nevertheless agree in substance.

". . . to the mountain . . ." What mountain is referred to here—the mountain of the transfiguration or that of the Sermon on the Mount? It might be better not to identify it geographically and merely think of a mountain opposite Mount Zion to the north.

". . . to which Jesus had directed them." According to verse 7 it was the angel; according to verse 10 it was Jesus himself, by means of the women, who directed the disciples, "his brethren," to go there. The order must have gone to the disciples, since now the eleven turn up. The combination with the appearance to the five hundred brethren (1 Cor. 15:6), as proposed by Olshausen and Schlatter, seems therefore unlikely.

VERSE 17

"And when they saw him . . ." This seeing (*idontes*) implies that the revelation of the fact of Jesus' resurrection and of the identity of the risen Lord with the crucified, earlier accorded to the women, is now to be granted to the disciples as well. The expression "he came" (*proselthōn*) in verse 18, however, suggests for the time being a certain distance and objectivity of this revelation.

". . . they worshiped him," as did the women in verse 9, and as all shall do again at the Ascension (Luke 24:51). Thomas's confession, "my Lord and my God," serves as a necessary commentary. Worship is offered in the presence of the revealed God. Jesus encountered them as God, and they encounter him now as worshipers.

". . . but some doubted," as in Luke 24:37f. and John 20:24f. (Thomas has suffered great injustice at the hands of exegetes. His insistence upon touching the body of Jesus to relieve his doubt is quite normal and apostolic!) Older exegetes (Starke, Rieger, Olshausen) found it inadmissible to ascribe the doubt to the apostles, and accordingly assumed the presence of others. But this is improbable in the light of verse 17. J. Weiss finds the phrase linguistically crude, disruptive, isolated, and "against the temper of this harmonious ending." Yet the comparison with Luke and John indicates the necessity of the element of doubt even for Matthew. Calvin correctly interpreted: worship and doubt have a common cause; the servant figure of the man Jesus was garbed in the glory of God. Revelation always has a *terminus a quo* and a *terminus ad quem* ["point of origin and final destination"]. Veiled, it arouses doubt; unveiled, it commands worship. All of us waver again and again between the two. Rieger is therefore right when he says that this sentence was included "as a reminder that faith requires struggle. Don't be surprised if your belief is a continuous conquest of unbelief." This element of doubt to be conquered by faith is represented here by "some" (*hoi de*), as in John by Thomas, and in Luke by almost all apostles. Only the gift of the Holy Spirit puts an end to the struggle and casts out doubt. Doubting apostles and a doubting church *after* Pentecost truly have no place in the New Testament. *"Spiritus sanctus non est scepticus"* ["the Holy Spirit is no sceptic"], said Luther. But here the apostles are only at the beginning. They stand in the shadow of the death of Christ. They reenact the doubtful role they displayed at the time of the Passion.

VERSE 18

"And Jesus came and said to them": with these words Matthew perhaps hints at the event of Pentecost, not mentioned elsewhere in his record. It is at any rate certain that when Jesus drew near, the objective revelation was

subjectively appropriated. Bengel comments, "*eo ipso dubitantibus fidem faciens*" ["by that very act creating faith for the doubters"]. By approaching them Jesus awakened faith in the doubters! This, then, is the "sequence" to the doubting in verse 17 which J. Weiss missed.

"'*All authority in heaven and on earth has been given to me.*'" According to the "*therefore*" (*oun*) of verse 19, this affirmation of power is the objective presupposition on the part of Jesus for the immediately following imperative. As the one described in verse 18, Jesus has the power and authority to address the disciples the way he does in verse 19. Hence the disciples' carrying out of the charge will not at all be determined by the excellency and strength of their own will and work; nor will it be jeopardized by their deficiencies. Behind the command of verse 19 stands the commander himself, Jesus, as described in verse 18. He assures the execution of the command over against both the disciples' weakness and any interference by a third party.

Exousia means "right and power" and corresponds to the Latin term *potestas*. The parallel is only seemingly missing in Luke. The fact that Jesus is invested with the highest authority as a guarantee for his command is also attested by Luke inasmuch as Jesus is there both the content and the interpreter of the Scriptures. According to Matthew's version, Jesus' prophecy to the high priests (26:64) has now been fulfilled, "Hereafter you will see the Son of man seated at the right hand of Power, and coming on the clouds of heaven," and with it Daniel 7:14, "To him was given dominion and glory and kingdom." The kingdom is truly his, and he will deliver it to the Father (1 Cor. 15:24). God has highly exalted him and bestowed on him a name above every name, the name of *kyrios*, that at this name every knee should bow, in heaven and on earth and under the earth (Phil. 2:9f.). He disarmed, according to 1 Corinthians 15:24 even destroyed, the principalities and powers and made a public example of them, triumphing over them in him (Col. 2:15). He is "far above all rule and authority and power and dominion, and above every name that is named, not only in this age, but also in that which is to come." God "has put all things under his feet" (Eph. 1:21-22). "The kingdom of the world has become the kingdom of our Lord and of his Christ, and he shall reign for ever and ever" (Rev. 11:15). What does all this mean? It means that the divine claim to all things created in heaven and on earth is, very concretely, Jesus' claim; the divine authority is Jesus' authority; the divine acting, ruling, and judging is Jesus' affair. As the holder of this *exousia*, Jesus stands behind the command in verse 19; he is the authority to those whom he sends out, and as such guarantees the implementation of the command to the disciples as well as against interference by third parties. Those who accept the command fall under this *exousia;* they are responsible to and covered by this authority.

All authority in heaven and on earth! This affirmation is exclusive. Objectively speaking, there is no authority besides the authority of Jesus.

All power, all right, belongs to Jesus. Remaining are only principalities and powers already subjected to him, of which he is the head (Col. 2:10). There are therefore no such things as natural law and natural power, asserting their own domain over against Jesus', deserving homage, trust, fear, and obedience in their own right. Thus it is impossible to postulate, on the basis of the *exousia* (Rom. 13:1f.) a secular power instituted by God alongside the kingdom of Christ, a political realm that would not be included in the kingdom of Christ.

But who is the holder of such *exousia*? Because all authority has been "given" to him we are prevented from thinking in the abstract of an eternal, nonincarnate Son of God, of the *logos asarkos* ["the body-less (i.e., pre-existent) word"]. To him authority need not be given; he holds it from eternity to eternity. The New Testament constantly speaks of this Son of God, yet never abstractly. The eternal Son is always man at the same time. Of him our text speaks. To the man Jesus is given the *exousia*. The man Jesus is the commanding Lord in verse 19.

That all authority has been "given" to him must however not be interpreted to mean that he received it only in his resurrection. Such an assumption is refuted by a number of very clear texts in the Gospels where the affirmation made in verse 18 undeniably refers to Jesus before his death. "'All things have been delivered to me by my Father'" (Matt. 11:27). "The Father . . . has given all things into his hand" (John 3:35). Jesus knew "that the Father had given all things into his hands" (John 13:3). "'Thou hast given him power over all flesh'" (John 17:2). "He taught them as one who had authority" (Matt. 7:29). "'The Son of man has authority on earth to forgive sins'" (Matt. 9:6). See also Matthew 21:23f. *Exousia* is given to the man Jesus as divine authority can alone be given to a human creature. Only when man prays for it, believes in God, is obedient to Him, is it given as free grace. Because God's free grace is eternal, authority is given everlastingly; potentially in God's design to create and save the world, actually in the incarnation of the Word. *Er ist ein Kindlein worden klein, der alle Ding erhält allein* ["He is a child born tiny, who alone sustains every thing"]. By forgiving sins and accomplishing signs and miracles, Jesus made at least a partly visible use of his authority long before his resurrection. There was never a time when he was devoid of it. His "emptying himself" (Phil. 2:7) was nothing but the hiddenness of his majesty, caused by human blindness. What he achieved in the state of utmost weakness, his death upon the cross, was truly a manifestation of his might. "*Sa divinité se tenoit pour un peu de temps comme cachée, c'est à dire elle ne démonstroit point sa vertu*" ["His divinity is put aside briefly, that is to say, it did not demonstrate in any way his virtue"] (Calvin). In the resurrection, however, Jesus reveals himself to the disciples as the one who held, holds, and will hold all authority, a fact that had hitherto been hidden from the disciples as well as from the world. It is of this revelation of the risen Lord that verse 18 speaks.

VERSES 19-20A

This is the crucial affirmation of the whole text. It is the charge and commission of the risen Jesus, the authority for which was asserted in verse 18.

"*Go therefore and make disciples. . . .*" Make them what you yourselves are! Have them learn here, with me, where you yourselves have learned! Call them into the twelve of the eschatological Israel! Let them share in its place and task in the world!

We have already noticed the strangeness of biblical arithmetic. The twelve are designed to be countless. In the same manner as Jesus "made" apostles from the first disciples (Mark 3:14-15), the apostles are called to make apostolic Christians of all others. The kingly ministry of the Messiah is here entrusted to the first disciples constituting the king's troops.

The sweeping imperative, "Go therefore," rests on the authority which is given to Jesus. As soon as his authority is announced in verse 18 there follows the charge, "make disciples!" The reminiscence of the "sending" in Matthew 10 and of its parallel in Mark 16:15, "'Go into all the world and preach the gospel to the whole creation,'" largely obscures the peculiarity of our text. The same reality is envisaged here as in chapter 10. Yet there it appears in its implicit and hidden form, while here in its explicit and visible form. In both instances the founding, through Jesus' word, of the *apostolic* church is envisaged. It is the church that receives the apostles' word and actively transmits it. "'As the Father has sent me, even so I send you'" (John 20:21). This apostolic church, existing not for itself, but "for Christ," on behalf of him (2 Cor. 5:20), is the decisive event of the *eschaton* that has broken into time. The existence of the new community consists not only in the apostles' preaching of the gospel and their fellow men's listening. It is constantly renewed as the listeners themselves become "apostolic" and, as new disciples, begin to proclaim the good news. Consequently the charge is not only *kēryxate* but *mathēteusate*, "make disciples." John 17:20-23 might well be the appropriate commentary to this charge. " 'I do not pray for these only, but also for those who are to believe in me through their word, that they may all be one; even as thou, Father, art in me, and I in thee, that they also may be in us, so that the world may believe that thou hast sent me . . . and hast loved them even as thou hast loved me.' "

And now the great problem of our text:

"*. . . all nations . . .*" *panta ta ethnē*. On the basis of these words the text is called "the great commission." What does "all nations" mean?

It means, first of all, *people* from among all nations who are received into discipleship. They become significant for the existence of their respective nations because the nations now come within reach of the apostolate and its proclamation and receive their concealed center through the Christian community living in their midst. Note the *autous,* which occurs twice. It cannot refer to *ethnē*. Not the nations as such are made disciples. This interpretation once infested missionary thinking and was connected with the painful fantasies of the German Christians. It is worthless.

"All nations" means, furthermore, people from Gentile lands, from the *goyim*. This does not exclude Israel. Her right of the firstborn, her *dignitas primogeniturae* ["dignity as the firstborn"], as Calvin called it, remains unimpaired. Yet the disciples are summoned to go out to the Gentile people and nations. For now the eschatological Israel shall appear, the people gathered by the Messiah who appeared at the end of time. This is the new eschatological community. It is gathered from among the Jews and Gentiles. The doors and windows of the house of Israel, so far closed, must open. The apostles' mission is "to the Jew first and also to the Greek" (Rom. 1:16). Accordingly, Mark 16:15 states, "'Go into all the world and preach the gospel to the whole creation.'" Matthew expresses the same idea, only in more concrete terms, when he speaks of "all nations." Through this mission the community of Jesus becomes manifest in his resurrection as the universal community. It is the eschatological Israel, the Israel which receives into its life and history the chosen ones from among the Gentiles. In fact, it had never been anything else. Even during his life before death Jesus had never given it any other foundation than that which now became apparent: not as a special community within Israel, and hence not as a new form of the previous Israel in history, but as the Israel of the end of time, fulfilling the destiny of the historical Israel, as "a covenant to the people, a light to the nations" (Isa. 42:6; 49:8). It is important to see this. Already the relationship to verse 18 and its parallels rules out any limitation of Jesus' dominion. How could he, to whom all power is given, have ever intended founding a pious little Jewish club? The name of the "Son of man" is the name of him whom "all peoples, nations, and languages" shall serve (Dan. 7:14). The field where the Son of man sows the good seed is the world (Matt. 13:38). The ransom for many (*anti pollōn*, Mark 10:45) and the shedding of blood for many (*hyper pollōn*) certainly imply Jesus' identification with the Suffering Servant of God in Isaiah 53 (see in particular verses 11-12). Of him it is said, " 'It is too light a thing that you should be my servant to raise up the tribes of Jacob and to restore the preserved of Israel; I will give you as a light to the nations, that my salvation may reach to the end of the earth'" (Isa. 49:6). "He shall be exalted and lifted up, and shall be very high. . . . So shall he startle many nations; kings shall shut their mouths because of him" (Isa. 52:13f.). From the very beginning Jesus calls his disciples "the salt of the earth" and "the light of the world" (Matt. 5:13-14). Already John the Baptist had proclaimed that God would raise up children to Abraham from the stones (Matt. 3:9). Jesus himself spoke of the many that will come from east and west and sit at table with the patriarchs (Matt. 8:11); of the angels whom the Son of man shall send out at the Parousia to gather his elect from the four winds, from one end of heaven to the other (Matt. 24:31; see also 25:31f.); of the servants that will go out to the streets and gather all they find, both bad and good (Matt. 22:9f.); even of the testimony his disciples will bear also before the Gentiles (Matt. 10:18).

Jesus at first kept this universality of the new community relatively hidden, as he did with the power and authority given him (verse 18), and with the name of Messiah (Matt. 16:20). Why? The previous, historical, Israel had not yet run its course before Jesus' death. His life had not yet been spent as a ransom for many. Not everything was ready yet. The table had not been set. The guests could not yet be invited. Israel was not yet fully prepared to fulfill its eschatological mission. Aware of this "not yet," Jesus understood his mission to be—temporarily—to the lost sheep of the house of Israel. But even as he pronounced this rule, he made an exception (Matt. 15:24). In the very strange passage of Mark 4:10-12 an even stricter rule is announced. Initially he did "not yet" address himself directly and properly to the whole people of Israel, but only to his disciples. Aware of this "not yet" he charged his disciples to go—temporarily—nowhere among the Gentiles and to enter no town of the Samaritans (Matt. 10:5). This "not yet" again overshadows the relative seclusion of the primitive apostles in Jerusalem. They had first to overcome their reluctance to get in touch with the Gentiles (Acts 10), and finally entrusted Paul with the mission to the Gentiles (Gal. 2). Nevertheless, while this "not yet" casts its shadows even over the time after Easter, it was in fact overcome. The great turning point in history had since been marked. The "delivering" of Jesus to the Gentiles, foretold in the second and third announcements of his imminent suffering, had taken place (Matt. 27:2). This event separates the times. Now the eschatological Israel begins. Jesus' rejection by the Jews becomes the offer of grace to the Gentiles. In the rejection and death of its Messiah, the history of Israel has reached its end and goal; the hidden church of Jews and Gentiles awaits its revelation. The messianic Israel is in fact revealed by the words of verse 19. What does it matter if the revelation was apparently not fully realized right away? The number twelve of the eschatological Israel is even externally again complete by the addition of Paul. The activity of the apostles must set in with this very revelation: "Make disciples of all nations."

This "all nations" in no way contradicts the earlier teaching and practice of Jesus. The narrow path within Israel had to branch out into the wide world of all nations, and the inroad into the wide world had to begin as the narrow path within Israel. "Salvation is from the Jews" (John 4:22). From the *Jews*—this is the first, limited, and hidden form of the eschatological community, represented by the eleven. Salvation *comes* from the Jews—to the Gentiles—this is its second, unlimited, and manifest form, represented by the eleven plus one.

To say that the primitive apostles acted as if they had not heard the Great Commission (J. Weiss, Klostermann) is misleading. Already the eleven, as Jesus saw and addressed them, are the eleven plus one who shall carry out the mission. The church as a body will obey the command: its proclamation, first exclusively addressed to Israel, is immediately understood by the Jews of all lands in their own language (Acts 2:6f.). Spread by Paul, the twelfth apostle, it becomes the message to the Gentiles.

It is therefore not necessary to draw upon the assumption of a "backward projection on the part of the later church" (Klostermann) in order to explain verse 19. Nor do we have to declare the commission as "interpolated," to justify the mission to the Gentiles by the "supra-Jewish substance of the Gospel," and to find its Magna Charta in the history of "early Christian missions" (J. Weiss). As recapitulation and anticipation, revealing the hidden reality of the eschatological community, the Great Commission is truly the most genuine utterance of the risen Jesus.

"*. . . baptizing them in the name of the Father and of the Son and of the Holy Spirit.*" The making of disciples is achieved by baptism and teaching.

Baptizing is the priestly function of objectively introducing others into the realm of God's reign. Initially it is the function of Jesus himself. Yet here he transmits it to his first disciples after he had them taste in advance the fruit of his sacrificial death—at the Last Supper—and then had suffered death.

Baptizing in a *name* meant, in the Jewish custom of the day, to administer to someone a cleansing bath intended to certify a state to be attained. A Gentile slave, for instance, was administered baptism as a sign of his liberation when he left. Baptizing in the name of the Father and of the Son and of the Holy Spirit means to give to someone the cleansing bath which certifies to him and to others that he belongs to this God. Father, Son, and Holy Spirit, then, are for him what the name of the triune God really stands for. He in turn has to confess and to confirm that he belongs to this God.

Some special observations:

1. If the BD reading[1] *baptisantes* ("after having baptized them") were correct, the administering of baptism would only be a secondary task to laying the groundwork for the primary task of teaching.

2. The text does not propose a liturgical formula to be used for baptism (as maintained by Zahn). Baptism "in the name of Jesus Christ" (Acts 2:38) therefore does not speak against the authenticity of the text (as has been suggested by J. Weiss).

3. Stress is laid, not on the act of baptizing itself, since cleansing rites attesting initiation were a current Jewish practice of the time; rather, the emphasis is on the particular kind of baptism the disciples are asked to administer. A Gentile becomes a disciple when he is assured of his belonging to the Father, Son, and Holy Spirit.

4. The external act of baptizing is a *signum pro re* ["a sign (standing) for the reality"]. The disciples are commanded, and therefore they expect to be able, to bring about the state of affairs to be certified. By the intermediary of the disciples the Gentiles shall be joined with those who belong to the

---

1. A reference to two Greek manuscripts: B—*Codex Vaticanus;* D—*Codex Bezae Cantabrigiensis.*

Father, the Son, and the Holy Spirit, thereby becoming themselves disciples. Luke 24:47 explains the meaning of this incorporation. Repentance and the forgiveness of sin shall be preached to the Gentiles in Jesus' name. They become disciples as sinners who, set free by God and thankful to God, are wrenched from the separation from God.

The command to baptize is to be understood in the same light. It is the transferral of the messianic power of Jesus, the priest of all men, to Peter. "I will give you the keys of the kingdom of heaven" (Matt. 16:19), a most genuine word of the risen Lord. Genuine and very significant, furthermore, is the invocation of the name of the triune God at the very moment when the universal existence of the apostolic church at the end of time is revealed. This is the only place in the New Testament where this name is invoked with such simplicity (cf. 1 Cor. 12:4-6; 2 Cor. 13:13; 2 Thess. 2:13-14; Eph. 4:4-6; 1 Pet. 1:2).

". . . *teaching them to observe all that I have commanded you.*" As baptism constitutes the existence and the nature of discipleship, teaching constitutes the ways and works of the disciples.

"Teaching," *didaskein,* is the function of the prophet and teacher by preaching and instruction. Now Jesus appoints his disciples to this teaching office. To become a Christian means to become a Christ to others by participating in Christ's kingly, priestly, and prophetic ministry. The apostles accede to this ministry after passing through the crisis, that is, through their failure during the Passion when their apostleship, humanly speaking, had become utterly discredited. They had failed in *tērein,* in observing what Jesus had commanded them. Yet without inquiring into the validity of their conversion (see, however, Luke 22:32), Jesus freely entrusts them, the undeserving, with teaching the Gentiles this "observance," and with guiding them in the ways and works of disciples. (*Tērein* means "to keep," "to preserve," to protect something entrusted to one's care.)

". . . *all that I have commanded you.*" What did Jesus command them to do? To follow him, in order "to be with him" (Mark 3:14). They are to live within the earthly confines of the kingdom of God and to submit to the order of life established there. All this not as an end in itself, for the sake of their own personal morals and salvation or of the well-being of society, but that the order of service be preserved which he had given them, his heralds and apostles. All "baptized" become *eo ipso* [by that very act] subservient to this order of service, the very foundation of the Christian community. They in turn need to be called to acknowledge, to keep, and to confirm their belonging to the Father, the Son, and the Holy Spirit. They need to be nurtured in this service in order that their works may become those of disciples and a Christian community may exist in the world. It exists only where the things commanded by Jesus are "observed." This nurturing of the Gentiles who, by baptism, become servants of the triune God, is the task of the apostles. As the witnesses to Jesus' life and resurrection, they are entrusted with the task for all times and in all places. All others receive it only from them, secondhand. The apostles, and they alone, are called to teach in the church. For there is no room in the church for any other object of *tērein* but the one commanded by Jesus to the apostles. What they have been commanded, they must teach without omission, the whole content of the order of service. This is the New Testament affirmation of the self-sufficiency of the Scriptures, the crossroad where we must part from the Roman Catholic Church. Teaching in the church can only be repetitive of apostolic teaching.

There remains one more question with regard to verses 19-20a. What about the explicitly stated task (Matt. 10:8f.) to heal the sick, to raise the dead, to make clean the lepers, to cast out evil spirits? We know from Acts and from several Letters that such special "gifts," though not widespread, were not lacking in the later church. Nevertheless, the part of Jesus' commandment dealing with doing signs has been fulfilled and become superfluous with the resurrection of Jesus, the sign of signs. Signs may happen again. But they cannot be postulated as essential marks of the eschatological community. In its past, the forty days, as in its future, the Second Coming, this community is surrounded by the one "sign of the Son of man." When in Mark 16:17ff. the gift of "accompanying" signs is declared to be an almost indispensable attribute of faith, it only shows the noncanonical character of that text. The task of the apostles, and therefore also of the apostolic church, consists in baptizing and teaching in the light of this sign—in the light of Easter morning, in the light of "the hope laid up for you in heaven" (Col. 1:5).

VERSE 20B

"And lo, I am with you . . ." The church of the *eschaton* which broke into time and now is manifest and recognized is not left alone. Its founder possesses not in vain all authority in heaven and on earth (verse 18). "Where two or three are gathered in my name, there am I in the midst of them" (Matt. 18:20). Jesus himself, with all his power and authority, stands behind the apostles when they carry out his command and commission. "He who hears you hears me" (Luke 10:16). "So every one who acknowledges me before man, I also will acknowledge before my Father who is in heaven" (Matt. 10:32). *Ergo nunquam plane exspirabit ecclesia christiana* ["Therefore, never will the Christian church completely expire"] (Bengel). This is why the Christian church can never speak or act on its own authority and for its own cause. The self-seeking and self-exalting idea of the Roman Catholic Church is thereby attacked at the very roots.

"I am with you" is, according to Genesis 28:15; Judges 6:12; Haggai 1:13, the affirmation of the immediate presence of God. In making it, Jesus once more says who he is. "I am *with you.*" This is not to say that he will always be with his people in the same way as he is now. These forty days are unique, only to be compared with the return in glory which, rightly understood, begins already with the forty days. However, the church between Ascension and Second Coming is not without a master. And because the church is in

the world, the world is not without a master either. The church has no right to consider the world as "masterless," merely neutral or even hostile, or else it has not grasped Jesus' "with you."

"I am with you": in remembrance of my past life, death, and resurrection, I speak and act today. In the Holy Spirit I fill and rule the present, any present, with my word. I will come with the future, any future. I stand at the door and knock. With my past, my present, and my future I shall be with you evermore.

This is the *promise* of the risen Lord, covering the time beyond the forty days. It is the point of departure for the subsequent events at the end of time. As the apostles receive and grasp this promise and stand on this firm ground, they are the rock on which Jesus builds his church, stronger than the gates of Hades.

"*. . . to the close of the age.*" We must reckon with three different times or ages. From creation to the appearance of Christ: the time as it passes, and is actually past, with the appearance of Christ. From Christ's appearance to his return in glory: the *eschaton* as revealed in Christ's resurrection. From his return in glory into eternity: God's own eternal time in which the temporal is suspended. Accordingly, "to the close of the age," of this age, must signify until the time when the *eschaton*, ushered in with the appearance of Christ, will have run its course, when the universe will be subjected to God's reign, when the distinct reign of Christ will come to an end, and God will be everything to everyone (1 Cor. 15:27f.). Because of Jesus' presence, the sum and substance of our text, the Great Commission of the risen Lord to baptize and evangelize is valid throughout the days of this "last" age.

Part II

HISTORY

3

Captivity and Liberation in the Modern Missionary Movement

Orlando E. Costas

Orlando E. Costas (1942-1987), a Puerto Rican ordained in the American
Baptist Churches and the United Church of Christ, was the Thornley B.
Wood Professor of Missiology and director of Hispanic studies at Eastern
Baptist Theological Seminary, Philadelphia, Pennsylvania. He later became
the Judson Professor of Missiology and dean of the Andover Newton
School of Theology. A pastor, missionary to Latin America, community
organizer, internationally known missiologist, contextual theologian, and
theological educator, he authored thirteen books in Spanish and English.
Costas served on the Commission on Human Rights and the Committee
on Evangelism and Education of the Baptist World Alliance.

Is the modern missionary movement an entrepreneurial force? That
is, is it a "business enterprise," a religious counterpart of the capitalist
movement? Is this the reason so many churches and Christians historically
related to the modern missionary movement have divorced themselves
from their respective cultures, have embraced an ethic of neutrality, and
have been more comfortable with structures of oppression than with
movements of liberation? Could it be a mere coincidence that Christian
mission has experienced its greatest expansion during the colonial era? Is
it a matter of simple semantics that missionary activity has been called an
"enterprise"? Could not this designation logically arise because missionary
activity is possible both thanks to the prosperity of those countries that have
enthusiastically sent missionaries to distant lands and because such activity
accompanies—or at least prepares the way for or follows in the steps of—
commercial, military, or political activities of such countries? Should we
not see behind this the reason why the modern missionary movement has
assumed the corporation model as its organizational structure?

These are not frivolous questions. They arise out of concrete historical
situations. Therefore, they cannot be brushed aside with simplistic defensive
answers.

First published in *Christ Outside the Gate: Mission Beyond Christendom* (Maryknoll,
NY: Orbis Books, 1982), 58-70. Reprinted here with permission.

The fact of the matter is that during the last five centuries Christian mission has shown features of a large entrepreneurial network. The agents of this network have been mission societies, with their stockholders (individual and collective supporters), boards of directors, administrators, and employees (missionaries). This system has succeeded not only in subjugating Christian mission, but also has turned it into a tool of domestication, thereby stripping it of its liberating content.

In this chapter we shall try to demonstrate why Christian mission has been joined to the world of free enterprise. This will allow us to explain the why and the wherefore of such a union, and will help us to distinguish between the effect of that process (the subjugation of the church insofar as it is the People of God as well as of those whom the church has been called to serve) and the basic purpose of Christian mission (to be a channel of wholeness and liberation).

MISSION AS ENTERPRISE: THE MISSIONARY SOCIETIES

For Latin Americans this issue dates back to the discovery of their continent. It is well known that the people who came to those shores from Spain were not only looking for gold and glory, but were also deeply motivated by religious concerns. Hence a representative of the church accompanied Columbus as early as his second voyage. Thus it was that conquest and colonization followed evangelization. (In fact, one pretext of the *encomiendas*—grants of slaves to the colonists—was to evangelize the Indians.)

If it is well known that the Iberian expansion was motivated by a genuine missionary zeal, it is no less well known that those missions also most effectively extended Spanish and Portuguese culture and rule. In 1493 Pope Alexander VI granted to the Spanish kings political and religious authority over all the territory already discovered or yet to be discovered that lay more than "one hundred leagues" west of the Azores in the western part of the Atlantic, provided that those territories did not already belong to a Christian monarch. One year later this privilege was amended to include Portugal, to whose lot fell the territory of Brazil. The papal bulls of Alexander VI do not represent merely political privilege, but also a missionary duty: "for the popes of the Renaissance who were more interested in the arts than religion, this was the easiest way to unload their responsibilities onto the kings of Spain and Portugal" (González 1970: 142-43). In this way these monarchs became the pope's vicars in the New World.

From 1516 on, all vessels heading to the New World were required to carry at least one missionary. Traditional mendicant orders such as the Franciscans and the Dominicans dedicated themselves to this task. To these were added the work of the Jesuits and the Mercedarians, in addition to some secular priests. In this way the chief Catholic missionaries early on became part of the Ibero-American colonial process. Centuries later their Protestant counterparts were to be absorbed into a new colonial process: North Atlantic neocolonialism.

For us who come from the Protestant tradition, the issue dates back to the Reformers. Melanchthon and Zwingli and Calvin and Bucer held that mission work was the responsibility of the civil authorities. Therefore it does not surprise us that Protestant mission work began with the political and economic expansion of such Protestant countries as Holland, England, and Denmark.

After becoming independent from Spain (1581), the Dutch set out to develop a naval empire. In 1602 they founded the East India Company. In addition to its obvious commercial goal, that company's objective was to propagate the Christian faith in the East Indies. Hence the company, and not the (Reformed) church, contracted missionaries, even going so far as to establish a seminary for their training. This also explains the commercial stimulus that was part of the beginnings of Dutch mission work: "Missionaries were paid for every baptism they performed" (ibid.: 190).

The corporation model as a means of commercial expansion had already been used by the English since the last decades of the sixteenth century. The idea of companies with limited liability, in which the owners were liable only for the actual stocks of the company and not for other economic interests they might have, produced an extraordinary incentive for English merchants and enormous dividends for the Crown. All the same, the deep religious feelings of the English made Parliament charge the mercantile companies with the duty to evangelize such pagan peoples with whom they might come into contact. Thus a missionary goal was added to the economic and political goals in the constitutional charter granted to Humphrey Gilbert in 1583 for the colonization of North America. The Virginia and Massachusetts Bay companies had the same responsibility written into their charters. In this way the English mission work, like that of Holland, was in its beginnings part of its mercantile expansion. When in 1648 Parliament decided to take care of mission work separately, it created a mission corporation, a company with limited liability, the Society for the Propagation of the Gospel in New England. This was the model that would characterize most modern mission work.

Denmark accompanied Holland and England in their mercantile and mission efforts. In 1622 this Lutheran nation founded an East Indian company (like England in 1600 and Holland in 1622), though it did not include mission work among its duties. This company established two colonies in India: Tranquebar in the south and Serampore in the north. In 1706 King Frederick IV felt compelled to add the missionary dimension to Tranquebar. Since he was not able to find candidates in his own country, he turned to the University of Halle in Germany, which since the time of its founder, Jacob Spener, had become the center of German pietism. Thus the first missionaries of the famous Tranquebar mission set out from Halle.

Later the Danes supported missionary efforts in Greenland and Labrador, with everything under the auspices of the Crown.

Interestingly, this Danish initiative, with its pietist link in Halle, greatly influenced the missionary work that the Moravians undertook in 1732 under Count Ludwig von Zinzendorf. I say that this is interesting because the Moravians were the first Protestants who put into practice the idea that missionary work was the responsibility of the *church*, and not of a corporation or a government. Besides this, the missionaries of the Unitas Fratrum, as the Moravians called themselves, used the experience of the Herrnhut community and developed a radically different mission focus. They would immigrate to their place of service, support themselves by manual labor, live in communities, and minister from them.[1] Beginning with the Danish colony of Saint Thomas in the Caribbean, the Moravian missionaries, most of whom were simple workers with little formal education but filled with love and evangelistic courage, soon spread to all parts of the world.

Because of the breadth of their work, however, the Moravians found it hard to pay passages and to start work in different mission fields. In the middle of this situation was founded a "mercantile enterprise to make profits for the Lord's work" (Danker 1971: 21)[2] At first Zinzendorf opposed the idea (partly due to his aristocratic background and partly for theological reasons), but he later agreed to the idea, provided that the profits were exclusively used for mission work. Under the leadership of Abraham Durninger, who has been called a "mercantile genius," the Moravians developed "a complex international business in textiles, especially linen, tobacco, and wholesale and retail sales" (ibid.: 23). Thus the Moravians added the principle "profit for the Lord" to their missionary "communalism" and thereby unconsciously helped develop an entrepreneurial identity for the missionary cause (ibid.: 31ff.).

Undoubtedly the Moravians' experience was a great inspiration for William Carey, who has been called the "father of modern missions." Carey, a self-taught person who earned his living as a cobbler, challenged himself

---

1. An excellent example of such missional communalism is the economic system set up at the Moravian settlement in Bethlehem, Pennsylvania (founded in 1742). According to J. Taylor Hamilton and Kenneth G. Hamilton, the system, which became known as the Economy, was "adopted . . . so as to develop the resources of the new settlement as quickly as possible and thus free the latent power of the community for the work of the Savior." They add that "Basic to the Economy was a community of labor rather than property. . . . Any member who owned property was permitted to retain it if he chose, but all were required to place their time, talents, and labor at the disposal of the Church. No private enterprises existed in the community; every form of business and manufacture belonged to the Church, as did all real estate. All branches of the common Economy came under the supervision of committees. . . . With all its defects . . . the Economy served its purpose remarkably well in its day. . . . The Economy supported about fifty evangelists and pastors and maintained some fifteen schools and provided the traveling expenses for missionaries to the West Indies and Surinam" (*History of the Moravian Church: The Renewed* Unitas Fratrum *1722-1957* [Bethlehem, PA; Interprovincial Board of Christian Education/Winston-Salem, N.C.: Moravian Church in America, 1967], 137).

2. Cf. Hamilton and Hamilton, *History,* 113.

and his English brothers and sisters to "expect great things from God" and to "undertake great things for God." He set out for India hoping to support himself by his trade, but that noble goal could not happen except through the formation of a missionary structure. So, the Particular Baptist Society for the Propagation of the Gospel among the Heathen was founded.[3] The English East India Company did not allow Carey, on his arrival in Calcutta, to enter as a missionary because it feared the subversive effect that his work could have among the Bengali people. The only way he could remain in India was to work in North Bengal as an administrator of an indigo plantation. When new missionaries arrived five years later, Carey was able to move with them to Serampore, fifty kilometers from Calcutta, thanks to the manager of the Danish East India Company.

Once settled in Serampore, the missionaries established a genuine commune in which they shared the little that they earned with their manual labor. Later in their free time they carried out impressive work: they founded churches and schools; developed botanical projects; undertook linguistic and cultural investigations; and established the first newspapers in the region. In 1818 they founded the first university in North India: Serampore College. Despite their English Baptist links, Carey and his colleagues attempted to develop a work with indigenous foundations. Perhaps this explains the many tensions between the Mission Society and the Serampore College and Mission. Finally the society refused to give Serampore financial support and dismissed Carey as one of its missionaries. In England false rumors flitted about regarding the lives and work of Carey and his colleagues. The work was seriously affected because of the struggle between the society and the local leaders—especially the missionaries—for the control of the mission and the college. Shortly after Carey's death the Serampore College and Mission had to submit to the control of the British Baptist Mission Society in order to survive.

This account of William Carey and his colleagues clearly shows the sad experience of mission work throughout the last three centuries. Mission work is so dependent on the world of free enterprise that it is practically impossible for it to exist without that support. Despite the progress of his work within the local reality and despite his profound commitment to the Bengali people (Carey never returned to England), this pioneer of modern mission work found himself forced time and again to depend on the prevailing economic system—from the banking system (which enabled the transfer of funds from England by the use of letters of credit) to the mercantile companies. On the other hand, because modern missions have been built along the lines of the corporation model, they have made Christian mission part and parcel of the colonial or neocolonial system. As a North American missionary colleague has aptly stated in an unpublished paper:

---

3. "Particular Baptists" were those who held to Calvinist theology as against "General Baptists" who were Arminian. Interestingly enough, it was Calvinist Baptists who championed the missionary cause among Baptists rather than the "freewill" Arminians.

The majority of missionary societies [have been] organized following the pattern of business corporations, operating in a given country or in their colonial extensions to make a profit through manufacture, sales, finance or whatever. The structure consists of a Board of Directors, administrative officers, and employees. The efficiency of this system depends on the fact that those who are involved are working within the same laws and economic conditions. The golden era of this type of mission was during the colonial system of the last century, and Marxists continue to remind us of the dependence of missions on the colonial powers. Even today, North American missionary societies work by and large in countries that have diplomatic relations with the USA and Canada. (Troutman 1976: 4)

The trouble with all of this is that it has branded the churches and Christian institutions of the third world that have arisen from mission work. Meanwhile the majority of these churches, institutions, and believers depend on the mother country, if not economically, at least in theology, ecclesiology, missiology, and political ideology. Educational agencies such as the Theological Education Fund, whose initial capital was donated by John D. Rockefeller, Jr.; organizations such as the World Council of Churches; ecumenical social programs such as Church World Service, Christian Aid, and Bread for the World; Catholic agencies such as Caritas, Adveniat, and Misereor; and Evangelical agencies such as World Vision, Tear Fund, World Relief, and World Concern are all made possible thanks to the economic power of the North American, Western European, and Australasian countries.

This reality is reinforced by the extraordinary missionary presence today in third world countries. In 1979 it was estimated that there was a worldwide Protestant missionary force of 81,500 and a Catholic force of 138,000 (Wilson 1980: 20-21). Nearly two-thirds of Protestant missionaries came from North America—the United States and Canada—and, of these, 33.2 percent were working in Latin America and the Caribbean. (Of the 9,958 North American Catholic missionaries serving overseas, 47 percent were concentrated in Latin America.) Although we do not have the data as to the approximate number of agencies through which this impressive number of missionaries carries on its work throughout the world, we do know that in regard to North America there are no fewer than 714 Protestant mission societies (Danker 1971: 20-22)[4] with a total annual income of $1,148,169,321.[5] These figures show, on the one hand, the uneven concentration of missionary personnel

---

4. There are approximately three hundred Catholic missionary societies in the United States, but their total-income figure is unavailable.

5. In 1976 Richie Hogg compared the income of the American Protestant overseas missionary enterprise to the "Fortune 500" list of the largest industrial corporations in the United States and found it stood only in 410th place. See Richie Hogg, "The Role of American Protestantism in World Mission," *American Missions in Bicentennial Perspective*, ed. R. Pierce Beaver (Pasadena, CA: William Carey Library, 1977), 370.

from the continent with one of the largest concentrations of missionaries in Latin America, which is both one of the least populated (with less than 10 percent of the total world population) and one of the most economically exploited parcels of the third world. They suggest, on the other hand, that missions are expressions of a definite entrepreneurial network, which, though not occupying a very high place among large corporations, is nevertheless alarming when we take into account the impact that such a presence is bound to have on their self-understanding, reflection on the faith, and social, political, and cultural attitudes of those churches and Christians that are related in one way or another with missionary and para-missionary agencies from the first world.

ENTERPRISE AS MISSION: THE LIBERAL PROJECT

The incorporation of the modern missionary movement into the world of free enterprise did not occur by accident; it fits into the great liberal project of Europe and North America. Although the modern missionary movement dates back to the sixteenth and seventeenth centuries for Catholics and Protestants respectively, this project did not begin to stand out until the end of the seventeenth century. All the same, liberalism's roots go back to the Renaissance, which is both economically and sociologically connected to mercantilism. The modern missionary movement, as we have noted, is a product of mercantile expansion. That is, it has obvious links with the platform that was used to launch the liberal project. For that reason we should not be surprised to find very early in modern missionary work key postulates of liberalism such as progress, liberty, and individualism.

Thus it was not by accident that mission work took an entrepreneurial shape. It occurred because the modern missionary movement is the child of the world of free enterprise. This is not to deny the fact that missions developed from theological influences, much less that the Holy Spirit's sovereign initiative, presence, and activity guided the motives of the missionary movement. However, it is an established sociological fact that religious movements always sprout in relation to concrete historical situations. In theological terms the work of God does not exist outside of history; instead it occurs amid history's tensions and conflicts. Hence there are relationships between faith and culture, theology and ideology, church and society. In the case of the modern missionary movement, Christian mission was not only made to depend on the model of the colonial-mercantile-imperial or neocolonial-liberal-capitalist enterprise, but also on its goal to reorganize society in terms of an economy free from state control, of a governmental structure based on voting rights, and of a universal vision founded on the idea of progress. From this perspective, the missionary movement was called to various tasks.

First, it had to legitimate the liberal project with symbols, doctrinal statements, and ecclesial practices. In order to do this, missionary societies organized churches with a representative or congregational form of government wherein liberal democracy could be exercised. They founded schools and religious-education programs based on personal honesty, dedication to work, temperance, and moderation, respect for civil authorities, self-control, and avoidance of vices and worldly pleasures. They established seminaries, institutes, or theological faculties where pastors, teachers, and administrators could be trained in accordance with liberal ideology. Finally there was the task of interpreting the faith in symbols and categories that corresponded to the liberal project through translated literary works and original publications.

In the second place, the missionary movement has sometimes been called to prepare the way for agents of liberal economics or politics. This was the task that the Wesleyan movement performed in the eighteenth century and David Livingstone in the nineteenth. The Wesleyan movement first set out to evangelize the English proletariat and then moved to evangelize the heathen. Thus it provided a religious alternative to the French Revolution's "Liberty, Equality, and Fraternity" in the form of what Bernard Semmel has called the "Methodist Synthesis." This synthesis combined the old and the new: a passion for liberty and respect for order, and the internal renewal of England along with its outward expansion. In addition it established the ideology of the Victorian era. In this way the Wesleyan movement's home-mission project preceded its worldwide mission work and also prepared the way for England's national mission, namely, the British Empire (Semmel 1973: vii, 20, 170ff.). We can talk in similar terms of the great explorer—missionary David Livingstone. Not only did Livingstone open up the routes into the heart of Africa for English business; he also set the foundation for Britain's colonization of Africa (Listowel 1974: 232-46; Jeal 1973: 370-74).

Third, and most recently, mission societies and other related agencies have enabled the church (both at home and abroad) and the nations they serve to adapt to the entrepreneurial system's new strategies. It is well known that since the mid-1950s the entrepreneurial world has been undergoing a profound change. Panamanian economist Xabier Gorostiaga has divided this process into two parts: the internalization of production (1955-65) and the internalization of capital (1965-75), which has resulted in the development of multinational companies and transnational financial centers.[6]

Curiously enough, the world missionary movement has been experiencing similar changes. In 1963 the Seventh World Missionary Conference, meeting in Mexico and sponsored by the World Council of Churches, developed the idea of "witness in six continents." Since then the idea of an internationalized mission has become popular in Protestant mission circles.

---

6. See Xabier Gorostiaga, "Notas sobre metodología para un diagnóstico económico del capitalismo latinoamericano," in *Capitalismo: violencia y antivida*, vol. 1, ed. Elsa Tamez and Saúl Trinidad, Colección DEI (San José, Costa Rica: EDUCA, 1978), 40-48; idem, *Los banqueros del imperio: Los centros financieros en los países sub-desarrollados*, Colección DEI (San José, Costa Rica: EDUCA, 1977), passim.

Among Catholics the impetus of Vatican II gave birth to the idea of "mutuality in mission"; that is, all of the church is to be involved in mission and not simply the church located in so-called mission lands. Thus many Catholic missionary societies have a multinational missionary staff serving in many lands and cultures.

In Evangelical Protestantism a series of missionary and evangelistic congresses has created an ever greater international awareness of mission work. This series began in 1966 with the Wheaton Congress on World Evangelization. It continued with the First and Second Latin American Congresses of Evangelization (Bogota, 1969; Lima, 1979) and other similar congresses in Asia, Africa, North America, and Europe, and culminated in the International Congress of World Evangelization held in Lausanne in 1974, which was followed by the Consultation on World Evangelization held in June 1980, in Pattaya, Thailand, and the Congress on Frontier Missions held in Edinburgh, Scotland, in October 1980.[7]

At Lausanne there was a discussion about a new missionary era (an expression that was also used in the 8th World Missionary Conference sponsored by the World Council of Churches in Bangkok, Thailand, in 1973). The meeting in Lausanne concluded that "the dominant role of Western missions is fast disappearing. God is raising up from the young churches a great new resource for world evangelization ("The Lausanne Covenant," 1975). The emerging mission societies of the third world are this new resource.[8]

During this time mission societies such as the Latin American Mission (nondenominational), the Paris Mission (Reformed), the World Mission Council (Congregational), and service agencies such as World Vision were turning into "multinational" organizations. The Latin American Mission (LAM) became part of the Community of Latin American Evangelical Ministries (CLAME), the Paris Mission became the Evangelical Community for Apostolic Action (CEVAA), and the Council for World Mission, successor to the London Missionary Society, went through a reorganization that has brought into its fellowship congregational churches in the United Kingdom, Australia, and New Zealand plus all of the other churches with which the old London Missionary Society was related. World Vision, an organization which for some time has had its financial base in the United

---

7. For a report on Edinburgh 1980, see William Cook, "A Church for Every People by the Year 2,000," in *Occasional Essays* 8, nos. 1-2 (December 1981): 18-19.

8. While no exact figures on the number of third world Protestant missionaries exist, there are some limited studies that have been able to identify several hundred. Third world missionary societies could include well over 5,000 missionaries. For outdated yet helpful statistical evidence, see James Wong, Peter Larson, and Edward Pentecost, *Missions from the Third World: A World Survey of Non-Western Missions in Asia, Africa and Latin America* (Singapore: Church Growth Study Center, 1972). For a discussion on issues related to the work of Protestant Third World missions, see Theodore Williams, ed., *World Missions: Building Bridges or Barriers* (Bangalore, India: World Evangelical Fellowship Missions Commission, 1979).

States, Canada, Australia, and New Zealand, has developed a separate international corporation with a board of directors and an executive and program staff from the first and third worlds.[9]

One of the most interesting examples of this process is the United States Center for World Mission, founded in 1977 and located in Pasadena, California. This center includes a consortium of new mission societies that function within historical churches as alternatives (shock troops) to the work of mission boards or official denominational departments. Furthermore, it has stimulated the organization of a national committee that brings together mission committees of local churches throughout the United States and offers, among other things, advice for the financial support of mission work. It also sponsors William Carey University, which offers opportunities to young university students who hope to serve either as career missionaries or (preferably) as missionary volunteers through secular employment abroad. The university attempts to be a link with several centers of missiological research and missionary activity that are located in strategic parts of the world. This mission complex focuses its attention on areas of the world where there are the greatest numbers of peoples as yet untouched by the gospel, such as China, animist groups, and the Muslim, Hindu, and Buddhist worlds. Its strategy is to spread the gospel to these places via the most workable method. In some instances this may involve business executives or members of the diplomatic corps. Its organizational principles are a combination of the old voluntary association (connected to missionary societies), computer technology (e.g., the use of computers to gather statistics and form a network of contacts with the financial bases of the churches), and the construction of a network of multinational operations.

It should be said at the outset that relationships of this sort are unconscious and indirect. They are not concocted by specific groups of people. We must avoid what Gorostiaga calls a "'detective view of history' that suspects Machiavellian plots whenever one mentions power elites that try to institute a structurally functioning system" (Gorostiaga 1978: 40). Christians who participate in the modern missionary movement do so, by and large, out of a sincere commitment to Jesus Christ and the Christian missionary mandate. Nevertheless, they are part of a worldwide system that often uses people, movements, and institutions for purposes other than the communication of the gospel and its liberating power.

Given the traditional alliance between the world of free enterprise and the missionary movement, it appears that whatever change occurs in the former would sooner or later affect the latter. The simple fact is that the missionary movement has been supported economically by women, men,

---

9. I have been referring specifically to the Protestant missionary movement, although the work of Catholic missions has similar links in countries such as the Federal Republic of Germany, The Netherlands, the United States, and Canada. It is interesting to note that the Catholic churches of Holland, Germany, France, Italy, the United States, and Canada also began to form missionary societies in the nineteenth century.

and agencies committed to the so-called free-enterprise system and its liberal capitalist ideology. Since many mission benefactors are people whose lives are involved directly or indirectly with multinational enterprises, it is natural that mission organizations not only develop work methods, organizational structures, and administrative techniques from the capitalist system, but also that they are part of that economic system. (Many missionary agencies as well as other religious institutions of the North Atlantic have invested substantially in large corporations.) Furthermore, the hope is that just as missions supported the ideological system in its early stages, so they will do it again in this new phase. For this reason it is deemed necessary to adapt the mission system to the new shape of the commercial system.

The evidence submitted thus far seems to indicate, at least, that one of the contemporary functions of the missionary movement is that of facilitating the process of adaptation of significant regions of the third world to the new mode of international capitalism. Such adaptation takes both negative and positive forms. Negatively it involves the rejection of any attempts to break with the system of international capitalism. Positively it involves the spreading and strengthening of ethical values, of doctrinal positions, of ecclesial practices, and of lifestyles that conform to that system.

This may partly explain the fantastic support that has been given in recent years by many missionary-minded churches and individuals to large evangelistic campaigns, social-assistance projects, activities that overemphasize numerical church growth and de-emphasize other dimensions of the church's life, the promotion of popular religious literature that tends toward spiritual sensationalism, and the development of church administration techniques. This may also partly explain the great opposition one notices in such circles to educational and theological-pastoral programs that attempt to be critically contextual; to literature of the same kind; to evangelistic efforts that do not conform to traditional patterns or contents; to social programs dedicated to macro-structural issues, and church activities that are based on a contextualized and liberating Christian ethic. By the same token it may explain why many mission societies and para-mission service agencies support (sometimes implicitly, sometimes explicitly) fascist governments in some parts of Asia, Africa, and Latin America. Finally, it may explain their displeasure with liberation movements (such as the Popular Coalition in Chile).

ENTERPRISE AS DOMESTICATION, MISSION AS LIBERATION

Earlier we stated that the issue of the missionary movement as an instrument of domestication is not frivolous but is based on concrete experiences that raise serious and penetrating questions. In the first section of this chapter we have pointed out the links between the modern missionary movement and the world of free enterprise. In the second section we have sought to understand the domesticating role that the Christian world mission—insofar as it is an entrepreneurial force—has played in the last five hundred years. But is this all that we can say about Christian mission? By no means!

We must bear in mind that Christian mission is grounded on the mission of God as revealed in the history of Israel and incarnated in the person and work of Jesus Christ. The Old Testament discloses a God who is opposed to any attempts to subjugate; a God who is on the side of the widow and the orphan, the poor and the stranger; a God who raises the humble and casts down the oppressor; who frees from slavery, demands justice, freedom, and peace. The New Testament witnesses to the incarnation of this mission in the person and work of Jesus Christ. Thus Jesus identified with the poor, proclaimed wholeness for the sick, liberty for the captives, and restoration for the marginated and deprived. It is in this perspective that the missionary mandate has been given. Jesus commands his disciples to continue his work under guidance through the power of the Holy Spirit.

Christian mission is therefore a liberation movement. To be sure, it is a liberation from the power of sin and death. As I have noted elsewhere in *Christ Outside the Gate*, in the Scriptures sin and death are understood in social and personal terms, cosmically and historically, that is, as opposition to God's work, as deformation and corruption of the way of life that God gives. They are understood as alienation and enmity among people and between humanity and creation. Therefore, forgiveness from sin means, on the one hand, liberation from all sorts of enmity, and, on the other, reconciliation with God, neighbor, and creation. Such an experience gains validity in concrete practice. It is verified in life. This is the message that the church has been sent to proclaim and to teach to the nations. The church should bear witness to the liberating God of the Bible; it should anticipate the shalom of God's kingdom; it should practice his justice; it should be a "free" servant community that celebrates God's love in daily life.

We must also remember that from its beginning the Christian world mission has had to struggle against the threat of subjugation. We find groups in the New Testament such as the Zealots, the Judaizers, and the Gnostics, which attempted to subdue the liberating cause of Jesus Christ. The Zealots tried to combine the liberating project of Jesus with their national chauvinism, but Jesus refused to allow that. The Judaizers wished to convert the early church into a Judeo-Pharisaic sect, but the disciples, especially Paul, turned back that attempt, emphasizing the interracial, international, anticlassist, and antisexist nature of Christian faith. The Gnostics intended to turn the gospel into an ahistorical and privatistic message, but leaders such as John the apostle vigorously attacked that by declaring the historicity of the gospel (the incarnation) and its apostolic and communal character.

We can point to similar attempts at domestication in later times.[10] Despite the cooptation of the gospel that followed the Edict of Milan

---

10. See, e.g., the historical analyses of Max Warren, *I Believe in the Great Commission* (Grand Rapids: Eerdmans, 1976), 56-127; and González, *Historia*, 41-132.

(A.D. 313), Christian mission was able to resist complete perversion in the Constantinian era by means of prophetic groups as disparate as the heretical Nestorians and the mendicant orders. Despite the intrusion of mercantile and imperialistic elements in the modern mission era, we can find many landmarks of liberation. Thus we find in sixteenth-century colonial Spanish America missionaries such as Bartolomé de Las Casas and Luis de Montesino; or such moving gestures as that of the Moravians in Saint Thomas, who were willing to become slaves in order to minister to the slave population; or William Carey in the beginning of the nineteenth century, who planted the seed that was to encourage the Bengali people to fight for Indian independence from the British colonial yoke; or Johannes Verkuyl in the twentieth century, who took the risks of excommunication from his own church in Holland, of expulsion from his mission society, and of being considered a traitor by his fellow citizens when he sided with Sukarno and his freedom fighters in the struggle for Indonesia's liberation.

Nowadays the vanguard of the missionary enterprise must contend with a minority of Christians who are committed to the liberating project of Jesus Christ. These Christians are not merely resisting the domesticating role that has been ascribed to the Christian world mission by the missionary movement. They are also developing a new missionary presence in the world. This minority is present on practically every level of the Christian church as well as in many mission circles. Those who identify with this stream need not be intimidated by the power structures of the missionary enterprise. There is no reason to worry or feel inferior when facing the missionary apostasy that we see in many parts of the Christian church today. On the contrary, such prophetic missionary minorities should join forces and with courage and commitment continue to unmask the secret alliance between the world missionary movement and the internationalist capitalist enterprise, repossessing the liberating character of mission by building new plans of action and missionary organizations, by changing the direction of those missionary, paramissionary, and ecclesiastical organizations that want to be renewed and are opening themselves to the winds of the Holy Spirit, and by letting the transforming power of the gospel work in their personal lives and ministries.

4

Shifting Southward
Global Christianity since 1945

Dana L. Robert

Dana L. Robert, professor of world Christianity and history of mission at Boston University School of Theology, is a United Methodist. For fourteen years, she has traveled annually to Zimbabwe, where she researches and helps facilitate a program in Theological Education by Extension among indigenous churches. Her books include *African Christian Outreach*, vol. 2: *Mission Churches* (Pretoria: South African Missiological Society, 2003); *American Women in Mission* (Macon, GA: Mercer University Press, 1997); and *Gospel Bearers, Gender Barriers: Missionary Women in the Twentieth Century* (Maryknoll, NY: Orbis Books, 2002). With her husband, M. L. Daneel, an expert on African indigenous religions, she co-directs the Center for World Christianity and Mission at Boston University.

From December 12 to 29, 1938, the most representative meeting of world Protestantism to date took place in Tambaram, India. Under the gathering storm clouds of World War II, with parts of China already under Japanese occupation, Hitler triumphant in the Sudetenland, and Stalinism in full swing, 471 persons from 69 different countries met at Madras Christian College for the second decennial meeting of the International Missionary Council.

For the first time, African Christians from different parts of the continent met one another. The African delegation traveled together for weeks on a steamer that proceeded from West Africa to Cape Town, and around the Cape of Good Hope to India. China, besieged by Japan and torn asunder by competing warlords, nationalists, and Communists, sent forty-nine official delegates, of whom nearly two-thirds were nationals and only one-third were missionaries. The women's missionary movement, then at the height of its influence, pushed for full representation by women at Madras. Their persistence was rewarded with sixty women delegates sent by their national Christian councils, and another ten women in attendance by invitation.

First published in *International Bulletin of Missionary Research* 24, no. 2 (April 2000): 50-58. Reprinted here with permission.

Europeans, whose countries would soon be at war, worked together in committee, as common Christian commitment overrode the tensions among Belgians, Danes, French, Germans, British, Dutch, Norwegians, and others.

The central theme that drew so many to India at a time of multiple global crises was "the upbuilding of the younger churches as a part of the historic universal Christian community."[1] With Protestant missions bearing fruit in many parts of the world, the time was ripe for younger non-Western churches to take their places alongside older Western denominations in joint consideration of the universal church's faith, witness, social realities, and responsibilities. The roster of attendees reads like a who's who of mid-twentieth-century world Christianity.[2]

Yet the 1938 IMC conference was a gathering of visionaries, for the global Christianity it embraced was a skeleton without flesh or bulk, a mission-educated minority who were leading nascent Christian institutions. At the beginning of the twentieth century, Europeans dominated the world church, with approximately 70.6 percent of the world's Christian population. By 1938, on the eve of World War II, the apparent European domination of Protestantism and Catholicism remained strong. Yet by the end of the twentieth century, the European percentage of world Christianity had shrunk to 28 percent of the total; Latin America and Africa combined provided 43 percent of the world's Christians. Although North Americans became the backbone of the cross-cultural mission force after World War II, their numerical dominance was being overtaken by missionaries from the very countries that were considered mission fields only fifty years before. The typical late twentieth-century Christian was no longer a European man, but a Latin American or African woman (Barrett and Johnson 2000: 24-25). The skeleton of 1938 had grown organs and sinew.

This article paints in broad strokes the transformation of world Christianity since the Second World War—a massive cultural and geographic shift away from Europeans and their descendants toward peoples of the Southern Hemisphere.[3] The shift southward began early in the century, and the 1938

---

1. *The World Mission of the Church: Findings and Recommendations of the Meeting of the International Missionary Council, Tambaram, Madras, India, Dec. 12-29, 1938* (London: International Missionary Council, 1939), 7.

2. In attendance were pioneer leaders such as Bishop Azariah, the first Indian Anglican bishop, and Toyohiko Kagawa, advocate of Japanese social Christianity. There were up-and-coming theologians such as Christian Baëta of Gold Coast and D. T. Niles of Ceylon, both thirty years old. Young leaders of future social struggles included Chief Albert Luthuli, future president of the African National Congress and first African recipient of the Nobel Peace Prize in 1960, and Y. T. Wu, author of the controversial anti-Western Chinese Christian Manifesto in 1950. Women leaders included Mina Soga, social worker and the first African woman to attend an international conference, and Michi Kawai, noted Japanese educationist. For attendance list, see *The World Mission of the Church*, 187-201.

3. An earlier draft of this article was presented at the meeting of the American Society of Church History in Washington, DC, on January 9, 1999. Following both the terminology of the New International Economic Order (Brandt Commission) and the geographic reality of

missionary conference was vivid proof of powerful indigenous Christian leadership in both church and state, despite a missionary movement trapped within colonialist structures and attitudes. But after World War II, rising movements of political and ecclesiastical self-determination materially changed the context in which non-Western churches operated, thereby allowing Christianity to blossom in multiple cultures. After examining the changing political context in which the growth of global Christianity took place, this essay will give examples of the emerging Christian movement and then comment on the challenge for historians posed by the seismic shift in Christian identity.

CHRISTIANITY AND NATIONALISM

Besides laying waste to Europe, North Africa, and western Asia, the Second World War revealed the rotten underbelly of European imperialism. In the new postwar political climate, long-simmering nationalist movements finally succeeded in throwing off direct European rule. With the newly formed United Nations supporting the rights of peoples to self-determination, one country after another reverted to local control. In 1947 India obtained its freedom from Britain, beginning a process of decolonization that continued with Burma in 1948, Ghana in 1957, Nigeria in 1960, Kenya in 1963, and on around the globe. British policies of indirect rule promoted orderly transitions in some places, but left open sores in others, for example in Sudan, where the Islamic north was left to govern the traditionalist and Christian south in 1956. Having introduced Western democratic institutions, the United States released the Philippines in 1946. Colonial powers such as Holland, France, and Portugal resisted the nationalist tide, ultimately to no avail. The Belgians were so angry at losing their colonies that they literally tore the phones off the walls in the Congo, leaving the colonial infrastructure in ruins. The French departed Algeria after six years of fighting the independence movement. Only a coup d'état in Portugal finally persuaded the Portuguese to free Angola and Mozambique in 1975, which, like many countries, erupted into civil war once the Europeans had departed. Different ethnic and political groups that had previously cooperated in opposition to European imperialism now found themselves fighting over control of nations whose boundaries, size, and even political systems had been created by foreigners. The success of anti-imperialist independence movements, with subsequent internal struggles for control in dozens of fledgling nation-states, was the most significant political factor affecting the growth of non-Western Christianity in the decades following World War II.

---

where most churches are growing, I have chosen to speak here of Christianity in the "South." "North"/"South" nomenclature nevertheless contains imprecisions and inadequacies, as do the terms "West"/"East," "First World"/"Third World," or "First World"/"Two-Thirds World."

To understand why decolonization profoundly affected the state of Christianity in the non-Western world, one must explore the prior ambiguous relationship between Western missions and European imperialism. On the one hand, although missionary work often predated the coming of Western control, imperialism's arrival inevitably placed missions within an oppressive political context that they sometimes exploited for their own benefit. In China, for example, the unequal treaties of 1842 and 1858 permitted missions to operate in selected port cities and to buy land. Foreign missions in China benefited from extraterritoriality, whereby they were not subject to Chinese laws and regulations.

In colonial Africa, missions received land grants. For example, in 1898 Cecil Rhodes awarded 13,000 acres to American Methodists for their Rhodesian Mission. Sometimes, however, the missionaries themselves stood between the indigenous peoples and their exploitation by Europeans. French Protestant missionary Maurice Leenhardt defended the land rights of the Kanaks in face of overwhelming pressure from French colonialists in New Caledonia. Presbyterian missionaries William Sheppard and William Morrison faced trial in 1909 for exposing the atrocities perpetrated on rubber gatherers in the Belgian Congo. While courageous individual missionaries mitigated the effects of imperialism on indigenous peoples, by and large the missions benefited materially from European control. Most missionaries saw themselves as apolitical and preferred the status quo of colonialism to the uncertainties of nationalist revolution.

Another important factor in understanding the ambiguous relationship between missions and imperialism before decolonization was the importance of missionary schools. Christian missions pioneered Western learning in the non-Western world. In 1935 missions were running nearly 57,000 schools throughout the world, including more than one hundred colleges. Mission schools promoted literacy in both European languages and vernaculars, and they spread Western ideals of democratic governance, individual rights, and the educability of women and girls. Despite their limitations, missions through education provided local leadership with the tools it needed to challenge foreign oppression. The Christian contribution to Asian nationalism was extremely significant, especially through the impact of mission schools. Korea, for example, was colonized by the Japanese in 1910. At that time, mission schools were the only form of modern education in the country. In 1911 the Japanese military police accused students at a Presbyterian school of plotting to assassinate the Japanese governor-general. The police arrested 123 Koreans for conspiracy, 105 of whom were Christian nationalists. In 1919, thirty-three Koreans signed the Korean Declaration of Independence. Fifteen signatories were Christians, even though Christians represented only 1 percent of the total population (Clark 1986: 8-10). Mission education, which combined vernacular literacy with Western learning, clearly played a key role in equipping nationalist leadership.

The role of mission schools in creating nationalist leadership was important not only in Asia, but also in Africa. Missions founded schools before those of colonial governments, including the first higher education for Africans in 1827 at Fourah Bay College in Sierra Leone, and higher education for South Africans at Fort Hare in 1916. By the Second World War, mission churches in Africa had produced a Christian elite poised to found independent governments. When independence came, even though Christianity was a minority religion, its adherents played a much larger role than their numbers warranted. Most black African leaders were churchmen. Kenneth Kaunda, first president of Zambia, was the son of a Presbyterian minister. Hastings Banda, first president of Malawi, received his early education in a mission school and attended college in the United States. Kwame Nkrumah, first president of Ghana, attended Catholic mission schools and began his career teaching in them. Leopold Senghor studied for the priesthood before entering politics and becoming first president of Senegal. Similarly, Julius Nyerere, first prime minister of Tanzania, both studied and taught in Catholic mission schools. Not only did mission schools train many nationalist leaders, but church-related institutions provided opportunities for developing indigenous leadership.

After World War II, with the process from decolonization to independence in full swing, Christianity in the non-Western world faced an entirely new context. In 1954, leading East Asian Christians wrote a volume entitled *Christianity and the Asian Revolution*. Reflecting on the social convulsions of the twentieth century, the Christian leaders defined the "Asian Revolution" not only as a reaction against European colonialism but also as a search for human rights and economic and social justice, ideas obtained from the West itself. The authors noted, "As the American colonists revolted in the name of English justice against British rule, so Asians, in the name of political and social doctrines which originated in large part in Europe and America, revolted against European colonialism" (Manikam 1954). The rejection of colonialism by Asian and African Christians included rejecting Western missionary paternalism, with its Eurocentrism and moral superiority (Shenk 1996: 51; Robert 1998: 563-70). From the 1950s through the 1970s, as nations shook off the legacy of European domination, churches around the world accused Western missionaries of paternalism, racism, and cultural imperialism. The refrain "Missionary, go home!" reached its peak in the early 1970s. In 1971 Christian leaders in the Philippines, Kenya, and Argentina called for a moratorium on missionaries to end the dependence of the younger churches on the older ones. In 1974 the All Africa Conference of Churches, meeting in Lusaka, Zambia, called for a moratorium on Western missionaries and money sent to Africa, because of the belief that foreign assistance created dependency and stifled African leadership.

The cries for a moratorium from Latin American, Asian, and African Christians shocked the Western missionary movement. But indigenous Christian protests against Western mission were insignificant compared with the wholesale rejection of Christianity that occurred within revolutionary movements led by non-Christians. At the International Missionary Council meeting of 1938, the largest delegations of Asian Christians came from the countries with the largest Western-style Christian infrastructures: India and China. Both Indian and Chinese Christianity boasted national Christian councils under indigenous leadership; both enjoyed thriving ecumenical movements that supported organic church unions; both hosted a range of Christian colleges and hospitals. Ironically, anti-Christian backlashes raged in both countries. Because Christianity was a minority religion in both China and India, its association with European domination widely discredited it as dangerous and foreign in the eyes of the majority non-Christians. Despite a community that traced its founding to the apostle Thomas, most Indian Christians were outcastes, members of ethnic groups despised in Hindu society. Practicing a double discrimination against both Christianity and low caste status, the postcolonial Indian government excluded Christian Dalits (outcastes) from the affirmative-action programs guaranteed to other ethnic minorities. The government of India began denying visas to missionaries in 1964, and Christians faced ongoing discrimination and intermittent persecution in both India and Pakistan (Quigley 1999: 10).[4]

In China, the place of the largest Western missionary investment in the early twentieth century, accession to power by the Communists in 1949 condemned Christianity as the religion of the colonialist oppressor. Chinese churches became sites for Marxist struggle against the "opium of the people." In 1950 the Communist government organized Chinese Protestants into the Three-Self Patriotic Movement and Catholics into the Catholic Patriotic Association. Under theologian Y. T. Wu, who had attended the Madras IMC meeting in 1938, the Three-Self Movement published the Christian Manifesto, which stated that missionary Christianity was connected with Western imperialism and that the United States used religion to support reactionary political forces. The document called for Chinese Christians immediately to become self-reliant and separate from all Western institutions (MacInnis 1972: 158-60). The Three-Self Movement began holding meetings at which Christian leaders were accused of betraying the Chinese people and were sent to labor camps for "reeducation." With the outbreak of the Korean War in 1950, the remaining foreign missionaries left China, for their presence was endangering the Chinese Christian community. The few missionaries who did not leave were imprisoned along with many leading Chinese Christians. The worst suffering of Chinese Christians occurred from 1966 to 1976 during the Cultural Revolution, a period in which no public worship was permitted in China. The very schools and hospitals that had seemed like the best contribution of foreign missions to China were held up as the proof of missionary imperialism and foreign domination of

---

4. The rise of Hindu fundamentalism in the late 1990s increased drastically the amount of anti-Christian violence. In Gujarat alone, sixty recorded incidents occurred in the second half of 1998 until Christmas, and roughly the same number occurred in the few weeks after (Thomas Quigley, "Anti-Christian Violence in India," *America*, April 3, 1999, p. 10).

Christianity. Millions of Chinese died as the government encouraged the destruction of all things religious or traditional. Except for a catacombs church of unknown strength, it seemed to China watchers in the 1970s that the Communist dictatorship had destroyed Chinese Christianity.

In parts of Africa, anticolonial movements sometimes took an anti-Christian stance. Nationalist leaders accused missions of telling Africans to pray and then stealing their land while their heads were bowed. Despite having been a resident mission pupil in childhood, Jomo Kenyatta, leader of the anti-Christian, pro-independence Mau-Mau rebellion in Kenya during the 1950s and later the country's first president, accused missionaries of trying to destroy African culture. During the Mau-Mau liberation struggle, which mobilized African traditional religion against Christianity, rebels killed African Christians who refused to drink the goats' blood and other sacrifices of the pro-independence cult. During the Cold War, Marxist ideology as well as funding from the Soviet Union and China began playing a role in African conflicts. Following the Cuban example, Communist-funded movements in Mozambique and Angola dismantled mission schools and attacked churches as supposed organs of capitalism and European religion.

By the 1970s, on a political and ideological level, world Christianity seemed in disarray. Although mission education, literacy training, and ideals of individual human worth had provided tools that initiated intellectual leadership of independence movements in Asia and Africa, the perceived alliance of foreign missions with European domination branded Christianity a henchman of colonialism. In the West, reacting against the colonial legacy, scholars and historians similarly indicted Christian missions as a tool of Western domination. As far as Western intellectuals were concerned, the non-Western Christian was a mercenary "rice Christian," and the missionary as outdated as a dinosaur. The teaching of missions and world Christianity began disappearing from colleges and seminaries, a casualty of the Vietnam-era rejection of "culture Christianity" and Western domination in world affairs. With indigenous church leaders calling for moratoriums on missionaries, Western mainline churches became highly self-critical and guilt ridden. Attempting to shift from paternalistic to partnership models of mission, they began cutting back on Western missionary personnel. During the long process from decolonization to independence, scholars, politicians, and leading ecclesiastics branded both Western missions and world Christianity failures because of their perceived social, theological, and political captivity to the despised colonialist interests.

REVIVAL AND RENEWAL IN WORLD CHRISTIANITY

The irony of world Christianity from the Second World War through the 1970s was that even as scholars were writing books implicating Christianity in European imperialism, the number of believers began growing rapidly throughout Asia, Africa, and Latin America. Perhaps if historians in the sixties and seventies had been studying Christianity as a people's movement rather than a political one, they might have noticed that growth among the grass roots did not mirror the criticisms of intellectual elites. The process of decolonization and independence began severing the connection between Christianity and European colonialism. The repudiation of missionary paternalism, combined with expanding indigenous initiatives, freed Christianity to become more at home in local situations.

Another fallacy of treating Christianity as a politicized Western movement is that scholarship ignored the way in which ordinary people were receiving the gospel message and retranslating it into cultural modes that fitted their worldviews and met their needs (Burrows 1998: 86-87). In retrospect it is evident that even during the colonial period, indigenous Christians—Bible women, evangelists, catechists, and prophets—were all along the most effective interpreters of Christianity to their own people. The explosion of non-Western Christianity was possible because Christianity was already being indigenized before the colonizers departed.

In the uncertainty of postcolonial situations, in the midst of civil strife and ethnic tensions in emerging nations, indigenous forms of Christianity spread quietly and quickly. Even in the so-called mission denominations, native leaders took over and indigenized positions held formerly by Western missionaries. In Kenya, for example, Mau-Mau rebels targeted Anglicanism as the religion of the colonizers during the 1950s. But after Mau-Mau independence and the subsequent instability of a struggling government, Anglicanism in Kenya emerged even stronger, with exponential growth among the Kikuyu from the 1970s onward. Not only was Anglicanism now led by Kenyan bishops and priests, but the new context transformed the liability of being an English religion under a colonial government into the advantage of being a global faith under an independent government. In the 1980s and 1990s, as political and economic institutions began collapsing under corrupt one-party dictatorships, the church became one of the few institutions with the moral authority and international connections to oppose the government, which it did on occasion. In some parts of Africa, the church's infrastructures and international connections provided more stability for supporting daily life than did the government (see Walls 1998: 8-14). The postindependence growth of Anglicanism occurred so steadily throughout former British colonies that Africa is now the continent with the most Anglicans. At the 1998 Lambeth Conference, the highest consultative body of the Anglican Communion, 224 of the 735 bishops were from Africa, compared with only 139 from the United Kingdom and Europe (Anglican Communion News Service 1998). Anglicans in Nigeria report 17 million baptized members, compared with 2.8 million in the United States (Libby 1998: 4).

Given its brutal suppression under Communism after 1949, the Chinese church provides the most stirring illustration of the resilience of Asian

Christianity. In 1979 five thousand Chinese Christians attended the first public worship service allowed since 1966. By suffering under Communism along with other citizens, Chinese Christians proved they were not the "running dogs" of imperialists but were truly Chinese citizens. With the end of the Cultural Revolution, Christians began reclaiming buildings that had previously been seized. The China Christian Council opened thirteen theological seminaries and began printing Bibles, creating a hymnal, and training pastors for churches that had gone without resources for fifteen years. Recent scholarship estimates that on the eve of the Communist takeover, one-fourth of all Chinese Christians were already members of indigenous, independent Chinese churches (Bays 1996, 310). It was these indigenized forms of Christianity that provided the most resistance to Communist domination of the churches. Biblically literalist, directly dependent on the power of the Holy Spirit, and emerging from the religious sensibilities of popular Chinese religion, indigenized forms of Chinese Christianity grew the most under Communist persecution. What had been 700,000 Protestants in 1949 grew to between 12 and 36 million Protestants by the end of the century (Robert 1998: 570). In addition to government-approved churches, millions of Chinese Christians meet in house churches characterized by spontaneous spoken prayer, singing and fellowship, miraculous healing, exorcisms of evil spirits, and love and charity to neighbors.

The translation of Christianity into African cultures was most obvious in the life and work of so-called African Independent or African Initiated Churches (AICs), defined by Harold Turner as churches founded in Africa, by Africans, primarily for Africans. By 1984 Africans had founded seven thousand independent, indigenous denominations in forty-three countries across the continent. By the 1990s over 40 percent of black Christians in South Africa were members of AICs. Chafing under white domination and racism, African-led movements began breaking off from mission churches in the 1880s. The earliest independent churches emphasized African nationalism in ecclesiastical affairs. They received the name "Ethiopian" in 1892 when a Methodist minister, Mangena Mokone, founded the Ethiopian Church in the Witwatersrand region of South Africa. Believing that Africans should lead their own churches, Mokone cited Psalm 68:31: "Ethiopia shall stretch out her hands to God" (Daneel 1987: 49). During the early twentieth century, important African prophets and evangelists emerged throughout the continent, often to be arrested and persecuted by colonial authorities who deemed spiritual independence a dangerous precursor to political independence.

By the mid-twentieth century, the largest group of AICs were known as Spirit churches, often called Aladura in western Africa and Zionist in southern Africa (Ayegboyin and Ishola 1997; Pobee and Ositelu II 1998). Spirit churches were characterized by a prophetic leader, a high emphasis on the Holy Spirit, Pentecostal phenomena such as speaking in tongues and exorcisms, and often a holy city or "Zion" as headquarters. With Bible translation into many African languages, prophetic African leaders interpreted the Scriptures for themselves in line with African cultural practices. Zionists, for example, permit polygamy, which exists both in the Bible and in traditional African cultures. Their leaders rely on dreams and visions for divine inspiration—also both a biblical and traditional African practice. Many people are attracted to AICs because they focus on healing the body and spirit through prayers, laying on of hands, and administration of holy water and other remedies. Women healers treat barren women and other sufferers, providing respite for them in healing colonies. In Zimbabwe more than 150 indigenous churches have extended the metaphor of healing by joining in a movement to heal the earth through planting trees (750,000 trees in 1997 alone; see ZIRRCON Trust 1997: n.p.). Spirit churches spread rapidly following political independence because they translated the Christian faith into African cultures, thereby both transforming the cultural forms and expanding the meaning of the gospel as received from Western missionaries. Spirit churches also spread because they mount vigorous missionary movements, sending out evangelistic teams that dance through the villages, singing, praying, preaching, healing, and drawing people into a vigorous worship life.

Another momentous change in the world church since the 1960s can be traced to the renewal of Catholicism, the largest branch of Christianity with approximately 980 million members in 1996. The Second Vatican Council (1962-65) brought to Rome the Catholic bishops, who together voted major changes in Catholicism's theological self-definition, customs, and attitudes. As these bishops returned to their homelands, they began putting into practice the idea of the church as the People of God, with Mass said in the vernacular and a new openness to current sociocultural realities. In particular, the more than six hundred Latin American bishops who attended the Vatican Council gained a new sense of their potential as the numerically largest bloc of Catholics in the world. Latin American bishops reflected on their common social problems—stark division between rich and poor, takeovers by military dictatorships, and a legacy of a church that took the side of the rich. At the meeting of Latin American bishops in Medellín, Colombia, in 1968, the bishops evaluated the social context of their continent and spoke with a powerful voice against the dependence of Latin America on the industrialized North—a dependence that perpetuated the poverty of the South. Calling the church to take the side of the poor, the bishops supported a new "theology of liberation" (Cleary 1985: chap. 2).

The "renewed commitment to democracy and human rights in the Catholic Church" supported a wave of democracy throughout Latin America, Eastern Europe, and the Philippines during the 1970s and 1980s (Marshall 1997: 9).

The movement toward democracy in traditionally Roman Catholic countries was not universally acclaimed by the church, as the route often entailed violent rebellion and upheaval of the status quo. The theology of liberation immediately came into conflict with powerful military dictatorships, which began persecuting the church. Militaries martyred an estimated 850 bishops, priests, and nuns in Latin America during the 1970s and early 1980s. Military governments targeted church leaders at all levels because they were conscientizing the poor—teaching them to read and defending their human rights. The Roman Catholic Church in Latin America gained a vitality it had long lacked as laypeople began meeting in Base Christian Communities, which functioned as Bible study groups that reflected on the relationship between the church as community and social injustices. But as the theology of liberation confronted the social and political power structures in Latin America, the Catholic Church became divided between those who supported liberation theology among the People of God and those more conservative, who felt the nature of the church was more hierarchical and otherworldly.

The renewal of Catholicism in Latin America since the Second Vatican Council underscores a major tension in the growth of non-Western Christianity since the mid-twentieth century: the forms and structures for the growth of late twentieth-century Christianity could not be contained within either the institutional or the theological frameworks of Western Christianity. The Base Christian Communities, for example, introduced Bible study and a more intense spirituality into what had been nominal Catholic practice. Faced with the severe shortage of priests, Latin American Catholics, once they became used to reading the Bible for themselves, began forming their own churches and breaking away from Catholicism. Ironically, the liberation theologies of the Base Christian Communities may have created heightened expectations that could not be fulfilled, and disillusioned Catholics began founding their own churches. Protestant growth has become so rapid in Latin America that scholars have predicted that Protestants, notably of Pentecostal persuasion, could constitute a third of the Latin American population by the year 2010, with their greatest strengths in Guatemala, Puerto Rico, El Salvador, Brazil, and Honduras (Berg and Pretiz 1994). These new Protestants are founding their own churches, such as the Universal Church of the Kingdom of God, a Pentecostal group begun in the late 1970s by Edir Macedo de Bezerra. By 1990 this home-grown denomination had eight hundred churches with two million worshipers led by two thousand pastors throughout Latin America. Neither Catholicism nor the classic churches of the Protestant Reformation can contain the vitality of Latin American Christianity today.

Reasons for the revival and renewal of global Christianity today are too complex and diverse to be encapsulated in a brief essay. In addition to increasing indigenization within a postcolonial political framework, many sociological factors affect church growth, including urbanization, dislocation caused by war and violence, ethnic identity, the globalizing impact of cyberspace, and local circumstances. Political contexts differ widely for Christian communities around the world. Nevertheless, Christianity throughout the non-Western world has in common an indigenous, grassroots leadership; embeddedness in local cultures; and reliance on a vernacular Bible. Where Christianity is growing in the South, it supports stable family and community life for peoples suffering political uncertainty and economic hardships. The time when Christianity was the religion of European colonial oppressors fades ever more rapidly into the past.

A GLOBAL/LOCAL CHRISTIAN FABRIC

As Christianity shifts southward, the nature of Christianity itself evolves. The movement of the faith from one culture to another typically has caused a major change in the self-understanding and cultural grounding of the Christian movement (Walls 1996a). Past cultural shifts occurred when Christianity moved from a Hebrew to a Greco-Roman milieu, and then from a Mediterranean to a European framework. With the voyages of discovery, Europeans began exporting their religion in the late 1400s. At that time Christian expansion was partly a function of the state, reflecting the Christendom model of church/state relations. Even the voluntarism of Protestant missions occurred within a largely Christendom model. But the end of European colonialism after the Second World War accompanied a decline of European religiosity relative to the rest of the world. The virtual destruction of Russian Orthodoxy under the Communist regime was also a major factor in the elimination of the Christendom model.

Now much of the dynamism within world Christianity is occurring below the equator. As Christianity shifts southward, the interpretations of Christianity by people in Latin America, Africa, and southern Asia are coming to the fore. This changing face of the world church also brings new interpretive challenges for historians.

One of the knottiest interpretive problems in understanding Christianity today is the tension between a worldwide community of people who call themselves Christians and a multitude of local movements for whom Christianity represents a particular culture's grappling with the nature of divine reality. Christianity is a world religion with a basic belief that God has revealed himself in the person of Jesus Christ, whose adherents are spread throughout the globe. Yet as Lamin Sanneh has so cogently argued, by virtue of its use of the vernacular in speaking of God and in spreading the Scriptures, Christianity has translated or incarnated itself into local cultures (Sanneh 1989). What at first glance appears to be the largest world religion is in fact the ultimate local religion. Indigenous words for God and ancient forms of spirituality have all become part of Christianity. Flexibility at the local level, combined with being part of an international network, is a major factor in Christianity's self-understanding and success today. The strength of world Christianity lies in its creative interweaving of the warp of a world religion with the woof of its local contexts.

The increasing cultural diversity within Christianity, with the recognition of the local within the global and the global within the local, complicates the writing of church history in the twenty-first century. The days are gone when the history of Christianity could be taught as the development of Western doctrine and institutions. Being in the middle of a large-scale transformation

in the nature of Christianity, we do not yet have an adequate interpretive
or even descriptive framework for what is happening. Australian historian
Mark Hutchinson advocates a paradigm shift in the history of Christianity to
a model of multiculturalism, a globalization of evangelicalism (Hutchinson
1998: 46-49).[5] Others interpret worldwide growth as the spread of Pentecostalism, since the majority of growing churches today express themselves
in Pentecostal worship styles (Hollenweger 1997; Cox 1994; A. Anderson
1992). A history-of-religions framework sees that the growing energy of
Christianity has always been drawn from primal spirituality (Walls 1996b:
68-75). Sociologists have explored the spread of Christianity today as a
process of modernization, a variant of the Weberian thesis in the growth
of capitalism (Martin 1990).[6] Historians influenced by liberation theology
stress that the central focus of history should be the poor and marginalized
rather than the ecclesiological elites of the Christendom model (Dussel
1981). Liberation theology has a strong influence on the ongoing history
projects of the Ecumenical Association of Third World Theologians.

While each of these models has something to offer in helping us speak and
teach about world Christianity, there is a danger in theories of globalization
that skip over the painstaking historical research necessary for each local
context. Global analyses need to begin with local history, with the internal
criteria of each movement as the starting point of our historical musings
(Shenk 1996: 56). As with the outdated nomenclature of mission history,
such as "younger churches," "developing churches," the "history of the
expansion of Christianity," and so on, there is a constant temptation to
define the changing global patterns in relation to the European and the
North American experience.

The tension between the global and the local is not merely an academic
exercise but is a struggle over identity. For example, some commentators
are describing the growing world church as Pentecostal. Pentecostal and
charismatic scholars want to claim the growth of world Christianity as part
of their own missionary success (Synan 1998).[7] Since Pentecostal phenomena
were so derided in Western Christianity into the 1980s, it is understandable
that Western Pentecostal scholars wish to include all phenomenologically
similar movements as somehow related to Azusa Street. Anthropologists
might similarly wish to describe new Christian movements as Pentecostal
because of the prominence of common phenomena such as speaking in
tongues, healing rituals, and the alleged marginalized social status of many
adherents. For political liberals who look down on what they perceive to

---

5. Hutchinson is one of the leaders of the Currents in World Christianity Project, funded
by the Pew Charitable Trusts, which seeks to understand the global spread of evangelicalism.

6. Sociologist Peter Berger of Boston University has led a research institute investigating
the growth of world Protestantism as an aspect of economic culture.

7. Pentecostal historian Vinson Synan told the Eighteenth Pentecostal World Conference
in 1998 that more than 25 percent of the world's Christians are Pentecostal or charismatic and
that "the renewal will continue with increasing strength into the next millennium" (*Current
News Summary*, Religion Today.com, October 5, 1998).

be narrow pietism, the word "Pentecostal" has been attractive as a negative descriptor, as part of an implied spillover from the Christian right in the United States.

For historians, however, unreflective use of the term "Pentecostalism" to summarize growing world Christianity has the same problem as calling all biblical Christianity "fundamentalism." It reduces local identity to a standardized set of criteria, in this case to phenomenology. Are Pentecostal phenomena the defining mark of identity for local practitioners, or are there other theological or communal identity markers that are more meaningful for them? Do all Pentecostal phenomena worldwide have an organic connection to Azusa Street and the missionary movement that spread from there, or is Pentecostal practice reflective of indigenous cultural initiative? Is the use of the word "Pentecostal" just the latest instance of categories originating from the North being used to explain and somehow take credit for what is going on in the South?

Non-Western historians are cautioning against blanket use of the word "Pentecostal" to describe indigenous Christianity. For example, Nigerian church historian Ogbu Kalu, head of the African history project for the Ecumenical Association of Third World Theologians, has criticized the Pentecostal terminology as reflecting the dominance of anthropology in ignoring essential historical and theological differences among current movements. Kalu insists that historians be more accurate and recognize the differences that arise within the movements themselves (Kalu 2000). Inus Daneel, the leading interpreter of African Initiated Churches in Zimbabwe, argues vigorously against the label of Pentecostalism being plastered onto indigenous churches. Not only have these churches been founded by African prophets, but they have recruited their members largely from the traditional population, not from so-called mission churches. Although they emphasize the Holy Spirit, the AICs deal with issues arising from African culture, not from Western Pentecostalism. To claim that AICs are otherworldly, for instance, ignores the holism that undergirds African religions (Daneel 1999b).

As scholars analyze and define what is happening in world Christianity today, we must apply such globalizing concepts as "Pentecostal" only after careful research into the local contexts.[8] Historians should take the lead in acknowledging the new Christianities as radically indigenous movements, not simply Pentecostalism or primal religiosity, or perhaps not even multicultural options within a global evangelicalism. Each movement should be studied from within its own internal logic, even as the universal

---

8. One possible paradigm is to distinguish between largely urban, modernizing movements and rural, neotraditionalist movements. In Singapore, for example, there are growing numbers of English-speaking, Internet-linked, young professional Pentecostals. These Christians are part of an international network replete with its own literature, hymnody, and global evangelistic consciousness. In rural Indonesia, however, nonliterate indigenous Christian movements, influenced by the spirit world of Javanese mysticism, are not connected to the nearby urban elites. (I am indebted to Graham Walker for this example.)

nature of Christianity is recognizable in the construction of local identities. Popular Korean Christianity is a case in point. David Yonggi Cho leads the largest church in the world, the Yoido Full Gospel Church in Seoul, Korea. Cho is by membership a Pentecostal, a minister in the Assemblies of God. Yet the emphasis of his congregation on material blessings and on such spiritualities as a prayer mountain is clearly attributable to the influence of Korean shamanism. Does Yoido Full Gospel Church exemplify globalized Pentecostalism or localized Spirit religion? As historians work within the tensions between the global and the local that characterize indigenous world Christianities today, we should recognize that each form of twenty-first century Christianity represents a synthesis of global and local elements that has its own integrity.

As Christianity declines in Europe and grows in the South, historians need to recognize what the International Missionary Council saw in 1938: the future of world Christianity rests with the so-called younger churches and their daily struggles. Ultimately, the most interesting lessons from the missionary outreach during the Western colonial era is what happened to Christianity when the missionaries weren't looking, and after the colonizers withdrew. The challenge for historians lies in seeing beyond an extension of Western categories and into the hearts, minds, and contexts of Christ's living peoples in Asia, Africa, and Latin America.

Part III

THEOLOGY, CHURCH, AND KINGDOM

5

Reconciliation as a Model of Mission

Robert J. Schreiter

Robert J. Schreiter, an internationally recognized expert in the areas of inculturation and the world mission of the church, specializes in how the gospel is communicated in different cultures and in how a theology of reconciliation might shape missionary activity today. Vatican II Professor of Theology at Catholic Theological Union in Chicago, he is also a priest of the Congregation of the Precious Blood. Among his published books are *Constructing Local Theologies* (Maryknoll, NY: Orbis Books, 1985) and *The Ministry of Reconciliation: Spirituality and Strategies* (Maryknoll, NY: Orbis Books, 1998).

CHANGING WORLD, CHANGING MISSION

As we stand at the end of a century and of a millennium, the surge of events sweeping over us has become nearly more than we can comprehend. When the Berlin Wall came down in 1989 and Nelson Mandela was released from prison in 1990, who did not think that a new age of hope and dignity would not soon be upon us? Confident proclamations of a "new world order" and even the "end of history" were sounded. Futurologists such as Alvin Toffler and John Naisbitt set forth visions of technological Gardens of Eden in which humanity would flourish and prosper. The dialectics of history seemed indeed to many to be in a penultimate phase, stretching toward a grand synthesis.

But history in fact seldom proceeds so elegantly as history in theory. A global capitalist order has quickly succeeded the bipolar capitalist-socialist conflict that marked most of [the twentieth] century. It has, within a few years, reconfigured the economic map of the world. While enriching many and creating new centers of wealth for the first time, it has also pushed the very poorest into even greater misery. The old economic system, which had inherited the center-periphery model of capital flow and production

First published in *Neue Zeitschrift für Missionswissenschaft* 50, no. 4 (1996): 243-50. Reprinted here with permission.

from the age of empire, was replaced with a polycentric model that distinguishes between those who are inside and part of the process from those who are excluded and forgotten. This new global economic system, a form of market capitalism, has carried with it a layer of homogenized hyperculture that has settled on the many cultures where it now operates. The signifiers of this hyperculture are items of consumption: clothing, food, and entertainment.

The global reach of this form of market capitalism is reinforced by a networked communication system that shrinks time and space, a single community of science and medicine and—increasingly—education. The grand uniformities of a globalized world are not the entire story, however. Precisely because of the polycentric character of this network—with its promise that new centers may begin anywhere—its grasp of the world is far from uniform. Particularities are asserting themselves at the very same time—and often in the very same place—where globalization seems to have the upper hand. In some instances, these particularisms are very old ones that had been contained or repressed during the colonial and later bipolar period. The wars in the former Yugoslavia and in parts of the former Soviet Union are examples of such particularisms alive today. Other particularisms are direct protests against the new global reality and represent efforts for communities and movements to redefine themselves in the face of globalization. The struggles in Islam in countries such as Turkey, Egypt, and Algeria; religious right-wing movements and parties in Israel and the United States; and competing religious movements in India are all such protest movements. They are mistakenly labeled as "fundamentalist" at times, but actually represent different and complex responses to the homogenizing forces of modernity.

And then there are what might be called apocalyptic particularisms that see themselves as the guardians of a beleaguered truth in an increasingly hostile world. Events in Japan and the United States have brought these small groups into the glaring spotlight of public attention by their acts of terrorism in Tokyo, Oklahoma City, and New York. The polycentric process of globalization is strong enough to provoke these various particularisms, but not strong enough to control them.

Even more chillingly, in those parts of the world now ignored, violent forms of such particularisms rage unabated. The horrors of Rwanda are like wounds being constantly reopened. The spread of global market capitalism, creating new centers of wealth and communication in the world, has also fostered a worldwide migration of peoples, either seeking some share in the wealth in the burgeoning cities or fleeing the poverty created by the widening gap between rich and poor. In some areas this has led to conflicts as cultures clash and peoples compete for the same scarce resources. Others still are refugees from civil and political violence. The United Nations High Commission for Refugees estimates, conservatively, that there are some twenty million political refugees and eighty to a hundred million economic refugees uprooted from their homelands in the world today [ca. 1996]. This churning of peoples and cultures is unprecedented in world history. Frequently in the past, regions of the world would experience such demographic flow. But never has it been on such a worldwide scale.

In the midst of all this ferment (seen positively) and violence (seen negatively), there have also been profound signs of hope. The end of political dictatorships in the southern cone of South America and across the great Eurasian landmass, the end of apartheid in South Africa—it was hardly conceivable that such violence could come to an end with such little counterviolence. In so many places it was human decency and integrity that came to prevail. But new societies do not arise phoenix-like from the ashes of morally and politically bankrupt societies. In some instances, as in Eastern Europe and the former Soviet Union, civil societies had been completely dismantled to permit direct state supervision of individuals. In other societies, such as Argentina and Chile, the divisions that had grown up in the dictatorships leave deep chasms after the dictatorship had ended. In societies such as South Africa, blacks and whites are struggling to live together for the first time. In all of these societies, the violence, trauma, and death that marked those savage pasts must still be reckoned with, lest they pull down the fragile new constructions of more just and equitable societies now being built.

All in all, the ending of the century and the millennium is a time of great ferment—a horizon of creativity and hope for some, a burgeoning tide of chaos for others. We need to ask: where is the church and its mission in all of this? To be sure, the church of Jesus Christ is a worldwide movement and organization as well. One-third of the world's population is Christian, distributed among more than twenty thousand identifiable communions and denominations. Nearly half of all these Christians live in Latin America, Africa, and South Asia.

These statistics remind us both of the success of the Christian missionary movement in the last two centuries, resulting in Christianity becoming a worldwide church for the first time, and of the fact that the Christian church is increasingly a church of the poor, those whose lives are not improving under global capitalism and, in some instances, are growing even worse. The worldwide movement of Christianity, therefore, is running counter to the globalizing movements of the world economic system.

What is the sense of the church's global mission in such a world? Where and how should the Good News be preached? The question presses upon us in a special way as we see the people whose lives have been tossed around in the political, economic and social upheavals that are marking our time: those who have been uprooted from their homelands; those who bear the memories and wounds of violence; those who face profound uncertainty about their own future and the future of their children; those who see no alternative to a life of poverty and oppression.

MODELS OF MISSION IN THE TWENTIETH CENTURY

In his masterful study of the history and theology of Christian mission, South African missiologist David Bosch spoke of "paradigms" of mission, borrowing the much-used term of historian of science Thomas Kuhn. While Bosch helpfully discerned a variety of such paradigms of mission throughout Christian history, many feel that he hesitated overmuch in proposing a paradigm for the present time. He speaks in his book *Transforming Mission* of an emerging ecumenical paradigm that is to serve as a meeting place for some fourteen of the trends he saw in late twentieth-century mission. If there was any organizing element to which all these trends were responding, it was the "postmodern" condition. His enumeration of the many things that mission had become is useful but does not present a compelling image or metaphor to galvanize missionary activity. Bosch completed his manuscript before the dramatic events of 1989 and the following years, and so he could not have foreseen how the world would change in such a very short time.

Language of paradigms and paradigm shifts remains very popular in theology and in popular literature, although such language has lost its cachet in science, at least in the Kuhnian sense of the term. Paradigms are rarely as self-enclosed as Kuhn first proposed them over thirty years ago. Nor does the new paradigm so utterly efface the old as Kuhn was read to have argued. "Model" might be a more modest word here, one that I prefer since, in Clifford Geertz's sense, it can provide both a model "of," that is, a description of what is happening, and a model "for," that is, a prescription for how to act in that world so described.

Before proposing a model of mission for the times we are now in, it may be useful to look at the immediate past, since that most often is the experience against which we gauge our future. I would propose that there have been two principal models of mission operating in the modern missionary period, dating roughly from the beginning of the nineteenth century. These two models were compelling for so many Christians precisely because they took careful measure of the times, providing both a model "of" and a model "for" mission. They each provide a root image or metaphor that helped organize and direct experience. Both models can still be seen today, although conditions and attitudes in any given place will favor one more than the other. The fact that there have been different operative models of mission in the church's history—Bosch's historical overview gives ample evidence of that—reminds us that mission happens neither in a vacuum nor in a privileged supracultural space. Mission is both challenge and response: a challenge to address a perceived need and a response intended to meet that need.

Throughout the modern missionary period—from the beginning of the nineteenth century to the middle of the twentieth—mission was characterized by metaphors of *expansion*. That this form of mission proceeded with the imperial expansion of countries of Europe is no accident. As contemporary debates on the relation between Christian mission and European colonialism indicate, it is a complex history, a history neither purely of mindless collaboration nor of uninterrupted resistance. Missionaries aided both in the subjugation of peoples and in the preservation of their cultures. The history and geography of nineteenth- and twentieth-century mission are such that generalizations will not carry one very far.

What does seem to be clear, however, is that mission took place within the context of European colonial expansion. That colonial expansion crept into missionary vocabulary, sometimes borrowing the former's military metaphors. Missionaries frequently shared the colonizers' view of the otherness of the people they encountered, seeing them as in need of education and civilization. The Great Commission of Matthew 28:20, which gained its preeminence as a biblical mandate in the expansionist period, sent forth missionaries to baptize and to teach.

The end of the colonial period, from 1945 through the 1960s, saw the emergence of a second model of mission, characterized by metaphors of *accompaniment*. While extending the church remained important, missionaries began to define their task increasingly as one of intense involvement with the changing societies of postcolonial times, including nation building and postcolonial identity. Images of expansion and conquest gave way to images of insertion and solidarity, to programs of contextualization and inculturation, to dialogue, and to commitments to join the struggle for justice and liberation. Luke 4:16-20, with its images of intense involvement with the marginalized, is to this model of mission what the Great Commission was to the first one. Arguments have persisted through the second half of the twentieth century as to how mission should be carried out (proclamation or dialogue? conversion or solidarity?) and whether there should be mission at all (which usually focused on the expansionist model). But what all this represents, in some way, is the shift of circumstances under which Christian mission was conducted. The forms of accompaniment that began to emerge clearly in the 1960s (although, of course, forms of accompaniment reach far back into mission history) represent a different (and to my mind, accurate reading) of how times had changed and therefore how God's Good News needed to be communicated and heard.

It seems to me that the way the world has changed at the end of this century calls for a rethinking of mission once again. Not that aspects of mission of previous models must now be abandoned: there are still those who have not heard the gospel, and the plight of the poor and the oppressed has changed little, except perhaps to have gotten worse. But the changes in the world that I have tried to describe above call out for a model of mission that takes us at once to the heart of the gospel and to the aching heart of the world that needs to hear God's word. That model is mission as reconciliation.

RECONCILIATION AS GIFT AND AS VOCATION

Because the word "reconciliation" is used in so many different ways, it is important to specify its meaning here. Reconciliation is, first of all, not about forgetting the violence or trauma of the past so that a people or a nation can get on with the business of reconstruction. Appeals to forgive and forget are quite simply misplaced here, since such hastily called truces do not deal with the demons of the past; those demons are only held at bay, and then but for a time. Such a tactic trivializes the suffering that people have gone through and, in effect, continues their victimization rather than overcomes it.

Nor can reconciliation be construed as an alternative to or substitute for the struggle for liberation. This was proposed on a number of occasions in Latin America in the 1980s as a right-wing stratagem to undercut theologies of liberation. Liberation is a condition for reconciliation, not an alternative to it. If reconciliation is about anything, it is about truth. The lie of oppression must be countered and overcome.

And finally, reconciliation as it will be understood here is not to be equated with arbitration of conflict. Arbitration and conflict management are important and necessary things, indeed often noble undertakings by believers and nonbelievers alike. But they are not the same as reconciliation, inasmuch as arbitration and conflict management remain beholden in some manner to the terms of the conflict itself and so suspend violence but do not really overcome it.

What, then, is reconciliation as it is being proposed here? First and foremost to remember is that reconciliation is the work of God, reconciling the world in Christ. To recognize that it is God, rather than any of us, who brings reconciliation is to acknowledge the breadth and the depth of pain and trauma that evil and violence wreak on the world. None of us can fathom the terrible impact they make on us. Nor are we able to assess the persisting damage they may continue to bring to human lives and to communities.

It is through us that God brings reconciliation. But it comes especially through the victim who experiences God's reconciling grace restoring the victim's humanity and so lifting the victim out of victimization. That God would begin with the victim should not surprise us—God sides with the outcast, the marginalized, those left to feel less than human. But that restoration of the victim's humanity, that enablement of a new subjecthood does not simply return the reconciled person to a prior state. As St. Paul reminds us in Second Corinthians, those who have been reconciled are made a new creation. They stand in a new place, from which they view both what has been done to them and also what the future might become.

In reconciliation, people frequently focus on the perpetrators of evil, how they might repent of their evildoing, and how forgiveness might take place. These are the most glaring dimensions of a situation in need of reconciliation. But they are usually also the most intractable. Evildoers are reluctant to come forward, and often show little remorse. Moreover, church people will urge victims to forgive and forget, since that is the "Christian" thing to do. But we must remember that the perpetrator of evil has been diminished in humanity by what has happened as well, which likely makes them less able to repent or show remorse. Perhaps that is why God first restores the victim. The free, reconciling gift of God's love, which restores a damaged humanity, makes it possible for the victim to love others. And very often those who have so experienced God's reconciling love discern in that love not only how to come to terms with the terrible things that have happened to them in the past, but also discover a vocation, a calling from God to be the healers and reconcilers in the shattered world around them. It is they who become agents of God's reconciliation and it is through them that reconciliation will eventually take place.

That reconciling grace does not come in an instant. A long and difficult journey precedes the welling up of God's grace in broken lives, a journey that involves untangling the skein of lies that have wrapped themselves around the victim. It involves the reordering of memories so that the past can no longer terrorize the present. And it sometimes requires finding one's bearings again after profound disorientation.

Nor does forgiveness come any more quickly. Well-meaning admonitions to forgive because it is the Christian thing to do are misplaced, and simply lay an additional burden on the victim. Being made to forgive makes a victim even more victimized. Forgiveness arises out of the autonomy of the reconciled victim, when the victim can call upon God to forgive, since the range of forgiveness needed reaches beyond our ken. This would follow the pattern of Jesus, who asked God to forgive his executioners, as depicted in the Gospel of Luke. Jesus does not forgive his executioners, but asks God to do so.

And forgetting? To "forgive and forget" are frequently paired together, as though forgetting is proof of real forgiveness. But forgetting is not part of the experience of reconciliation. What is remembered is now cast in a different way, but it is not forgotten. To forget such matters is to trivialize them, and so to trivialize the experience (and therefore the person) of the victim. Memories remain, although they are transformed. The rage arising out of them no longer consumes the present. Nor is there vengeance, although the demand for justice remains. For me the most powerful image of this memory is the story of the risen Jesus with the disciple Thomas in John 20. Jesus appears to the disciples in his glorified form. But that transformed body still bears the clear marks of his torture and death. And it is these wounds that heal Thomas. The wounds, the scars are still there, but they become the source of healing. They are not forgotten.

From all of this it should be apparent that reconciliation is no easy road. Nor is it a graduated, therapeutic path. Reconciliation is about a healing, a change of view that cannot be programmed. It is more of a spirituality than a strategy, and one cultivates it as a spirituality and not as a task with a beginning and an end.

RECONCILIATION AS A MODEL OF MISSION

So how might reconciliation be a model of mission today? What would developing such a spirituality involve, and how might it be translated into a ministerial praxis? Is the ministry of reconciliation, of which Paul speaks in 2 Corinthians 5, indeed given to us and open to all?

To begin, one cannot really speak of a "right" to be a reconciler. Church people sometimes arrogate this ministry to themselves, but this is something that comes to one through the reconciling experience of God's grace and the calling to be a reconciler and healer. Or one may participate in the ministry of reconciliation by having stood by the victims in their struggle and being accepted by those victims. To come in after the struggle and appoint oneself a minister of reconciliation lacks any credibility. Church people sometimes do this, and so impede the process of reconciliation rather than foster it.

What might a ministry of reconciliation look like? As has been already said, it is God who makes reconcilers, yet we can create a ministry around such people that supports and extends the work of reconciliation. This might be achieved, I would suggest, by creating communities of memory and communities of hope.

Communities of memory bear the narrative of a people, the fount and source of their identity. They struggle to maintain that narrative in the face of the lies propagated about that community by acts of violence and oppression. When persons and communities have been traumatized by violence and oppression, the narratives of who a community is and has been need to be rebuilt and restored.

A community of memory is first of all a community of *hospitality;* that is to say, it sees in the victim a person, a subject, not just a victim degraded by violence. A community of hospitality gives a space of recognition and safety wherein damaged personhood might be restored. In such a place, persons and communities might tell their stories and restore their narratives.

Second, a community of memory is a place of *truth telling,* where the lies of violence, injustice, and oppression are overcome. They are not just safe enclaves where shattered lives may be restored; they advocate and struggle for truth in the public forum as well. Here is one of the places where the ministry of reconciliation continues the struggle for justice, for full reconciliation requires justice. Without full justice, the lie still finds a place in a society.

Third, a community of memory is a place of *connection,* forging bonds in many directions. It connects the shreds of stories of violence and trauma into the larger narratives of individuals and communities, stories now shorn of their power to consume the present but stories that are part of the larger narratives of our identity. A community of memory reconnects those who have been separated out and reweaves them into the fabric of the community. And perhaps most importantly, a community of memory connects the story of the community with the narrative of the passion, death, and resurrection of Jesus, in order (to echo Philippians 3) to be so conformed into the pattern of his death as to come to know the power of the resurrection.

A ministry of reconciliation also fosters communities of hope. The call to reconciliation is not only one of coming to terms with the past. Reconciliation cannot occur without that. But reconciliation is also about coming to a new place from which a new society is constructed.

Communities of hope work, first of all, to give shape to the vocation that grows out of the reconciling experience. The vocation grows out of the gift, a gift meant to be shared further with others. But concrete programs and projects must be formed to help make this happen. A community of hope manifests its hope by looking to the future, the building of a new and just society.

Second, by being a community of hope, the reconciling community shows its conviction that there can be an alternative to the present order. It is suspicious of inevitabilities that constrain the creative spirit. It holds fast to the vision of the Colossians hymn of all things being reconciled to God in Christ.

A NEW MODEL OF MISSION?

Having attempted to describe reconciliation, both as an experience and as a ministry, we are left with the question: can it be the model of mission we need at this point in our history? Is this the form the Good News of Jesus Christ takes at the end of the century and of the millennium?

I would propose that it is. The message of reconciliation seems especially apt for so many of the situations we encounter in our world today. When one surveys the profound brokenness growing out of violence, trauma, and oppression that must be overcome in the construction of a new society in places such as South Africa, Argentina, El Salvador, and Cambodia, a ministry of reconciliation is urgently needed. Where societies have seen their civil life for so long ruled by lies, such as in Eastern Europe, communities of truth telling and memory are so necessary. Where long-seated hatreds have boiled over into civil war in the former Yugoslavia and Rwanda, a restored humanity and community are called for. And in societies that suppress violently the contradictions that allow some to prosper and the rest to sink in poverty and degradation, or call such contradictions necessary and inevitable, the truth needs to be told. Reconciliation is about the healing of humanity, the pursuit of justice, telling the truth. It is about connecting together the shreds of broken lives, and a vision of a healed planet.

Reconciliation, I would therefore suggest, may well be the response to a time where globalization permits no alternative to itself, and for that reason gives some forms of particularism a special virulence. A ministry in which one can hold on to hope against the apparent odds of broken lives and communities; in which the truth will not be stilled by webs of lies; in which the human community can be imagined from a new place: this is surely the Good News of Jesus Christ in our time. The Good News of one who has known our suffering, who now knows glory but still bears the scars of his torture and death: this is the mission, at the end of the century and the end of the millennium, to which we are called.

6

The Unity of the Church and the Homogeneous Unit Principle

C. René Padilla

René Padilla grew up in Ecuador and Colombia, and served in Buenos Aires, Argentina. He participated in prison ministry, preached on radio and in the streets, and led InterVarsity Christian Fellowship student ministries in Latin America. The church he planted among slum dwellers and drug addicts became a model for integrating evangelism and social action. At the Lausanne Congress and consultations, he was instrumental in advocating a more active role among evangelicals in addressing social issues. He was president of the Micah Network, a worldwide group of organizations aimed at mobilizing Christians against poverty, and wrote *Mission Between the Times: Essays on the Kingdom* (Grand Rapids: Eerdmans, 1985).

Throughout the entire New Testament the oneness of the People of God as a oneness that transcends all outward distinctions is taken for granted. The thought is that with the coming of Jesus Christ all the barriers that divide humankind have been broken down and a new humanity is now taking shape *in* and *through* the church. God's purpose in Jesus Christ includes the oneness of the human race, and that oneness becomes visible in the church. In the first part of this article we shall examine the New Testament teaching on the oneness of the church in which God's purpose to unite all things in Jesus Christ is expressed. In the second part we shall examine the historical unfolding of God's purpose of unity in apostolic times. Finally, in the last part, we shall evaluate Donald McGavran's homogeneous unit principle, according to which "men like to become Christians without crossing racial, linguistic or class barriers" (1970: 198), in the light of our previous analysis of scriptural teaching and apostolic practice.

First published in *International Bulletin of Missionary Research* 6, no. 1 (January 1982): 23-31. Reprinted here with permission.

I. GOD'S PURPOSE OF UNITY IN JESUS CHRIST

The Bible knows nothing of the human being as an individual in isolation; it knows only of a person as a *related* being, a person in relation to other people. Much of its teaching is colored by the Hebrew concept of human solidarity, for which H. Wheeler Robinson coined a well-worn label—"corporate personality." Accordingly, the church is viewed in the New Testament as the solidarity that has been created in Jesus Christ and that stands in contrast with the old humanity, represented by Adam. The Adam-solidarity is humankind under the judgment of God. Its oneness is a oneness of sin and death. But where sin abounded, grace has abounded all the more. As a result, the Adam-solidarity can no longer be viewed in isolation from Christ's world, in which God has justified sinners. Over against the darkness of death that fell on humanity through the first Adam, the light of life has broken into the world through the last Adam (Rom. 5:12-21). By means of the first Adam, the kingdom of death was established among humankind; humanity as a whole slipped into the void of meaningless existence out of fellowship with God and under his judgment. By means of the last Adam, a new humanity comes into existence, in which the results of the fall are undone and God's original purpose for humanity is fulfilled.

The letter to the Ephesians assembles a number of insights regarding the new humanity brought into being by Jesus Christ. It opens with a doxology (1:3-14) in which the unity of Jew and Gentile in the church is viewed in the light of God's eternal purpose, which includes the creation of a new order with Christ as the head. The whole universe is depicted as intended by God to be "summed up" or "recapitulated" in Christ, moving toward an *anakephalaiōsis*—a harmony in which "all the parts shall find their centre and bond of union in Christ" (Lightfoot quoted in Bruce 1961: 33). In that context, the unity of Jew and Gentile (vv. 13-14) can only be understood as a proleptic fulfillment of that which God is to accomplish in the "fullness of time" (v. 10).

Both Jews and Gentiles may now receive the seal of the Spirit by faith. Circumcision, which in former days was the sign of participation in the Abrahamic covenant, in the new order becomes irrelevant—it is merely an outward sign and it has been superseded by the "circumcision made without hands" (Col. 2:11). With the coming of Christ, "neither circumcision counts for anything, nor uncircumcision, but a new creation" (Gal. 6:15; cf. 5:6). God has brought into being a new humanity in which the barriers that separated the Gentiles from the Jews are broken down (Eph. 2:11ff.). Out of the two large homogeneous units whose enmity was proverbial in the ancient world God has made one; two enemies have been reconciled in "one body" (v. 16). In his death Jesus Christ removed the wall that stood between the two systems under which "the people" (*'am*) and "the nations" (*goyim*) had lived in former days. Now both Jews and Gentiles stand as equal in the presence of God (v. 18), as members of a new fellowship that may be described as a city, a family, and a building (vv. 19-20). Thus the unity that

God wills for the entire universe according to the first chapter of Ephesians becomes historically visible in a community where reconciliation both to God and to one another is possible on the basis of Christ's work.

Further on, in chapter 3, Paul claims that God's purpose of unity in Jesus Christ has been made known to him "by revelation" (v. 3). He is a steward of a "mystery" that was hitherto faintly perceived but that has now been revealed, namely, that in Christ "the nations" have a share in the blessings of the gospel, together with "the people," on the common ground of God's grace. Unmistakably, the unity of Jew and Gentile is here said to be *the gospel*—not simply a result that should take place as the church is "perfected," but an essential aspect of the kerygma that the apostle proclaimed on the basis of Scripture (vv. 8-9). Furthermore, it is conceived as an object lesson of God's manifold wisdom, displayed for the instruction of the inhabitants of the celestial realms, both good and evil (v. 10).

The unity resulting from Christ's work is not an abstract unity but a new community in which *life in Christ* becomes the decisive factor. The only peoplehood that has validity in the new order is that related to the church as "a chosen race, a royal priesthood, a holy nation, God's own people" (1 Pet. 2:9). Although made up of Jews and Gentiles, the church is placed together with Jews and Greeks (non-Jews), as a third group (1 Cor. 10:32). It is viewed as "the seed of Abraham," in which, since one is incorporated without any conditions apart from faith in Jesus Christ, "there is neither male nor female, neither Jew nor Gentile, there is neither slave nor freeman," for all are one (*heis*) in Christ (Gal. 3:28). No one would, on the basis of this passage, suggest that Gentiles have to become Jews, females have to become males, and slaves have to become free in order to share in the blessings of the gospel. But no justice is done to the text unless it is taken to mean that in Jesus Christ a new reality has come into being—a unity based on faith in him, in which membership is in no way dependent on race, social status, or sex. No mere "spiritual" unity, but a concrete community made up of Jews and Gentiles, slaves and free, men and women, all of them as equal members of the Christ-solidarity— that is the thrust of the passage. And, as Donald Guthrie puts it, "Paul is not expressing a hope, but a fact" (Guthrie 1969: 115).

A similar idea is conveyed again in Colossians 3:11, where Paul states that for those who have been incorporated into the new humanity created in Jesus Christ, the divisions that affect the old humanity have become irrelevant: "Here there cannot be Gentile and Jew, circumcised or uncircumcised, barbarian, Scythian slave, free man, but Christ is all and in all." Race loses its importance because all the believers, whether Jews or Gentiles, belong to the "Israel of God" (Gal. 6:16). Religious background is neither here nor there because "the true circumcision" (Phil. 3:3) is made up of Jews who are Jews inwardly, whose circumcision is "real circumcision . . . a matter of the heart, spiritual and not literal" (Rom. 2:28-29). Social stratifications are beside the point because in the new humanity the slave becomes his own master's "beloved brother" (Philem. 15); the slave is called to serve

the Lord and not humankind (Col. 3:22) and the free person is to live as
one who has a master in heaven (Col. 4:11). Here—in the corporate new
human, in the new homogeneous unit that has been brought into being in
Jesus Christ—the only thing that matters is that "Christ is all and in all."
Those who have been baptized "into one body" (1 Cor. 12:13) are members
of a community in which the differences that separate people in the world
have become obsolete. It may be true that "men like to become Christians
without crossing racial, linguistic or class barriers," but that is irrelevant.
Membership in the body of Christ is not a question of likes or dislikes, but a
question of incorporation into a new humanity under the lordship of Christ.
Whether a person likes it or not, the same act that reconciles one to God
simultaneously introduces the person into a community where people find
their identity in Jesus Christ rather than in their race, culture, social class,
or sex, and are consequently reconciled to one another. "The unifier is Jesus
Christ and the unifying principle is the 'Gospel'" (Mackay 1953: 84).

God's purpose is to bring the universe "into a unity in Christ" (Eph. 1:10,
NEB). That purpose is yet to be consummated. But *already,* in anticipation
of the end, a new humanity has been created in Jesus Christ and those who
are incorporated in him form a unit wherein all the divisions that separate
people in the old humanity are done away with. The original unity of the
human race is thus restored; God's purpose of unity in Jesus Christ is thus
made historically visible.

II. THE UNITY OF THE CHURCH
AND APOSTOLIC PRACTICE

A cursory examination of the New Testament shows the way in which
the teaching on the new unity of the church developed in the foregoing
section was implemented by the apostles. Furthermore, it brings into focus
the difficulties that the early church faced as it sought to live in the light of
God's purpose of unity in Jesus Christ. The breaking down of the barriers
between Jew and Gentile, between slave and free, and between male and
female, could no more be taken for granted in the first century than the
breaking of the barriers between black and white, between rich and poor,
and between male and female today. But all the New Testament evidence
points to an apostolic practice consistent with the aim of forming churches
in which God's purpose would become a concrete reality.

Jesus' Example

The apostles had no need to speculate as to what a community in which
loyalty to Jesus Christ relativized all the differences would look like; they
could look back to the community that Jesus had gathered around himself
during his earthly ministry. True, he had not demanded a rigidly structured

uniformity, yet he had attained the formation of a community that had been held together by a common commitment to him, in the face of which all the differences that could have separated them had been overcome. Members of the revolutionary party (such as "Simon who was called the Zealot," Luke 6:15) had become one with "publicans"—private businessmen in charge of collecting taxes for the government of the occupying power (such as Matthew, in Matt. 9:9-13; cf. Luke 19:1-10). Humble women of dubious reputation (see Luke 7:36-39) had mixed with wealthy women whose economic means made the traveling ministry of Jesus and his followers possible (Luke 8:1-3). Women had been accepted on the same basis as men, despite the common view, expressed by Josephus, that a woman "is in every respect of less worth than a man" (Jeremias 1971: 223ff.).

To be sure, Jesus had limited his mission to the Jews and had imposed the same limitation to his apostles before his resurrection. Yet, as Jeremias has demonstrated, he had anticipated that the Gentiles would share in the revelation given to Israel and would participate in God's people (Jeremias 1958). Accordingly, he had commanded his disciples to proclaim the gospel to "all nations"; the Gentile mission was to be the means through which the Gentiles would be accepted as guests at God's table (Matt. 8:11; cf. Isa. 25:6-8).

The Jerusalem Church

On the day of Pentecost, the gospel was proclaimed to a large multitude of pilgrims that had come to Jerusalem for the great Jewish Feast of Weeks (Acts 2:1-13). The heterogeneous nature of the multitude is stressed in the narrative by reference to the variety of languages (vv. 6-8) and lands and cultures (vv. 9-11) represented among them. Granted that the "devout men" (*andres eulabeis*) mentioned in verse 5 should be taken as Jews rather than as Gentile God-fearers, the fact that Luke wants to press home upon us is that "every nation under heaven" was represented and that the mighty works of God were proclaimed in the indigenous languages and dialects of many lands. The worldwide proclamation of the gospel—the proclamation to be portrayed in the succeeding chapters of Acts—was thus anticipated in one single event in which even the linguistic barriers were miraculously broken down for the sake of the spread of the gospel "to the ends of the earth" (1:8). The point here is that at Pentecost people became Christian with people from "every nation under heaven" (2:5), including "visitors from Rome, both Jews and proselytes" (v. 10). Accordingly, Peter understood Pentecost—the gift of the Spirit—as the means whereby the promise of the gospel (that "all the nations of the earth shall be blessed," Gen. 12:3) was extended not only to those present but also to their descendants as well as to "all that are far off" (v. 39).

The Christian community that resulted from Pentecost was, of course, made up mainly of Jewish Christians. What else could be expected before

the Gentile mission? Yet it would be a great mistake to conclude that it was
in their Jewishness that they found their identity. Not racial homogeneity,
but Pentecost, was the basis of their unity. Only in the light of the outpouring
of the Spirit are we able to understand how it was possible for the early
Jerusalem church to include in its constituency "unlearned and ignorant
men" (*agrammatoi . . . kai idiotai*, Acts 4:13; *'amme ha-'aretz*, "people
of the land," according to rabbinical terminology), and educated priests
(6:7), and, at a later stage, Pharisees (15:5; cf. 11:2); poor people in need
of help and wealthy landlords (2:44-45; 4:32-37), possibly members of a
well-to-do foreign community (Judge 1960: 55); Jews (Aramaic-speaking,
most of them natives of Palestine), "Hellenists" (Greek-speaking Jews
from the Dispersion) (6:1ff.), and at least one Gentile from Syrian Antioch
(v. 5).

Luke's record shows that the basic ecclesiastical unit for both preaching
and teaching was the house church (Acts 2:46; 5:42; cf. 12:12, 17; 21:18).
But there is nothing in Acts to support the view that "the mixed church at
Jerusalem divided along homogeneous unit lines,"[1] or to lead us as much
as to imagine that there were different house churches for the educated and
for the uneducated, for the rich and for the poor, for the Palestinian Jews
and for the Jews of the Dispersion. All the evidence points in the opposite
direction. One of Luke's main emphases as he describes the church growing
out of Pentecost is, in fact, that the believers were "together" (*epi to auto*,
with a quasi-technical sense; cf. 2:44); that they had "all things in common"
(2:44; 4:32); that they were "of one heart and soul" (4:32). The burden of
proof lies with anyone who, despite Luke's description, continues to hold
that the early church in Jerusalem was organized according to homogeneous
units.

A problem that soon arose in the early Jerusalem church was due
precisely to the heterogeneous nature of the community—the "Hellenists"
complained against the "Hebrews" because their widows were not receiving
a fair share from the common pool that had been formed (Acts 6:1). No
clearer illustration of the way in which the apostles faced the problems of
division in the church can be found than the one recorded here. A modern
church-growth expert might have suggested the creation of two distinct
denominations, one for Palestinian Jews and another one for Greek Jews.
That would have certainly been a *practical* solution to the tensions existing
between the two conflicting homogeneous units! We are told, however, that
the apostles called the community together and asked them to choose seven
men who would be responsible for the daily distribution (vv. 2-6). The unity
of the church across cultural barriers was thus preserved.

---

1. C. Peter Wagner, *Our Kind of People: The Ethical Dimensions of Church Growth
in America* (Atlanta: John Knox, 1979), 122-23. If both Jews and Gentiles were divided into
"numerous important homogeneous units" (ibid., 114), why does Wagner argue that the
Jerusalem church was divided into only two groups, the Hellenists and the Hebrews?

The Church in Syrian Antioch

Following Stephen's martyrdom, a great persecution arose against the Jerusalem church, apparently mainly against the Hellenist believers with whom Stephen had been identified (Acts 8:1). A result of the persecution, however, was that the first large-scale evangelization outside Palestine was launched by exiles who traveled as far as Phoenicia, Cyprus, and Syrian Antioch (11:19).

According to Luke's report, these exiles, aside from a few, shared the gospel with "none except Jews" (v. 19). Why so, one may ask. No explicit answer is given in the narrative, yet this statement is used by Donald McGavran to support the claim that in the years following Pentecost the church made "early adjustments" that favored the spread of the gospel and resulted in "one-race congregations" that "arose by the dozens; perhaps by the hundreds"(McGavran 1974: 23). Luke's record, however, does not substantiate the thesis that the apostles deliberately promoted the formation of "one-race congregations" and tolerated Jewish prejudices against the Gentiles for the sake of numerical church growth. In order to claim that it does, one needs to come to Scripture with the preconceived idea (1) that the apostles shared the modern theory that race prejudice "can be understood and should be made an aid to Christianization" (McGavran 1955: 10), and (2) that the multiplication of the church invariably requires an adjustment to the homogeneous unit principle. Without this unwarranted assumption, one can hardly miss the point made by Acts that the extension of the gospel to the Gentiles was such a difficult step for the Jerusalem church that it took place only with the aid of visions and commands (8:26ff.; 10:1-16) or under the pressure of persecution (8:1ff.; 11:19-20). No suggestion is ever given that Jewish Christians preached the gospel to "none except Jews" *because of strategic considerations.* All the evidence points to the fact that restrictions placed on the proclamation of the gospel even by Greek-speaking Jews was due to scruples that would have to be overcome (as in Peter's case when he was sent to Cornelius) if the Gentiles were to receive the Word of God and if the Jews were to see that "God shows no partiality" (as in the case of those in Judea who heard that Cornelius and his kinsmen and friends had believed). As long as Jewish Christians allowed inherited prejudices to persist, probably because of their fear that this contact with Gentiles might be interpreted by fellow Jews as an act whereby they were "traitorously joining a strange people" (to borrow McGavran's expression), they could only preach "to none except the Jews." Who would have thought that their approach, based on such a limited outlook, would be used as a pattern for evangelism in the twentieth century?

The evangelists who took the new step of preaching the gospel to Gentiles in Syrian Antioch were unnamed "men of Cyprus and Cyrene" (11:20). The importance of this step can hardly be overestimated. Antioch was the third largest city in the world, "almost a microcosm of Roman antiquity in the first century, a city which encompassed most of the advantages, the problems, and the human interests, with which the new faith would have to grapple" (Green 1970: 114). Soon the church there would become the base for the Gentile mission.

There is no evidence that those who received the gospel in Antioch were relatives to the exiles coming from Jerusalem. Perhaps they were, but this is merely a conjecture and lends no solid support to the idea that "in Antioch for both the Jerusalem refugees and the resident Christians we have bridges of relationship into the Greek people" (McGavran 1955: 24). Furthermore, nothing is said by Luke to lead us to the conclusion that the evangelization of Gentiles in this city took place in the synagogue. That might have been the case, but if the correct reading in verse 20 is *hellenas* rather than *hellenistas*, Gentiles of Greek culture would be meant. Floyd Filson may be right in believing that the evangelized were "Gentiles who had had no previous contact with the synagogue" (1965: 191). The message that was preached to them was centered in Jesus as Lord (*kyrios*) and was thus cast in terms not entirely unfamiliar to people living in a cosmopolitan city where salvation was being offered by many cults and mystery religions in the name of other lords. God's power was with the evangelists and as a result many believed. Unless we are to assume that for the sake of numerical growth the "great number" of those who believed were immediately separated into homogeneous unit house churches (Wagner 1979: 124) the clear implication is that the church that came into being embraced both Jewish and Gentile believers *on an equal basis* and that there was no thought that the latter had to accept Jewish practices as a prerequisite. At a later stage, as we shall see, the question of the place of Jewish ceremonial law in the church was to become a matter of debate. But there is no evidence that at the start of the Antioch church the evangelists resorted to the homogeneous unit principle in order to accomplish their task. How was unity preserved when there were many members who did not keep the Jewish ceremonial law and there were others who did? We are not told. We can imagine that difficulties would arise. "But," as Adolf Schlatter has commented, "the early Church never shirked difficulties: it attacked bravely. So nothing more is said about these difficulties, and we do not hear how intercourse in the mixed communities was secured" (1961: 59).

An insight into the degree to which people from a variety of backgrounds worked together in the Antioch church is found in the list of leaders provided by Luke in Acts 13:1: "Barnabas, Symeon who was called Niger, Lucius of Cyrene, Manaen a member of the court of Herod the tetrarch, and Saul." A more heterogeneous group could hardly be suggested! Barnabas was a Levite, a native of Cyprus (4:36). Symeon, as his nickname Niger ("Black") suggests, was a Jew (or proselyte?) apparently of dark complexion, perhaps to be identified with Simon of Cyrene who carried Jesus' cross. Lucius was a Gentile (or a Jew with a Roman name?), a native of the African city of Cyrene, perhaps one of the men who had first preached the gospel in Antioch. Manaen was a "foster-brother" (*synthrophos*) to Herod Antipas, the tetrarch of Galilee, with whom he had been reared. Saul was an ex-Pharisee, a "Hebrew of Hebrews" and (as a Roman citizen) a member of a small privileged minority in the eastern Mediterranean (Judge 1960: 52, 58). What could glue these men together aside from a common experience?

The Early Gentile Churches and the "Circumcision Party"

As long as the church was made up mainly of Jews, apparently it was not a great problem for Jewish Christians to accept Gentile converts as full members of the church without demanding that they become Jews. Peter's report on the way Cornelius and his household had received the Word of God was enough to silence the criticism that the circumcision party in Jerusalem had raised against the apostle (Acts 11:1-18). Later on, the news concerning the numerical growth of the church in Syrian Antioch was welcomed in the mother church, which then sent one of its most outstanding leaders with the commission to instruct the new believers (11:22ff.). When the leaders of the Gentile mission (Barnabas and Saul) visited Jerusalem in connection with the relief sent from Antioch for the brethren in Judea (11:27-30), they had a meeting with James (Jesus' brother), Peter, and John, as a result of which they were given "the right hand of fellowship"; the understanding was reached that "we," says Paul, "should go to the Gentiles and they to the circumcised" (Gal. 2:9). The presence of a young Greek convert, named Titus, with the delegation from Antioch at that time could be taken as a further confirmation that the Jewish Christian would not expect Gentile converts to be circumcised (Gal. 2:1-3).

The spread of the gospel throughout south Galatia brought about by the travels undertaken by Paul and Barnabas, with the resulting increase of Gentile converts, finally raised the whole issue of the basis on which the Gentiles could participate as full members in the People of God. Was faith to be regarded as sufficient, as the missionaries were preaching? Granted that the gospel was meant to be preached to all men and women, whether Jews or Gentiles, should not the Gentile converts be circumcised? Should they not be required to conform to Jewish ceremonial laws and food regulations? Should they not be expected to "take upon themselves the yoke of the commandments," like the proselytes to Judaism? The issue was pressed by a circumcision party within the Jerusalem church, made up of people who had previously been associated with the Pharisees (Acts 15:1, 5).

It is likely that the episode that Paul narrates in Galatians 2:11-14 should be viewed in connection with the visit that according to Acts 15:1 these members of the circumcision party made to Antioch. Before their coming Peter had felt free to share a common table with Gentile Christians, for he had learned in Joppa not to call anything "common" (or "unclean") if God had purified it. When they came, however, "he drew back and separated himself, fearing the circumcision party" (Gal. 2:12). His attitude can best be understood when it is viewed in the light of a historical context in which those Jews who sat at a table where food would not be kosher thereby opened themselves to the accusation of "traitorously joining a strange people." According to Paul, those who induced Peter to act inconsistently with his Gentile brethren had been sent by James. Paul's words need not mean that they had been personally commissioned by James to spy out the Jewish-Gentile relations, but from all we know the conservative party may have forced James to take action against a practice that went against their own taboos. T. W. Manson's suggestion therefore carries weight, that a message from James was brought to Peter, couched more or less in the following terms: "News has come to Jerusalem that you are eating Gentile food at Gentile tables, and this is causing great scandal to many devout brethren besides laying us open to serious criticism from the Scribes and Pharisees. Pray discontinue this practice, which will surely do great harm to our work among our fellow-countrymen" (Manson 1962: 181).

Be that as it may, Peter's action, however justified it may have been in his own opinion, was strongly opposed by Paul, who saw in it a "play-acting" (*hypokrisis*) that compromised the truth of the gospel (v. 13). To be sure, Peter had not agreed with the conservative party on the question of keeping the law as a Christian requirement. His failure had been to give up table fellowship with his Gentile brethren, not because of his own convictions but because of a fierce pragmatism in the face of the danger of being regarded as a traitor to his own race. Although he himself believed with Paul that "neither circumcision counts for anything, nor uncircumcision, but a new creation" (6:15), prompted by fear of others he had adopted a course of action that was totally inconsistent with that conviction. And because of his influence, he had carried with him the rest of the Jewish Christians, including Barnabas (2:13), thereby destroying Christian fellowship and denying the truth of the gospel, according to which for those who have been incorporated into Jesus Christ all the barriers that separate people have been abolished (3:28).

Peter's action showed how real was the danger facing the apostolic church to be divided into two "denominations"—a Jewish Christian church and a Gentile Christian church, each with its own emphases, serving its own homogeneous unit. The situation was so serious that a meeting was held in Jerusalem in order to discuss the problem, with the apostles and elders of the local church and with Paul and Barnabas as delegates from Antioch (Acts 15:2ff.). The circumcision party that had provoked the Jewish–Gentile incident in Antioch presented its case, but the "council" vindicated Paul and Barnabas and sent them back to Antioch with a letter summarizing the decision that had been reached (vv. 22-29).

The "Jerusalem Decree" provided the basis for Jewish and Gentile Christians to live in unity, as equal members of the body of Christ. It clearly exemplifies the apostolic practice in the face of problems arising out of racial, cultural, or social differences among Christians. In the first place, the Gentile converts would not have to be circumcised in order to be accepted as full members of the People of God. Faith in Jesus Christ was thus affirmed as the only condition for salvation. And the repudiation of the attempt made by the conservative party of the Jerusalem church to impose circumcision on the Gentile Christians was archetypical of the Christian rejection of every form of "assimilationist racism" (to use Wagner's expression). Clearly the apostles would have agreed with the claim that "any teaching to the effect that Christianity requires a person to adapt to the culture of another homogeneous unit in order to become an authentic Christian is unethical because it is dehumanizing" (Wagner 1979: 99).

In the second place, it was taken for granted that Jewish and Gentile Christians would continue to have regular social intercourse as members of interracial local congregations, and provision was therefore made to prevent conflicts arising out of cultural differences. There is nothing at all in the book of Acts or the epistles to lend support to the theory that the apostles ever contemplated the idea of adopting Peter's approach as described in Galatians 2:11-14: the separation of Jews and Gentiles in different one-race churches that would then endeavor to show their unity in Christ exclusively in "the supracongregational relationship of believers in the total Christian body over which Christ himself is the head . . . " (Wagner 1979: 182). *The apostles rejected imperialistic uniformity, but they also rejected segregated uniformity.* It was precisely because they assumed that Christians, whether Jews or Gentiles, would normally eat and worship together that they took measures to remove the most obvious obstacle to Christian fellowship in interracial churches. As F. F. Bruce has rightly observed:

> The Jerusalem decree dealt with two questions—the major one, "Must Gentile Christians be circumcised and undertake to keep the Mosaic law?" and the subsidiary one, "What are the conditions with which Gentile Christians should comply if Jewish Christians are to have easy social relations with them?" The second question would not have been raised had the first question been answered in the affirmative. If Gentile Christians had been required to follow the example of Gentile proselytes to Judaism, then, when these requirements were met, table-fellowship and the like would have followed as a matter of course. But when it was decided that Gentile Christians must not be compelled to submit to circumcision and the general obligations of the Jewish law, the question of table-fellowship, which had caused the recent trouble in Antioch, had to be considered. (1969: 288)

The decision reached was that the Gentiles would abstain from practices that were particularly offensive to Jews, namely (according to the most probable reading), from the flesh of animals that had been offered in sacrifices to idols, from meat with blood (including therefore the flesh of animals that had been strangled), and from "unchastity" in the sense of the degrees of consanguinity and affinity contemplated in Leviticus 18:6-18. If the Jerusalem "Council," having set out to deal with the question of circumcision, ended with regulations related to table fellowship, the obvious explanation is that, once the matter of principle was settled, the effort was made to provide a modus vivendi for churches in which Jews and Gentiles would continue to have table fellowship together. And it is quite likely that the regulations included in this arrangement were basically the same as those that had always provided a basis for intercourse between Jews and "God-fearing" Gentiles in the synagogues throughout the empire.[2]

According to Alan R. Tippett, the Jerusalem Decree "against the forcing of the cultural patterns of the evangelizing people on the unevangelized is written into the foundation of the Church and cries aloud today at the expressly westernizing missionary" (Tippett 1970: 34). True. But a closer look at the historical situation shows that the Jerusalem Decree also cries aloud at every attempt to solve the conflicts arising out of cultural differences among Christians by resorting to the formation of separate congregations, each representing a different homogeneous unit. The regulations given by the Jerusalem conference were formulated on the assumption that table fellowship between Jewish and Gentile Christians was to continue despite the difficulties. *Unity in Christ is far more than a unity occasionally expressed at the level of "the supracongregational relationship of believers in the total Christian body"; it is the unity of the members of Christ's body, to be made visible in the common life of local congregations.*

The working arrangement represented by the Jerusalem Decree was entirely consistent with Paul's attitude expressed later in 1 Corinthians 8:7ff. and Romans 14:13ff. There was no compromise on a matter of principle, but the Gentiles were asked to forgo their freedom with regard to practices that caused offense to their Jewish brethren. At least for Paul, the way to solve the conflicts in the church was neither imperialistic uniformity nor segregated uniformity but love, for love alone "binds everything together in perfect harmony" (Col. 3:14).

The Gentile Mission

A well-attested fact regarding evangelism in the early church is that almost everywhere the gospel was first preached to both Jews and Gentiles *together*, in the synagogues. Luke provides no evidence to support McGavran's claim that family connections played a very important role in the extension of the faith throughout the Roman Empire (McGavran 1955: 27ff.), but there is

---

2. W. M. Ramsay, *St. Paul the Traveler and the Roman Citizen* (Grand Rapids: Baker Book House, 1949), 169. C. Peter Wagner recognizes that "Most synagogue communities in the Roman provinces were made up of a core of Hellenistic Jewish residents, some Gentile proselytes who had converted to Judaism and been circumcised, and a number of so-called God-fearers who *were* Gentiles attracted to the Jewish faith but who had not wished to be circumcised and keep the Mosaic law" (*Our Kind of People*, 127). If that kind of pluralism was possible in a Jewish context, Wagner's thesis that "New Testament churches were homogeneous-unit churches" (p. 117) can be discarded a priori as an unwarranted assumption.

no doubt that the "God-fearers" on the fringe of the Jewish congregation served in every major city as the bridgehead into the Gentile world (Ramsay 1949: 276-77). That these Gentiles who had been attracted to Judaism should be open to the Christian message is not surprising. If (according to the Mishnah) even proselytes could only refer to God as "O God of *your* fathers," how much less would the "God-fearers"—who were not willing to be circumcised and to comply with food laws—be regarded as qualified for membership in the chosen people. In F. F. Bruce's words:

> By attending the synagogue and listening to the reading and exposition of the sacred scriptures, these Gentiles, already worshippers of the "living and true God" were familiar with the messianic hope in some form. They could not inherit this hope and the blessings which accompanied it until they became full converts to Judaism, and this was more than most of them were prepared for. But when they were told that the messianic hope had come alive in Jesus, that in him the old distinction between Jew and Gentile had been abolished, that the fullest blessings of God's saving grace were as readily available to Gentiles as to Jews, such people could not but welcome this good news just as every ancestral instinct moved Jews to refuse it on these terms. (Bruce 1969: 276f.)

A cursory study of the Pauline mission shows that time after time on arriving in a city the apostle would first visit the synagogues and then, when the break with the Jewish authorities was produced, he would start a Christian congregation with the new Gentile believers and a handful of converted Jews (Acts 13:5; 14:1; 17:1, 10, 17; 18:4, 19; 19:8). Such an approach had a theological basis—the offer of the gospel was to be made "to the Jews first" (Rom. 1:16; 2:9, 10; cf. Acts 3:26), according to a conviction going back to Jesus himself, that the Gentiles could only be incorporated into the kingdom after Israel had had the opportunity to return to the Lord (Jeremias 1955: 71ff.; cf. Manson 1955). But it also made it possible for the church to start almost everywhere with a nucleus of believers who already had the background provided them by Judaism, with all the obvious advantages that this background implied. From that nucleus the gospel would then spread to Gentiles with a completely pagan outlook.

It would be ridiculous to suggest that Jews and Gentiles heard the gospel *together* in the synagogues, but then those who believed were instructed to separate into segregated house churches for the sake of the expansion of the gospel. Such a procedure would have been an open denial of apostolic teaching concerning the unity of the church. It would have also meant that the door of the church was made narrower than the door of the synagogue, where Jews and Gentiles could worship together. The suggestion is so farfetched that it can hardly be taken seriously. All the New Testament evidence, however, points in the opposite direction, namely, in the direction of an apostolic practice whose aim was the formation of churches that would live out the unity of the new humanity in Jesus Christ. The apostles knew very well that if the acceptance of "people as they are" was to be more than lip-service acceptance it had to take place at the level of the local congregations. Accordingly, they sought to build communities in which right from the start Jews and Gentiles, slaves and free, poor and rich would worship together and learn the meaning of their unity in Christ, although they often had to deal with difficulties arising out of the differences in backgrounds or social status among the converts. That this was the case is well substantiated by a survey of the dealings of the apostles with the churches in the Gentile world, as reflected in the New Testament. For the sake of brevity two examples will suffice.

The Church in Corinth. It is in the context of a chapter dealing with the diversity not of homogeneous unit *churches* but of the *members* of the church that Paul states: "For just as the body is one and has many members, and all the members of the body, though many, are one body, so it is with Christ. For by one Spirit we were all baptized into one body—Jews or Greeks, slaves or free—and all were made to drink of one Spirit" (1 Cor. 12:12-13). The emphasis on the nature of the oneness of Christians representing various racial and social groups can be best explained when it is viewed in relation to the situation of the church in Corinth.

According to Luke's report in Acts, the initiation of the church in that city followed the pattern characteristic of the Gentile mission. Paul began his preaching ministry in the synagogue, where Jews and Gentiles heard the gospel *together* (Acts 18:4). Later on he was compelled to leave the synagogue, but by then there was a nucleus of converts, including "God-fearing" Gentiles such as Gaius Titius Justus (Acts 18:7; 1 Cor. 1:14) and Stephanas and his household (1 Cor. 1:16; according to 16:15, "the first converts in Achaia"), and Jews such as Crispus, the ruler of the synagogue, and his household (Acts 18:8; 1 Cor. 1:14). Gaius's house was located next door to the synagogue (Acts 18:7), and it became the living quarters for Paul and the meeting place for "the whole church," consisting of Jews such as Lucius, Jason, and Sosipater, and Gentiles such as Erastus and Quartus (Rom. 16:21, 23).

There are other hints regarding the constituency of the Corinthian church given in 1 Corinthians. The clear inference from 1:26 is that the majority of the members came from the lower strata of society—they were not wise, or powerful, or of noble birth "according to worldly standards." At least some of the members were slaves, while others were free (7:21-22). On the other hand, the community also included a few well-to-do members, notably Gaius (presumably a Roman citizen), Crispus (the ex-ruler of the synagogue), Erastus (the city treasurer, Rom. 16:23), and possibly Chloe (as suggested by the reference to her "dependents," who may have been slaves, 1 Cor. 1:11).

It would be absurd to take Paul's exhortation to each Corinthian Christian to remain "in the state in which he was called" (1 Cor. 7:20) as lending support to the idea that each one was to belong to a homogeneous unit church representing his or her own race or social class (Wagner 1979: 133). The whole point of the passage (1 Cor. 7:17-24) is that in the face of God's call both race and social status have become irrelevant; the only thing that really matters is faithfulness to Jesus Christ. The apostle is teaching here neither that slaves should remain in slavery nor that they should take freedom, should the opportunity for manumission come, but that the Christian's existence is no longer determined by one's legal status but by the fact that he or she has been called by God. The slave's slavery is irrelevant because the slave is "a freedman of the Lord"; the free man's freedom is equally irrelevant because he is "a slave of Christ" (v. 22). This is not a piece of advice to reject or to accept manumission—to leave or to remain in one's homogeneous unit—but an exhortation to see that, whatever one's social status may be, he or she is to "remain with God" (v. 24). In S. Scott Bartchy's words, "Since God had called the Corinthians into *koinonia* with his crucified Son, it was *this* fellowship and not any status in the world which determined their relationship to God" (1973: 182). This relationship to God was in turn to be the basis for the relationship among Christians.

The racial, social, and cultural diversity among the people that made up the church in Corinth goes a long way to explain the problems of dissension that Paul addresses in 1:10ff. Although the Christians continued to meet together at Gaius's house (Rom. 16:23), they tended to divide into at least four groups, each claiming to follow a different leader (1:12). We cannot be certain regarding the distinctive claims made by each group, but the least we can say is that the Petrine party was made up of Jews who insisted on the food regulations formulated by the Jerusalem Council (cf. 1 Cor. 8:1ff; 10:25ff), while the "Christ party" was probably made up of Gentiles who regarded themselves as "spiritual men," opposed Jewish legalism, and denied the Jewish doctrine of the resurrection (Manson 1962: 190ff.). To complicate things even further, the communal meals, in the course of which the believers participated in the Lord's Supper, had become a sad picture of the division of the church according to economic position. C. K. Barrett is probably right in inferring from the text that "the members of the church were expected to share their resources, the rich, presumably, to bring more than they needed and to make provision for the poor" (1971: 263). Instead of sharing, however, the rich would go ahead and eat their own supper and even get drunk, while the poor would go hungry. The natural result was that the poor felt ashamed and the supper became a display of unbrotherliness (1 Cor. 11:20-22). It seems clear that, despite the divisions, the whole Christian community in Corinth continued to come together regularly in one assembly (11:17, 20; 14:23, 26; cf. Rom. 16:23). There may be some exaggeration in Johannes Munck's description of the Corinthian church as "The Church Without Factions" (1959: 135ff.), but it is undeniable that all the evidence points in the direction of disunity and bickering, but not of separate churches representing the various positions in conflict.

The important thing here is to notice that the whole epistle exemplifies again the apostolic practice in the face of problems of division caused by racial, cultural, or social differences among the members of the church. Not the least suggestion is ever made that the solution to such problems is to be found in homogeneous unit churches that would then seek to develop "intercongregational activities and relationships" (Wagner 1979: 150). Again and again the emphasis falls on the fact that the believers have been incorporated into Jesus Christ, as a result of which all the differences deriving from their respective homogeneous units are now relativized to such a degree that in the context of the Christian community they can be viewed as nonexistent. Indeed the call to unity is central to the whole epistle.

The Church in Rome. This church, in contrast with the one in Corinth, seems to have broken up into separate groups, some of which may have been made up of people representing diverse homogeneous units in society. In Bruce's words, "Perhaps some local groups consisted of Jewish Christians and others of Gentile Christians, and there were few, if any, in which Jewish and Gentile Christians met together" (Bruce 1969: 394). It may well be that it was because of this situation that Paul addressed his epistle to the Romans "to all God's beloved in Rome" (1:7) rather than "to the Church of God which is at Rome." A better sign of this situation, however, is the mention made in chapter 16 of at least five house churches, associated with the names of Prisca and Aquila (v. 3), Aristobulus (v. 10), Narcissus (v. 11), Asyncritus (v. 14), and Philologus (v. 15).

If this reconstruction of the situation of the church in Rome is correct, are we then to conclude that it lends support to the theory that the apostolic practice was aimed at the formation of homogeneous unit churches? So to conclude would be to disregard completely what was undoubtedly Paul's main purpose in writing the epistle, namely, "to bring about the obedience of faith" (1:5) in congregations where, as Paul S. Minear has argued (1971), Christians representing a given position would not worship side by side with Christians representing another position. Only by a partial reading of Minear's work can the evidence adduced by him be used as lending support to the theory that the apostolic church consisted largely of homogeneous unit congregations or that the situation of the church in Rome reflected the apostolic practice (Wagner 1979: 130-31). Quite to the contrary, Minear's claim is that the epistle to the Romans was written with the hope that "a larger number of segregated house-churches would at last be able to worship together—Jews praising God among Gentiles and Gentiles praising God with his people" (Minear 1971: 16-17). Accordingly, he shows how the entire epistle develops the idea that through the coming of Jesus Christ all human distinctions have been broken down, and concludes that faith required that the various groups in Rome should welcome one another notwithstanding their opposing views on foods and days. Thus, for Minear the situation viewed by Paul in chapters 14 and 15 was "the target of the whole epistle" (Minear 1971: 33).

Paul's approach to the problem in Rome was consistent with the apostolic practice with regard to churches threatened by division. There is no evidence that he would have approved of the modern device to solve the problem of disunity, that is, the forming of segregated congregations open to communications with other segregated congregations. All his letters make it overwhelmingly clear that he conceived oneness in Christ as an essential aspect of the gospel and therefore made every effort to see that Christians would together "with one voice glorify the God and Father of our Lord Jesus Christ" (Rom. 15:5).

Other New Testament writings reflect the same apostolic concern for church unity across all the barriers separating people in society. And no research is necessary to verify that the congregations that resulted from the Gentile mission normally included Jews and Gentiles, slaves and free, rich and poor, and were taught that in Christ all the differences derived from their respective homogeneous units had become irrelevant (see Eph. 6:5-9; Col. 3:22-4:1; 1 Tim. 6:17-19; Phlm. 16; James 1:9-11; 2:1-7; 4:13; 1 Pet. 2:18; 1 John 3:17).

The impact that the early church made on non-Christians *because of Christian brotherhood across natural barriers* can hardly be overestimated. The abolition of the old separation between Jew and Gentile was undoubtedly one of the most amazing accomplishments of the gospel in the first century. Equally amazing, however, was the breaking down of the class distinction between master and slave. As Michael Green comments, "When the Christian missionaries not only proclaimed that in Christ the distinctions between slave and free man were done away as surely as those between Jew and Greek, but actually lived in accordance with their principles, then this had an enormous appeal" (Green 1970: 117-18). In F. F. Bruce's words, "Perhaps this was the way in which the gospel made the deepest impression on the pagan world" (Bruce 1957: 277).

III. AN EVALUATION OF THE "HOMOGENEOUS UNIT PRINCIPLE"

How are we to evaluate the use of the homogeneous unit principle, advocated by Donald McGavran and his followers, in the light of the foregoing discussion of the apostolic teaching and practice regarding the unity of the church?

Before attempting to answer that question, two observations are necessary for the sake of clarity. In the first place, it cannot be denied that from a biblical perspective the (quantitative) growth of the church is a legitimate concern in the Christian mission (Costas 1981: 2ff.). If God "desires all men to be saved and to come to the knowledge of the truth" (1 Tim. 2:4), no Christian is in harmony with God's desire unless he or she also longs to see all coming to Jesus Christ. Moreover, it is clear that this longing will have to be expressed in practical terms (which may well include the use of anthropological and sociological insights) so that the gospel is in fact proclaimed as widely as possible. The issue in this evaluation, therefore, is not the employment of principles that can help in the expansion of the church. In the second place, it is a fact that hardly needs verification that the growth of the church takes place in specific social and cultural contexts and that people generally *prefer* to become Christians without having to cross the barriers between one context and another. This, again is not the issue in this evaluation.

The real issue is whether church planting should be carried out so as to enable people to become Christians without crossing barriers (McGavran 1970: 198ff.), whether this principle is "essential for the spread of the gospel" and biblically and theologically defensible. Enough has been said in the two previous sections on the apostolic teaching and practice bearing on the subject for me to draw the following conclusions, all of which are amply supported by exegesis:

1. In the early church the gospel was proclaimed to all people, whether Jews or Gentiles, slaves or free, rich or poor, without partiality. More often than not during the Gentile mission *Jews and Gentiles heard the gospel together.* The New Testament provides no indication that the apostolic church had a missionary strategy based on the premise that church planting would be "more effective" if carried on within each separate homogeneous unit and was therefore to be conducted along racial or social lines.

2. The breaking down of the barriers that separate people in the world was regarded as *an essential aspect of the gospel,* not merely as a result of it. Evangelism would therefore involve a call to be incorporated into a new humanity that included all kinds of people. Conversion was never a merely religious experience; it was also a way of becoming a member of a community where people would find their identity in Christ rather than in their race, social status, or sex. The apostles would have agreed with Clowney's dictum that "The point at which human barriers are surmounted is the point at which a believer is joined to Christ and his people" (1976: 145).

3. The church not only grew, but *it grew across cultural barriers.* The New Testament contains no example of a local church whose membership had been taken by the apostles from a single homogeneous unit, unless that expression is used to mean no more than a group of people with a common language. By contrast, it provides plenty of examples of how the barriers had been abolished in the new humanity.

4. The New Testament clearly shows that the apostles, while rejecting "assimilationist racism," never contemplated the possibility of forming homogeneous unit churches that would then express their unity in terms of interchurch relationships. Each church was meant to portray *the oneness of its members* regardless of their racial, cultural, or social differences, and in order to reach that aim the apostles suggested practical measures. If "authentic unity is *always* unity in diversity" (Wagner 1979: 96), the unity fostered by the apostles could never be one that eliminated plurality in the membership of local churches. Unity was not to be confused with uniformity

either among local congregations or among individual church members. In Ignatius's words, "Where Jesus Christ is, there is the whole church." Each local congregation was therefore to manifest both the unity and the diversity of the body of Christ.

5. There may have been times when the believers were accused of traitorously abandoning their own culture in order to join another culture, but there is no indication that the apostles approved of adjustments made in order to avoid that charge. They regarded Christian community across cultural barriers, not as an optional blessing to be enjoyed whenever circumstances were favorable to it or as an addendum that could be left out if deemed necessary to make the gospel more palatable, but as *essential to Christian commitment*. They would have readily included any attempt to compromise the unity of the church among those adjustments to which Christianity objects as "adjustments which violate essential Christian teachings" (McGavran 1974: 20).

If these conclusions are correct, it is quite evident that the use of the homogeneous unit principle for church growth has no biblical foundation. Its advocates have taken as their starting point a sociological observation and developed a missionary strategy; only then, a posteriori, have they made the attempt to find biblical support. As a result, the Bible has not been allowed to speak. A friendly critic of the "Church Growth" movement has observed that "lack of integration with revelation is the greatest danger in Church Growth anthropology" (McQuilkin 1973: 43). The analysis above leads us to conclude that the "Church Growth" emphasis on homogeneous unit churches is in fact directly opposed to the apostolic teaching and practice in relation to the expansion of the church. No missionary methodology can be built without a solid biblical theology of mission as a basis. What can be expected of a missiology that exhibits dozens of books and dissertations dealing with the "Church Growth" approach, but not one major work on the theology of mission?

We must admit that, at times, "The witness of separate congregations in the same geographical area on the basis of language and culture may have to be accepted as a necessary, but provisional, measure for the sake of the fulfillment of Christ's mission" (Newbigin 1977: 124). But the strategy of forming homogeneous unit churches for the sake of (quantitative) church growth has nothing to say in the face of "the fear of diversity and the chauvinistic desire to ignore, barely tolerate, subordinate or eliminate pluralism," which, according to C. Peter Wagner, "has perhaps done more to harm church life in America than has heretofore been recognized" (Wagner 1979: 147). Because of its failure to take biblical theology seriously, it has become a missiology tailor-made for churches and institutions whose main function in society is to reinforce the status quo. What can this missiology say to a church in an American suburb, where the bourgeois is comfortable but remains enslaved to the materialism of a consumer society and blind to the needs of the poor? What can it say to a church where a racist "feels at home" because of the unholy alliance of Christianity with racial segregation? What can it say in situations of tribal, caste, or class conflict? Of course, it can say that "men like to become Christians without crossing racial, linguistic, and class barriers." But what does that have to do with the gospel concerning Jesus Christ who came to reconcile us "to God *in one body* through the cross"?

The missiology that the church needs today is not one that conceives the People of God as a quotation taken from the surrounding society, but one that conceives it as "an embodied question-mark" that challenges the values of the world. As John Poulton says, referring to the impact of the early church on society: "When masters could call slaves brothers, and when the enormities of depersonalizing them became conscious in enough people's minds, something had to go. It took time, but slavery went. And in the interim, the People of God were an embodied question-mark because here were some people who could live another set of relationships within the given social system" (Poulton 1973: 112). Only a missiology in line with the apostolic teaching and practice with regard to the extension of the gospel will have a lasting contribution to make toward the building of this kind of church—the first fruits of a new humanity made up of persons "from every tribe and tongue and people and nation" who will unitedly sing a new song to the Lamb of God (Rev. 5:9).

Part IV

EVANGELISM
AND
CONTEXTUALIZATION

7

Five Theses on the Significance of
Modern African Christianity: A Manifesto

Kwame Bediako

Kwame Bediako (d. 2008) (a minister of the Presbyterian Church of Ghana) served as general secretary for the African Theological Fellowship. A visiting lecturer in African theology at the University of Edinburgh, Scotland, he was also honorary professor at the School of Theology, University of Natal, Pietermaritzburg, South Africa. He wrote extensively in the fields of gospel, culture, and Christian identity, and in the development of new contextual theologies in Africa. His publications include *Theology and Identity: The Impact of Culture upon Christian Thought in the Second Century and Modern Africa* (Oxford: Regnum, 1992); *Christianity in Africa: The Renewal of a Non-Western Religion* (Maryknoll, NY: Orbis Books, 1995), and *Jesus and the Gospel in Africa: History and Experience* (Maryknoll, NY: Orbis Books, 2004).

This paper is a further refinement of "A Manifesto,"[1] recently published in the maiden issue of *Studies in World Christianity: The Edinburgh Review of Theology and Religion* 1, no. 1 (1995): 51-67. In the present form it was delivered as the keynote address at the recent African Christianity Project conference held in March 1995 in Edinburgh and also at the Oxford Centre for Mission Studies Summer School on Institutional Development, in June-July 1995.

First published in *Transformation* 13, no. 1 (March 1996): 20-29. Reprinted here with permission.

1. This Manifesto started as a series of brief reflections, related on the one hand to my Alexander Duff Lectures given in New College, Edinburgh, between 1988 and 1992, and on the other hand, to the larger agenda of the "African Christianity Project" of the Centre for the Study of Christianity in the Non-Western World. This project is intended to explore the various dimensions of the significance of Christianity in Africa in the closing decades of the twentieth century, and as we look to the coming one. Though developed in the course of two research seminars in the Edinburgh Centre, the Manifesto is now being published for the first time. The Duff Lectures were published in July 1996 by Orbis Books as *Christianity in Africa: The Renewal of a Non-Western Religion*.

INTRODUCTION

In our time, there has been much allusion to the marginalization of Africa, following the end of the Cold War era, and in the expectation that Africa will hold a less strategic place in a world no longer dominated by the ideological rivalries between East and West, between capitalism and communism. However, in *Christianity in Africa* (Maryknoll, NY: Orbis Books, 1996), I have argued that in one particular respect, it may not be possible to marginalize Africa. That one area is the field of Christian theology, studies in Christian history and religious scholarship generally.

I do not wish to make exaggerated claims for Africa, but the essential point of my argument was made nearly twenty years ago by Harold Turner (1974) in an article in a volume of essays in honor of the late Harry Sawyerr of Fourah Bay College, Sierra Leone, and published as *New Testament Christianity for Africa and the World*. The article was entitled "The Contribution of Studies on Religion in Africa to Western Religious Studies." In that article, Turner sought to show that in all the regular religious disciplines—biblical studies, Christian history, missiology and ecumenics, systematic theology, and Christian ethics, as well as in the general phenomenology and history of religion—the African field threw new light on old issues, because it yielded data that were both vital and contemporary. Turner stated quite clearly the basis on which he was commending the serious study of African Christianity, and I would like to quote him fully here:

> Theology as a science depends upon access to its appropriate *data* in their most authentic and vital forms. If we regard the *data* of theology as being the revelations and acts of the Divine, the post-biblical and contemporary manifestations of these *data* will occur less vividly in a dispirited Western Church with declining numbers and morale. On the other hand, the *data* will be more evident and accessible in unsophisticated churches where the living God is taken seriously as present in the healing and conquering power of the Spirit, with a gospel-generated growth and a spiritual creativity and confidence. Here at the growing edges of Christianity in its most dynamic forms, the theologian is encouraged to do scientific theology again, because he has a whole living range of contemporary *data* on which to work. It is not that these dynamic areas of the Christian world are free from imperfection; but being full of old and new heresies, they need theology and offer it an important task. (Turner 1974: 177-78)

I have quoted Turner at some length to show that he was neither uncritical nor naive regarding the African field he was commending, and I hope the same can be said about my own perspective on the subject.

Nearly twenty years ago, Andrew Walls wrote: "Theology that matters will be theology where the Christians are" (1976: 183). And, he went on, as "it looks as if the bulk of Christians are going to be in Africa, and Latin America and in certain parts of Asia"—with Africa having a particular significance in this *southward* shift of "the centre of gravity of Christianity"—he felt able to state:

> It follows from this that what happens within the African churches in the next generation will determine the whole shape of Church history for centuries to come. Whether, and in what way, world evangelization is carried on may well be determined by what goes on in Africa; what sort of theology is most characteristic of the Christianity of the twenty-first century may well depend on what has happened in the minds of African Christians in the interim. (Walls 1976: 183)

Perhaps, it is worth indicating what the title of Andrew Walls's article was "Towards Understanding Africa's Place in Christian History." Like the volume from which I cited Harold Turner's article, this one too was in honor of a modern African Christian leader: in this case, Christian Baëta of Ghana.

In the two recensions of the Manifesto, which has been somewhat cast in the role of *agent provocateur* in this consultative conference, what I have done is to offer the five theses as a framework for understanding modern African Christianity, and for assessing the value of such an enhanced appreciation of it for religious and theological scholarship, and for the understanding of Christianity itself generally in the wider world. As I understand it, herein lies the particular significance of the African Christianity Project, which is coordinated by the Centre for the Study of Christianity in the Non-Western World, New College, University of Edinburgh, in association with a number of African academic institutions as represented at this conference.

The five theses are proposed only as a starter for further reflection, and also as a provocation to more intensive study of Christian presence in African life, in the light of the largely accepted view that Christianity, in the course of the twentieth century, has in fact acquired a high degree of significance in modern Africa, and that this has happened in ways that require fresh systematic study in order to achieve new interpretative depth.

What follows is an exposition of the Manifesto which offers some further comments, and perhaps in the process, provides something like a third recension!

Thesis 1: African Christianity Must Be Distinguished from the Literature of African Christianity

As I indicate, this may seem so self-evident that it might appear not to need to be stated, and yet, in point of fact, it has not always been universally recognized, so that the pivotal argument here may bear rehearsing. When John Mbiti wrote in 1986 that "the Christian way of life is in Africa to stay, certainly within the foreseeable future" (229), he was not only stating what seemed to him an obvious fact; he was also modifying one of his own earlier judgments. For in the 1960s, amid the many calls for the "indigenization of Christianity" in Africa, and for an African theology that would bear the marks of an authentic African meditation and reflection—largely, in my view, because there was a constant flogging from a critical Western public impatient with Africa and largely without understanding the continent— John Mbiti was among those African writers who lamented the absence of such a theology in African Christianity (1969: 232), and he even wrote of the lack of a "theological consciousness and concern" in African churches.[2]

Nearly twenty years later, however, Mbiti would make a distinction between, on the one hand, an African theology that was there, existing in the living experiences of Christians "in the open, from the pulpit, in the marketplace, in the home, as people pray or read and . . . discuss the Scriptures . . ." and, on the other hand, academic theology, which could only come afterwards, in order to "understand and interpret retrospectively, as it were," the features of that "prior theology."

Thus, Mbiti could write, "African Christianity cannot wait for [academic] written theology to keep pace with it" (1986: 229). Stated in these terms, the thesis obviously has relevance beyond the African field. For indeed, the very "birth of theology" in the New Testament, as has been argued by Daniel von Allmen (1975: 37-52), was consequent on a prior experience of faith in the early Christian communities. According to von Allmen, a process of theological contextualization could emerge only because there did exist a *substratum* of vital Christian experience and consciousness, itself of a theological nature. These two elements are neither to be confused, nor is the latter to be treated as of scant significance.

In a published article in which I argue for the need to take seriously this existing African "oral theology" (Bediako 1993: 7-25), I have sought to show that this element of a spontaneous or implicit theology constitutes an abiding ingredient in every tradition of the Christian presence, and is not to be regarded as a sort of "primitive" stage preceding "real" Christian thought, which then emerges in academic form and comes to subsume it. Rather, the existence of such a tradition of vital Christian apprehension and consciousness, even without a substantial literary form, is the sign of a Christianity that has come of age. An authentic tradition of literary Christian scholarship can exist only where a living reality of Christian experience is, and is felt to be, relevant to daily life. It is in this regard that African Christianity, in its significance in African life, must be distinguished from the scholarly literature on it.

---

2. See his "Some African Concepts of Christology," in Georg F. Vicedom, ed., *Christ and the Younger Churches* (London: SPCK, 1972), 51-62. For an even more critical African view, see Bolaji Idowu, *Towards an Indigenous Church* (London: Oxford University Press, 1965); for a measured Western response, see Philip Turner, "The Wisdom of the Fathers and the Gospel of Christ: Some Notes on Christian Adaptation in Africa," *Journal of Religion in Africa* 4, no. 1 (1971): 45-68.

And yet, it seems that it is possible to make the point even more forcefully. I wish to suggest that *we recognize, and speak generally of Christianity as Africa's "new" religion and understand the continent's primal religions as its "old" religions.* Obviously, I do not mean this to be taken as an undifferentiated, sweeping generalization that could be easily falsified. Nonetheless, I am stating it as generally valid for Tropical Africa. In other words, a sub-Saharan African, unless otherwise qualified, is to be assumed to be a Christian. Of course, I use the term "Christian" in a broad sense, but I consider it legitimate—as a description of persons who identify with a view of Jesus as ultimately significant, and of the Bible as the authoritative deposit of divine revelation, with a special use of water, bread, and wine, and recognize themselves as a community distinguished by their relation to Jesus, which relates them to others who claim a similar relation to Jesus. The recognition of Africa as a largely "Christian" continent has been suggested by others on demographic grounds. I suggest that there are other grounds also for this recognition.

The clue to what I am suggesting must lie not so much in the African genius in religion nor in the evident African capacity for adapting and developing indigenous forms of Christianity; it must lie, surely, in the nature of the Christian faith itself, as it has been demonstrated in its more recent history of transposition through the modern missionary movement. Unlike, say in Islam, where the word of Allah is fully heard only through the medium of Arabic, in Christianity the perception of the word of God is achieved in our mother-tongues (Acts 2:11). And here, it is to the credit of the modern missionary movement from the West that in contrast to the missionary thrust into northern and western Europe in earlier times, the history of modern mission could be written as the history of Scripture translation.[3]

I am arguing therefore that there has occurred in modern Africa the most notable demonstration for a long time of Christianity's essential character as "infinitely culturally translatable" (Walls 1981). In the case of Africa, the significance of this has been far-reaching. For, as Lamin Sanneh has graphically put it, the import of Scripture translation and its priority in missionary work is an indication that "God was not disdainful of Africans as to be incommunicable in their languages" (1983a: 166). This, Sanneh goes on, not only "imbued African cultures with eternal significance and endowed African languages with a transcendent range"; it also "presumed that the God of the Bible had preceded the missionary into the receptor-culture." As, through the very process of Scripture translation, "the central categories of Christian theology—God, Jesus Christ, creation, history—are transposed into their local equivalents, suggesting that Christianity had been adequately anticipated," they create in indigenous languages resonances far

---

3. See Philip Stine, ed., *Bible Translation and the Spread of the Church: The Last Two Hundred Years* (Leiden: Brill, 1990).

beyond what the missionary transmission conceived.[4] For the centrality
of Scripture translation points to the significance of African pre-Christian
religious cultures, not only as a "valid carriage for the divine revelation,"
but also as providing the idiom for Christian apprehension, as anyone who
knows the origins of African Christian names for God will understand. In
contrast, for example, to what had happened in the earlier evangelization
of Europe, in Africa, the God whose name had been hallowed in indigenous
languages in the pre-Christian tradition was found to be the God of the Bible,
in a way that neither Zeus, nor Jupiter, nor Odin could be. Onyankopon,
Olorun, Ngai, Nkulunkulu are the names of the God and Father of Jesus
Christ; Zeus, Jupiter, and Odin are not.

The wider implications of all this are enormous for our subject, in that
the relatively early possession of mother-tongue Scriptures meant that
many Africans gained access to the original sources of Christian revelation
as mediated through African traditional religious terminology and ideas.
Through these, Jesus Christ the Lord had shouldered his way into the African
religious world, and was to be discovered there by faith, not invented by
theology. It is because John Mbiti came to appreciate this fact that his later
comments regarding the presence of theology in African Christianity were
significant, and are a pointer to the need to make the distinction between
African Christianity itself and the scholarly literature on it, if we are to take
seriously the apprehension of Christianity at the specific level of religious
experience, where the faith has to live.

In this regard, in a recent article on "The Impact of the Bible in Africa,"
I have suggested that in view of the fact that the vast majority of African
Christians perceive and articulate their Christian experience through the
medium of African mother-tongues, the extent to which the practitioners of
African academic theology take seriously these languages in the present and
the future may not be an irrelevant question (Bediako 1994: 243-54).

Thesis 2: The Scholarly Penetration of African Christianity, Working from the Most Helpful Perspectives, Will Constitute One of the Most Important Tasks of the Future

This thesis was intended to balance the first one, which, valid as it is,
cannot stand alone. Historically, the Christian faith has developed as a
religion savante, continually stimulating an intellectual tradition through
a process of inward and outward self-definition which it produces in its
converts. Becoming a Christian, that is, through faith in Jesus Christ,
becoming the seed of Abraham and heir together with Israel—as taught in

---

4. On this subject, see Kwame Bediako, "The Missionary Inheritance," in Robin Keeley,
ed., *Christianity: A World Faith* (Tring: Lion Publishing, 1985), 303-11; also Lamin Sanneh,
Translating the Message: The Missionary Impact on Culture (Maryknoll, NY: Orbis Books,
1989).

Pauline theology—means, for the vast majority of the human race, coming into the inheritance of an "adoptive past" (Walls 1978: 13). All this raises important questions that require the necessary intellectual penetration for the establishment of a unified vision of identity and selfhood, which is inherent in the Christian experience of salvation. For biblical salvation, *shalom,* is wholeness.

The predominant concern with culture in the early literature of African academic theology has sometimes been regarded by some Western interpreters as an unhealthy inward-looking preoccupation with an imagined African traditional past (Hastings 1989: 30-35). On the other hand, African non-Christian critics have also berated African theologians for "Christianizing" and so "distorting" African tradition (p'Bitek 1970; Mazrui 1980). In the long term, the more incisive observation, in my view, is that of the African non-Christian critics. Ali Mazrui poses the question, not without a certain frustration: "Why should African students of religion be so keen to demonstrate that the Christian God had already been understood and apprehended by Africans before the missionaries came?"[5]

It is a pointer to what African theological scholarship had in fact achieved. African theologians, in setting about to demonstrate, from their Christian standpoint, that "the African religious experience and heritage were not illusory," but rather contained a valid preparation for the gospel, have made their own vital contribution not only toward the rehabilitation of that heritage itself but also to the reestablishment of African self-respect (Tutu 1978: 366). It might be held against African theology that it has for far too long failed to address the profound injustices and social ills of African societies. However, with equal validity, it may be asked how a theological tradition can ever address the ills of its context when it has not yet established its own sense of identity? From a settled sense of coherence in relation to the divine purpose in history, then even harder questions may be faced. Ali Mazrui has argued that African peoples, though, perhaps not the most brutalized in human history, are probably the most humiliated. If Mazrui is right then a pertinent question could be: why has there been so little reflection in African Christian thought so far on the African collective experience of suffering? Certainly, compared with, say, the frequent Western reflection and agonizing over the subject of the Holocaust, there seems as yet nothing to show in mainstream African theological reflection on the four centuries of trade in African humanity as merchandise, mainly promoted by the predominantly Christian nations of the world. And yet, is such a reflection possible without an African theodicy? And can an African theodicy come into place until it is demonstrated that the Christian God was at work in Africa before Christian missionaries proclaimed him? May the nineteenth-century "black spokesman," Edward Wilmot Blyden, yet be proved right that the African capacity to suffer has made "Africa's lot not unlike that of the ancient people of God, the Hebrews" and, perhaps even

---

5. See Ali Mazrui's "Epilogue" in p'Bitek 1970, 125.

more telling still, resemble "also him who made Himself of no reputation, but took upon Himself the form of a servant and having been made perfect through suffering, became the 'captain of our salvation'" (1967: 120-21).

Such questions mean, then, that the scholarly penetration of African Christianity which is meant here seeks not only new information, but more important still, greater depth, more insight. What is needed is not only access to sources of the Christian stories of various African peoples, but also the ability to embrace such stories as part of the total historical experiences of the peoples themselves.

To this end, one of the more helpful academic disciplines which, in my view, will prove useful to African Christian scholarship will be *African history*. Perhaps the major aim in the quest for the depth that I have in mind is a modern African *City of God*, in which, from a Christian standpoint in scholarship, an attempt is made to understand the divine guidance, as well as the human responses to the divine impulses in the total African experience. By this approach, it would also be important to understand the failures no less than the successes in the African past in order to appreciate the significance that Africans attach to their adherence to the Christian faith.

But, not to lose sight of the religious, and the particularly Christian, dimension of our subject, it seems to me that one can be more precise on this point too. I have always regarded John Mbiti's *African Religions and Philosophy* (1969) as a sort of religious history of African peoples perceived as a cultural unit within humanity, incorporating its *substratum* of the continent's primal religions and its fulfillment in the apprehension of Jesus Christ in African experience. Since most subsequent treatments of African primal religions have tended to avoid general studies and to favor, instead, more individual or area studies, it may be equally interesting, and perhaps even important, to apply Mbiti's insight to particular studies of limited range. In this regard, it is interesting that a historian of African religion such as Terence Ranger, in his study of Christianity in Zimbabwe, should conclude so firmly that the Christian faith has been an intrinsic part of the definition of "African identity." According to Ranger, it is precisely "*because* the Christian movement has been one of the great realities of twentieth century Africa [that] it has also been, by definition, an aspect of African identity" (1987: 29-57).

In my view, however, the making of this "Christian" Africa in the twentieth century should be regarded as a "surprise story" in the modern expansion of the Christian movement, and that on two counts. At the Edinburgh 1910 World Missionary Conference, the official report stated: "If things continue as they are now tending, Africa may become a Mohammedan continent" (World Missionary Conference, 1910a: 5-6). No one at that time could have foreseen the emergence of a vibrant Christian presence in Africa. But perhaps more importantly, in view of the fact that Africa's primal religions were then presumed not to contain "any preparation for Christianity" (World Missionary Conference, 1910b: 24), the present evidence of an African experience of the Christian faith bearing the marks of the continuing impact of the worldview of primal religions must carry its own significance. In that sense Africa has played a major role in bringing about the realization that we may now take for granted, that the primal religions of the world have provided the religious background of the faith of the majority of Christians everywhere in Christian history to the present. Far from not containing "any preparation for Christianity," they have been "the most fertile soil for the gospel," as Andrew Walls has pointed out (1978: 11; Turner 1977: 27-37).

This leads me to the essential point I wish to make: The persistent concentration by Africa's Christian theologians on the continent's primal religions in the formative period of African theology may have brought us to a new creative stage in Christianity's encounter with the primal religions of the world. It seems to me, therefore, that in Africa the opportunity for a serious *theological* encounter and cross-fertilization between the Christian religion and the primal religions, which was lost in the earlier evangelization of Europe, can be regained. In African Christianity, the peculiar historical connection between Christianity and primal religions can be studied on the basis of data that are both vital and contemporary, and on a scale that is probably unequalled in all Christian history.

In this regard, the scholarly penetration of African Christianity that I am urging brings us fully into important investigations in the history and phenomenology of Christianity within the broad field of the history and phenomenology of religion, and of the social and cultural interactions of religion in history. Speaking as a theologian myself, it seems to me that theology has not been in greater need than now of the skills and insights of historians and the benefits of historiography.

Thesis 3: The Aim of Seeking Interpretative Depth of African Christianity Will Require That Due Stress Be Placed on the Observation and Study of the Actual Life of African Christian Communities

It is not intended to set the study of the actual life of African Christian communities off against the study of documents. Obviously both are important. However, it is because the phenomenon studied cannot be fully circumscribed within the literature on it that one needs to pay particular attention to the more "informal" expressions of Christian presence in the African scene. For example, what use is made of the Scriptures in resolving problems in daily life? Does the use of the Scriptures relate to the well-known general African inclination toward seeking guidance for living and making decisions? What is the place and role of the Christian pastor or minister, or other "religious specialists," in African communities? Are the roles they are expected to play related to what is known from the practice of Africa's primal religions? How far does Christian theological training prepare Christian ministers for these roles? If there are relations between the two, might it be justified to speak of, or expect to discover, African patterns, or even "traditions" of Christian ministry?[6] In what does the appeal of Christianity to Africans consist? Why does religion still continue to play a dominant role in African life even when all the signs of a so-called Western secular life are also found to be invading African social and economic existence? In other words, what factors explain the continuing resilience of religion, and of Christianity in particular, in the conditions of modern life in Africa, including political life?

Answers to such questions as these are not always found in official documents. The decisions that go to make up their significance are often taken in small groups and in "informal" ways, in which religious choices are made in situations that may not appear to be religious.

But, a further, perhaps more important, implication may lie here for African religious scholarship. If it retains and maintains a vital link with the Christian presence in Africa, and with the spontaneous and often *oral* articulation of Christian faith and experience that goes on, it will be in a position to contribute significantly to understanding, as well as shaping, Christian thought generally for the coming century. An indication that the early concentration by African theology on the African primal heritage was appropriate is the fact that a later generation of African theologians, while exploring other themes, have been able to do so by taking off from genuinely African categories. This is most markedly so in relation to christological discussion, which was rather conspicuously minimal or absent in earlier writings. But the current christological explorations revolve around such categories as Christ as Healer, as Master of Initiation and as Ancestor—all of which are derived directly from the worldview and from the apprehension of realty and the Transcendent within African primal religions (Bediako 1984: 81-121; Nyamiti 1984; Pobee 1979; Sanon and Luneau 1982; Schreiter, ed. 1991; Bujo 1992). It is interesting and perhaps instructive that those who have made the more helpful contributions in this connection have been writers who, on the whole, have maintained a close contact with and involvement in African church life. It seems to me reasonable to suggest that the further sharpening of these insights is more likely to occur where such vital participation in African Christian communities continues. Insofar as these now African christological titles are not abstract concepts but African categories of experience, their future significance will be determined not in the minds of academic theologians alone, but also, and perhaps more importantly, in the lives and experiences of African Christians. It is the theology that touches the greatest number of Christians, and resonates with their perceptions, that will have a future.

It seems to me that this predominantly theological discussion may also require an important interaction with history, and with historical

---

6. For a study that demonstrates that the "role" of the African Christian minister may not necessarily be determined by Western expectations, missionary or secular, see John Middleton, "150 Years of Christianity in a Ghanaian Town," *Africa* (1983): 1-8.

investigation. For, the process of attaining the interpretative depth of the actual and present life of African Christian communities as I am urging involves necessarily understanding also how such communities came into being, and how they came to be what they are. In other words, the interpretative depth that I have in view will require also the appropriate historical framework for understanding African Christian communities. Perhaps what I am suggesting is that we may be on the threshold of a completely new conception of African church history. In some "polemic thoughts on African church history," the archivist of the Basel Mission, Paul Jenkins, wrote a few years ago: "An African Church history that begins with missionary institutions—and especially one that begins with missionary initiatives—is almost bound to stress the foreign nature of the faith and its practices" (1986: 67).

That this was the dominant frame of reference for understanding Christianity in Africa in the 1960s and 1970s is seen in the early direction that the then-emergent movement of African theology took, a direction which, to me, indicates the skewing effect of that frame of reference on the development of African theological thought and agenda.

In the circumstances of the time, all who were concerned with the fortunes of Christianity in Africa naturally felt the urgency to demonstrate the African credentials of the faith. But understandably, it was African Christian scholars and churchmen themselves upon whom that burden fell most heavily. A comparison of the intellectual careers of two African Christian academics who were destined to become influential in the growth of African theology in the subsequent decades will make clearer my point. These were Bolaji Idowu (of Nigeria) and John Mbiti (of Kenya). Both scholars were present at the important Seventh International African Seminar that was held in Accra, Ghana, in April 1965, and delivered papers. Idowu's paper, under the title, "The Predicament of the Church in Africa," presented a disturbing picture of the church in Africa as "still dependent . . . looking to missionaries from outside for manpower and material resources, dependent in its theology, its liturgy and its church discipline, in fact in its whole expression of the Christian life" (Baëta 1968: 353). For Idowu, "the Church in Africa came into being with prefabricated theology, liturgies and traditions" (Idowu in Baëta 1968: 426). Mbiti's paper was on "ways and means of communicating the gospel" to ensure effectiveness and relevance (in Baëta 1968: 329-50).

This is, perhaps, not the place for a detailed exposition of those papers. But these men were testifying to what they, together with others, perceived to be the "predicament of the church," to use Idowu's language, and were also showing an awareness of the intense pressure that this perceived predicament was exerting on African churchmen, compelling them to find (one might even say, almost invent) a theological identity, a theological idiom, and a Christian *modus vivendi* which would be more appropriate to the African context and reality. They seemed united in the concern that the "massive and unavoidable fact and factor" of the Christian presence still needed deeper rooting in the African scene, at least to the extent that it should cease to be and be seen as a foreign plant, and to become instead, a home-grown and indigenous reality.

Not surprisingly, therefore, in the subsequent few years, the major concern became "indigenization"—of Christianity, church, and theology. Idowu quickly earned a status as a doyen among African theologians, certainly in the West African region, and took up the challenge of indigenization in a spirited publication, *Towards an Indigenous Church* (1965), though some of the material had been developed for three radio talks as far back as 1961 on the "problem of indigenization of the church in Nigeria." This was probably the first and clearest statement by a leading African theologian, setting forth specific proposals which an African church might consider in order to transform itself into an authentic African Christian community, if it found itself "heavily tinged with Western culture." For Idowu, Christianity was in Africa, but not of Africa . . . not yet. In other words, for Idowu, the "foreignness" of Christianity in Africa was a fundamental *datum* and the starting point of the discussion; indigenization was as much about discarding "foreignness" as it was about rooting the faith in local realities. Accordingly, Idowu specified five areas which, in his view, needed attention: (1) the Bible in Nigerian languages; (2) the language of evangelization; (3) theology; (4) liturgy; (5) dress and vestments. It may seem odd that for all his insistence on the church in Nigeria bearing "the stamp of originality," Idowu decided that ministers' vestments was one area in which "the Church in Nigeria must preserve something as token of her being part and presence of the Universal Church." On the other hand, it could also be argued that Idowu was seeking a far more fundamental indigenization than merely external features. We are unable to pursue our discussion into the details of Idowu's thinking, but whatever the merits of Idowu's arguments, the reason for replacing, in his words, "the European complexion of the Church" with an indigenous complexion was that "Christian Nigerians cease to see Jesus Christ as an imported divinity from a European pantheon" and that they come to see him as "God's Messiah to Nigerians, their own personal Savior and Lord."

The really important question to ask for our present purposes is why this spirited apologia for indigenization has not been followed through in the theological and intellectual career of Idowu. We have to explain why, eight years later, in his *African Traditional Religion: A Definition*, Idowu could conclude that, "African traditional religion is *the* religion practiced by the majority of Africans, nakedly [i.e., overtly] in most cases, but also in some cases under the veneers supplied by Westernism and Arabism" (1973: 208).

We must explain why, when Idowu quoted the biblical text of 1 John 3:2: "It does not yet appear that we shall be," he applied it not to the church in Nigeria, but to the prospect of African traditional religion. The task of vindicating and establishing "a satisfying African self-consciousness and dignity," which in *Towards an Indigenous Church* was laid upon the

Christian church, now came to be confidently entrusted to the old traditional religion, now revitalized with its "God-given heritage and indigenous spiritual treasures" (Idowu 1973: 205).

Idowu, through the years, it seems, remained haunted by the "foreignness" of Christianity, and having started from that foreignness, was never able to arrive at indigeneity.

Like Idowu, Mbiti also early on deplored the lack of sufficient and positive engagement by Western missions with African cultural and religious value. He saw the result of this in an African church which had "come of age *evangelistically,* but not *theologically*"; "a church without theology, without theologians and without theological concern" as he was writing in 1967 and also in 1969 (1969: 232-33; 1972: 51-62).

However, Mbiti soon came to make a distinction between "Christianity" which "results" from the encounter of the gospel with any given local society and so is always indigenous and culture-bound, on the one hand, and the gospel, which is "God-given, eternal and does not change," on the other. In 1970 he wrote:

> We can add nothing to the Gospel, for this is an eternal gift of God: but Christianity is always a beggar seeking food and drink, cover and shelter from the cultures it encounters in its never-ending journeys and wanderings. (1970b: 438)

Mbiti had already given an indication of this trend of thought in his paper at the Accra Seminar of 1965, when he stated:

> We cannot artificially create an "African theology" or even plan it; it must evolve spontaneously as the Church teaches and lives *her* Faith and in response to the extremely complex situation in Africa. (In Baëta 1968: 332)

But the definitive break came later, when Mbiti rejected the very idea of the quest for indigenization of Christianity or of theology in Africa. In a response to a study of his theology by John Kinney (1979: 65-67), Mbiti wrote:

> To speak of "indigenizing Christianity" is to give the impression that Christianity is a ready-made commodity which has to be transplanted to a local area. Of course, this has been the assumption followed by many missionaries and local theologians. I do not accept it any more. (1979: 68)

It may be of interest also to compare the attitudes of our two representative thinkers to the African Independent Churches. Idowu found no place for them in his drive for indigenization. He saw them instead as "syncretistic sects which have spread all over the country like the seed of contagion . . . , the product of syncretizing Christianity with some dominant practices of the national cults." He saw no positive contribution coming through the ministries of these churches.

Mbiti, on the other hand, though not an uncritical admirer of the Independents, nevertheless saw in them an African Christian consciousness and experience having its own integrity. They represented not only a massive rejection of imported forms of the Christian life; they also bore witness to the fact that "African peoples have taken seriously to Christianity." Through them and their distinctive styles of ministry and community, God was speaking to the world church and to the world. Mbiti looked forward to a time when they would not be "as far apart from the historical churches as they are at present" (1970a: 34f.).

Therefore, for Mbiti, the gospel is genuinely at home in Africa, is capable of being apprehended by Africans at the specific level of their religious experience, and in fact has been so received through the missionary transmission of it. The Western missionary enterprise, from this perspective, has a place within a religious history which properly belongs to African tradition. Since God is One, Mbiti maintains, "God the Father of our Lord Jesus Christ is the same God who has been known and worshipped in various ways within the religious life of African peoples" and who, therefore, was "not a stranger in Africa prior to the coming of missionaries." They did not bring God; rather God brought them, so that by the proclamation of the gospel through missionary activity, Jesus Christ might be known, for "without Him [Jesus Christ] the meaning of our religiosity is incomplete."

> The Gospel enabled people to utter the name of Jesus Christ . . . that final and completing element that crowns their traditional religiosity and brings its flickering light to full brilliance. (1979: 68)

By this approach, Mbiti in effect "exorcises" the "Westernism" and "foreignness" in the Western transmission of the gospel, and internalizes whatever was of the gospel. By the same process, he affirmed the missionary endeavor, but without making the missionary central; for the whole operation began with God and was carried through by God. The encounter was, at its deepest levels, not the meeting of Western ideas and African traditions, rather it was the meeting of the African in his and her religiosity with Jesus Christ, whose "presence in the world is not a historical [i.e., chronological] but a geographical presence in the world made by Him and through Him" (1979: 68).

I suggest that the theological principle we see operating in Mbiti's thought is that of translatability—the capacity of the essential impulses of the Christian religion to be transmitted and assimilated in a different culture so that these impulses create a dynamically equivalent response in the course of such transmission. In terms of this principle, it is possible to say that the earlier concern to seek an "indigenization" of Christianity in Africa, as though one were dealing with an essentially "Western" and "foreign" religion, was, in effect, misguided because the task was conceived as the correlation of two entities thought to be independent. Therefore the effort was bound to lead to a dead end, as we have noted in Idowu's case, precisely because it fastened too intently on the "foreignness" of the modes of the transmission of the faith, and correspondingly paid too little attention to actual achievement "on the ground." But the achievement meant here is not measured in terms of the Western missionary transmission, but rather in terms of the African assimilation of the faith. As Ajayi and Ayandele point out, in a critique of the 1965 seminar in their article "Writing African Church History," evangelization is not simply the "communication of foreign ideas to passive recipients who have to swallow every bit whether or not they approve" (1969: 91). It was misguided therefore to assume that African converts to Christianity assimilated the missionary message in Western terms rather than in terms of their own African religious understandings and background.

To recall another of Paul Jenkins's "polemical thoughts" on African church history:

> African Church history must be concerned with the free dialogue that is already taking place between questions and problems as formulated in the different traditional cultures and the answers and solutions latent in the Christian message. (1986: 68)

It is by doing this that we come to recognize the extent of indigenization, which is already present in the very process of indigenous assimilation. In this regard, it seems to me that the scholarly investigation of the actual life of African Christian communities is of interest not only to those whose primary concern is to promote the fortunes of the Christian faith, but also to those who are keen to understand how, in the course of the present century, the faith has moved from being the religion of white people to being more associated with the religious lives of black people.

Thesis 4: An Understanding of the African Accession to Christianity Helps toward an Understanding of the Recession from Christian Faith in the Modern West

The study of Christianity in Africa should not be isolated from the study of the Christian presence elsewhere in history. In other words, one must guard against making the African field (or any non-Western field of reference) so unique in the features it presents that it ceases to have any relation to what happens to Christianity elsewhere. Rather, the African phenomenon must be seen within the wider setting of the general history of the transformations of Christianity. In other words, it is important to avoid an "us" and "them" syndrome. The significance of the modern shift in the center of gravity of Christianity is not that its former centers of dominance cease to matter, but rather that the faith now acquires new centers of its universality. Accordingly, the study of one manifestation of it must help toward understanding its character in general.

In the present circumstances, it is important, therefore, to take together the modern significant *accession* to the Christian faith in Africa and some other parts of the non-Western world, and the equally marked *recession* from the faith in the modern West.[7] It will then become possible to explore how far the accession to Christianity in the predominantly religious world of Africa has also coincided with the erosion of a religious outlook in the West, particularly in Europe. The modern shift may thus have secured the faith and ensured for it a future which, in a secularized environment, would be more precarious. Religious accession and religious recession thus both come to belong within Christian history and help to show all church history as *mission* history. Thus, following the Western missionary impact on the non-Western world, the Western world itself, according to Karl Rahner, "a milieu that has become unchristian" (1974: 32), now needs to be reevangelized, and Christian history seems to indicate that there is nothing unusual in this.

By relating Christian accession to Christian recession in the way indicated, it may then become possible to find a viable alternative to the current dominant anthropology-based missiology, which tends to reduce everything into such terms as "the West and the rest." Rather, by reading and interpreting all Christian history as *mission history,* it will become possible to discover that some of the clues for understanding the issues confronting Christian witness in the modern West lie in the history of similar encounters elsewhere in the meeting of the gospel with other cultures. Missiology will become, thus, not just learning techniques for communicating the gospel to other peoples and cultures different from one's own; it becomes also an exercise in self-understanding within Christian scholarship (Bediako 1989: 52-68). In this sense, the re-evangelization of the modern West may require Western Christian scholarship to discover the universal relevance of the church's missionary learning experience gained in the non-Western world.

There are obvious parallels here with the thought and action of the early Christian centuries. The promoters and vindicators of the Christian faith in that early period seemed convinced that the nature of the past operations of the God whose Good News they were claiming to announce had something to do with the people to whom they were addressing themselves. Since the God of Israel was the same God who was at work in the gospel of Jesus Christ, even if somewhat differently, the early heralds of the Christian faith appeared to take it for granted that the Old Testament, when interpreted from their new point of view, yielded meaning that would be evident to new Gentile converts. For early Christianity, the Old Testament, for all practical purposes, became a Christian book, capable of explaining Gentile,

---

7. For my use of the terms "accession" and "recession," see Andrew F. Walls, "Structural Problems in Mission Studies," *International Bulletin of Missionary Research* 15, no. 4 (October 1991): 146-55.

no less than it did Jewish, religious history. One early Gentile Christian, Justin, even dared to declare to a non-Christian Jew, to the latter's evident discomfiture, that the prophecies concerning Christ "are laid up in your Scriptures, or rather not in yours but in ours, for we obey them but you, when you read you do not understand their sense" (*Dialogue with Trypho* 29.2). Justin could hold such a view because he had come to the conclusion that a particular reading and interpretation of the religious history of Israel gave that history a significance for him, a significance which he ought to take seriously. No reader of Justin can miss the excitement that Justin must have felt at the prospect that it was predominantly Gentiles like himself who were increasingly finding their spiritual home in the inheritance of Israel. Indeed, we might even say that the future of the Christian movement lay not with Jewry nor in Jerusalem but with those ill-rated Gentiles, those "foolish" and fickle Galatians, those unreliable and quarrelsome Corinthians, and that new "Babylon," Rome. The explanation of this remarkable turn of history Justin found in the universal significance of Jesus Christ as the divine Word, the source and norm of all truth and knowledge wherever these may be found. By the same token, the Christian faith became disengaged from any cultural possessiveness of it.

The polarity of *engagement* and *disengagement* could accurately be a recurring motif in all subsequent Christian history. This is a perspective which might he profitably explored in relation to our suggested linking of *accession* and *recession* in our study of Christianity in history, and the modern African field may yield some fruitful results.

In relation to our present purposes, it is worth recalling that Europe shares with Africa an identical pre-Christian heritage in the primal religious traditions of the world. But it is in Africa (as in the rest of the non-Western world) that the significance of the primal religions in the history of Christianity has been seen for what it is. And this relocation of African primal religions "at the very center of the academic stage" (Hastings 1976: 50) may prove a benediction to Western Christian scholarship as it also seeks to be communicative, evangelistic, and missionary in its own context. For the African vindication of the positive theological significance of African primal religions, if it has validity, also goes to affirm that the European primal heritage was not illusory, to be consigned to oblivion as primitive darkness. The nature of the meeting of Christianity with European primal religions may hold more significance for understanding the modern West than may have been assumed. A serious Christian theological interest in the European primal traditions and early Christianity amid those traditions, could provide a fresh approach to understanding Christian identity in Europe too, as well as opening new possibilities for Christian theological endeavor today. And the primal worldview may turn out to be not so alien to Europe after all, even in a post-Enlightenment era.

For the signs of what appears to be a postmodernist rejection, in the West, of the Enlightenment, seen partly in the resurgence of the phenomenon of the occult as well as in some of the more disturbing features of the "New

Age," bearing the marks of a primal worldview, are sufficient indicators that a primal religious tradition, suppressed rather than purged and integrated, can rise to haunt the future. In this connection, the viability of a Christian consciousness that retains its link with the living forces of the primal tradition, as well as the theological cross-fertilization between the primal worldview and Christian faith that is evident in African theology—all these are an implicit challenge to the notion that humanity can be fully defined in exclusively post-Enlightenment terms. It seems, then, that the world's primal religions, in Europe as in Africa and elsewhere, the religious traditions that have been most closely associated with the continuing Christian presence historically in the world so far, may yet again point the way into the Christian future. If this expectation proves right, the African contribution will have been an important one.

Thesis 5: The Study of Christianity in Africa in Its Total Religious and Sociopolitical Context Will Help Point the Way for the Church to Exist in a Post-Christendom Era

There is a further sense in which the correlation of Christian *accession* and Christian *recession* can become illuminating for Christian scholarship. At the heart of the Christian faith is the affirmation of the incarnation, whereby God intervened in human history and life in a paradigmatic way which remains permanently significant. In sum, the incarnation is the strongest claim that human experience of transcendence is real and contemporary, not imaginary or outworn. Faith in the living God is thus the only true basis for human existence and the human response in prayer, worship, and obedient discipleship is entirely appropriate.

Consistent with such a claim is the affirmation that God has indeed made known his will, again in a paradigmatic manner which remains operative and permanently relevant. Hence, trust in the Bible as revelation—translatable and therefore available to all people everywhere on the same terms is quite defensible. It is possible, therefore, through the Word of God made relevant through the presence of the transcendent Spirit of the Incarnate God, to know divine guidance for human existence.

It becomes possible, therefore, to affirm that Jesus is Lord in the midst of other claims to lordship. The very affirmation is made within a frame of reference that includes the awareness of other spiritual presences (Bediako 1994-95: 50-61; Cragg 1977, 1986).

In these statements I have attempted to express some features of African Christian existence which, it seems to me, in view of the generalized acceptance of a post-Enlightenment secularity, as well as the impact of the long tradition of Christendom, are difficult to sustain in the modern West. In this sense, the "normal" African experience of pluralism, as well as the general capacity to expect to experience transcendence in the context of the modern conditions of life, may help to show how the church may live, worship, and witness in a post-Christendom, and a "World-Christianity" era.

The African (as indeed the rest of the non-Western) experience may indicate that secularity as an ideological posture may not be regarded as "normal" and need not be accepted as a necessary accompaniment of modernity. Africa (as the rest of the non-Western world), may thus become, at least for a period in the foreseeable future, a privileged Christian laboratory for the world, to the extent that the "normal" African (as other non-Western) experience of religious pluralism as the framework for Christian affirmation may indicate that "Christian uniqueness" or distinctiveness need not be lost in the midst of religious and cultural pluralism.

But the challenge is to African Christian scholarship too. If the theses being advanced here on the significance of African Christianity are valid, then African Christian scholarship is going to have to discover and assume some amount of responsibility for carrying forward these items of the Christian agenda of the future. However, to say so is not to suggest that it can be taken for granted that this will happen. African Christianity and African Christian scholarship will have to show their spiritual and intellectual credentials for what they are. In other words, it is hard to see how the scholarly penetration of African Christianity by African Christian scholarship in its multifarious dimensions in the coming decades can be pursued with integrity apart from taking some responsibility also for the major tasks of Christian witness in our time. Modern African Christianity is inheritor to twenty centuries of Christian tradition. Its task thereby is made not less, but more onerous.

CONCLUSION

The overall basis of these five theses on understanding modern African Christianity's significance is that, in the course of the twentieth century, the Christian presence has undergone literally a sea-change in Africa. It has gone from being, and from being perceived as, a Western factor in African life, to becoming, and being experienced as, an African reality. It seems that it is now time for scholarship to recognize generally, and work with, this transformation of African Christianity.

But, perhaps there is even more to what now confronts us than simply the transformation of African Christianity. In *Christianity in Africa,* I have suggested that part of the significance of the striking level of Christian accession in Africa in the course of this century may be that it provides the opportunity for the recovery and renewal of an essentially "non-Western religion," a notion that brings us round to the theme of Andrew Walls's seminal article that I mentioned near the beginning of this presentation, "Towards Understanding Africa's Place in Christian History." Understanding Africa's place may well be an indicator of where we are in Christian history as a whole. In seeking to understand African Christianity, we are investigating, in the words of John Foster, a former professor of ecclesiastical history in Glasgow, some of "the urges of essential Christianity." African Christianity has the marks of "representative" Christianity in our time (Andrew Walls).

Lamin Sanneh, at the end of his *West African Christianity: The Religious Impact,* one of the rare comprehensive treatments of the theme which helpfully points to the significant "indigenous" factor in the Christian story of Africa, felt able to state that no one can miss the vitality of the Christian religion in much of the continent, and that African Christianity may well have entered upon a universal vocation in the onward march of the people of God in history, a destiny comparable to that of Gentile Christianity in the early Christian centuries (1983b).

This cannot mean that the African field will resolve all questions. Rather, it may well mean a new creative stage in how we understand those questions, while it will also raise new questions not asked before, or else, old questions too lightly dismissed, such as the relationship of Christian faith to the spiritual universe of the primal religions of the world. As Andrew Walls has more recently pointed out, "The conditions of Africa . . . are taking Christian theology into new areas of life, where Western theology has no answers, because it has no questions" (1991: 147-48).

One of those areas, posing fresh questions, was what lay behind my use of the statement by the Ivorian philosopher Paulin Houtondji, discussing the "continuing encounter between Africa and itself," in order to draw my own conclusion about seeing the significance of Christianity in Africa as one *African* reality encountering other African realities.[8] In a post-Christendom world, which, we are told, is also "postmodern," with its resurgence of

---

8. Paulin J. Houtondji, *Sur la "philosophie africaine": critique de l'ethnophilosophie* (Yaoundé: Editions Clé, 1980). The passage of Houtondji in which he discusses the encounter between so-called "traditional" African culture and so-called "Western" thought is as follows:

We speak of African civilisation as "traditional" in contrast to Western civilisation, as if there could be African civilisation, Western civilisation, in the singular, and as if civilisation were not by nature, a permanent clash of contradictory cultural forms. . . . European civilisation is not a closed system of values but a set of irreducible cultural products which have appeared on the European continent; or, at a deeper level, it is the set of these products and of the creative tensions which underlie them . . . in the forms they have assumed in the past and in the as yet unpredictable forms they will assume tomorrow. . . . Nor is African civilisation a closed system in which we may imprison ourselves (or allow ourselves to be imprisoned). It is the unfinished history of a similar contradictory debate as it has proceeded, and will continue to proceed, in that fraction of the world we call Africa. . . .

What we must recognize today is that pluralism does not come to any society from outside but is inherent in every society. The alleged acculturation, the alleged "encounter" of African civilisation with European civilisation, is really just another mutation produced from within African civilisations. . . . The decisive encounter is not between Africa as a whole and Europe as a whole: it is the continuing encounter between Africa and itself. (226-27, 233)

new quests for transcendence, the African evidence may help toward a fresh understanding of the resilience and the dynamism of religion itself.

Finally, I recall yet another seminal thought of Andrew Walls, made in connection with the intellectual career of the British Christian scholar who has been among the most influential in establishing the academic respectability of African pre-Christian religions in religious studies in the United Kingdom, not to mention his achievements in Africa, Geoffrey Parrinder:

> The recognition that religions are not unitary mutually exclusive entities which replace each other in the process of religious change, but that a person's or a community's religious experience has to be taken in itself and within its own social setting, was perhaps more readily learned in Africa than elsewhere. (Walls 1980: 145)

If I may dare to make a comment on the statement, it is to say that what has occurred to Christianity in Africa in the twentieth century now provides the opportunity for that recognition, and many others besides, to be learned.

8

Recasting Theology of Mission
Impulses from the Non-Western World

Wilbert R. Shenk

Wilbert R. Shenk served with the Mennonite Central Committee in Indonesia (1955–59), and in administration (1963–65), and with the Mennonite Board of Missions (1965–90). He taught at Associated Mennonite Biblical Seminary, and later became professor of mission history and contemporary culture at Fuller Theological Seminary. From 1990 to 1993 he worked with The Gospel and Our Culture Project in Birmingham, England. He has written a wide array of essays and books, including *Write the Vision: The Church Renewed* (Eugene, OR: Wipf & Stock, 1995) and *Changing Frontiers of Mission* (Maryknoll, NY: Orbis Books, 1999).

David J. Bosch completed writing his magisterial *Transforming Mission: Paradigm Shifts in the Theology of Mission* in 1990. Although Bosch intimated in articles in 1983 and 1984 that new, non-Western patterns and paradigms were emerging (1983b: 485-510; 1984: 14-37), in *Transforming Mission* he worked out his analysis within the framework of the missionary movement from the Western Christian tradition. The last third of *Transforming Mission* is a study of the way the logic of "mission in the wake of the Enlightenment" has been played out as an essentially Western initiative.

The past decade has proved to be pivotal in geopolitical terms. Along with the end of the Cold War and the globalization of the world economy, a sea change in the locus of Christian initiative has taken place. Churches in Asia, Africa, and Latin America are now sending thousands of missionaries to other regions and countries, while the decline and disorientation of the churches in the West is a matter of mounting concern. Today the West presents a particularly demanding missiological challenge.

Recent surveys of mission theology reveal the continued domination of Western voices, with no discernible shift during the 1990s (Kirk 2000; Van

First published in *International Bulletin of Missionary Research* 25, no. 3 (July 2001): 98-107. Reprinted here with permission.

Engen 1996). Western theology of mission has continued on an essentially unchanged trajectory. Even recent initiatives to develop a theology that engages contemporary Western culture as a missionary frontier—an urgent priority—have been significantly stymied by the historical burden of the Western theological tradition.

Since the Christian majority is now to be found outside the West, and missionary initiatives from the churches of Asia, Africa, and Latin America are at the cutting edge of the Christian world mission, we must ask: What kind of theology of mission will best serve the global Christian mission in the future? What fresh theological resources can be brought to bear on this new phase of the Christian mission? It is time to listen to voices from the non-Western world that can help construct a theology capable of empowering the global church for participation in the *missio Dei*.

My thesis is that (1) a dynamic theology of mission develops where there is vigorous engagement of culture by the gospel, accompanied by critical reflection on that process; that (2) this process is decisive for shaping Christian identity; and that therefore (3) we must look to the evolving Christian movement in Asia, Africa, and Latin America to discern defining themes. Although various scholars have argued for the term "missionary theology" (on the grounds that all theology ought to be missionary in character, a position with which I sympathize), to minimize confusion I will retain the conventional terminology "theology of mission."

ROOTED IN CULTURAL ENGAGEMENT

Vital theology of mission flows from missionary engagement. As Bosch emphasized, the New Testament provides us with the example par excellence of theology animated by mission. In the New Testament, theological concerns are grounded in the *missio Dei*. The New Testament writings reflect the historical, social, religious, and political context in which the missionary encounter of the Christian gospel with Middle Eastern culture took place. These documents show how the disciples of Jesus Christ responded to the existential questions they faced as the movement spread through the Mediterranean world. Christian identity was forged as the evangelization process progressed.

The contrast with Western academic theology could not be sharper. From as early as the fourth century, Western theology has pursued an inward-focused, intellectual, and pastoral agenda rather than an outward-looking evangelistic and missional agenda. With the coming of the Enlightenment in the late seventeenth century, the West became convinced that its culture, through the process of modernization and growing scientific knowledge, was destined to be the universal culture. As Western theology moved into the university and was professionalized, it became increasingly detached from ecclesial reality and cultural context (Pauck 1959: 270-83).[1] In the twentieth century it was left to missionary statesmen and a few theologians sympathetic to mission to develop the theology of mission; the academy—in both its dominant seminary and university forms—largely ignored it.

The global domination of Western theology remains largely unaddressed. Theological education in the non-Western world is still captive to the Western tradition and curriculum. Describing Protestant theology in Japan, Masaya Odagaki calls the period before 1970 the classic age of contemporary theology. He notes that "theological giants such as Barth, Bultmann, and Tillich were playing active roles, and dialogue with these great theologians was the basic method of doing theology in this country. In fact, some have called this the period of the 'Germanic captivity'" (Odagaki 1997). In his review of developments since 1970, Odagaki concludes that Japanese theology has not yet begun to address the Japanese context effectively.

Nonetheless, in some non-Western areas, another variety of theology is emerging. Surveying African theology, Johannes Verkuyl observes, "It goes without saying that African theology does all the things which theology in general does, but in African theology (as in Asian) all these other functions are embraced in the missionary or communicative function. It is not primarily an intra-ecclesiastical exercise, but a discipline whose practitioners keep one question central: How can we best do our theology so that the gospel will touch Africans most deeply?" (1978: 277). The answer to that probing question will emerge only in the context of active evangelization.

In noting the shift from a Western to a non-Western locus of theological vitality, we do not intend to encourage the development of new, parochial theologies. The Christian movement is more global than ever. The local, wherever that be, must be held in a dialectical relationship with universal Christian experience. Instead of being preoccupied with intra-ecclesiastical debates, theology must engage with those seminal historical periods when issues of faith and culture were wrestled with effectively in the light of the *missio Dei.*

---

1. Pauck noted the irony that although American churches were shaped by dynamic evangelization on the Western frontier, this fact has had no influence on American theology. Pauck then makes a general historical observation: "It is a remarkable fact that the missionary enterprise does not engender theological creativity. With the possible exception of the early Church, whose theology was decisively shaped by the missionary spirit, no part of Christendom has produced major theological responsibility and creativeness in connection with evangelistic endeavors. This is strange because one should expect that precisely that encounter with other religious claims would cause the missionary to justify and explicate the grounds and reasons for his own faith by means of theological thinking" (p. 278). Cf. José Míguez Bonino, *Faces of Protestantism in Latin America* (Grand Rapids: Eerdmans, 1997), chap. 6; Andrew Kirk, *The Mission of Theology and Theology as Mission* (Harrisburg, PA: Trinity Press International, 1997); and J. Verkuyl, *Contemporary Missiology* (Grand Rapids: Eerdmans, 1978), 5-6.

SHAPING CHRISTIAN IDENTITY

A critical issue for Christians at the beginning of the twenty-first century is Christian identity. Human identity is the product of particular historical and social contexts with their peculiar interplay between external and internal forces. Christians in Latin America, Asia, and Africa who have been associated with Western missions in the modern period have struggled to overcome the stigma of being identified with a "foreign" religion. The economic, military, political, and cultural hegemony of the West, in which Christians have been implicated during the past three centuries, has greatly complicated the issue of identity for non-Western Christians. But it also must be emphasized that the question of identity is as urgent for Christians in the West as in any other part of the world. Western Christians face disturbing questions as to how to overcome the enervating syncretism that saps the vitality of Christian life today.

Whenever the Christian gospel truly encounters a culture, it disturbs the status quo, altering the normal state of things that gives human beings identity. It exposes the fact that no culture is wholly submitted to the kingdom and rule of God. In every culture an array of principalities and powers contends for human allegiance. In the face of this reality the gospel asserts that in Jesus the Messiah, God has acted decisively to liberate humankind from sin. In the incarnation "the Logos became flesh" precisely to expose the false claims of these other powers and establish the means for men and women to be reconciled to God in Jesus Christ. Thus, the question at stake in every context is always that of allegiance: is Jesus Christ Lord? And wherever Jesus Christ is not acknowledged as Lord, the church is called to evangelize.

Conversion to Jesus Christ means embracing a new identity. Working out the implications of this identity in Christ will have profound and unanticipated consequences. For many believers in the earliest Christian community, it seemed clear that one could become a Christian only by first becoming a Jew. This issue was resolved only after hard struggle (Filson 1963). To be converted is to embrace Jesus Christ as sovereign and take on the identity defined by Christ rather than the identity imprinted by the status quo. Conversion means that all rival authorities are dethroned and relativized. We dare not mistake cultural change for conversion. "Christianization" that merely replaces one culture with another has a long history but is patently not conversion. Superficial cultural changes leave undisturbed the issues of allegiance and Christian identity.

The conflict over conversion and identity centers on the issue of the relationship between the universal (that which is not conditioned by any culture) and the particular (that which is unique to a culture or religion). How does the gospel relate to each and every local religious and cultural manifestation without compromising the gospel's supracultural character? The temptation is always present to reify one culture and make it the standard for judging Christian faith and practice in other cultures. At times a cultural requirement has been imposed from the outside by a missionary or by the "mother" church; at other times the issue has arisen as an individual or church has struggled to decide how to practice faithful discipleship in a culture where historical precedents were lacking.

The dilemma in its latter form is vividly illustrated by the great Japanese Christian intellectual Uchimura Kanzo (1861-1930), who wrote:

> When a Japanese truly and independently believes in Christ, he is a Japanese Christian, and his Christianity is Japanese Christianity. . . . A Japanese by becoming a Christian does not cease to be a Japanese. On the contrary, he becomes more Japanese by becoming a Christian. A Japanese who becomes an American or an Englishman or an amorphous universal man is neither a true Japanese nor a true Christian. . . . I love two J's and no third; one is Jesus and the other is Japan. I do not know which I love more. . . . For Jesus' sake, I cannot own any other God than his Father as my God and Father; and for Japan's sake, I cannot accept any faith which comes in the name of foreigners. (Cited in Lee 1981: 97-99)

Christian identity starts from the premise that in Jesus Christ God is creating a new humanity whose identity is not dependent on any of the usual elements: race, language, social class, territory, and nationality. All of these are among the powers that must be relativized and transformed by the work of Christ. That is to say, these elements are not abolished but are to be brought into captivity to the purposes of Jesus Christ. Christian identity will be based on the decisive reconciling action of God in Jesus Christ to create a new humanity (Eph. 2:15). In the quest to embrace authentic Christian identity, no one culture is privileged over other cultures. Within the economy of the new humanity, all cultures are valued equally and are worthy of respect. Cultural and ethnic diversity becomes the means by which the richness and glory of God's grace is more perfectly revealed to us.

Since at least the fourth century A.D., the quest for Christian identity has been complicated by elements of political, cultural, and ecclesiastical coercion. The Christian missionary movement too often has been co-opted as an instrument for imposing unwanted identities on people. A widely held perception is that the way in which the Christian gospel was introduced, first to Europeans, and then to Latin Americans, Africans, and Asians, has contradicted the essential meaning of Jesus Christ for humankind; this feeling continues to fuel tensions between the Western church and other churches.

The seventeenth-century Enlightenment further reinforced this attitude by its quest for an approach to knowledge that was universally valid. As Charles R. Taber (1991) has shown, until well into the nineteenth century European culture was assumed to be the sacred vessel carrying to other cultures this universal vision that alone would deliver them from their unenlightened condition. During the modern mission movement this assumption became a source of profound tension between missionaries and the peoples to whom they went.

A METHODOLOGICAL CLUE

For several decades Andrew F. Walls has argued that the contemporary churches of Asia, Africa, and Latin America have more in common with the second-century church than with present-day Western churches. He maintains that they will find important resources for forging their identity by entering into dialogue with the early church.[2] More recently he has suggested that the early church father Origen (ca. 185–ca. 254) was the pioneer of mission studies, including theology of mission (Walls 1999: 98-105). Origen and his fellow theologians were converts from pagan backgrounds. They worked through the issues of Christian identity as Gentiles who had been grafted into the biblical faith without being cut off from their cultural and historical roots.

Great cultural and historical distance separates the early church and the modern Western church, whereas contemporary Asian, African, and Latin American Christians have considerable affinity with those of the first and second centuries. Because Western theologians largely lack the experience of becoming Christian from radically different backgrounds, they find it difficult to enter into the existential situation of present-day Christians outside the West, where religious and cultural pluralism is the norm. Yet this limitation has not inhibited Western theology from assuming that it is uniquely qualified to determine the theological canons by which contemporary African, Asian, and Latin American churches ought to live.

This methodological suggestion has important implications. It encourages the theologian of mission to range over the whole of Christian history rather than being tied to a particular institutional or ecclesiastical tradition, or to a particular historical period. When theologians are tethered to particular ecclesiastical traditions, Western history is given disproportionate weight. It is more promising to cede to the Asian, African, and Latin American churches the freedom to seek out natural links between their experiences and those historical periods when the church confronted similar issues.

---

2. Walls, who taught in Sierra Leone in the 1950s, remarks: "I still remember the force with which one day the realization struck me that I . . . was actually living in a second-century church" (*The Missionary Movement in Christian History* [Maryknoll, NY: Orbis Books, 1996], xiii). In 1942 John Foster made the same observation in *Then and Now: The Historic Church and the Younger Churches* (London: SCM, 1942). Also see Foster's *After the Apostles: Missionary Preaching of the First Three Centuries* (London: SCM, 1951) and *The First Advance: A.D. 29-500*, 2d ed. (London: SPCK, 1992).

OPENNESS TO CULTURE

During the past decade four issues have been at the top of the agenda of the theology of mission: culture, pneumatology, Christology, and ecclesiology. These issues, while not new, are being addressed in fresh ways.

From the beginning of the Christian movement, and particularly during the modern period, when intercultural contacts were increasing rapidly, the missionary attitude was to treat culture as a problem to be solved. In his critique of modern mission, Roland Allen (1930: 178-80) charged the missionary movement with operating on the basis of a "Judaizing" viewpoint.

Although many missionaries struggled to understand culture and work with it constructively, the Western intellectual framework assumed the primacy of Western culture. This stance is reflected in the work of the eminent missionary and Africanist Diedrich Westermann, regarded as a progressive thinker in his day. In the Duff Missionary Lectures for 1935, in a discussion of African cultures, Westermann argued: "The avowed aim of missionary work is to give the African a life-power which is able to remake not only individuals but tribes and peoples as a whole. *Giving the new, means taking away the old.* . . . In trying to build up a new society, the missionary cannot help destroying age-old institutions and ideals" (1937: 2). Radical displacement of the old is assumed to be the only way forward.

A generation later, Islamicist Kenneth Cragg put a question to Westermann: "If the old is taken away, to whom is the new given?" Instead of radical displacement of the old, Cragg insisted that evangelization means that the old is encountered in such a way as to engender "the revolution that will both fulfill and transform it" (1968: 57). Rather than refusing the risks involved in the struggle to find new expressions of the faith in the idiom of new believers, Cragg called for courageous engagement. Only in this way will the deepest spiritual yearnings of new believers be satisfied and the full resources of the gospel be brought to bear on a culture.

The model of "continuity" and "discontinuity" focused attention on how much of a person's religious and cultural inheritance could be retained and how much had to be discarded in order to embrace the Christian faith. Too often Western theologians, emphasizing the fall and alienation of humankind from God, concluded that the entire pre-Christian inheritance must be set aside. The emphasis on discontinuity was applied disproportionately with regard to cultures outside the West. Because the measuring rod was Western sensibilities, it was non-Western cultures that were stigmatized. This approach encouraged a dismissive attitude toward traditional culture and religion. The psychological wounds caused by Western cultural "Judaizers" have been slow to heal.

Increasingly in the postcolonial period the tide has turned against this formulation, thereby opening the way for a more constructive approach to all cultures. In Africa the study of traditional religion now enjoys full academic respectability, and generally the attitude is open and positive. Over the past thirty years theologians of Asia, Africa, and Latin America have been "attempting to make clear the fact that conversion to Christianity must be coupled with cultural continuity" (Fasholé-Luke 1975: 267-68). But the task is incomplete. In spite of the gains made through the development of theories of enculturation and contextualization, these views still bear the imprint of the modern Western missions model. The struggle to find a more adequate approach continues (Walls 1996a; Sanneh 1989).

A constructive theology of mission will be based on Christological openness to culture, not rejection. Three fundamental affirmations characterize such openness: First, God has modeled openness to culture in the incarnation of Jesus Christ. Second, through redemption the creation is transformed and renewed; Scripture shows all peoples and cultures to be equally in need of redemption. Third, the apostolic principle adopted by the Jerusalem Council has continuing validity and should guide the church in responding to the issues raised by cultural and religious pluralism in each generation.

Ghanaian theologian Kwame Bediako has emerged as a leading figure in the effort to rethink and develop a missionary theology of culture based on Christological openness. Methodologically, Bediako follows the lead of Andrew Walls in seeking precedents and dialogue partners in the first two centuries of Christian history (see Sebastian 1998: 40-50). Contemporary African theologians, observes Bediako (1990: 5-6), find in the apostle Paul an important ally. Paul understood that whoever encounters Jesus Christ does so as a whole person—a person in a web of relationships, with a history, living in a particular culture, speaking the vernacular. The work of redemption takes place in the individual's indigenous environment. Conversion is meaningless if it does not connect to the individual's entire context. Furthermore, the apostle Paul made clear that if adaptation is called for with respect to religious and cultural rules, it is the missionary who must accommodate (1 Cor. 9:15-23). Christian identity can be constructed only out of the cultural materials at hand, not on the basis of materials imported or imposed.

This thinking should not be interpreted to mean that the missionary is required to approve of a culture as it is. Rather, it is a call for the missionary to cooperate with the Holy Spirit in the confidence that the Spirit is already at work in the situation. The missionary's role is to bear witness to what it means to be "in Christ" and live within the new order of the kingdom of God. Christological openness toward culture does not begin with judgment but with relationship.

Among the most contested issues in mission studies and practice has been Asian and African views of the community's relationship to ancestors. In many cultures the ancestors are a key element in a people's worldview and essential to group identity. Asian and African theologians recognize that Christian identity will remain confused so long as the relationship to the ancestors is not clarified. Congolese theologian Bénézet Bujo argues that Jesus is essential to a constructive answer concerning ancestor theology. "This importance does not come from looking at Jesus Christ simply as an ancestor," Bujo insists. "The term 'ancestor' can only be applied to Jesus in an analogical, or eminent, way, since to treat him otherwise would be to make of him only one founding ancestor among many." Jesus did not merely fulfill the ideal of the ancestors but "transcended that ideal and brought it to a new completion" (Bujo 1992: 80).

Although Christian theology will continue to depend on the work of specialists in biblical, theological, and historical studies, it is increasingly recognized that other sources must be included. In preliterate societies or cultures where narrative continues to play an important role, the theologian must draw on these materials and theologize in forms that are culturally appropriate. For example, too little attention has been paid to the fundamental importance in many churches of hymnody. In many non-Western societies theologizing is done primarily through the creation of hymns. Recent studies indicate this genre to be a rich source of theological insight (Krabill 1990; 1995; Kiernan 1990; Molyneux 1990).

EMPOWERMENT OF THE SPIRIT

Two developments were of overriding importance for the Christian movement in the twentieth century. The first was the shift in the center of gravity from the West to Africa, Latin America, and Asia. The second was the rise and spread of the Pentecostal movement (Hollenweger 1972 and 1997). Pentecostalism emerged at the beginning of the twentieth century as a socially nonconformed and racially inclusive movement among the lower classes in the United States. Though the U.S. movement did not retain its racially inclusive stance for long (A. Anderson 1992a: 32-35; Cox 1994), the Pentecostal/charismatic phenomenon today comprises a global community of some 534 million adherents (Barrett and Johnson 2001: 25). The movement has been a major force in world evangelization and has exerted deep influence on the global Christian community.

Recent historical and sociological studies have advanced the argument that the Pentecostal movement has contributed not only to the redefinition of religion worldwide but also to constructive change in the wider society. David Martin traces the historical genealogy of Puritanism, Methodism, and Pentecostalism. He shows how these religious movements have contributed to the transformation of culture. Each movement has emphasized the experiential character of religion and the role of the laity at the grass roots. Space has been thus created for challenging institutional rigidities in church, politics, and economic systems. Martin (1990: 20) provides case studies from throughout Latin America of the role of evangelicals and Pentecostals in fostering societal change in the twentieth century. For the past three centuries the main arbiters of meaning have been scientific modernity and traditional religion. Today both of these sources of authority are largely spent, and alternatives are needed.

Harvey Cox (1994: chap. 15) argues that the contest is now between fundamentalism and experientialism. Fundamentalism, a reaction to modernity, looks to the past for its inspiration by asserting fidelity to tradition but does so in a rationalistic mode that is characteristic of modernity. Experientialism also calls for a return to tradition, but its proponents are temperamentally pliable and express their quest experientially. "This emerging mode of spirituality, therefore, finds its cohesion not in the system but in the person, not in the institution itself but in the people who draw on its resources to illuminate their daily lives" (Cox 1994: 305).

Pentecostalism is distinguished by its emphasis on an immediate and personal experience of the Holy Spirit and the urgency of evangelization. The starting point is not rational discourse about the person and work of the Spirit but direct personal encounter with the Holy Spirit and the release of the charismata of the Spirit in the life of the believer. This emphasis on experience and a desire to see the experiences of the first Christians reproduced today has resulted in vigorous missionary activism among Pentecostals.

The present strength of Pentecostalism arises in large measure from the fact that it has become indigenous throughout the world to an extent unmatched by other Christian traditions. It can be categorized in two types: (1) indigenous churches and (2) mission-founded churches, the first being by far the largest. African Initiated Churches (AICs, or sometimes Indigenous African Christian Churches) are perhaps the best-known example of indigenous Pentecostalism. The origins and motivations of these movements have been the subject of considerable study, and various classification schemes have been proposed (Daneel 1987: 68-88; 1998; 1999b). Theories based on such factors as political aspirations, economic dissatisfaction, social deprivation, and racial discrimination have been advanced to explain the rise of these churches. Based on research carried out among the Akan of Ghana, Kofi Appiah-Kubi concludes "that spiritual hunger is the main cause of the emergence of the Indigenous African Christian Churches." What Appiah-Kubi describes as spiritual hunger is the felt-need to worship in a way that responds to the full range of human experience: "The most significant and unique aspect of these churches is that they seek to fulfill what is lacking in the Euro-American missionary churches" (1979: 117-18). These indigenous churches emphasize healing, dreams, visions, and prophesying. Worship is dramatic and participatory. There is a sense of the immediacy of the presence of the Holy Spirit.

The Pentecostal focus on the Holy Spirit has been accompanied by ethical sensitivity. On the one hand, Pentecostals typically have developed strict codes of Christian behavior. On the other, perplexing issues such as what the attitude of the Christian should be toward the ancestor cult have been addressed with sensitivity and clarity. Allan Anderson (1993) concludes that in the African experience "we have evidence of a Spirit-inspired confrontation with the ancestor cult which has replaced the traditional beliefs with a truly Christian alternative." This step has been achieved without negating indigenous culture. "[The] revelations of the Holy Spirit in African Pentecostalism point to a realistic encounter and confrontation between the new Christian faith and the old traditional beliefs. Christianity thereby attains an authentically African character, realistically penetrating the old and creating the new" (Anderson 1993: 38-39).

Another important area of encounter between gospel and culture for African churches has been the response to the liberation of creation. Traditionally, Africans have placed a high value on the environment and their place in it. It was understood that human well-being depended on respecting and caring for the physical environment. In many areas around the world industrialization and urbanization have contributed to the destruction of the environment, and the church has failed to give clear guidance. M. L. Daneel (1991: 99-121; 1993: 311-32; and 1996: 130-88) has reported extensively on the practical efforts undertaken in Zimbabwe by the AICs to restore the environment and to develop a theological framework for doing so. Significantly, much of this theological response has been "in ritual activity rather than in written theology" (Daneel 1991: 113). These churches readily combine their evangelizing with stewardship of the environment.

The sense of the immediacy of the Holy Spirit in the life of the faith community has fostered an ethos in which women are free to acknowledge and exercise their gifts, including leadership roles in the churches. Pentecostal/charismatic churches have long recognized the leadership of women. Indeed, numerous prophetesses have founded churches. Now a shift is under way as women in these churches are being encouraged, in the freedom of the Spirit, to forge their own style of ministry rather than fitting into the conventional patterns of ministry of the past (Asamoah-Gyadu 1998: 27).

Pentecostal theologian Veli-Matti Kärkkäinen (1999), noting that Pentecostals "have given experience a privileged place in mission," observes that "a distinctively *Pentecostal* theology of mission is still in the making." Emphasizing the urgency of the task, Pentecostals have devoted little time to reflecting and writing about their vast experience in evangelization. Kärkkäinen stresses the importance of Pentecostals undertaking this task and asks, "What would a distinctive Pentecostal-Charismatic *missionary pneumatology* look like?" (Kärkkäinen 1999: 75, 87).

Clearly the emergence of the Pentecostal movement in the twentieth century has resulted in a rich and extensive experientially based variety of Christian faith. Having produced contextually appropriate churches in diverse cultures, the movement holds promise of a new understanding of theology, including theology of mission, no longer bound to the categories of Western rationality.

A MISSIONAL CHRISTOLOGY

Christology has been at the center of theological work, and often controversy, throughout history. Jaroslav Pelikan (1985) explores eighteen metaphors that have been used over the course of nearly two thousand years to describe and interpret who Jesus Christ is. Pelikan shows the historical context of each metaphor and explains how each metaphor has highlighted an important dimension of Jesus that appealed to a particular culture or group. Such studies remind us that perceptions of Jesus are at best partial and always conditioned by the historical context.

In any given situation the critical question is, What is the *functional* understanding of Jesus Christ in the life of this faith community? Saul Trinidad and Juan Stam, in their study of Protestant preaching in Latin America, observe: "Protestant preaching has by and large been characterized by a functional Docetism in its Christology. . . . The 'heavenly' and 'spiritual' Christ has been real and personal for believers. But he has not been Jesus of Nazareth in all his humanity and historicity" (1984: 44). This Docetic Christ is not known as companion to the poor and oppressed in their everyday world (see Luke 4: 18-19).

In sub-Saharan Africa Charles Nyamiti, speaking from a Roman Catholic perspective, reports a situation in ferment. Describing the range and variety of Christologies, he observes, "Perhaps for the first time in the history of sub-Saharan Africa new African categories are systematically employed to express and expound upon the mystery of our Savior" (1991). Terms and categories drawn from indigenous culture are being used to describe the work of Christ, including "healer," "ancestor," "master of initiation," and "chief." At the same time Nyamiti is compelled to add that none of this recent theological work has found its way into the curricula of Catholic seminaries and theological institutes. Consequently, it has yet to exert "influence in the life of the African churches" (Nyamiti 1991: 14, 17, 18). In contrast to AICs, Catholic and Protestant churches with historical ties to Western Christian traditions have been inhibited from incorporating theological and institutional innovations. The traditional European or North American curriculum still controls theological education. Procedures for fostering theological development in a dialectical relationship with the church have not been developed.

Since the end of the colonial era we have become intensely aware of social and political conditions in Latin America, Africa, and Asia that are characterized by dehumanizing injustice and poverty as a consequence of forces controlled by the global economy and the powerful, rich nations. Who do we say Jesus Christ is in relation to such conditions? How is the gospel heard in such situations? In this situation the church is challenged to ask afresh, What is the church, and what is the mission of the church? How does it relate to the *missio Dei*?

C. René Padilla (1986), Latin American biblical scholar, has stressed the urgency of a missional Christology, that is, a Christology that is historically situated and responds to the cries of the poor and disenfranchised of the world. Such a Christology is based on the historical reliability of the biblical account of Jesus.[3] The humanity of Jesus is essential to establishing the link

---

3. C. René Padilla, "Toward a Contextual Christology from Latin America," in *Conflict and Context: Hermeneutics in the Americas,* ed. C. René Padilla and Mark Lau Branson

"between his mission and that of his followers." For Padilla it is important that social ethics arise from Christology: "If the Christ of faith is the Jesus of history, then it is possible to speak of social ethics for Christian disciples who seek to fashion their lives on God's purpose of love and justice concretely revealed. If the risen and exalted Lord is Jesus of Nazareth, then it is possible to speak of a community that seeks to manifest the kingdom of God in history" (Padilla 1986: 84, 89).

Based on the account of Jesus in the Gospels, Padilla shows that the ministry of Jesus is the enactment of his message. Padilla identifies the following elements in Jesus' ministry: (1) Jesus presented himself as a prophet with prophetic authority. (2) He had a unique and intimate relationship with God and called God *abba*. (3) Jesus associated freely with "publicans and sinners," a radical departure from the conventional wisdom that held that such folk had no favor with God. (4) Jesus insisted that God's kingdom had entered history, the evidence for which was that the sick were being healed, the dead were being raised, and the poor were hearing good news. He was in the vanguard of a new order that rejected the sword as its foundation. The new order was subverting the old. (5) As a Galilean Jesus knew what it meant to live on the margin of Jewish society. As if to emphasize the point, he made the marginal people of that society—those forgotten, abandoned—his priority. (6) Jesus attacked the religious establishment for its hypocrisy, false piety, and dependence on good works. Contrary to the practice of the religious leaders, he championed the standards of justice and mercy called for by the Jewish law. (7) Jesus denounced the idolatry of wealth. His own lifestyle identified him as one of the poor, yet this status did not prevent him from gaining access to other social classes. (8) Jesus defined power as nonviolent love expressed as sacrificial service. (9) Jesus called his disciples to a life of social nonconformity in "a community of love and justice, forgiveness and sharing" (Padilla 1986: 89) and commissioned them to continue his work of making disciples and responding to peoples' needs in compassionate ministry.

According to Peruvian missiologist Samuel Escobar, during the past generation evangelicals have been searching for a *missional* Christology. This search is signaled by the shift from Matthew 28:18-20 as the basis for mission to John 20:19-23. The emerging Christological paradigm "is incarnational and is marked by a spirit of service" (Escobar 1999: 70-91). The example of Jesus as the servant Messiah wholly dedicated to the realization of the *missio Dei* establishes a model for our discipleship. A missional Christology secures Christian identity by linking it to the *missio*

(Grand Rapids: Eerdmans, 1986), 83-84. Cf. Kwame Bediako, "Five Theses on the Significance of Modern African Christianity: A Manifesto," *Transformation* 13, no. 1 (March 1996): 20-29, also chapter 7 of this volume; and John Mbiti, "Response to the Article by John Kinney," *Occasional Bulletin of Missionary Research* 3, no. 2 (April 1979): 68; and Samuel Escobar, "Evangelical Theology in Latin America: The Development of a Missiological Christology," *Missiology* 19, no. 3 (July 1991): 315-32.

Dei, thereby drawing every believer into active discipleship that continually thrusts the community of disciples into the world as the first fruit of the kingdom of God.

A MISSIONAL ECCLESIOLOGY

It has been observed that the churches of Asia, Africa, and Latin America know at first hand what it means to be a missionary church because they are much closer in time to missionary action. Persecution and suffering for the sake of Christ continues to take place. Being a Christian requires personal decision in the face of risk. Unfortunately, while this risk taking is undoubtedly present in many non-Western churches, the formal ecclesiology these churches have inherited from the Western tradition largely reflects a church focused on pastoral care and maintenance.

An important dimension of liberation theology was its critique of traditional ecclesiology. In the wake of Vatican II, the Base Ecclesial Communities were understood as an attempt to "reinvent the church." The church was viewed as being encumbered with burdensome institutions and procedures controlled by a hierarchy that seemed out of touch with the people. These structures were not associated with missionary action. Against this background, the Base Ecclesial Communities began in Brazil as a lay-led grassroots evangelization movement (Boff 1986: 3).

Among the leading proponents of missional ecclesiology are Samuel Escobar, René Padilla, and the late Orlando Costas. Instead of traditional Western Christology and ecclesiology developed in a context where the religious and cultural center seeks to maintain control, they advocate a vision of missional ecclesiology integrally related to missional Christology. Only in this way will the church be empowered for its missionary responsibility in the world. But this vision entails a change in perspective as to the actual *social location* of the church. Realistically, the church must learn to do its theological work from a minority position—and often on the margins— since that is the position of the church in many countries.

Using the Gospel of Mark as his primary text, Costas (1989: chap. 4) developed "a theology of contextual evangelization." The whole of Jesus' ministry, argues Costas, is framed by his being a Galilean. Galilee is a metaphor for both the political and the social backwater of the nation. Mark's Gospel furnishes a model of contextual evangelization that includes three elements: (1) the sociohistorical foundation—the periphery is the base; (2) the public character of evangelization—the gospel of the kingdom is proclaimed amid the multitudes; and (3) the global scope of evangelization—the gospel is proclaimed from the periphery of the nations (Costas 1989: chap. 4). In this situation, evangelization is carried out with full awareness that Jerusalem is the center of power. Jesus challenged Jerusalem, knowing full well that he would face crucifixion because he threatened the religious and political establishments.

Escobar and Padilla have urged the need for an ecclesiology that is consistent with this missional Christology. Padilla asserts, "The basic question that this new ecclesiology seeks to answer is how to be the Church of Jesus Christ in the midst of poverty and oppression?" (1987: 342). Padilla points to three things that will characterize a missional ecclesiology. First, it is grounded in a church of the people. Liberation theology emphasized the importance of "the poor." But the official church has long been the church controlled from the center and catering to the interests of those who had the power. The church belongs neither to the center nor to the periphery, neither to the powerful nor to the poor. It belongs solely to Jesus Christ. The importance of the insight introduced by liberation theologians was to expose the way in which the church has long been held captive by powerful interest groups, thereby marginalizing the poor and powerless.

In the second place, says Padilla, a missional ecclesiology depends on developing the priesthood of all believers. In the words of Leonardo Boff, "The mission of the People of God is not entrusted only to a few but is given to all. . . . All are sent out to proclaim the good news about the bright future of history" (quoted in Padilla 1987: 347). In other words, the mission entrusted to the church is too important and of such scope that it cannot be left in the hands of the hierarchy or an earnest minority. The church dare not squander the gifts the Holy Spirit bestows on each member. A missional church will nurture and call forth all gifts for ministry and evangelization.

Third, a missional ecclesiology will embrace the prophetic mission of the church. This feature is consistent with Jesus' own ministry (Luke 4:18-19). All the forces and powers that touch human life come under scrutiny. Those that oppress the poor and destroy life are to be exposed and denounced. Good News means that men and women can be set free from life-destroying powers. The vocation of the Old Testament prophets was to proclaim this message. Jesus intensified the prophetic witness and made it foundational to his messianic work. The witness from the periphery ultimately is to create space for the emergence of God's new order, the kingdom of God.

A missional ecclesiology starts by recalling that when God wanted to do a new thing, God sent the Messiah to Galilee—the periphery of Jewish life. It was from this vantage point that God chose to announce that the kingdom was now breaking into history in the person and ministry of God's Messiah (Matt. 4:17; Mark 1:14-15).

CONCLUSION

The thrust of this essay has been to argue that in the decade since David Bosch's *Transforming Mission* was published, theology of mission has been moving toward a new stage of development. Four themes characterize this emerging phase.

First, the Christian movement requires a reconceptualization of missionary theology from two angles. The nature of theology needs to be rethought. Formally, mission theology is the effort to understand and interpret the *missio Dei* in the light of Scripture, the experience of the church in mission throughout history, and the present sociopolitical context in order to give guidance to the church in fulfilling its missionary calling. Although we may readily agree that this is the only kind of theology the Christian movement requires, there is little clarity as to its content. Furthermore, the Western captivity of all theology, including theology of mission, must be broken. The task in the twenty-first century is to conceptualize theology in light of the fact that the Christian faith is global with multiple heartlands. The churches in Asia, Africa, and Latin America are at the cutting edge. In the past, mission thinking was cast in terms of a movement directed from the Western center to far-flung geographic frontiers. With multiple centers of initiative and the church encircling the globe, mission theology must be freed from the traditional Eurocentric bias.

Second, a new criterion of theological validity ought to be adopted: *Only theology that motivates and sustains the church in witness and service in the world deserves to be accredited.* This criterion means that the whole church needs to recover the kind of theology modeled by the earliest Christians and found today among the churches of Asia, Africa, and Latin America. The distinction between theology and theology of mission only serves to perpetuate a false dichotomy and ought to be abolished. The church can ill afford any theology that does not equip it for faithful witness to the world concerning Jesus Christ as Lord and Savior.

Third, the experience of the churches of Africa, Latin America, and Asia offers important guidance for the next stage of the Christian movement. As minority groups in their societies, reflecting on the challenges they face in mission, non-Western churches have insights to share with the West. The clues proposed here—Christological openness to culture, dynamic pneumatology, missional Christology, and missional ecclesiology—suggest some key elements for this theological agenda. In each case new approaches ought to be explored out of the interaction between contemporary missionary witness, the New Testament, and the experience of Christians who faced parallel issues in other historical periods.

Fourth, the churches in the West urgently need resources for responding to the challenge of evangelizing their own culture, which regards itself as postreligious, resources that may well be found outside the West (Bosch 1995). Contemporary Western culture takes pride in its multiple pluralisms—religious, cultural, ethnic, linguistic, and esthetic. Clearly, however, this culture intends to keep religion sequestered in the private sphere so that public culture remains wholly secular, free of religious influence. Neither pluralism nor fundamentalism can effectively meet the demands of this situation. Does not the church in modern and postmodern Western culture need to embrace the agenda of Christological openness to culture, a dynamic pneumatology, missional Christology, and missional ecclesiology as urgently as the churches of other continents? (Ramachandra 1996). The renewal of the church is intimately linked to the recovery of the *missio Dei* as the reason for the church's existence. Apart from this focus, renewal serves no purpose (Shenk 1995). Nineteenth-century mission leaders spoke of the time in the future when the Western church would be the beneficiary of "a blessed reflex." They anticipated the time when the so-called sending churches in the West would be challenged and renewed by the churches then springing up in Africa, Asia, and Latin America. May it now, finally, be so.

9

The Gospel as Prisoner and Liberator of Culture

Is There a "Historic Christian Faith"?

Andrew F. Walls

Andrew F. Walls served in West Africa beginning in 1957, and began at the University of Nigeria, Nsukka, in 1962 as head of the Department of Religion. He became professor of religious studies in Aberdeen in 1966 and was Riddoch Lecturer in Comparative Religion there from 1970 to 1985. He founded the Center for the Study of Christianity in the Non-Western World at Aberdeen in 1982, whence he moved it to the University of Edinburgh in 1986. He has been visiting professor of world Christianity at Yale and at Harvard Universities and guest professor of ecumenics and mission at Princeton Theological Seminary. He is author of *The Missionary Movement in Christian History* (Maryknoll, NY: Orbis Books, 1996) and *The Cross-Cultural Process in Christian History* (Maryknoll, NY: Orbis Books, 2002); and, with Christopher Fyfe, of *African Christianity in the 1990s* (Edinburgh: Centre of African Studies, University of Edinburgh, 1996). Currently he serves as professor emeritus at the University of Edinburgh and adjunct professor of the history of missions at Liverpool Hope University. He is also director of the Scottish Institute of Missionary Studies at the University of Aberdeen, and professor at the Akrofi-Christaller Memorial Centre in Ghana.

Let us imagine a long-living, scholarly space visitor—a professor of comparative interplanetary religions perhaps—who is able to get periodic space-grants which enable him to visit Earth for field study every few centuries. Let us further assume that he wishes to pursue the study of the earth-religion Christianity on principles of Baconian induction, observing the practices, habits, and concerns of a representative sample of Christians, and that he exploits the advantage he has over any earthbound scholar by taking his sample across the centuries.

Published in *The Missionary Movement in Christian History: Studies in the Transmission of Faith* (Maryknoll, NY: Orbis Books, 1996), 3-15. This article was originally published in *Faith and Thought* 108, nos. 1 and 2 (1982): 39-52. A *slightly* revised form appeared in *Missionalia* 10, no. 3 (1982). Reprinted here with permission from the Orbis Books version.

Let us assume his first visit to be to a group of the original Jerusalem Christians, about 37 C.E. He notes that they are all Jews; indeed, they are meeting in the Temple, where only Jews can enter. They offer animal sacrifices. They keep the seventh day punctiliously free from work. They circumcise their male children. They carefully follow a succession of rituals, and delight in the reading of old law books. They appear, in fact, to be one of several "denominations" of Judaism. What distinguishes them from the others is simply that they identify the figures of Messiah, Son of Man, and Suffering Servant (figures all described in those law books) with the recent prophet-teacher Jesus of Nazareth, whom they believe to have inaugurated the last days. They live normal family lives, with a penchant for large, close families; and they have a tightly knit social organization, with many common meals taken in one another's houses. Law and joyful observance strike our spaceman observer as key notes of the religion of these early Christians.

His next visit to Earth is made about 325 C.E. He attends a great meeting of church leaders—perhaps even the Council of Nicea. The company come from all over the Mediterranean world and beyond it, but hardly one of them is Jewish; indeed on the whole they are rather hostile to Jews. They are horrified at the thought of animal sacrifices; when they talk about offering sacrifices they mean bread and wine used rather as it was in the house meals our observer noticed in Jerusalem. They do not have children themselves, since church leaders are not expected to marry, and indeed most of them regard marriage as an inferior, morally compromised state; but they would regard a parent who circumcised his children as having betrayed his faith. They treat the seventh day as an ordinary working day: they have special religious observances on the first day, but do not necessarily abstain from work or other activities. They use the law books that the Jerusalem Christians used, in translation, and thus know the titles Messiah, Son of Man, and Suffering Servant; but "Messiah" has now become almost the surname of Jesus, and the other titles are hardly used at all. They give equal value to another set of writings, not even composed when the Jerusalem Christians met, and tend to use other titles, "Son of God," "Lord," to designate Jesus.

Their present preoccupation, however, is with the application of another set of words to Jesus—words not to be found in either set of writings. The debate (and they believe it of absolutely fundamental importance) is over whether the Son is *homo-ousios* with the Father, or only *homoi-ousios* with him.

The dominant factors that the outsider notices as characteristic of these Christians are the concern with metaphysics and theology, an intense intellectual scrutiny, an attempt to find precise significance for precise terms. He thinks of the Jewish Christians in the Temple nearly three centuries back, and wonders.

The best cure for his wonderment is the still greater wonder of a journey to Ireland some three centuries later still.

A number of monks are gathered on a rocky coastline. Several are standing in ice-cold water up to their necks, reciting the psalms. Some are standing immobile, praying—with their arms outstretched in the form of a cross. One is receiving six strokes of the lash because he did not answer "Amen" when the grace was said at the last meal of brown bread and dulse. Others are going off in a small boat in doubtful weather with a box of beautiful manuscripts and not much else to distribute on islands in the Firth of Clyde, calling the astonished inhabitants to give up their worship of nature divinities and seek for joy in a future heavenly kingdom. Others are sitting quite alone in dark caves by the seashore, seeking no intercourse with men.

He ascertains from these curious beings that their beautiful manuscripts include versions of the same holy writings that the Greek fathers used. He notices that the Irish use the same formula that he heard being hammered out in Nicea in 325 C.E., somewhat to his surprise, because they do not in general seem very interested in theology or very good at metaphysics. They attach great importance to the date on which they celebrate their main festival, Easter; an outsider is most likely to notice their desire for holiness and their heroic austerity in quest of it.

Our spaceman delays his next visit until the 1840s, when he comes to London and finds in Exeter Hall a large and visibly excited assembly hearing speeches about the desirability of promoting Christianity, commerce, and civilization in Africa. They are proposing that missionaries armed with Bibles and cotton seeds be sent a distance of four thousand miles to effect the process. They are also proposing a deputation to the British government about the necessity of putting down the slave trade, raising a subscription to promote the education of black mechanics, agreeing that letters be written, pamphlets and articles published. The meeting has begun with a reading from the same book (in English translation) that the other Christians used, and there have been many other quotations from the book; indeed, a large number of people in the meeting seem to be carrying it. On enquiry, the observer finds that most also accept without question the creed of Nicea. Like the Irish, they also use the world "holy" quite a lot; but they are aghast at the suggestion that holiness could be connected with standing in cold water, and utterly opposed to the idea of spending life praying in an isolated cave. Whereas the Irish monks were seeking to live on as little as possible, most of this group look remarkably well fed. What impresses the outsider is their activism and the involvement of their religion in all processes of life and society.

In 1980 he comes to Earth again, this time to Lagos, Nigeria. A white-robed group is dancing and chanting through the streets on their way to their church. They are informing the world at large that they are Cherubim and Seraphim; they are inviting people to come and experience the power of God in their services. They claim that God has messages for particular individuals and that his power can be demonstrated in healing. They carry and quote from the same book as the Exeter Hall gentlemen. They say (on being shown the document in a prayer book) that they accept the creed of Nicea, but they display little interest in it: they appear somewhat vague about the relationship of the Divine Son and the Holy Spirit. They are not politically active, and the way of life pursued by the Exeter Hall gentlemen is quite foreign to them; they fast like the Irish, but only on fixed occasions and for fixed purposes. The characteristic that springs most readily to the spaceman's mind is their concern with power, as revealed in preaching, healing, and personal vision.

Back in his planetary home, how does our scholar correlate the phenomena he has observed? It is not simply that these five groups of humans, all claiming to be Christians, appear to be concerned about different things; the concerns of one group appear suspect or even repellent to another.

Now in no case has he chosen freakish examples of Christians. He has gone to groups which may, as far as such statements can be permissible at all, be said to reflect representative concerns of Christians of those times and places, and in each case the place is in the Christian heartlands of that period. In 37 C.E. most Christians were Jews. Not only was Jerusalem the Christian center; Jerusalem Christians laid down the norms and standards for other people. By 325 C.E. few Christians were Jews, the main Christian centers lay in the Eastern Mediterranean and the key language for Christians was Greek. By 600 C.E., the balance had shifted westward, and the growing edge of Christianity was among the northern and western tribal and semitribal peoples—and Ireland was a power center. In the 1840s Great Britain would certainly be among the outstanding Christian nations, and certainly the one most notably associated with the expansion of the Christian faith. By 1980, the balance had shifted again, southwards; Africa is now the continent most notable for those that profess and call themselves Christians.[1]

So will our visitor conclude that there is no coherence? That the use of the name Christian by such diverse groups is fortuitous, or at least misleading? Or does he catch among the spheres some trace of Gilbert Murray's remark that representative Christians of the third, thirteenth, and twentieth centuries would have less in common than would a Catholic, Methodist, and Free-thinker, or even (glancing round the College Common Room and noting the presence of Sir Sarvepalli Radhakrishnan) "a well-educated Buddhist or Brahmin at the present day"? (Murray 1935: 174). Is shared religion in the end simply a function of shared culture?

Our spaceman may, however, note that between the five groups he has visited there is a historical connection. It was Christians scattered from Jerusalem who first preached to Greeks and founded that vast Greek edifice

---

1. See David B. Barrett, "A.D. 2000: 350 Million Christians in Africa," *International Review of Mission* 59 (1970): 39-54; A. F. Walls, "Towards Understanding Africa's Place in Christian History," in J. S. Pobee, ed., *Religion in a Pluralistic Society: Essays Presented to Professor C. G. Baëta* (Leiden: Brill, 1976), 180-89.

he observed in 325; it is in Eastern Christianity that we must seek some of the important features and some of the power of Celtic Christian religion. That Celtic religion played a vital part in the gradual emergence of the religion of Exeter Hall. And the Cherubim and Seraphim now in Lagos are ultimately a result of the very sort of operations which were under discussion at the Exeter Hall meeting.

But besides this historical connection, closer examination reveals that there are other definite signs of continuity. There is, in all the wild profusion of the varying statements of these differing groups, one theme which is as unvarying as the language which expresses it is various: that the person of Jesus called the Christ has ultimate significance. In the institutional sphere, too, all use the same sacred writings; and all use bread and wine and water in a special way. Still more remarkable is the continuity of consciousness. Each group thinks of itself as having some community with the others, so different in time and place, and despite being so obviously out of sympathy with many of their principal concerns. Still more remarkable, each thinks of itself as in some respect continuous with ancient Israel, even though only the first have any conceivable ethnic reason to do so, and though some of the groups must have found it extremely hard to form any concept of ancient Israel, or any clear idea of what a Jew might be or look like.

Our observer is therefore led to recognize an essential continuity in Christianity: continuity of thought about the final significance of Jesus, continuity of a certain consciousness about history, continuity in the use of the Scriptures, of bread and wine, of water. But he recognizes that these continuities are cloaked with such heavy veils belonging to their environment that Christians of different times and places must often be unrecognizable to others, or indeed even to themselves, as manifestations of a single phenomenon.

THE "INDIGENIZING" PRINCIPLE

Church history has always been a battleground for two opposing tendencies; and the reason is that each of the tendencies has its origin in the gospel itself. On the one hand, it is of the essence of the gospel that God accepts us as we are, on the ground of Christ's work alone, not on the ground of what we have become or are trying to become. But, if he accepts us "as we are" that implies he does not take us as isolated, self-governing units, because we are not. We are conditioned by a particular time and place, by our family and group and society, by "culture" in fact. In Christ, God accepts us together with our group relations; with that cultural conditioning that makes us feel at home in one part of human society and less at home in another. But if he takes us with our group relations, then surely it follows that he takes us with our "dis-relations" also; those predispositions, prejudices, suspicions, and hostilities, whether justified or not, which mark the group to which we belong. He does not wait to tidy up our ideas any more than he waits to tidy up our behavior before he accepts us sinners into his family.

The impossibility of separating an individual from his social relationships and thus from his society leads to one unvarying feature in Christian history: the desire to "indigenize," to live as a Christian and yet as a member of one's own society, to make the Church (to use the memorable title of a book written in 1967 by F. B. Welbourn and B. A. Ogot about Independent churches in Africa) *A Place to Feel at Home.*

This fact has led to more than one crisis in Christian history, including the first and most important of all. When the elders at Jerusalem in the council of Acts 15 came to their decision that Gentiles could enter Israel without becoming Jews, had they any idea how close the time would be when most Christians would be Gentiles? And would they have been so happy with their decision had they realized it? Throughout the early years the Jerusalem church was in a position to set the standards and to make the decisions, because of its direct connection with the Savior, and its incomparably greater knowledge of the Scriptures. And when its historic decision opened the door wide for Gentile believers in the Jewish Messiah, there must have been many who assumed that nevertheless Gentile Christians, as they matured, would come to look as much like Jerusalem Christians as was possible for such benighted heathen. At least Acts 21:20 suggests that, while being decently glad of the "mission field" conversions recounted by Paul, they continued to think of Jerusalem as the regulative center of God's saving word. What were the thoughts of those who fled from Jerusalem as the Roman armies moved in to cast down the Temple? Did they realize that the future of the Messiah's proclamation now lay with people who were uncircumcised, defective in their knowledge of Law and Prophets, still confused by hangovers from paganism, and able to eat pork without turning a hair? Yet this—and the fact that there were still many left to speak of Jesus as Messiah—was the direct result of the decision of the Jerusalem Council to allow Gentile converts "a place to feel at home." So also was the acceptance of Paul's emphatic teaching that since God accepts the heathen as they are, circumcision, food avoidances, and ritual washings are not for them. Christ has so made himself at home in Corinthian society that a pagan is consecrated through his or her Christian marriage partner (1 Cor. 7:14). No group of Christians has therefore any right to impose in the name of Christ upon another group of Christians a set of assumptions about life determined by another time and place.

The fact, then, that "if any man is in Christ he is a new creation" does not mean that he starts or continues his life in a vacuum, or that his mind is a blank table. It has been formed by his own culture and history, and since God has accepted him as he is, his Christian mind will continue to be influenced by what was in it before. And this is as true for groups as for persons. All churches are culture churches—including our own.

THE "PILGRIM" PRINCIPLE

But throughout church history there has been another force in tension with this indigenizing principle, and this also is equally of the gospel. Not only does God in Christ take people as they are: he takes them in order to transform them into what he wants them to be. Along with the indigenizing principle which makes his faith a place to feel at home, the Christian inherits the pilgrim principle, which whispers to him that he has no abiding city and warns him that to be faithful to Christ will put him out of step with his society; for that society never existed, in East or West, ancient time or modern, which could absorb the word of Christ painlessly into its system. Jesus within Jewish culture, Paul within Hellenistic culture, take it for granted that there will be rubs and frictions—not from the adoption of a new culture, but from the transformation of the mind toward that of Christ.

Just as the indigenizing principle, itself rooted in the gospel, associates Christians with the *particulars* of their culture and group, the pilgrim principle, in tension with the indigenizing and equally of the gospel, by associating them with things and people outside the culture and group, is in some respects a *universalizing* factor. The Christian has all the relationships in which he was brought up, and has them sanctified by Christ who is living in them. But he has also an entirely new set of relationships, with other members of the family of faith into which he has come, and whom he must accept, with all their group relations (and "disrelations") on them, just as God has accepted him with his. Every Christian has dual nationality, and has a loyalty to the faith family which links him to those in interest groups opposed to that to which he belongs by nature.

In addition—as we observed to be the case in all the spaceman's varied groups of representative Christians—the Christian is given an adoptive past. He is linked to the People of God in all generations (like him, members of the faith family), and most strangely of all, to the whole history of Israel, the curious continuity of the race of the faithful from Abraham. By this means, the history of Israel is part of church history,[2] and all Christians of whatever nationality are landed by adoption with several millennia of someone else's history, with a whole set of ideas, concepts, and assumptions which do not necessarily square with the rest of their cultural inheritance; and the church in every land, of whatever race and type of society, has this same adoptive past by which it needs to interpret the fundamentals of the faith. The adoption into Israel becomes a "universalizing" factor, bringing Christians of all cultures and ages together through a common

---

2. ". . . the first fact of the Church [is] that we are Gentiles who worship the God of the Jews"—with *their* psalms, in Gentile languages, but with their concepts (Paul van Buren, "The Mystery and Salvation and Prayer," in *Ecumenical Institute for Advanced Theological Studies Yearbook* [Jerusalem, 1977-78], 37-52).

inheritance, lest any of us make the Christian faith such a place to feel at home that no one else can live there; and bringing into everyone's society some sort of outside reference.

THE FUTURE OF CHRISTIAN THEOLOGY AND
ITS CULTURAL CONDITIONING

In the remainder of this paper I would like to suggest something of the relevance of the tension between the indigenizing and the pilgrim principles for the future of Christian theology.

First, let us recall that within the last century there has been a massive southward shift of the center of gravity of the Christian world, so that the representative Christian lands now appear to be in Latin America, sub-Saharan Africa, and other parts of the southern continents. This means that Third World theology is now likely to be the representative Christian theology. On present trends (and I recognize that these may not be permanent) the theology of European Christians, while important for them and their continued existence, may become a matter of specialist interest to historians (rather as the theology of the Syriac Edessene church is specialist matter for early church historians of today, not a topic for the ordinary student and general reader, whose eyes are turned to the Greco-Roman world when he studies the history of doctrine). The future general reader of church history is more likely to be concerned with Latin American and African, and perhaps some Asian, theology. It is perhaps significant that in the last few years we have seen for the first time works of theology composed in the Third World (the works of Latin American theologians of liberation, such as Gutiérrez, Segundo, and Míguez Bonino) becoming regular reading in the West—not just for missiologists, but for the general theological reader. The fact that particular Third World works of theology appear on the Western market is not, however, a necessary measure of their intrinsic importance. It simply means that publishers think them sufficiently relevant to the West to sell there. Theology is addressed to the setting in which it is produced.

This is perhaps the first important point to remember about theology: that since it springs out of practical situations, it is therefore occasional and local in character. Since we have mentioned Gutiérrez, some words of his may be quoted here. Theology, he says, arises spontaneously and inevitably in the believer, in all who have accepted the gift of the word of God. There is therefore in every believer, and every community of believers, at least a rough outline of a theology. This conviction leads to another: whatever else theology is, it is what Gutiérrez calls "critical reflection on Christian praxis in the light of the word" (1973: 6-15). That is, theology is about testing your actions by Scripture.

In this, of course, we are hearing the typical modern Latin American theologian, who is stung by the fact that it has taken Marxists to point out things that Amos and Isaiah said long ago, while Christians have found good theological reasons to justify the position of Jeroboam, Manasseh, and Dives, and is nagged by the remark of Bernanos that "God does not choose the same men to keep his word as to fulfill it." But it is likely to be the way of things also in Africa. The domestic tasks of Third World theology are going to be so basic, so vital, that there will be little time for the barren, sterile, time-wasting by-paths into which so much Western theology and theological research has gone in recent years. Theology in the Third World will be, as theology at all creative times has always been, about doing things, about things that deeply affect the lives of numbers of people. We see something of this already in South African black theology, which is literally about life-and-death matters (as one South African black theologian put it to me, "Black Theology is about how to stay Christian when you're a Black in South Africa, and you're hanging on by the skin of your teeth"). There is no need to go back to wars of religion when men shed blood for their theologies; but at least there is something to be said for having a theology about things which are worth shedding blood for. And that, Third World Theology is likely to be.

Because of this relation of theology to action, theology arises out of situations that actually happen, not from broad general principles. Even the Greek Church, with centuries of intellectual and rhetorical tradition, took almost two hundred years to produce a book of theology written for its own sake, Origen's *De principiis*. In those two centuries innumerable theological books were written, but not for the sake of producing theologies. The theology was for a purpose: to *explain* the faith to outsiders, or to point out where the writer thought someone else had misrepresented what Christians meant.

It is therefore important, when thinking of African theology, to remember that it will act on an African agenda. It is useless for us to determine what we think an African theology ought to be doing: it will concern itself with questions that worry Africans, and will leave blandly alone all sorts of questions which we think absolutely vital. We all do the same. How many Christians belonging to churches that accept the Chalcedonian definition of the faith could explain with any conviction to an intelligent non-Christian why it is important not to be a Nestorian or a Monophysite? Yet once men not only excommunicated each other, they shed their own and others' blood to get the right answer on that question. The things that we think are vital points of principle will seem as far away and negligible to African theologians as those theological prize fights among the Egyptian monks now seem to us. Conversely, the things that concern African theologians may seem to us at best peripheral. Remembering the emergence of theology at a popular level, it is noteworthy how African Independent Churches sometimes seem to pick on a point which strikes us by its oddity or irrelevance, like rules about worship during the menstrual period. But this is usually because the topic, or the sort of topic, is a major one for certain African Christians, just as it apparently was for the old Hebrews, and it needs an answer, and an answer related to Christ.

There often turns out to be a sort of coherence in the way in which these churches deal with it, linking Scripture, old traditions, and the church as the new Levitical community—and giving an answer to something that had been worrying people. In short, it is safe for a European to make only one prediction about the valid, authentic African biblical theology we all talk about: that it is likely either to puzzle us or to disturb us.

But is not the sourcebook of all valid theology the canonical Scriptures? Yes, and in that, as the spaceman found, lies the continuity of the Christian faith. But, as he also found, the Scriptures are read with different eyes by people in different times and places; and in practice, each age and community makes its own selection of the Scriptures, giving prominence to those which seem to speak most clearly to the community's time and place and leaving aside others which do not appear to yield up their gold so readily. How many of us, while firm as a rock as to its canonicity, seriously look to the book of Leviticus for sustenance? Yet many an African Independent Church has found it abundantly relevant. (Interestingly, Samuel Ajayi Crowther, the great nineteenth-century Yoruba missionary bishop, thought it should be among the first books of the Bible to be translated.)

The indigenizing principle ensures that each community recognizes in Scripture that God is speaking to its own situation. But it also means that we all approach Scripture wearing cultural blinkers, with assumptions determined by our time and place. It astonishes us when we read second-century Christian writers who all venerated Paul, and to whom we owe the preservation of his writings, that they never seem to understand what we are sure he means by justification by faith. It is perhaps only in our own day, when we do not read Plato so much, that Western Christians have begun to believe that the resurrection of the body is not the immortality of the soul, or to recognize the solidly material content of biblical salvation. Africans will have their cultural blinkers, too, which will prevent, or at least render it difficult for them to see some things. But they will doubtless be different things from those hidden in our own blind spots, so they should be able to see some things much better than we do.

That wise old owl, Henry Venn, of the Church Missionary Society, reflecting on the Great Commission in 1868, argued that the fullness of the church would only come with the fullness of the national manifestations of different national churches:

> Inasmuch as all native churches grow up into the fullness of the stature of Christ, distinctions and defects will vanish. . . . But it may be doubted whether, to the last, the Church of Christ will not exhibit marked national characteristics which, in the overruling grace of God, will tend to its perfection and glory.[3]

---

3. Instructions of the Committee of the Church Missionary Society to Departing Missionaries, June 30, 1868, reproduced in W. Knight, *The Missionary Secretariat of Henry Venn* (1880), 284.

Perhaps it is not only that different ages and nations see different things in Scripture—it is that they *need* to see different things.

The major theological debate in independent Africa[4] just now—item 1 on the African theological agenda—would appear to be the nature of the African past. Almost every major work by an African scholar in the field of religions—Harry Sawyerr (1970), Bolaji Idowu (1962, 1973), J. S. Mbiti (1969, 1970c, 1971), Vincent Mulago (1968)—is in some way dealing with it. Now each of the authors named was trained in theology based on a Western model; but each has moved into an area for which no Western syllabus prepared him, for each has been forced to study and lecture on African traditional religion—and each has found himself writing on it. It seems to me, however, that they all approach this topic, not as historians of religions do, nor as anthropologists do. They are still, in fact, Christian theologians. All are wrestling with a theological question, the prime one on the African Christian's intellectual agenda: who am I? What is my relation as an African Christian to Africa's past?

Thus, when Idowu concludes with such passion that the *orisas* are only manifestations of Olódùmare, and that it is a Western misrepresentation to call Yoruba religion polytheistic, the urgency in his voice arises from the fact that he is not making a clinical observation of the sort one might make about Babylonian religion: he is handling dynamite, his own past, his people's present. One can see why a non-Christian African writer such Okot p'Bitek, who glories in pre-Christian Africa, accuses John Mbiti and others so bitterly of continuing the Western missionary misrepresentation of the past (1970). It is as though he were saying, "They are taking from us our own decent paganism, and plastering it over with interpretations from alien sources." Here speaks the authentic voice of Celsus.

The mention of Celsus reminds us perhaps that African Christians are not the first people to have a religious identity crisis. Gentile Christians had precisely the same issue to face—an issue that never faced the Jewish missionaries Paul, Peter, Barnabas. They knew who they were ("circumcised the eighth day, of the tribe of Benjamin . . ."), just as Western missionaries for more than 150 confident years knew who *they* were. It is our past which tells us who we are; without our past we are lost. The man with amnesia is lost, unsure of relationships, incapable of crucial decisions, precisely because all the time he has amnesia he is without his past. Only when his memory returns, when he is sure of his past, is he able to relate confidently to his wife, his parents, or know his place in a society.

Early Gentile Christianity went through a period of amnesia. It was not so critical for first-generation converts: they responded to a clear choice, turned from idols to serve the living God, accepted the assurance that they had been grafted into Israel. It was the second and third generations of Christians who felt the strain more. What was their relation to the Greek past? Some of them

4. "Independent Africa" is here distinguished from South Africa, where different conditions have produced different priorities and a different debate.

(some indeed in the first generation, as the New Testament indicates) solved the problem by pretending their Greek past did not exist, by pretending they were Jews, adopting Jewish customs, even to circumcision. Paul saw this coming and roundly condemned it. You are *not* Jews, he argues in Romans 9-11; you *are* Israel, but grafted into it. And, defying all the realities of horticulture, he talks about a wild plant being grafted into a cultivated one. But one thing he is saying is that Gentile Christianity is part of the *wild* olive. It is different in character from the plant into which it is grafted. Such is the necessity of the indigenizing principle.

Later Gentile Christians, by then the majority in the church, and in no danger of confusing themselves with Jews, had a major problem. Yes, they were grafted into Israel. The sacred history of Israel was part of their history. Yes, the idolatry and immorality of their own society, past and present, must have nothing to do with them. But what was God doing in the Greek world all those centuries while he was revealing himself in judgment and mercy to Israel? Not all the Greek past was graven images and temple prostitution. What of those who testified for righteousness—and even died for it? Had God nothing to do with their righteousness? What of those who taught things that are true—that are according to reason, *logos,* opposed to the Great Lies taught and practiced by others? Had their *logos* nothing to do with the *Logos,* the light that lighteth every man coming into the world? Is there any truth which is not God's truth? Was God not active in the Greek past, not just the Jewish? So Justin Martyr and Clement of Alexandria came up with their own solutions, that there were Christians before Christ, that philosophy was—and is—the schoolmaster to bring the Greeks to Christ, just as was the Law for Jews.

This is no place to renew the old debate about continuity or discontinuity of Christianity with pre-Christian religion, nor to discuss the theology of Justin and Clement, nor to consider the correctness of Idowu and Mbiti. My point is simply that the two latter are wrestling with essentially the same problem as the two former, and that it seems to be the most urgent problem facing African Christians today, on their agenda. Until it is thought through, amnesia could make African Christianity tentative and unsure of its relationships, and unable to recognize important tasks. More than one answer may emerge; the early centuries, after all, saw the answer of Tertullian as well as of Clement. And there may be little that outsiders can do to assist. Once again Paul saw what was coming. "Is he not," he asks his Jewish interlocutor, and on the most thoroughly Jewish grounds, "the God of the Gentiles also?" (Rom. 3: 29f.).

The debate will certainly reflect the continuing tension between the indigenizing and the pilgrim principles of the gospel. Paul, Justin, and Clement all knew people who followed one without the other. Just as there were "pilgrims" who sought to follow, or to impose upon others the modes of thought and life, concerns and preconceptions which belonged to someone else, so there were Greek-educated "indigenizers" who sought to eliminate what they considered "barbarian" elements from Christianity such as the resurrection and the last judgment. But these things were part of a framework which ultimately derived from the Christian faith, and thus they played down, or ignored, or explicitly rejected, the Old Testament, the Christian adoptive past. Perhaps the most important thing to remember about the opponents of these Gnostics is that they were just as Greek as the Gnostics themselves, with many of the same instincts and difficulties; but they knew instinctively that they must hold to their adoptive past, and in doing so saved the Scriptures for the church. Perhaps the real test of theological authenticity is the capacity to incorporate the history of Israel and God's people and to treat it as one's own.

When the Scriptures are read in some enclosed Zulu Zion, the hearers may catch the voice of God speaking out of a different Zion, and speaking to the whole world. When a comfortable bourgeois congregation meets in some Western suburbia, they, almost alone of all the comfortable bourgeois of the suburbs, are regularly exposed to the reading of a non-bourgeois book questioning fundamental assumptions of their society. But since none of us can read the Scriptures without cultural blinkers of some sort, the great advantage, the crowning excitement which our own era of church history has over all others, is the possibility that we may be able to read them together. Never before has the Church looked so much like the great multitude whom no man can number out of every nation and tribe and people and tongue. Never before, therefore, has there been so much potentiality for mutual enrichment and self-criticism, as God causes yet more light and truth to break forth from his word.[5]

---

5. I have quoted here sentences from my paper "African and Christian Identity," which first appeared in the Mennonite journal *Mission Focus* and was later reprinted in W. R. Shenk, ed., *Mission Focus: Current Issues* (Scottdale, PA: Herald, 1980).

Part V

CHRISTIANITY
AND
THE RELIGIONS

10

The Gospel and the Religions

Lesslie Newbigin

Lesslie Newbigin (1909-1998), one of the most respected and gifted theologians of the twentieth century, whose writings spanned six decades, modeled contextualization for Christian witness by immersing himself in languages and cultures in particular rural and urban contexts. Ordained in the Presbyterian Church of Scotland in 1936, he served as a missionary to India, in Madras, from 1936 to 1946 and from 1965 to 1974. Appointed the youngest bishop to be elected to the Church of South India, he became a pillar of the ecumenical movement, ardently advocating for Christian unity in pluralistic societies, and emphasizing the importance of evangelism in preserving the catholic church. From 1959 to 1965 he was general secretary of the International Missionary Council and then the World Council of Churches. He was also moderator of the General Assembly of the United Reformed Church. Toward the end of his life, he urged the church to take the gospel anew to post-Christian Western culture and wrote his important works, *Foolishness to the Greeks* (Grand Rapids: Eerdmans, 1986) and *The Gospel in a Pluralist Society* (Grand Rapids: Eerdmans, 1989).

1. If, as I have affirmed, we are to reject religious pluralism and acknowledge Jesus Christ as the unique and decisive revelation of God for the salvation of the world, what is the proper attitude that believers in that revelation ought to take toward the adherents of the great world religions? Perhaps one should begin by making the elementary point that the word "religion" covers an extremely wide and varied range of entities, and the way in which we relate to them as Christians will vary accordingly. One might divide the religions, as Nicol Macnicol does in his fine book *Is Christianity Unique?*, into those which understand God's self-revelation in historical terms—Judaism, Christianity, Islam—and those for whom the essential religious experience is a-historical—Hinduism, Jainism, Sikhism, Buddhism. Within the first group one would again have to distinguish between Judaism, which looks for a Messiah still to come, Christianity, which confesses Jesus as the Messiah

First published in *The Gospel in a Pluralist Society* (Grand Rapids: Eerdmans, 1989), 171-83, by permission of the Society for Promoting Christian Knowledge. Reprinted here with the kind permission of Wm. B. Eerdmans Publishing Company.

who has come and is to come, and Islam, which affirms not a Messiah but a succession of messengers culminating in the Prophet. One should perhaps also include in this list Marxism, which functions in some respects as a religion in which the proletariat is the messianic people whose victory will inaugurate the final removal of human alienation from the sources of being. Clearly the gospel is related to each of these in differing ways.

One could also classify the religions in a different way which takes account of the very important group of religions which are known as primal religions. Dr. Harold Turner, well known as a student and interpreter of new religious movements in primal societies, says that there are only three possible ways of understanding the world: the atomic, the oceanic, and the relational—symbolized respectively by billiard balls, the ocean, and the net. This is a classification of worldviews rather than of religions, but all religions embody some kind of worldview. The atomic, which is characteristic of contemporary Western society and has deep roots in Greek philosophy, sees reality in terms of its individual units. The atom, conceived as a minute piece of matter, is the ultimate constituent of the visible world. The human individual, conceived as an autonomous center of knowing and willing, is the ultimate constituent of society. The oceanic view, on the other hand, sees all things ultimately merged into one entity which is both the soul and all that exists. Atma is Brahma. The third view sees everything as constituted by relationships, whether it is the material world or human society. This view, characteristic of what we are accustomed to call primitive societies and primal religions, is also the view of the Bible. That is probably why the gospel is more readily accepted by so-called primitive peoples than by those who inhabit atomic or oceanic worldviews. It also calls into question the conventional use of the term "higher religions" to denote the other world faiths.

2. These preliminary remarks about classifications of religions and worldviews should serve to remind us that in using the word "religion" we are already making assumptions that need to be examined. In most human cultures, religion is not a separate activity set apart from the rest of life. Neither in practice nor in thought is religion separate from the rest of life. In practice all the life of society is permeated by beliefs which Western Europeans would call religious; and in thought what we call religion is a whole worldview, a way of understanding the whole of human experience. The sharp line that modern Western culture has drawn between religious affairs and secular affairs is itself one of the most significant peculiarities of our culture and would be incomprehensible to the vast majority of people who have not been brought into contact with this culture. It follows that in thinking about the implications of the claim that Jesus is God's unique self-revelation for our relation to the world religions, we must take into view more than what we call religion. The contemporary debate about Christianity and the world's religions is generally conducted with the unspoken assumption that "religion" is the primary medium of human contact with the divine. But this assumption has to be questioned. When the New Testament affirms that God has nowhere left himself without witness, there is no suggestion

that this witness is necessarily to be found in the sphere of what we call religion. The parables of Jesus are notable for the fact that they speak of secular experiences. When the Fourth Gospel affirms that the light of the *Logos* who came into the world in Jesus shines on every human being, there is no suggestion that this light is identified with human religion. The text goes on to say that this light shines in the darkness, and the ensuing story constantly suggests that it is religion which is the primary area of darkness, while the common people, unlearned in religious matters, are the ones who respond to the light. And it is significant that Justin Martyr, one of the earliest apologists to use this Johannine teaching in making contact with the unbelieving world, affirms that the true light did indeed shine on the great philosophers such as Socrates, but that the contemporary religion was the work of devils. Our thought must therefore be directed not just to the religions so called; we must ask about the relation of the gospel to all who live by other commitments, whether they are called religious or secular.

3. We must look first at the strictly exclusivist view which holds that all who do not accept Jesus as Lord and Savior are eternally lost. We shall look later at the question whether this is in fact what fidelity to Scripture requires us to hold. There are several reasons which make it difficult for me to believe this. If it were true, then it would be not only permissible but obligatory to use any means available, all the modern techniques of brainwashing included, to rescue others from this appalling fate. And since it is God alone who knows the heart of every person, how are we to judge whether or not another person truly has that faith which is acceptable to him? If we hold this view, it is absolutely necessary to know who is saved and who is not, and we are then led into making the kind of judgments against which Scripture warns us. We are in the business of erecting barriers: Has she been baptized? Has he been confirmed by a bishop in the historic succession? Or has she had a recognizable conversion and can she name the day and the hour when it happened? We are bound to become judges of that which God alone knows. Moreover, every missionary knows that it is impossible to communicate the gospel without acknowledging in practice that there is some continuity between the gospel and the experience of the hearer outside the Christian church. One cannot preach the gospel without using the word "God." If one is talking to a person of a non-Christian religion, one is bound to use one of the words in her language which is used to denote God. But the content of that word has necessarily been formed by his experience outside the church. By using the word, the preacher is taking the non-Christian experience of the hearer as the starting point. Without this there is no way of communicating. This fact by itself does not refute the position we are considering, but it makes it impossible to affirm a total discontinuity between Christian faith and the religions. And anyone who has had intimate friendship with a devout Hindu or Muslim would find it impossible to believe that the experience of God of which his friend speaks is simply illusion or fraud.

4. An important group of writers who reject both this exclusivism on the one hand and a total pluralism on the other take an inclusivist position which acknowledges Christ as the only Savior but affirm that his saving work extends beyond the bounds of the visible church. Probably the most influential exponent of this view has been Karl Rahner with his conception of anonymous Christianity. It is important to note here that Rahner is not merely affirming that individual non-Christians can be saved—certainly no new doctrine—but that the non-Christian religions as such have a salvific role. Rahner (1966) set out his position in four theses:

a. Christianity is the absolute religion, being founded on the unique event of the incarnation of the Son of God. But, since this event occurred at a certain point in history, we have to ask about God's relation to those who lived before it occurred or before it was brought to their knowledge. This question will not be just about individuals but about the religions, to which they adhered. To quote Rahner, "Man who is required to have a religion is also commanded to seek and accept a social form of religion" (1966: 120).

b. It follows that non-Christian religions, even if they contain error (as they do), are lawful and salvific up to the time at which the gospel is brought to the attention of their adherents. The gospel requires us to assume that God's grace is offered to all, and that "in a great many cases at least" it is accepted (1966: 124). But after the time when the gospel has been preached and heard, the non-Christian religion is no longer lawful.

c. The faithful adherent of a non-Christian religion must therefore be regarded as an "anonymous Christian." He can be saved through his faithful practice of his religion. But the one who accepts Christ "has a greater chance of salvation than the anonymous Christian" (1966: 132).

d. The other religions will not be displaced by Christianity. Religious pluralism will continue and conflict will become sharper.

5. While Rahner's idea of "anonymous Christianity" has not proved widely acceptable, the idea that the non-Christian religions as such are to be understood as vehicles of salvation is widely accepted. It has indeed become a sort of orthodoxy, and those who are not willing to accept it are dismissed as simply out-of-date (as by Wesley Ariarajah [1988a: 419-20]). He attacks the position of those who are not willing to make this judgment but wish to leave it in God's hands as "theological neutrality," and says that we cannot now afford this neutrality because we urgently need to have a basis for praying together with people of other faiths for world peace. An alleged practical need overrides the question of truth. What are we to say, on the basis of a scriptural faith, about the status and role of the great world religions?

6. I believe that we must begin with the great reality made known to us in Jesus Christ, that God—the creator and sustainer of all that exists—is in his own triune being an ocean of infinite love overflowing to all his works in all creation and to all human beings. I believe that when we see Jesus eagerly welcoming the signs of faith among men and women outside the house of Israel; when we see him lovingly welcoming those whom others cast out;

when we see him on the cross with arms outstretched to embrace the whole world and when we hear his whispered words, "Father, forgive them; they know not what they do," we are seeing the most fundamental of all realities, namely, a grace and mercy and loving-kindness that reaches out to every creature. I believe that no person, of whatever kind or creed, is without some witness of God's grace in heart and conscience and reason, and none in whom that grace does not evoke some response—however feeble, fitful, and flawed.

7. The same revelation in Jesus Christ, with its burning center in the agony and death of Calvary, compels me to acknowledge that this world which God made and loves is in a state of alienation, rejection, and rebellion against him. Calvary is the central unveiling of the infinite love of God and at the same time the unmasking of the dark horror of sin. Here not the dregs of humanity, not the scoundrels whom all good people condemn, but the revered leaders in church, state, and culture combine in one murderous intent to destroy the holy one by whose mercy they exist and were created.

8. All true thinking about this, as about every matter, must be held within the magnetic field set up between these two poles: the amazing grace of God and the appalling sin of the world. To live in this magnetic field is to live in an atmosphere which is charged with power, tingling, as it were, with electricity. One is always in the (humanly speaking) impossible position of knowing that one is—along with all others—at the same time the enemy of God and the beloved child of God. To live in this charged field of force is always at the same time supremely demanding and supremely affirming. But we are always tempted to slacken the tension by drawing away from one or other of the two poles. Nowhere is this more clear than in the attitude we take to people outside the household of faith. We can opt for a solution which relies wholly on the universality and omnipotence of grace and move toward some form of universalism. Here the sharpness of the issue which God's action in Christ raises for every human soul is blunted. There is no life-or-death decision to be made. We can relax and be assured that everything will be all right for everybody in the end. Over much theological writing about the gospel and the world's religions one is tempted to write the famous words of Anselm: *Nondum considerasti quanti ponderis sit peccatum*—"You have not yet taken full account of sin." Or, on the other hand, the Christian may be so conscious of the abyss of sin from which only the grace of God in Jesus Christ could rescue him that he is unwilling to believe that the same grace can operate in ways beyond his own experience and understanding. His relation to the man or woman outside the church, or outside the particular embodiment of Christianity to which he adheres, can only be that of the saved to the lost. In both cases, genuine dialogue is impossible. In the first case there is no real dialogue because nothing vital is at stake; it is merely a sharing of varied experiences of the same reality. In the second case dialogue is simply inappropriate. The person in the lifeboat and the person drowning in the sea do not have a dialogue. The one rescues the other; the time to share their experiences will come only afterward.

9. If we are to avoid these two dangers, if we are to live faithfully in this spiritual magnetic field between the amazing grace of God and the appalling sin of the world, how are we to regard the other commitments, faiths, worldviews to which the people around us and with whom we live and move adhere? I believe that the debate about this question has been fatally flawed by the fact that it has been conducted around the question "Who can be saved?" It has been taken for granted that the only question was "Can the good non-Christian be saved?" and by that question what was meant was not "Can the non-Christian live a good and useful life and play a good and useful role in the life of society?" The question was "Where will she go when she dies?" I am putting this crudely because I want to make the issue as clear as possible. The quest for truth always requires that we ask the right questions. If we ask the wrong questions we shall get only silence or confusion. In the debate about Christianity and the world's religions it is fair to say that there has been an almost unquestioned assumption that the only question is, "What happens to the non-Christian after death?" I want to affirm that this is the wrong question and that as long as it remains the central question we shall never come to the truth. And this for three reasons:

a. First, and simply, it is the wrong question because it is a question to which God alone has the right to give the answer. I confess that I am astounded at the arrogance of theologians who seem to think that we are authorized, in our capacity as Christians, to inform the rest of the world about who is to be vindicated and who is to be condemned at the last judgment. There has been an odd reversal of roles here. There was a time when Protestants accused Catholics of lacking assurance of salvation, and Catholics accused Protestants of being too sure. Today Roman Catholic theologians accuse Protestants of a failure in responsibility when they say that God alone knows the ultimate fate of unbelievers. Hans Küng (1976: 99) is scathing in his contempt for Protestant theologians who say that we must leave the question of the ultimate fate of non-Christians in the hands of God. Rahner is equally sure that it is the duty of Christian theologians to tell the faithful adherent of a non-Christian religion that he can be saved but that he will have a better chance of salvation if he becomes a Christian and no chance at all if he refuses this invitation. And Wesley Ariarajah rebukes Visser 't Hooft for what he calls a "theology of neutrality" because the latter said, "I don't know whether a Hindu is saved: I only know that salvation comes in Jesus Christ" (1988a: 419-20). I find this way of thinking among Christians astonishing in view of the emphatic warnings of Jesus against these kinds of judgments which claim to preempt the final judgment of God. Nothing could be more remote from the whole thrust of Jesus' teaching than the idea that we are in a position to know in advance the final judgment of God. It would be tedious to repeat again the innumerable warnings of Jesus in this matter, his repeated statements that the last day will be a day of surprises, of reversals, of astonishment. In his most developed parable of the last judgment, the parable of the sheep and the goats, both the saved and the lost are astonished. Surely theologians at least should know that the judge on the last day is God and no one else. Perhaps the "feel" of Jesus' teaching is best captured in the brief story of the rich young ruler who had kept all God's commandments but turned away from the call to surrender his wealth, prompting Jesus' famous statement that for a rich man to enter the kingdom of God was harder than for a camel to go through the eye of a needle. When Peter protests, "Then who can be saved?" Jesus answers, "With men it is impossible, but with God all things are possible." I repeat that I find it astonishing that a theologian of the stature of Küng can so contemptuously reject the position of writers such as Barth and Kraemer who refuse to pronounce on the final salvation of the non-Christian. If a theologian is really serious he must learn to understand the impossible possibility of salvation.

In St. Paul we find this same tension of confidence and awareness of the abyss that lies beneath. Paul, who is certain that nothing can separate him from the love of God in Christ Jesus, also tells his friends that he has to exercise severe self-discipline "lest having preached to others I myself should be disqualified" (1 Cor. 9:27). The Christian life, lived in the magnetic field between the two poles of the amazing grace of God and the appalling sin in which I share, has a corresponding synthesis of a godly confidence and a godly fear. The fear is lest I should put my trust in anything other than God's grace in Jesus Christ; the confidence is in the infinite abundance of his grace to me and to every one of his creatures.

b. The second reason for rejecting this way of putting the question is that it is based on an abstraction. By concentrating on the fate of the individual soul after death, it abstracts the soul from the full reality of the human person as an actor and sufferer in the ongoing history of the world. Once again we have to insist that the human person is not, essentially, a soul that can be understood in abstraction from the whole story of the person's life. This reductionist move is as misleading as the corresponding move of the materialists and behaviorists who want to explain the human person simply as a bundle of physical activities. If we refuse both these forms of reductionism, then the question we have to ask is not, "What will happen to this person's soul after death?" but "What is the end that gives meaning to this person's story as part of God's whole story?" It has often been pointed out that the verb "to save" is used in the New Testament in three tenses—past, present, and future. We were saved, we are being saved, and we look for salvation. By common consent it is agreed that to understand the word we must begin from its eschatological sense, from the end to which it all looks. Salvation in this sense is the completion of God's whole work in creation and redemption, the summing up of all things with Christ as head (Eph. 1:10), the reconciling of all things in heaven and earth through the blood of the cross (Col. 1:20), the subjecting of all hostile powers under the feet of Christ (1 Cor. 15:24-28). The other uses of the verb (we have been saved, we are being saved) must be understood in the light of the end to which they look. The question of salvation is wrongly posed if it is posed in respect of the human soul abstracted from God's history of salvation, abstracted therefore from the question, "How do we understand the human story?" Being saved has to do with the part we are playing now in God's story and therefore with the question whether we have understood the story rightly. It follows that our dialogue with people of other faiths must be about what is happening in the world now and about how we understand it and take our part in it. It cannot be only, or even mainly, about our destiny as individual souls after death. Insofar as the debate has concentrated on this latter question, it has been flawed.

 c. The third reason for rejecting this way of putting the question is the most fundamental: it is that the question starts with the individual and his or her need to be assured of ultimate happiness, and not with God and his glory. All human beings have a longing for ultimate happiness, and the many worldviews, religious or otherwise, have as part of their power some promise of satisfying that longing. We must believe that this longing is something implanted in us by God. He has so made us that we have infinite desires beyond the satisfaction of our biological necessities, desires which only God himself can satisfy. Our hearts are restless till they find rest in him. On our journey he gives us good things that whet our appetite but do not finally satisfy, for they are always corrupted by the selfishness that desires to have them as our own possession. The gospel, the story of the astonishing act of God himself in coming down to be part of our alienated world, to endure the full horror of our rebellion against love, to take the whole burden of our guilt and shame, and to lift us up into communion and fellowship with himself, breaks into this self-centered search for our own happiness, shifts the center from the self and its desires to God and his glory. It is true, God forgive us, that Christians have turned even this into something that they thought they could possess for themselves; they have privatized this mighty work of grace and talked as if the whole cosmic drama of salvation culminated in the words "For me; for me"; as if the one question is "How can I be saved?" leading inevitably to the question "How can anyone be saved?" But this is a perversion of the gospel. For anyone who has understood what God did for us all in Jesus Christ, the one question is: "How shall God be glorified? How shall his amazing grace be known and celebrated and adored? How shall he see of the travail of his soul and be satisfied?" The whole discussion of the role of the world religions and secular ideologies from the point of view of the Christian faith is skewed if it begins with the question, Who is going to be saved at the end? That is a question which God alone will answer, and it is arrogant presumption on the part of theologians to suppose that it is their business to answer it. We have to begin with the mighty work of grace in Jesus Christ and ask, How is he to be honored and glorified? The goal of missions is the glory of God.

 What are the practical consequences of taking this as the starting point in our relation to people of other faiths? I suggest four immediate implications.

The first is this: we shall expect, look for, and welcome all the signs of the grace of God at work in the lives of those who do not know Jesus as Lord. In this, of course, we shall be following the example of Jesus, who was so eager to welcome the evidences of faith in those outside the household of Israel. This kind of expectancy and welcome is an implication of the greatness of God's grace as it has been shown to us in Jesus. For Jesus is the personal presence of that creative word by which all that exists was made and is sustained in being. He comes to the world as no stranger but as the source of the world's life. He is the true light of the world, and that light shines into every corner of the world in spite of all that seeks to shut it out. In our contact with people who do not acknowledge Jesus as Lord, our first business, our first privilege, is to seek out and to welcome all the reflections of that one true light in the lives of those we meet. There is something deeply repulsive in the attitude, sometimes found among Christians, which makes only grudging acknowledgment of the faith, the godliness, and the nobility to be found in the lives of non-Christians. Even more repulsive is the idea that in order to communicate the gospel to them one must, as it were, ferret out their hidden sins, show that their goodness is not so good after all, as a precondition for presenting the offer of grace in Christ. It is indeed true that in the presence of the cross we come to know that, whoever we are, we are sinners before the grace of God. But that knowledge is the result, not the precondition, of grace. It is in the light of the amazing grace of God in Jesus Christ that I am compelled to say, "God, be merciful to me a sinner." Indeed, as the Fourth Gospel teaches us, it is only the presence of the living Holy Spirit that can convict the world in respect of sin and righteousness and judgment. The preacher of the gospel may well be mistaken in regard to these matters; he may see sin where no sin is, and may be blind to the sins of which he himself is a party. As a fellow human being and a fellow sinner, his relation to the man or woman of another faith must be modeled on that of Jesus to all who came to him.

The second consequence of the approach I suggest is that the Christian will be eager to cooperate with people of all faiths and ideologies in all projects which are in line with the Christian's understanding of God's purpose in history. I have repeatedly made the point that the heart of the faith of a Christian is the belief that the true meaning of the story of which our lives are a part is that which is made known in the biblical narrative. The human story is one which we share with all other human beings—past, present, and to come. We cannot opt out of the story. We cannot take control of the story. It is under the control of the infinitely patient God and Father of our Lord Jesus Christ. Every day of our lives we have to make decisions about the part we will play in the story, decisions which we cannot take without regard to the others who share the story. They may be Christians, Muslims, Hindus, secular humanists, Marxists, or of some other persuasion. They will have different understandings of the meaning and end of the story, but along the way there will be many issues with which we can agree about what should be done. There are struggles for justice and for freedom in which we can and should join hands with those of other faiths and ideologies to achieve specific goals, even though we know that the ultimate goal is Christ and his coming in glory and not what our collaborators imagine.

Third, it is precisely in this kind of shared commitment to the business of the world that the context for true dialogue is provided. As we work together with people of other commitments, we shall discover the places where our ways must separate. Here is where real dialogue may begin. It is a real dialogue about real issues. It is not just a sharing of religious experience, though it may include this. At heart it will be a dialogue about the meaning and goal of the human story. If we are doing what we ought to be doing as Christians, the dialogue will be initiated by our partners, not by ourselves. They will be aware of the fact that, while we share with them in commitment to some immediate project, our action is set in a different context from theirs. It has a different motivation. It looks to a different goal. Specifically—and here I am thinking of the dialogue with secular ideologies—our partners will discover that we do not invest our ultimate confidence in the intrahistorical goal of our labors, but that for us the horizon is one that is both nearer and farther away than theirs. They will discover that we are guided by something both more ultimate and more immediate than the success of the project in hand. And they will discover that we have resources for coping with failure, defeat, and humiliation, because we understand human history from this side of the resurrection of the crucified Lord. It is—or it ought to be—the presence of these realities that prompts the questions and begins the dialogue. And, once again, the dialogue will not be about who is going to be saved. It will be about the question, "What is the meaning and goal of this common human story in which we are all, Christians and others together, participants?"

Therefore, the essential contribution of the Christian to the dialogue will simply be the telling of the story, the story of Jesus, the story of the Bible. The story is itself, as Paul says, the power of God for salvation. The Christian must tell it, not because she lacks respect for the many excellencies of her companions—many of whom may be better, more godly, more worthy of respect than she is. She tells it simply as one who has been chosen and called by God to be part of the company which is entrusted with the story. It is not her business to convert the others. She will indeed—out of love for them— long that they may come to share the joy that she knows and pray that they may indeed do so. But it is only the Holy Spirit of God who can so touch the hearts and consciences of the others that they are brought to accept the story as true and to put their trust in Jesus. This will always be a mysterious work of the Spirit, often in ways which no third party will ever understand. The Christian will pray that it may be so, and she will seek faithfully both to tell the story and—as part of a Christian congregation—so conduct her life as to embody the truth of the story. But she will not imagine that it is her responsibility to insure that the other is persuaded. That is in God's hands.

It has become customary to classify views on the relation of Christianity to the world religions as either pluralist, exclusivist, or inclusivist, the three positions being typically represented by John Hick, Hendrik Kraemer, and Karl Rahner. The position that I have outlined is exclusivist in the sense that it affirms the unique truth of the revelation in Jesus Christ, but it is not exclusivist in the sense of denying the possibility of the salvation of the non-Christian. It is inclusivist in the sense that it refuses to limit the saving grace of God to the members of the Christian church, but it rejects the inclusivism which regards the non-Christian religions as vehicles of salvation. It is pluralist in the sense of acknowledging the gracious work of God in the lives of all human beings, but it rejects a pluralism that denies the uniqueness and decisiveness of what God has done in Jesus Christ. Arguments for pluralism and inclusivism usually begin from the paramount need for human unity, a need hugely increased by the threats of nuclear and ecological disaster. We must surely recognize that need. But the recognition of the need provides no clue as to how it is to be met and certainly does not justify the assertion that religion is the means by which human unity is to be achieved. The question of truth must be faced. C. S. Song is one of those who wishes to play down the role of truth because, as he says, truth judges, polarizes, divides. Truth, he says, cannot unite the ununitable; only love can. So the Christian mission must be an affair of love, not an affair of truth (1984: 114). But it is not love that encourages people to believe a lie. As a human race we are on a journey and we need to know the road. It is not true that all roads lead to the top of the same mountain. There are roads that lead over the precipice. In Christ we have been shown the road. We cannot treat that knowledge as a private matter for ourselves. It concerns the whole human family. We do not presume to limit the might and the mercy of God for the ultimate salvation of all people, but the same costly act of revelation and reconciliation which gives us that assurance also requires us to share with our fellow pilgrims the vision that God has given us the route we must follow and the goal to which we must press forward.

11

The Uniqueness of Christ in Mission Theology

Charles E. Van Engen

Charles E. Van Engen is the Arthur F. Glasser Professor of Biblical Theology of Intercultural Studies at Fuller Theological Seminary. Previously, he was a missionary in Mexico, where he was born of missionary parents, and president of the General Synod of the Reformed Church in America from 1997 to 1998. He and his wife, Jean, are co-founders of Latin American Christian Ministries Inc. He has written many books, including *God's Missionary People* (Grand Rapids: Baker, 1991); *Mission on the Way: Issues in Mission Theology* (Grand Rapids: Baker, 1996); and *Communicating God's Word in a Complex World* (Lanham, MD: Rowman & Littlefield, 2003).

My thesis is this: "Jesus Christ is Lord" is a foundational biblical, personal faith-confession that corrects the traditional pluralist, inclusivist, and exclusivist positions held by Christians concerning other religions and calls God's missionary people to be mobilized by the Holy Spirit to participate in Christ's mission which is culturally pluralist, ecclesiologically inclusivist, and faith particularist.

INTRODUCTION

Many of us would agree with Clark Pinnock when he says, "By all accounts the meaning of Christ's lordship in a religiously plural world is one of the hottest topics on the agenda of theology in the nineties."[1]

First published in Edward Rommen and Harold Netland, eds., *Christianity and the Religions: A Biblical Theology of World Religions* (Pasadena, CA: William Carey Library, 1995), 183-217. Reprinted here with permission.
    1. Pinnock 1992: 7. Chapman quotes Max Warren as saying, "The challenge of agnostic science will turn out to have been child's play compared with the challenge to Christian theology of the faith of other (people)" (Colin Chapman 1990: 16). See also Robert Coote 1990: 15; Ralph Covell 1993: 162. Harold Netland quotes Gerald Anderson as saying, "The most critical aspect of the task of forging a viable theology of mission today 'deals with the Christian attitude toward religious pluralism and the approach to people of other faiths'" (Netland 1991: 9, quoting from G. H. Anderson 1988: 114).

The topic has been a matter of the church's reflection since the first century. Since the late 1400s, the missionary expansion of the churches (both Roman Catholic and Protestant) has tried conquest, accommodation, adaptation, indigenization, acculturation, contextualization, and inculturation in its relationship to other religious traditions. At the International Missionary Council's meeting in Tambaram, Madras, India, in 1938,[2] Hendrik Kraemer replied to William Hocking's earlier criticisms that led to the "Laymen's Foreign Mission Inquiry," by presenting "The Christian Message in a Non-Christian World," based on his missiological interpretation of Karl Barth.[3]

The matter has received increasing attention, particularly from the Roman Catholics after the Second Vatican Council,[4] and from the World Council of Churches after the Second World War.[5] Four years ago Gerald Anderson documented 175 books published in English between 1970 and 1990 that dealt with the subject of "Christian Mission and Religious Pluralism" (Anderson 1990). Three years later Anderson wrote, "No issue in missiology is more important, more difficult, more controversial, or more divisive for the days ahead than the theology of religions" (Anderson 1993: 200).

Evangelicals have only recently begun to give attention to this matter (Covell 1993: 162-63). At the 1979 Evangelical Consultation on Theology and Mission, held at Trinity Evangelical Divinity School, and in spite of the fact that the title of the published papers was "New Horizons in World Mission," no major presentation dealt with the topic of other religions (see Hesselgrave 1979). Fortunately, during the 1980s, a number of evangelicals have made significant contributions to the conversation.[6]

---

2. See International Missionary Council, *The World Mission of the Church: Findings and Recommendations of the Meeting of the International Missionary Council* (London: IMC, 1938). An excellent series of articles on Tambaram, 1938, appeared in *International Review of Mission* 78, no. 307 (July). See also Carl Hallencreutz 1969.

3. See "The Revelation of God as the Abolition of Religion," in John Hick and Brian Hebblethwaite, eds., *Christianity and Other Religions* (1980), 32-51.

4. See *International Bulletin of Missionary Research* 14, no. 2 (1990): 56-63. See Mikka Roukanen 1990.

5. See, e.g., Stanley Samartha 1977, 1981; Wesley Ariarajah 1988b; Wilfred Cantwell Smith 1980; Kenneth Cragg 1986; Charles Forman 1993; C. S. Song 1975, 1987; Jerald Gort et al. 1992; D. C. Mulder 1985; Anton Wessels 1992; Paul Tillich 1980; David Lowes Watson 1990; and the writings of M. M. Thomas and Paul D. Devanandan.

6. An excellent survey is given by David Bosch 1988. See also David Hesselgrave 1990; and Richard Bauckham 1979. Folks like Clark Pinnock 1992 and John Sanders 1992, along with others such as John Stott 1975, 1981, 1989; Harold Netland 1991; David Hesselgrave 1981, 1988; Michael Green 1977; Carl Braaten 1981; Ajith Fernando 1987; Ken Gnanakan 1992; Andrew Kirk 1992; Mark Heim 1985; William Crockett and James Sigountos 1991; together with J. I. Packer, Carl Henry, Kenneth Kantzer, and others have begun to offer us some very substantial food for thought. David Bosch, Gerald Anderson, and Lesslie Newbigin, along with John V. Taylor, Max Warren, Johannes Verkuyl, and Arthur Glasser, are among those who have consistently kept before all missiologists, including us evangelicals, the importance of continued and careful reflection on the subject. See also Jack Cottrell and Steve Burris 1993.

In this chapter, I will present my understanding of three generally accepted positions or paradigms, suggest a fourth, examine two foundational assumptions that impact all four, and draw three major missiological implications from the fourth paradigm.

THREE WELL-KNOWN PARADIGMS
OF CHRISTIAN ATTITUDES TO OTHER RELIGIONS

It is now common to subdivide the subject into three broad perspectives: pluralist, inclusivist, and exclusivist (or restrictivist). But the use of these terms is a rather recent phenomenon, and we need to examine their use.[7]

One of the earliest uses I have found of the three-part typology appeared in 1989 in *Religious Studies Review* articles by Paul Knitter and Francis Clooney.[8] By 1991 and 1992, the three-part typology had become common currency, at least among evangelicals.[9]

Harold Netland (1991: 8-35) follows this structure, but qualifies his acceptance of it. "The use of the term 'exclusivism,'" says Netland, "is somewhat unfortunate since it has for many people undesirable connotations of narrow-mindedness, arrogance, insensitivity to others, self-righteousness, bigotry, and so on. In the context of the current debate, however, the term is unavoidable, because of the widespread use today to refer to the position represented by the Lausanne Covenant" (1991: 34-35).[10]

---

7. In 1985, when Paul Knitter published *No Other Name?* he spoke of "models" of Christian attitudes to other religions: the Conservative Evangelical, the Mainline Protestant, the Catholic, and the Theocentric. In doing so, he downplayed the "pluralist, inclusivist, and exclusivist" typology. In 1982, in *God Has Many Names*, John Hick refers to the three major types of approaches, but the words themselves as typological categories are not strongly emphasized. Harold Netland pointed this out in his response to the original reading of this chapter as a paper at the Spring 1994 ETS/EMS Midwestern Conference. In a good reader on *Christianity and Other Religions* (1980), John Hick and Brian Hebblethwaite mention "religious pluralism" and "Christian absolutism," but do not use the three-part typology either. On the evangelical side, Mark Heim 1985 and Ajith Fernando 1987 do not structure their work around these three perspectives.

8. *Religious Studies Review* 14, no. 3 (July 1989): 198-207. Carl Braaten seemed to accept the threefold typology in 1987, mentioning Gavin D'Costa and Alan Race as utilizing it, but he does not indicate where it came from (Braaten 1987: 17).

9. Clark Pinnock 1992: 14-15; John Sanders 1992: 1-7; Millard Erickson in his introductory chapter to William Crockett and James Sigountos 1991: 27-33; J. Andrew Kirk 1992: 9-15; and Ken Gnanakan 1992 all follow this organization. David Bosch follows a similar typology, but uses the words relativism, fulfillment, and exclusivism (Bosch 1991: 478-83) to describe the three major perspectives.

10. In his response to this paper, mentioned above, Harold Netland commented, "It is probably safe to assume that the term 'exclusivism' was not first introduced into the discussion by adherents of that perspective, but rather is a pejorative term first introduced by those who did not accept that view, who wished to cast it in a particularly unappetizing light. Unfortunately, by default, we Evangelicals have allowed others involved in the debate over religious pluralism to define the category of 'exclusivism,' and to do so in unacceptable terms . . ." (Netland 1994: 1).

Have we evangelicals given away too much by too easily accepting these terms? First, notice that "pluralist" is positive in terms of a multicultural and multireligious world of which we are all increasingly conscious. The word "inclusivist" is positive in terms of wanting to open our arms to receive all those who are loved by God. But "exclusivist" is a negative word. Is this by accident, or by design? Few of us would like to be accused of being individually, institutionally, culturally, economically, politically, or socially "exclusive."

Second, what is the basis on which these words are being compared? If the basis is tolerance, the pluralist and inclusivist would seem to espouse tolerance, the exclusivist intolerance. If the basis is love? The pluralist loves everyone, as does the inclusivist, for they "(refuse) to limit the grace of God to the confines of the church," says Pinnock (1992: 15). It is the so-called exclusivist, or restrictivist, who, as Pinnock says, "restricts hope . . ." and therefore relegates people of other religions to "zones of darkness," refusing to love all peoples enough to offer them a "wider hope" (1992: 14). If the basis of comparison is global openness vs. parochialism, the exclusivist position looks ancient and out-of-date, and narrow.

Third, if the basis of comparison is optimism vs. pessimism, the inclusivist position is, in Pinnock's words, "optimistic of salvation" (e.g., 1992: 153), while the so-called "restrictivists" demonstrate a "negative attitude toward the rest of the world" (1992: 13), a "pessimism of salvation, or darkly negative thinking about people's spiritual journeys" (1992: 182). Thus Pinnock is forced to assess the exclusivist view of judgment in rather harsh terms.

> We have to confront the niggardly tradition of certain varieties of conservative theology that present God as miserly, and that exclude large numbers of people without a second thought. This dark pessimism is contrary to Scripture and right reason. (1992: 153-54)

John Hick describes the exclusivists in equally strong terms.

> [The exclusivist's] entirely negative attitude to other faiths is strongly correlated with ignorance of them. . . . Today, however, the extreme evangelical Protestant who believes that all Muslims go to hell is probably not so much ignorant . . . as blinded by dark dogmatic spectacles through which he can see no good in religious devotion outside his own group. (Hick 1982: 30)[11]

As evangelicals, we need to gain a better understanding of the basis for this caricature of the exclusivist position by both inclusivists such as

---

11. For similar sentiments, see, e.g., Eugene Hillman 1968: 25-27. Hick's sentiment echoes that of Ernst Troeltsch, expressed in a lecture at the University of Oxford in 1923; see Ernst Troeltsch 1980: 26-28; and Wilfred Cantwell Smith 1980: 96-98.

Pinnock and pluralists such as Hick. In order to do this, we need to lay the three paradigms side by side. To do this in a short space, and at the risk of severe oversimplification, I will represent each paradigm graphically and briefly describe my own summarized interpretation of its overall theological and missiological contours. The reader may wish to examine these summarizations to see if their description is close to the reader's perception of these paradigms.

Pluralist—A Creation Paradigm

1. Starting point: creation and the fact of religious pluralism
2. Relativism as to both culture and faith
3. Prior choice: common humanity
4. Concern about peoples of various faiths coexisting together
5. Understanding of Romans 5:12-19: "in Adam" all were created good[12]
6. Predominantly horizontalist orientation
7. Religion regarded as expression of individual subjectivity or culture
8. Weak theology of the fall and sin
9. Optimism about culture/faith
10. Bible regarded as only the Christian's book (one of many holy books)
11. Jesus Christ regarded as equal to the leaders of other religions
12. No conversion, no transformation
13. No concern for personal relationship with Jesus Christ
14. Holy Spirit viewed as working everywhere in the world, but with no relation to Christ or to the church
15. Pessimism about the church
16. No recognition of the kingdom of darkness or demonic
17. Ultimately an illogical view (pluralists cannot dialogue so conversation stops)
18. Little relationship to issues in folk religions
19. Close relationship to academic views of world religions
20. Mission regarded as irrelevant, unnecessary, demeaning, disrespectful

Inclusivist—A Paradigm of Universal Soteriology

1. Starting point: the unique Christ event as ontologically affecting all people
2. Absolutism about Jesus Christ, but weakness in personal relationship to the living Jesus Christ, and relativism about the form of universal christological soteriology

---

12. The question of what Paul meant in Rom. 5:12-19 as to the extent and nature of the symmetry between Adam and Jesus is beyond our scope here. Yet the implications of one's hermeneutic of that passage are profound and deep for our subject.

3. Prior choice: ultimate salvation of all by a loving God (Hick 1982)
4. Concern about peoples of various faiths coexisting together
5. Understanding of Romans 5:12-19: "in Christ" all are saved
6. Rather strongly verticalist soteriology, weakly horizontalist
7. Many religious forms regarded as ultimately based on the Christ event
8. Weak theology of the fall and sin
9. General optimism about culture/faith
10. Bible regarded as God's inspired revelation for all
11. Strong concern about the ontological uniqueness of Christ
12. Conversion regarded as good, but not necessary; transformation de-emphasized
13. Personal relationship to Jesus Christ regarded as desirable, not normative
14. Holy Spirit separated from Christology (Bradley 1993)
15. Pessimism about the institutional church
16. No recognition of the kingdom of darkness or demonic
17. Ultimately a patronizing attitude—all are saved in the Christ event whether or not they know or want it
18. Little relationship to issues in folk religions
19. Close relationship to academic views of world religions
20. Mission defined as telling people they are already saved in Jesus Christ

Exclusivist—An Ecclesiocentric Paradigm

1. Starting point: the church as the ark of salvation
2. Absolutism regarding personal allegiance to Jesus Christ *in the church* (a rather medieval, institutional understanding of *extra ecclesiam nulla salus*)
3. Prior choice: salvation only in the (my) institutional church
4. Concern that all non-Christians become Christians in the church
5. Understanding of Romans 5:12-19: "in Adam" all sinned
6. Strong verticalist orientation
7. All religious systems and cultures outside the church regarded as sinful (religious coexistence is possible only as people become Christian and part of the institutional church)
8. Heavy emphasis on theology of the fall and sin
9. Pessimism about culture/faith
10. Bible regarded as God's inspired revelation proclaimed through the church
11. Strong concern about uniqueness of Christ
12. Strong emphasis on conversion and transformation in and through Jesus Christ (and the church)
13. Personal relationship with Jesus a necessity
14. Holy Spirit predominantly mediated in word, worship, sacrament

15. Great optimism about the church—ecclesiocentric focus[13]
16. Overemphasis on kingdom of darkness; not much about the demonic
17. Ultimately a triumphalistic, dominating, self-serving approach
18. Success among folk religions
19. Lack of success among world religions
20. Mission defined as rescuing people out of sinful cultures into the church

A FOURTH POSSIBILITY: AN EVANGELIST PARADIGM

Let me suggest a fourth paradigm: the "evangelist." I have chosen this name because I want to present a paradigm whose starting point and center is the evangel, the confession by his disciples that *"Jesus is Lord."*[14] The "evangelist" paradigm may be presented as follows.

Evangelist—A Fourth Paradigm

1. Starting point: the confession "Jesus Christ is Lord"[15]
2. Absolutism regarding a personal faith relationship with the risen Jesus Christ as Lord; relativism in terms of the shape this takes in church and culture
3. Prior choice: personal faith in Jesus Christ (he was born, lived, ministered, died, rose, ascended, and is coming again) by grace and in the power of the Holy Spirit
4. Concern about human coexistence amidst multiple cultures and religions
5. Understanding of Romans 5:12-19: "as in Adam . . . so in Christ" is not completely symmetrical
6. Equally verticalist and horizontalist orientation
7. All cultures (including our own) regarded as fallen, but also as able to teach us something new about how "Jesus Christ is Lord"[16]
8. Seriousness regarding the consequences of the fall and of sin
9. Some optimism about cultures—affirmation of culture yet pessimism about human sinfulness

---

13. Wilfred Cantwell Smith 1980: 90 argues that "traditional missions are the exact extrapolation of the traditional theology of the church."

14. See Lesslie Newbigin 1978: 190-91. I have been helped here by an article by John Howard Yoder, "'But We Do See Jesus': The Particularity of Incarnation and the Universality of Truth," (John Howard Yoder 1983: 66-67).

15. For some discussion of this most essential kerygmatic confession by the early church and some of its missiological implications, see Van Engen 1991b: 92-94.

16. See Van Engen 1989 for some initial insight into how this seems to work through time in the midst of multiple cultures.

10. Bible regarded as God's inspired revelation for all humanity—it has new things to say to each new culture where the gospel takes root
11. Strong emphasis on confessing anew in word and life, "Jesus is Lord"
12. Strong emphasis on conversion and sometimes on transformation
13. Personal relationship with Jesus Christ a necessity
14. Holy Spirit viewed as working simultaneously but differently in the world, in and through the church, and in the believer for mission in the world
15. Moderate optimism about the institutional church—the orientation is more toward the kingdom of God
16. Consciousness of the kingdom of darkness and the demonic both in the world and in the church
17. Ultimately creative, ever-changing theology-on-the-way approach that calls for new Christologies in new cultural settings
18. Success among folk religions
19. Tendency to be confrontational with other global religious systems
20. Mission defined as calling people in multiple cultures to conversion, confession, and new allegiance, personally and corporately, to Jesus Christ as Lord

Before we look at the missiological implications of this fourth paradigm, we need to clarify two foundational presuppositions that influence all four options: (1) our understanding of the relation of faith and culture and (2) the relation of Christology and soteriology.

THE RELATION OF FAITH AND CULTURE

As the church becomes more and more a global community, it is increasingly clear that faith and culture cannot be entirely separated from each other. The gospel does not take place in a cultural vacuum, but is always incarnated in a specific cultural context. That is, it is infinitely "translatable," as Lamin Sanneh has said (1989: 50-51). Yet we must affirm also that culture and faith are not identical. As Charles Kraft says, "We deduce then, that the relationship between God and culture is the same as that of one who uses a vehicle to the vehicle that he uses. . . . Any limitation of God is only that which he imposes upon himself—he chooses to use culture, he is not bound by it in the same way human beings are" (1979: 115).

Not only must we distinguish God from culture, but we must also separate the faith of the individual from his or her culture.[17] We need to affirm

---

17. What I mean by "faith" here is not the same thing as "revelation," which is primarily the action of God, by God's initiative, in God's way. Neither do I mean "faith" in terms of an existential or subjective experience of the numinous, of the "Wholly Other," or of the "Real." Nor do I mean "faith" in terms of an assent to a number of propositions (and concomitant

approaches to other faiths that take seriously the culturally appropriate shape given the gospel in each time and place. But that is a far cry from equating culture and faith. Thus Paul Hiebert affirms,

> The gospel must be distinguished from all human cultures. It is divine revelation, not human speculation. Since it belongs to no one culture, it can be adequately expressed in all of them. The failure to differentiate between the gospel and human cultures has been one of the great weaknesses of modern Christian missions. (1985: 53)

The difference between faith and culture is not only anthropologically accurate, it is also supported historically and biblically. Historically, one needs only review the history of the church to realize that the gospel of faith in the lordship of Jesus Christ has always tended to break out of the cultural molds that would imprison it. Originally the gospel was not Western at all—it was Middle Eastern. It began among Aramaic-speaking Jews. Then it took shape in Greek culture, Roman culture, North African cultures, and on to Ethiopia, India, the Near East, the Arabian peninsula, then on to Europe, and so forth. To associate any culture too closely with biblical faith is to ignore the historical expansion of the church.

But more profoundly, the distinction between faith and culture is biblically essential. This issue is at the heart of Acts and Romans.[18] In Acts and Romans the issue is precisely how the same faith in Christ's lordship can take shape in a variety of cultures. The difference between faith and culture is also essential for our understanding of Galatians, Ephesians, and Colossians, for example. "The mystery," says Paul, "is that through the gospel the Gentiles (the *ethnē*, comprising a multiplicity of cultures) are heirs together with Israel, members together of one body, and sharers together in the promise of Christ Jesus" (Eph. 3:6, 15). The First Letter of Peter and Revelation would not make much sense either, without a distinction between faith and culture. We now know that people of many cultures can have the same faith, and people of the same culture can have many faiths—or, in the case of the secularized post-Christian West, no faith at all.

---

participation in a number of rituals) which allow for the person to be accepted in a specific religious context. Of course, I recognize the validity of all of these as part of a much larger picture. However, at the risk of oversimplification, I believe I am on firm Scriptural grounds to define "faith" in this context as including at its most foundational meaning a personal allegiance that derives from a covenantal RELATIONSHIP, an "assurance of things hoped for" (Heb. 11:1) that flows from a personal encounter with Jesus Christ by grace, through faith, in the power of the Holy Spirit.

Charles Kraft is developing a fascinating approach to this in his investigation of three encounters: "allegiance, truth, and power" that go on in Christian witness (Kraft 1991b: 258-65; 1992: 215-30).

18. See C. Van Engen 1991a: 191-93.

Now this issue is more important than it may seem. One of the most disturbing aspects of the literature relevant to our topic is the close, nearly synonymous, relationship that is assumed to exist between faith and culture. (See, for example, Ernst Troeltsch 1980: 27.) Whether we are speaking of Wilfred Cantwell Smith, Karl Rahner, Paul Knitter, John Hick, John Cobb, or Wesley Ariarajah, there is a disturbingly close relationship between faith and culture in their writings.[19] Interestingly, a close examination of the writings of inclusivists such as Clark Pinnock, John Sanders, and David Lowes Watson reveals the same almost total identification of culture with faith. However, the so-called "exclusivists" also tend to closely equate culture and faith—and in that case, conversion to Jesus Christ sometimes too easily becomes conversion to a particular version of culture-Christianity.

The distinction between faith and culture is important theologically and missiologically because the increasing cultural pluralism of our world seems to create the assumption that cultural pluralism should lead naturally to religious relativity. In today's world, Christians and non-Christians, pluralists, inclusivists, and exclusivists are beginning to share one thing in common. We are all being radically impacted by the largest re-distribution of people the globe has ever seen. In this new reality, all of us are seeking ways to affirm *cultural relativity:* tolerance, understanding, justice, equality, and co-existence of a new multicultural reality. The cities of our world are especially impacted by this.

But cultural relativity can impact our theology and missiology in strange ways, particularly if we hold faith and culture too close to each other. If one views faith and culture as nearly synonymous and one also begins to be open to cultural relativism, the next, seemingly obvious step is some form of *religious pluralism.* If one goes all the way with this process, one arrives at the pluralist position.[20] If one cannot go that far and feels strongly constrained to hold tightly to the uniqueness of the cosmic Christ-event, one arrives at the inclusivist position. If one refuses to accept *cultural* relativism, but holds faith and culture to be synonymous, one arrives at an exclusivist position reminiscent of a cultural Protestantism like that of the nineteenth century: conversion is adoption of certain cultural practices, rather than a matter of faith-relation to Jesus Christ. As the Evangelical community has become more culture-affirming, the distinction between faith and culture has become harder to maintain, and its impact on our missiology more pervasive.

---

19. For some references to this, see Van Engen 1991a: 189 n. 16.

20. W. A. Visser 't Hooft emphasized the importance of this faith/culture distinction. "To transform the struggle between the religions concerning the ultimate truth of God into an intercultural debate concerning values is to leave out the central issue at stake . . . ignoring the central affirmation of the faith, that God revealed himself once for all in Jesus Christ" (1963: 85).

THE RELATION OF CHRISTOLOGY AND SOTERIOLOGY

Second, we need to be conscious of the radically different forms the soteriological question takes among pluralists and inclusivists on the one hand, and the exclusivists and "evangelists" on the other. The bottom-line question of the pluralist and inclusivist positions is, "Given the fact that humanity is basically good, and God is a God of love, how is it possible that God could condemn so much of humanity to eternal punishment?" The exclusivists and evangelists would ask the question differently. We would ask, "Given the fact of the fall, and that 'all have sinned and fall short of the glory of God' (Rom. 3:23), how is it possible that so much of humanity may be saved?"

I believe that our theological work concerning Christology in relation to non-Christian faiths must expand beyond the soteriological questions to questions of creation, fall, the nature of humanity, and the nature of sin and holiness. Without examining these, we cannot fully clarify the issues at hand. This is where I believe Pinnock and Sanders are both quite unrealistic about their Christological re-thinking. One cannot make such a substantive change in one's Christology without it being either the beginning of a change in all the other loci of one's theology—or the result of changes already made or assumed.[21]

MISSIOLOGICAL IMPLICATIONS

Let me emphasize that I am making a conscious choice here to highlight the Christian's personal relationship with the living Jesus Christ who was born, lived in Palestine during a specific historical time, ministered, died, rose, ascended, and is coming again. The absolutely radical claim of the canonical text of the Bible is that this Jesus lives today, and is the one with whom the Christian disciple relates personally by faith. John Hick recognized in 1980 both the validity and the implications of this perspective (1980: 19). As Hick admitted, "If Jesus was literally God incarnate, the second Person of the holy Trinity living in human life, so that the Christian religion was founded by God-on-earth in person, it is then very hard to escape from the traditional view that all (sic) mankind must be converted to the Christian faith" (1980: 19).

Of course, this is the crucial point, and sadly John Hick opted to understand the narrative about Jesus Christ in what he called a "metaphorical" manner, rather than a literal description of a verifiable historical person (1982: 19). That decision was coupled, in Hick's view, with his prior commitment that "any viable Christian theodicy must affirm the ultimate salvation of all God's creatures" (1982: 17). The combination of these two prior commitments is

---

21. James Bradley pointed this out in relation to the *Logos* Christology that forms the basis of Pinnock's inclusivist position (Bradley 1993: 20-22).

not a neutral position, but rather involves an initial faith-choice that leads logically to a "pluralist" position.

Although there are many missiological implications that flow from the "evangelist" paradigm, I will limit myself to three basic ones. An "evangelist" paradigm of Christian attitude to other religions offers a perspective that is (1) faith particularist, (2) culturally pluralist, and (3) ecclesiologically inclusivist.[22]

The "evangelist" paradigm recognizes the need to integrate both the particularity and the universality of Jesus Christ. The particularity of Jesus Christ's incarnation, ministry, death, and resurrection in history continues to stand in dialectical tension with the universality of Jesus Christ's claim to be the Savior of the world. In the midst of this universal-particularism, the disciples of Jesus confess that "Jesus Christ is Lord."

JESUS CHRIST IS LORD: FAITH PARTICULARIST

The first element of this new paradigm that we need to stress is that it is *personal*. It deals not with religious systems, or theoretical religions as such, but with matters of people and of personal faith (Taber and Taber 1992). Thus we need to be able to deal with these matters in terms of "fuzzy sets," as Paul Hiebert has called them (1983: 427), for they have to do with personal faith allegiance to Jesus who lived and ministered in Palestine at a specific time in history.[23] As Gnanakan says, "God's revelation has a historicality and a universality that will need to be reconciled" (1992: 19). And such reconciliation is to be found, first of all, in a personal relationship of the Christian with the resurrected and ascended Jesus Christ of history. As Mark Heim (along with many others) has noted, the only truly unique, truly distinctive aspect of Christian faith is "a personal relationship between the Christian and the living Christ" (Heim 1985: 135).

Thus in the diagram of the "evangelistic" paradigm, all the figures are drawn with dotted lines. Confession in *Jesus* as Lord involves a personal faith-relationship that breaks the bonds of all religious systems. This relationship involves all of life with all its contradictions. It is not neat, logical, coherent. Sometimes it may involve what Hiebert has called "the excluded middle" (1982). This relationship is not exclusive, nor arrogant, nor triumphalistic. Rather, it is humble confession, repentance, and obedience. Thus the major question is not in what box or religious system does a person belong. Rather, we are dealing here with a relational "centered set," where the ultimate question is one of discipleship, one of proximity to, or distance from, Jesus the Lord.

---

22. I am following Paul Hiebert's lead here in calling missiology to move "Beyond Anti-Colonialism to Globalism" (1991).

23. See also Paul Hiebert 1979.

This perspective calls into question the institutional structures of all churches, and especially of "Christianity" as a religious system, for the churches are now seen to be the fellowship of disciples of Jesus, whose allegiance is to Jesus more than to a particular institution (contra the "exclusivist" perspective). This also calls into question the inclusivist perspective in its cosmic Christ-event that is salvific for all persons regardless of their personal relationship with Jesus Christ. And it questions the "pluralist" perspective in its relativistic reduction of the confession to Jesus being only "a" christ among many.

The confession of Jesus as Lord calls for stripping away all the layers of the artichoke[24] of cultural accretions that Christians have added to the basic confession. As Paul demonstrates in Romans, and as one sees modeled in Acts, to confess with one's mouth and believe in one's heart that Jesus is Lord—that is all there is. Nothing else really matters.

Thus when I call people of other cultures and faiths to confess "Jesus is Lord," it is not *my* Jesus (exclusivist), nor is it *a* or *any* Jesus (pluralist), nor is it the cosmic amorphous idea of Jesus Christ (inclusivist). Rather, it is Jesus *the* Lord, who calls for conversion and transformation of ALL who confess His name. Only in humility, in personal repentance and prayer, and expectation of great cultural diversity may I invite others to join me in confessing JESUS as Lord. Many Evangelical theologians and missiologists have affirmed this perspective. Such broad agreement does not minimize the radicalness of the affirmation.[25]

JESUS *CHRIST* IS LORD:
CULTURALLY PLURALIST

Along with the historicity and relationality of Jesus Christ, we must also affirm the universality of Christ's messianic lordship. As John 1, Ephesians 1, and Colossians 1 state, Jesus the Christ is the creator and sustainer of all the created order. Here we listen carefully to the so-called pluralist concerns. For we *are* concerned about the whole of humanity, and about the care of God's creation. We are concerned about how humans can live together in peace and justice, especially in the midst of increasingly difficult clashes between conflicting religious allegiances.

We need a trinitarian missiology that is kingdom oriented, as Johannes Verkuyl has so masterfully pointed out (1993). We need to remember that Christ's lordship is not only over the church (contra the "exclusivist"), but

---

24. I used to say "layers of the onion," but onions have no center; artichokes do.

25. The reader may consult, e.g., J. Verkuyl 1989; Arthur Glasser 1989; Mark Thomsen 1990; Michael Green 1977; Carl Braaten 1981; John V. Taylor 1981; Waldron Scott 1981; Norman Anderson 1950: 228-37; Mark Heim 1985: 135; John Howard Yoder 1983; Stephen Neill 1970; William Pickard 1991; and Ken Gnanakan 1992.

also over all the world. The pluralist and inclusivist perspectives confuse the manner, scope, and nature of Christ's kingly rule in relation to the church (the willing subjects), Christ's rule over all humanity in the world (many unwilling subjects), and over the unseen world. These need to be differentiated.[26]

However, this does not warrant our ignoring matters that deal with all peoples. Rather, Christ's lordship will radically question the "exclusivist" position in terms of other cultures and religions, and will instead open up a much greater breadth for contextualized encounter of Christians with their multiple cultures. Not all so-called non-Christian culture is sinful (contra the exclusivist). But neither is it all relative (contra the pluralist). For all is brought together under the lordship of Christ. Neither all creation nor every human is ontologically determined to be included in Christ's salvation against their will (contra the inclusivist). Rather, we are called to "test the spirits" (1 John 4:1-3). Those who confess "that Jesus Christ has come in the flesh" are to be recognized as related to God.

This broad, all-encompassing Christology means that we need to continue to listen carefully to the new Christologies that are arising in Asia, Africa, and Latin America. Maximally, all that which does not contradict the biblical revelation concerning the historical Jesus Christ our Lord is open for consideration. Even in the New Testament, we are becoming aware of a multiplicity of Christologies that draw from the greatness of Jesus Christ and shape themselves for specific cultural and historical contexts, as Robert Gundry recently pointed out in a paper entitled "Diversity and Multiculturalism in New Testament Christology" (1994).

Thus John Levison and Priscilla Pope-Levison (1994) have called us to join them in a search for "an ecumenical Christology for Asia" that is neither the cosmic Christ who loses touch with real life, nor the suffering Jesus who has no power to transform. In Latin America we inherited either the impotent Jesus hanging on the cross as a symbol of domination, or the distant Christ who is irrelevant to today's issues.[27]

Clearly, we need to be very careful here (H. Berkhof 1979: 48) and must follow a very sensitive process that Paul Hiebert has called "critical contextualization" (1987). As David Hesselgrave has warned, we are constantly faced here with twin dangers: "the risk of going too far" and "the risk of not going far enough" (1988: 152).[28]

---

26. I have sought to make just such a distinction in Van Engen 1981: 277-305 and 1991b: 108-17.

27. The development of new Christologies in Latin America has been extensive and creative. For Evangelical perspectives on this, see, e.g., Samuel Escobar 1991; Padilla 1986; and John Mackay 1933.

28. See also J. Andrew Kirk 1992: 171-87; Ajith Fernando 1987: 69ff.; Bruce Nicholls 1979, 1984; Lesslie Newbigin 1978; and Carl Henry 1991: 253.

JESUS CHRIST IS *LORD:*
ECCLESIOLOGICALLY INCLUSIVIST

Any discussion of the lordship of Jesus Christ must begin with a recognition of the kingdom of God, Jesus Christ's kingly rule in the lives of people and in the church. J. Verkuyl said it well.

A theology and missiology informed by the biblical notion of the rule of Christ will never fail to identify personal conversion as one of the inclusive goals of God's kingdom. . . . The good news of the Kingdom also has to do with the formation and in-depth growth of the Body of Christ throughout the world and to the end of time. . . . The Kingdom is, of course, far broader than the Church alone. God's Kingdom is all-embracing in respect of both point of view and purpose; it signifies the consummation of the whole of history; it has cosmic proportions and fulfills time and eternity. Meanwhile, the Church, the believing and active community of Christ, is raised up by God among all nations to share in the salvation and suffering service of the Kingdom. The Church consists of those whom God has called to stand at His side to act out with Him the drama of the revelation of the Kingdom come and coming. (1993: 73)

The kingdom leads to the church, the disciples of Jesus Christ the Lord. For the church is not only a gathering of individuals, it is much more. "Though faith may be intensely personal," comment Charles and Betty Taber, "religion is irreducibly social" (1992: 76). Jesus Christ is Lord not only of creation, he is also head of the church (Col. 1). Thus Jesus Christ sent his Spirit (contra Pinnock's *Logos* Christology) at Pentecost to constitute the church. Because Jesus Christ is head of the church, no one else is. The church belongs to no human person, and church growth must be growth in the numbers of disciples of Jesus, as Donald McGavran always affirmed— not proselytism with a view to expanding someone's little ecclesiastical kingdom. The "evangelist" paradigm seeks to correct the triumphalism and arrogance of which the "exclusivists" have sometimes been accused. [29]

Because Jesus Christ the Lord is the head of the church, the church's mission is therefore to participate in the mission of Jesus the Christ. This means that the church's mission is *no less* than that which Jesus declares in Luke 4. And it is *as much as* what Paul says in Acts 13: the church is to be a "light to the nations." The church is therefore to focus itself on the whole of humanity. There is always room for one more forgiven sinner. But this also means (contra the inclusivists) that it is the church as church, and not some cosmic idea that gathers disciples. This also signifies (contra the pluralists) that the church of whom Christ is head is called to proclaim that Jesus is *the* Lord of all humanity, not just a christ (see Van Engen 1991b: 93-94).

---

29. See Gnanakan 1992: 154.

This world-encountering church is as broad as all humanity, as accepting as Christ's cosmic lordship and as incorporating and gathering as Christ's disciples. The church is always the same: it is the disciples of Jesus Christ the Lord of creation, of all peoples, and of the Church.[30]

CONCLUSION

Ultimately our conviction, reflection, and proclamation involves a restatement of the mystery of the gospel for all peoples. In Paul's words, it involves a mystery that "for ages past was kept hidden in God, who created all things. His intent was that now, through the church, the manifold wisdom of God should be known . . . according to his eternal purpose which he accomplished in Christ Jesus our Lord. In him and through faith in him we may approach God with freedom and confidence" (Eph. 3:9-12 NIV). If Paul and the early church could say that in the midst of their cultural and religious diversity, we can feel confident in doing so as well. *"Jesus Christ is Lord."* In the midst of many cultures and peoples of many faiths, let's learn to be bold evangelists: faith particularist, culturally pluralist, and ecclesiologically inclusivist.

---

30. See, e.g., Johannes Verkuyl 1978: 354-68; 1993; David Bosch 1991: 474-89; Bruce Nicholls 1984: 131-35; and J. Andrew Kirk 1992.

Part VI

ANTHROPOLOGY

12

The Flaw of the Exluded Middle

Paul G. Hiebert

Paul G. Hiebert (1932-2007), born in Shamshabad, India, represented the third generation of a Mennonite Brethren missionary family. A missiologist and missionary to India under the Mennonite Brethren Board of Missions, he published more than 150 articles and 10 books, integrating insights and skills of anthropology with the theory and practice of Christian mission, and contributing to the critical realist approach to epistemology. A creative pioneer in anthropology and Christian missions, he taught missions and anthropology at Fuller Seminary in Pasadena, California (1977-1990), and was Distinguished Professor of Mission and Anthropology at Trinity Evangelical Divinity School in Deerfield, Illinois (1990-2007).

John's disciples asked, "Are you he that should come, or do we look for another?" (Luke 7:20). Jesus answered not with logical proofs, but by a demonstration of power in the curing of the sick and casting out evil spirits. This much is clear. Yet when I read the passage as a missionary in India, and sought to apply it to missions in our day, I had a sense of uneasiness. As a Westerner, I was used to presenting Christ on the basis of rational arguments, not by evidence of his power in the lives of people who were sick, possessed, and destitute. In particular, the confrontation with spirits that appeared so natural a part of Christ's ministry belonged in my mind to a separate world of the miraculous—far from ordinary everyday experiences.

The same uneasiness came to me early in my ministry in India. One day, while teaching in the Bible school in Shamshabad, I saw Yellayya standing in the door at the back of the class. He looked tired, for he had walked many miles from Muchintala where he was an elder in the church. I assigned the class some reading and went with him to the office. When I asked why he had come, he said that a few weeks earlier smallpox had come to the village and had taken a number of children. Doctors trained in Western medicine had tried to halt the plague but without success. Finally, in desperation, the

First published in *Missiology: An International Review* 10, no. 1 (January 1982): 35-47. Reprinted here with permission.

village elders had sent for a diviner who told them that Maisamma, goddess of smallpox, was angry with the village.

To satisfy her and stop the plague the village would have to perform the water buffalo sacrifice. The village elders went around to each household in the village to raise money to purchase the buffalo. When they came to the Christian homes, the Christians refused to give them anything, saying that it was against their religious beliefs. The leaders were angry, pointing out that the goddess would not be satisfied until every household gave something as a token offering—even one *paisa* would do.[1] When the Christians refused, the elders forbade them to draw water from the village wells, and the merchants refused to sell them food.

In the end some of the Christians had wanted to stop the harassment by giving the *paisa*, telling God they did not mean it, but Yellayya had refused to let them do so. Now, said Yellayya, one of the Christian girls was sick with smallpox, and he wanted me to pray with him for God's healing. As I knelt, my mind was in turmoil. I had learned to pray as a child, studied prayer in seminary, and preached it as a pastor. But now I was to pray for a sick child as all the village watched to see if the Christian God was able to heal.

Why my uneasiness both in reading the Scriptures and in the Indian village? Was the problem, at least in part, due to my own worldview—to the assumptions I as a Westerner made about the nature of reality and ways I viewed the world? But how does one discover these assumptions? They are so taken for granted that I am rarely even aware of them. One way is to look at the worldview of another culture and to contrast it with the way we view the world.

ILLS AND REMEDIES IN AN INDIAN VILLAGE

There are many illnesses in an Indian village. People become sick with hot diseases such as smallpox and must be treated with cold medicines and foods; or they have cold diseases such as malaria and need hot foods and medicines. Some need treatment for boils, cuts, and broken bones, others for mental illnesses. Women may be cursed with barrenness. Individuals or whole families may be plagued by bad luck, by constantly being robbed or by having their houses burn down. Or they may be seized by bad temper, jealousy, or hate; be possessed by spirits; or be injured by planetary forces or black magic.

Like all people, Indian villagers have traditional ways to deal with such diseases. Serious cases, particularly those that are life-threatening or had to do with relationships, they take to the *sadhu*, or "saint." This would be a person of God who claims to heal by prayer. Because God knew everything, including the nature and causes of the illness, the saints ask no questions.

---

1. A *paisa* is the smallest coin in India, now worth about .03 of one penny.

Moreover, because they are spiritual, they charge no fees, although those healed are expected to give a generous offering to God by giving it to the saint.

Other cases villagers took to a *mantrakar* or magician, particularly cases in which the villagers suspected some evil human or supernatural cause. The magician cured by means of knowledge and control of supernatural spirits and forces believed to exist on earth. If, for example, one were to venture out on an inauspicious day when the evil forces of the planets are particularly strong, they might be bitten by a viper. To cure this the magician would have to say the following magical chant (*mantra*) seven times for each stripe across the viper's back: OM NAMO BHAGAVATE. SARVA PEESACHI GRUHAMULU NANU DZUCHI PARADZURU. HREEM, KLEM, SAM PHAT, SVAHA.

This combines a powerful formula to counter the evil forces and a series of powerful sounds (*hreem, klem, sam, phat, svaha*) that further empower the formula. Sometimes the magician uses visual symbols (*yentras;* see fig. 1) or amulets to control spirits and forces in this world. Because they can divine both the nature and the cause of the evil plaguing the patient, they need ask no question, and, like the saints, they receive the offerings of those who have been helped.

A third type of medical practitioner was the *vaidyudu* (doctors), who cure people by means of scientific knowledge based on the *ayyurvedic* or *unani* systems of medicine. Because of their skills in diagnosis, these, too, ask no questions. Villagers report that these *vaidyudu* would feel their wrists, stomachs, and bodies and be able to determine their illness. They charged high fees, for this knowledge was powerful, but they give a guarantee: medicines and services were paid for only if the patient was healed.

In addition there were village quacks who healed people with folk remedies. Their knowledge was limited so they had to ask questions about the illness—where it hurt and for how long, had they been with someone sick and what had they eaten. For the same reason they charged low fees and gave no guarantees. People have to pay for the medicines before receiving them. (It should not surprise us that Western doctors are often equated at the beginning with the quacks.)

What happens to villagers who become Christians? Most of them took problems they formerly took to the saints to the Christian minister or missionary. Christ replaced Krishna or Siva as the healer of spiritual diseases. Many of them in time turned to Western allopathic medicines for many of the illnesses they took to the doctor and quack. But what of the plagues that the magician cured? What about spirit possession, or curses, or witchcraft or black magic? What is the Christian answer to these?

Neither the missionary evangelist or doctor had an answer. These do not really exist, they said. But to people for whom these were very real experiences in their lives, there had to be an answer. It is not surprising, therefore, that many of them returned to the magician for cures.

Figure 1
Magical Charms in an Indian Village

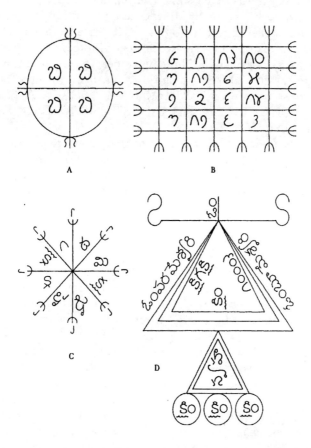

A

B

C

D

Magical charms, when properly used in a south Indian village, will automatically bring about the desired results. These charms combine powerful figures, sounds, and words. A: Yantra for a headache, including writing it on a brass plate, lighting a candle before it after it is wrapped in string, covering it with red and yellow powders, and tying it to the head. B: Yantra for assuring conception, involving inscribing it on a piece of paper or copper sheeting and tying it to the arm of the barren woman. C: Used for malaria. D: To the god Narasimha, for power and general protection.

This survival of magic among Christians is not unique to India. In many parts of the world, the picture is the same. In the West, magic and witchcraft persisted well into the seventeenth century, more than a thousand years after the coming of the gospel.

AN ANALYTICAL FRAMEWORK

In order to understand the biblical texts, the Indian scene and the failure of Western missionaries to meet the needs met by magicians, we need an analytical framework. To create this, we need two dimensions of analysis (see fig. 2).

The Seen-Unseen Dimension

The first dimension is that of immanence-transcendence. On one end is the empirical world of our senses. All people are aware of this world, and develop folk sciences to explain and control it. They develop theories about the natural world around them—about how to build a house, plant a crop, or sail a canoe. They also have theories about human relationships—how to raise a child, treat a spouse, and deal with a relative. When a Naga tribal person attributes the death of the deer to an arrow, or a Karen wife the cooking of a meal in terms of the fire under the pot, they are using explanations based on empirical observations and deductions. Western science, in this sense, is not unique. It may be more systematic in the exploration of the empirical world, but all people have folk sciences that they use to explain many of the ordinary, immediate experiences of their lives.

Above this level are beings and forces that cannot be directly perceived but are thought to exist *on this earth*. These include spirits, ghosts, ancestors, demons, and earthly gods and goddesses who live in trees, rivers, hills, and villages. These live not in some other world or time, but are inhabitants with humans and animals of this world and time. In medieval Europe these beings included trolls, pixies, gnomes, brownies, and fairies, who were believed to be real. This level also includes supernatural forces, such a mana, planetary influences, evil eyes, and the powers of magic, sorcery, and witchcraft.

Furthest from the immediate world of human experience are transcendent worlds beyond this one—hells and heavens; and other times such as eternity. Here are African concepts of a high god, and Hindu ideas of Vishnu and Siva. Here is located the Jewish concept of Jehovah, who stands in stark contrast to the Baals and Ashtaroth of the Canaanites, who were deities of this world, of the middle zone. To be sure, Jehovah entered into the affairs of this earth, but his abode was above it. On this level, too, are the transcendent cosmic forces such as karma and kismet.

Figure 2
An Analytical Framework for the
Analysis of Religious Systems

ORGANIC ANALOGY
Based on concepts of living beings relating to other living beings. Stresses life, personality, relationships, functions, health, disease, choice, etc. Relationships are essentially moral in character.

MECHANICAL ANALOGY
Based on concepts of impersonal objects controlled by forces. Stresses impersonal, mechanistic, and deterministic nature of events. Forces are essentially amoral in character.

UNSEEN OR SUPERNATURAL Beyond immediate sense experience. Above natural explanation. Knowledge of this based on inference or on supernatural experiences	**HIGH RELIGION BASED ON COSMIC BEINGS** cosmic gods angels demons spirits of other worlds	**HIGH RELIGION BASED ON COSMIC FORCES** kismet fate Brahman and karma impersonal cosmic forces
	FOLK OR LOW RELIGION local gods and goddesses ancestors and ghosts spirits demons and evil spirits dead saints	**MAGIC AND ASTROLOGY** mana astrological forces charms, amulets and magical rites evil eye evil tongue
SEEN OR EMPIRICAL Directly observable by the senses. Knowledge based on experimentation and observation.	**FOLK SOCIAL SCIENCE** interaction of living beings such as humans, possibly dead saints	**FOLK NATURAL SCIENCE** interaction of natural objects based on natural forces

OTHER WORLDLY
Sees entities and events occurring in some other worlds and in other times

THIS WORLDLY
Sees entities and events as occurring in this world and universe

The Organic-Mechanical Continuum

Scholars have widely noted that humans use analogies from everyday experience to provide them with pictures of the nature and operations of the larger world. Two basic analogies are particularly widespread: (1) to see things as living beings in relationship to each other; (2) to see things as inanimate objects that act upon one another like parts in a machine.

In the first or "organic" analogy, the elements being examined are thought to be alive in some sense of the term, to undergo processes similar to human life, and to relate to each other in ways that are analogous to interpersonal relationships. For example, in seeking to describe human civilizations, Spengler and Toynbee speak of them as living things: Civilizations are born, they mature and they die. Similarly, traditional religionists see many diseases as caused by evil spirits that are alive, that may be angered, and that can be placated through supplication or the offering of a sacrifice. Christians see their relationship to God in organic terms. God is a person and humans relate to him in ways analogous to human relationships.

Organic explanations see the world in terms of living beings in relationship to one another. Like humans and animals, they may initiate actions and respond to the actions of others. They may be thought to have feelings, thoughts, and wills of their own. Often they are seen as social beings who love, marry, beget offspring, quarrel, war, sleep, eat, persuade, and coerce one another.

In the second or "mechanical" analogy things are thought to be inanimate parts of greater mechanical systems. They are controlled by impersonal forces or by impersonal laws of nature. For example, Western sciences see the world as made up of lifeless matter that interacts on the basis of forces. Gravity pulls a rock down to the earth not because the earth and rock wish to meet—neither earth nor rock have any thought in the matter. In Western science even living beings often are seen as being caught up in a world ultimately made up of impersonal forces. Just as we have no choice about what happens to us when we fall out of a tree, so it is often thought that we have no control over the forces in early childhood that are believed to have made us what we are today.

Mechanical analogies are essentially deterministic; living beings in a mechanistic system are subject to its impersonal forces. But if they know how these forces operate, they can manipulate or control them for their own advantage. In a sense they become like gods who control their own destiny.

Mechanistic analogies are basically amoral in character. Forces are intrinsically neither good nor evil. They can be used for both. Organic analogies, on the other hand, are characterized by ethical considerations. One being's actions always affect other beings.

Many of the similarities between modern science, magic, and astrology that have been pointed out by anthropologists are due to the fact that they use mechanistic analogies. Just as scientists know how to control empirical forces to achieve their goals, the magician and astrologer control supernatural forces of this world by means of chants, charms, and rituals to carry out their purposes.

One of the greatest cultural gaps between Western people and many traditional religionists is found along this dimension. The former have bought deeply into a mechanical view of this universe and of the social order (cf. Berger, Berger, and Kellner 1973). To them the basis of the world is lifeless matter controlled by impersonal forces. Many tribal religionists

Figure 3
A Western Two-Tiered View of Reality

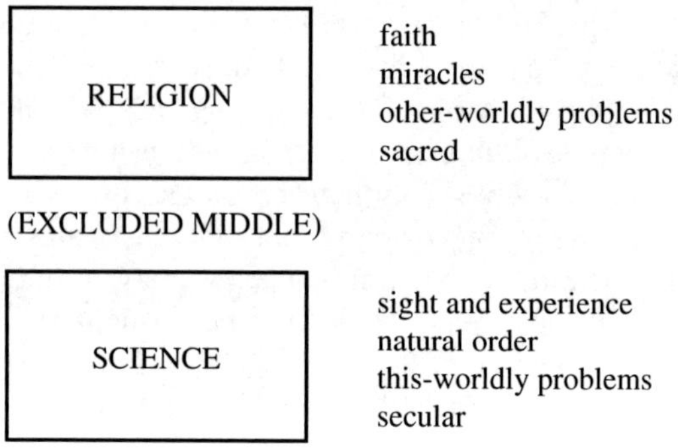

| RELIGION | faith
miracles
other-worldly problems
sacred |

(EXCLUDED MIDDLE)

| SCIENCE | sight and experience
natural order
this-worldly problems
secular |

see the world as alive. Not only humans, but also animals, plants, and even rocks, sand, and water are thought to have personalities, wills, and life forces. Theirs is a relational, not a deterministic, world.

THE EXCLUDED MIDDLE

The reasons for my uneasiness with the biblical and Indian worldviews should be clear: I had excluded the middle level of supernatural this-worldly beings and forces from my own worldview. As a scientist I had been trained to deal with the empirical world in naturalistic terms. As a theologian I was taught to answer ultimate questions in theistic terms. For me the middle zone did not really exist. Unlike Indian villagers, I had given little thought to spirits of this world, to local ancestors and ghosts, or to the souls of animals. For me these belonged to the realm of fairies, trolls, and other mythical beings. Consequently I had no answers to the questions they raised (see fig. 3).

How did this two-tiered worldview emerge in the West? Belief in the middle level began to die in the seventeenth and eighteenth centuries with the growing acceptance of a Platonic dualism (Bufford 1981: 30), and with it, of a science based on materialistic naturalism. The result was the secularization of science and the mystification of religion. Science dealt with the empirical world using mechanistic analogies, leaving religion to handle other-worldly matters, often in terms of organic analogies. Science was based on the certitudes of sense experience, experimentation, and proof. Religion was left with faith in visions, dreams, and inner feelings. Science sought order in natural laws. Religion was brought in to deal with miracles and exceptions to the natural order, but these decreased as scientific knowledge expanded.

It should be apparent why many missionaries trained in the West had no answers to the problems of the middle level—they often did not even see it. When tribal people spoke of fear of evil spirits, they denied the existence of the spirits rather than claim the power of Christ over them. The result, as Newbigin has pointed out, is that Western Christian missions have been one of the greatest secularizing forces in history (Newbigin 1966).

What are the questions of the middle level that Westerners find so hard to answer, and how do they differ from questions raised by science and religion? Science as a system of explanation, whether folk or modern, answers questions about the nature of the world that is directly experienced. All people have social theories about how to raise children and organize social activities. All have ideas about the natural world and how to control it for their own benefit.

Religion as a system of explanation deals with the ultimate questions of the origin, purpose, and destiny of the individual, a society, and the universe. In the West the focus is on the individual; in the Old Testament it was on Israel as a society.

What are the questions of the middle level? Here one finds the questions of the uncertainty of the future, the crises of present life, and the unknowns of the past. Despite knowledge that seeds once planted will grow and bear fruit, that travel down this river on a boat will bring one to the neighboring village, the future is not totally predictable. Accidents, misfortunes, the intervention of other persons, and other unknown events can frustrate human planning.

How can one prevent accidents or guarantee success in the future? How can one make sure that a marriage will be fruitful and happy, and endure? How can one avoid getting on a plane that will crash? In the West these questions are left unanswered. They are "accidents," "luck," or "unforeseeable events," hence unexplainable. But many people are not content to leave so important a set of questions unanswered, and the answers they give are often stated in terms of ancestors, demons, witches, and local gods, or in terms of magic and astrology.

Similarly, the cries and misfortunes of present life must be handled: sudden disease and plagues, extended droughts, earthquakes, failures in business, and the empirically unexplainable loss of health. What does one do when the doctors have done all they can and a child grows sicker, or when one is gambling and the stakes are high? Again, many seek answers in the middle level.

And there are questions one must answer about the past: why did my child die in the prime of life, or who stole the gold hidden in the house? Here again transempirical explanations often provide an answer when empirical ones fail.

Because the Western world no longer provides explanations for questions on the middle level, it is not surprising that many Western missionaries have no answers within their Christian worldview. What is a Christian theology of ancestors, of animals and plants, of local spirits and spirit possession; and of "principalities, powers and rulers of the darkness of this world" (Eph. 6: 12)? What does one say when new tribal converts want to know how the Christian God tells them where and when to hunt, whether they should marry this daughter to that young man, or where they can find the lost money? Given no answer, they return to the diviner who gave them definite answers, for these are the problems that loom large in their everyday lives.

IMPLICATIONS FOR MISSIONS

What implications does all of this have for missions? First, it points out the need for missionaries to develop holistic theologies that deal with all areas of life (see fig. 4), that avoid the Platonic dualism of the West, and that take seriously both body and soul.

On the highest level, this includes a theology of God in cosmic history: in the creation, redemption, purpose, and destiny of all things. Only as human history is placed within a cosmic framework does it take on meaning, and only when history has meaning does human biography become meaningful.

On the middle level, a holistic theology includes a theology of God in human history: in the affairs of nations, of peoples, and of individuals. This must include a theology of divine guidance, provision, and healing; of ancestors, spirits, and invisible powers of this world; and of suffering, misfortune, and death.

On this level, some sections of the church have turned to doctrines of saints as intermediaries between God and humans. Others have turned to doctrines of the Holy Spirit to show God's active involvement in the events of human history. It is no coincidence that many of the most successful missions have provided some form of Christian answer to middle-level questions.

On the bottom level a holistic theology includes an awareness of God in natural history—in sustaining the natural order of things. So long as the missionary comes with a two-tier worldview with God confined to the supernatural, and the natural world operating for all practical purposes according to autonomous scientific laws, Christianity will continue to be a secularizing force in the world. Only as God is brought back into the middle of our scientific understanding of nature will we stem the tide of Western secularism.

A second implication is that the church and mission must guard against Christianity itself becoming a new form of magic. Magic is based on a mechanistic view—a formula approach to reality that allows humans to control their own destinies. Worship, on the other hand, is rooted in a relational view of life. Worshipers place themselves in the power and mercy of a greater being.

The difference is not one of form, but of attitude. What begins as a prayer

Figure 4
A Western Two-Tiered View of Reality

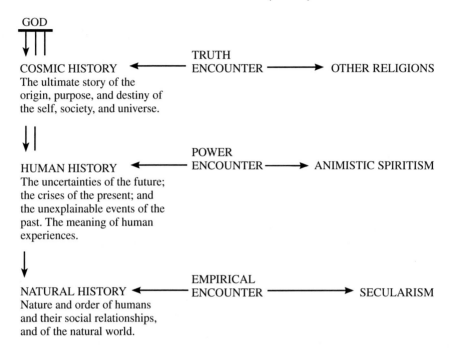

GOD

COSMIC HISTORY ←———— TRUTH ENCOUNTER ————→ OTHER RELIGIONS
The ultimate story of the
origin, purpose, and destiny of
the self, society, and universe.

HUMAN HISTORY ←———— POWER ENCOUNTER ————→ ANIMISTIC SPIRITISM
The uncertainties of the future;
the crises of the present; and
the unexplainable events of the
past. The meaning of human
experiences.

NATURAL HISTORY ←———— EMPIRICAL ENCOUNTER ————→ SECULARISM
Nature and order of humans
and their social relationships,
and of the natural world.

of request may turn into a formula or chant to force God to do one's will by saying or doing the right thing. In religion, we want the will of God for we trust in his omniscience. In magic we seek our own wills, confident that we know what is best for ourselves.

The line dividing them is a subtle one, as I learned in the case of Muchintala. A week after our prayer meeting, Yellayya returned to say that the child had died. I felt thoroughly defeated. Who was I to be a missionary if I could not pray for healing and receive a positive answer? A few weeks later Yellayya returned with a sense of triumph. "How can you be so happy after the child died?" I asked.

"The village would have acknowledged the power of our God had he healed the child," Yellayya said, "but they knew in the end she would have to die. When they saw in the funeral our hope of resurrection and reunion in heaven, they saw an even greater victory, over death itself, and they have begun to ask about the Christian way."

In a new way I began to realize that true answers to prayer are those that bring the greatest glory to God, not those that satisfy my immediate desires. It is all too easy to make Christianity a new magic in which we as gods can make God do our bidding.

13

Being Ecumenical in the Barrio

Daisy L. Machado

Daisy L. Machado, the first U.S. Latina ordained in the Christian Church (Disciples of Christ) in 1981 in the Northeast Region, has served inner-city Latino congregations in Connecticut, Spanish Harlem, Brooklyn, Houston, and Fort Worth. A native of Cuba, she was raised in New York and presently serves as professor of the history of Christianity at Union Theological Seminary, New York City, with a special focus on U.S. Christianities. The former dean of Lexington Theological Seminary, she was Luce Lecturer in Urban Ministry, Harvard Divinity School. In June 2004 the Academy of Catholic Hispanic Theologians in the United States gave Dr. Machado the "Virgilio Elizondo Award" for "her stature within the Hispanic/Latino/a theological community . . . and [for] her singular efforts to build bridges across religious, denominational, and theological boundaries." *Borders and Margins: Hispanic Disciples in the Southwest, 1888-1942* (New York: Oxford University Press, 2003) is among her many publications.

INTRODUCTION

The development of what is today called the "Ecumenical Movement" can be traced historically to the International Missionary Conference held in Edinburgh in 1910. Prior to that conference the Evangelical Alliance (1846) and the World's Student Christian Federation (1895) represented Protestant efforts that cut across denomination lines in an attempt to provide Christian service without the constraints of denominational creeds and doctrine. As the initiators and precursors of the movement first met, they helped to open the doors for interdenominational dialogue; and as they got to know one another, they realized they had much more in common with other Christians than they had supposed. Their goal was to "evangelize the world in their generation [and] this youthful spirit is

First published in *Journal of Hispanic/Latino Theology* 3 (November 1995): 6-13. Reprinted here with permission.

evidenced in the fact that the first great contributing organizations were student groups" (Marty 1986: 340). These groups became the centers of missionary fervor and the young men they attracted became the leaders of later missionary efforts.

Edinburgh became the setting for the great meeting of missions and the ecumenical movement began to take shape as the International Missionary Conference was formed. Participating churches "resisted any idea of a super church [yet] they preserved their distinctive character" (Marty 1986: 340) as they worked together in missions. The missionary field became a place for cooperative efforts as Protestant denominations moved around the globe in an effort to Christianize all nations.

Much, of course, has been accomplished, and much has changed in the ecumenical movement since 1910. Each ecumenical gathering—the Universal Christian Conference on Life and Order (Stockholm, 1925), the World Conference on Faith and Order (Lausanne, 1927), the Missionary Conference (Jerusalem, 1928), the Conference on Life and Work (Oxford, 1937), and the inauguration of the World Council of Churches (Amsterdam, 1947)—has led those involved to consider at different points in history the need for unity and the need to discern the many obstacles in the way of that unity.

Today's Protestant church sees ecumenism as a given, a reality for Christianity in the world, what historian Martin Marty calls the "fact of our era." For many Protestants in the United States the ecumenical movement has not fulfilled the vision of those leaders in the early organizations who saw evangelism as a task to be taken seriously. For other Protestants the ecumenical movement needs to be reexamined as today's pluralism poses yet another challenge in the search for Christian unity. Terms such as "evangelism" and "missions" need to be questioned as modern technology has shrunk our world so that meeting another culture and religion, or meeting Christians who speak a different language or relate to God in what would be considered a nontraditional Protestant manner, does not require one to cross an ocean or a mountain range, but simply to go across town or merely across the street.

Yet it is very interesting that while ecumenism is indeed a fact for most Protestant denominations, and the idea of missionary work overseas remains an area for valid funding and support, the work by these same denominations in the missions fields *within* the borders of the continental United States has become an area of denominational hesitancy, theological inconsistency, and economic neglect. Our postmodern world asks the Protestant churches (who pride themselves on their historical ecumenical spirit): Are not the multicultural, multiracial, and multiethnic inner cities of this country also valid areas for mission personnel and mission dollars? Are not the unchurched, literally, right next door? Why do we still insist on defining "missions work" as something done on another continent, in conjunction with other social issues (such as justice, economic opportunity, health, and education issues) yet neglect to raise the same relevant issues for those marginalized communities right here within our own borders?

PLURALISM AND ECUMENISM

Traditionally, the word "ecumenical" was used to understand the concept of "worldwide." It was used to talk of the church's councils and creeds that were accepted universally in contrast to those more local councils and decisions. In the late-nineteenth and early-twentieth centuries the word came to be used to describe an *ideal* for the Christian community. This ideal points to what the separated churches of Christendom have in common despite their divisions, as well as to their will to attain to the unity they ought to display (Vidler 1985: 257). "Worldwide," "ideal," "unity," "common ministries" are the concepts of ecumenism that are being challenged by the new millennium. They are challenged not because they are no longer valid, nor because they are theologically inaccurate, but because they have become so narrowly defined that they are exclusive.

We find that at the end of the twentieth century and at the dawn of a new millennium, the nineteenth-century ideal for unity and mission have become bureaucratic departments within most, if not all, oldline or mainstream denominations.[1] These departments are funded for work overseas with specific denominational guidelines and goals. This, of course, is not necessarily bad, but the reality remains that if this understanding of ministry in a pluralistic world becomes the only vehicle for ministries with people of other cultures and races, then something has been lost in application of the word ecumenical as indeed meaning "worldwide" as we reach the end of our century and as we face the reality of a diverse population. The problem has been that for Latinos becoming a part of Protestantism in the United States has meant assimilation into a religious culture that is in many ways alien to Latinos. The thinking is that one can have a different style of worship, sing different religious music, and celebrate non-Anglo events *outside* the U.S. borders. When *inside* the U.S. border Latinos sing translated hymns and not *coritos;* celebrate sweet sixteens and not *quinceañeras;* and use organ music and not guitars, congas, *güiros, panderetas, maracas.* If the style of worship in any Protestant Latino church does include these elements (and most do) it is then considered exotic, ethnic, loud, lacking reverence, and not very Protestant.[2]

---

1. The use of "mainstream or oldline" when talking about Protestantism in the United States is done to more clearly define those Protestant groups that are still considered the major denominations of the country: Methodists, Presbyterians, Baptists, Episcopalians, Disciples of Christ, Lutherans, etc. In this paper the emphasis is not upon theology—conservative or liberal—but on the presence of these denominational bodies throughout the history of the United States and their identification and contribution to the values of U.S. culture.

2. I have personally been involved as pastor in the development of two new Latino church starts, both of which were begun in a facility owned and shared by an older Anglo congregation. In both cases, in two different cities in Texas, members of these congregations complained about our music, the instruments we used, and some even said we were not "worshiping right." While this was not the feeling shared by all Anglos in these congregations, there was a sense that the Latino church start was indeed a different brand of Protestantism.

It seems that for many denominations the idea of being ecumenical has remained static, that is, it is something to be done overseas, "over there." In this static state the ecumenical ideal of worldwide is so narrowed that it does not and cannot consider embracing the pluralism and diversity of the people who today populate the United States "right here." The challenge that pluralism poses for today's denominations is the need to understand the interconnected nature of our global problems and what this means for our theological and ethical presuppositions.

The problems facing our global community do not remain overseas but are visible right here, along the Rio Grande border, in our inner cities, in the continued debate over "illegal" immigration. The cries for justice and peace are not just those heard in South Africa or Palestine or Bosnia—they were also the cries heard in the riot of Los Angeles in 1992 (Miles 1992)[3]; they are the cries of those victims of the drug trade; they are the cries of a nation that lives in fear and suspicion of the immigrant and has become accustomed to politicians who use the language of blaming the victim (the Other) to explain national concerns without having to take a proactive stance on behalf of peace and justice within the very borders of the United States.

The fact of the matter is that today's plurality of race, culture, and language makes many mainline denominations uncomfortable. Gone are the days of the racially homogenous communities. Despite the fact that many denominations in the early twentieth century focused their energies and resources in the developing cities of the United States, with such leaders of urban evangelism as Dwight Moody, B. Fay Mills, and Sam Jones, the immigrants pouring into the cities were for the most part European. Immigration figures show that 90.4 percent of legal U.S. immigration for the years 1820-1900 was from Europe, and that the bulk of these immigrants came from Germany, Ireland, and England (*1991 U.S. Hispanic Market* 1991: 34). Today the patterns of immigration tell a different story.

Demographics tell us that as recently as 1981-1989, 34.7 percent of legal immigrants to the United States were from Central/Latin America, and 42.8 percent were from Asia (ibid.: 36). Projections say that by the year 2020 the number of U.S. residents who are Hispanic or nonwhite will have more than doubled, to nearly 115 million, while the white population will not be increasing at all (Herrera 1992). Most of this population growth for Latinos is occurring in the following five metropolitan areas: Los Angeles (5 million Latinos), New York (2.9 million), Miami (1.1 million), San Antonio (998,000), and San Francisco (986,000) (*1991 U.S. Hispanic Market* 1991: 172-378).[4]

---

3. For an excellent article on the economic issues that were at the root of the riot in Los Angeles see Iack Miles, "Blacks vs. Browns, the Struggle for the Bottom Rung," *The Atlantic Monthly* (October 1992).

4. These figures, from 1991, are already dated given the continuous migration to the

Yet the fact that oldline denominations have been slow in accepting this irreversible population growth seems to be historically consistent. For example, it called the "second disestablishment." William McKinney, professor of religion and society, explains it this way:

> In the early days what we now call the oldline churches were dominant. To use a baseball metaphor, they were the only teams on the field. With disestablishment in the early nineteenth century, the oldline groups were forced to admit other teams, but they still owned the stadium. They gave up their established status, but retained their cultural and economic power. (1989: 1)

But times are changing. Euro-American Protestantism is no longer at the center of religious life in the United States. The issue goes beyond advocating restoration, and it is not enough for denominations to dwell on their former greatness. Today's mainstream denominations are caught up in a "religious and cultural realignment" (Roof and McKinney 1988: 237). McKinney says,

> The real issue is how we will deal with fundamental change in the relationship between oldline churches and mainstream culture. . . . The issue is whether we are not now able, perhaps for the first time in [North] American history, to shape a relationship to [North] American culture based not on our being here first, or on what the culture expects of us, but on a biblically oriented vision of the church's role in the world. . . . The oldline churches have no hope of reaching out to the new populations of [North] America . . . if they remain bound to the notion that it is possible or desirable to restore our churches to their earlier position of dominance. (1989: 3)

Protestant denominations in the United States will find that in this realignment the ideal of ecumenism, as an open and welcoming worldwide encounter of people at God's feast, can become a useful paradigm for Christian ministry for the coming millennium right here within U.S. borders. But before this can take place certain internal changes must occur. It is only when the notions of imperialism, superiority, and chosenness (which are tied into racial ideology) are finally removed from oldline denominations that a liberating ecumenical church can become flesh in our country.

United States from Mexico, Central and South America, as well as the Caribbean. For a more exhaustive analysis of the top fifty U.S. Latino markets/cities., see *1991 U.S. Hispanic Market*, Strategy Research Corporation (1991) 172-378.

A CHALLENGE TO THE PROTESTANT HEARTLAND

The realignment or disestablishment that today's Protestant churches face can be understood as a challenge to rethink how appropriate are the methods and the strategies used to reach and to minister to our multiracial communities around the country. The rigidity and high regard with which we hold our denominational history and guidelines, budget priorities, ordination requirements, and bureaucratic machinery point to what has been called an "institutional fundamentalism." This type of mentality can make most mainstream denominations off-limits to a large segment of the population. For example, most denominations can be a nonwelcoming place for pastors who cannot complete a graduate seminary degree program; for churches in poor communities that cannot be self-supporting or contribute their "share" to the denomination's pot; for those leaders whose dominant language is not English and have to deal with church structure; for those who are illiterate and find themselves surrounded by a worship environment predicated on the written word (hymnals, worship bulletins, Sunday School material). The call is for Protestant mainstream denominations to accept the new realities of our culture and to understand that North American society requires new institutions that have moved beyond a 1950s establishment mentality that assumes cultural supremacy. And even beyond this, the call is for Protestantism in the United States to open its eyes to the global reality that knocks on our national door.

Some of the questions that need to be asked require a reexamination of the theological and ethical implications for the churches in the United States. These are necessarily difficult questions because they challenge the assumption about our church life that "come not from the New Testament but from periods of [North] American life in which the [Protestant church] enjoyed a certain cultural hegemony" (McKinney 1989: 4). We need to ask what it means for the church in the United States when:

- 95 percent of the twofold increase in the world's population expected before the middle of the next century will occur in poor countries?
- the population of the United States is expected to rise by 29 percent by 2025, while its southern neighbors Mexico and Guatemala may grow 63 percent and 135 percent respectively (Connelly and Kennedy 1994: 76)?
- *maquiladora* workers along the Mexico/U.S. border make 38 cents an hour working for U.S.-owned companies?[5]
- in the Rio Grande Valley of Texas the percentages of persons and families in poverty are almost triple that of all Texas families and persons ("Poorest of the Americans" 1991: 2)?

---

5. On a class trip to the Rio Grande Valley made with a group of seminary students, March 12-15, 1995, this was the hourly pay we calculated from a Reynosa *maquiladora* worker's pay stub.

- there are at least 600 gangs with an estimated 100,000 gang members operating in Los Angeles county (Harris 1994: 289)?

These statistics point to what is happening here in the heartland, within our national borders. In light of these figures and the reality they denounce it is all the more urgent for Protestant mainstream churches to see their role not as one of establishment but instead one of disestablishment, off center, in the margins, outside the gate.

Theologian Douglas John Hall puts it this way:

Christianity was born in the situation of disestablishment. It would be hard to conjure up anything less "established" than the cross and the community that formed around it. Whenever Christianity has become part of the established order, it has exhibited at least a certain hypocrisy in relation to its own roots. Usually what it has demonstrated . . . has been nothing less than a betrayal of Christ himself, who keeps turning up on the side of the disestablished and disposed. (Hall 1975: 141)

ECUMENISM IN THE BARRIO

Through this [twentieth] century the Protestant oldline or mainstream denominations have participated in a great ecumenical effort that has sought relief for victims of war, famine, disease, and has investigated human rights violations and denounced dictatorships. Beyond U.S. borders these same denominations have sought to participate as one of many Christian advocates that have sought to be worldwide in their ministry: worldwide in a ministry to Third World countries working with a conviction that God does not call the church to be neutral in regard to human misery. The historical record can prove as much. And despite the many obstacles to Christian unity and the many critics of ecumenical efforts, the ecumenical ministries of overseas departments have not shut their doors.

But despite the gains and successes of the ecumenical witness of mainstream denominations away from home, this same ecumenical witness has failed to embrace that Third World which lives right within its borders. There is a Third World nation within the United States whose history is not European and whose tradition is not that of the "fathers" of this country. This is a Third World nation of refugees from poor countries and dictatorial governments, of victims of wars in which the United States has played an active role; these people are the pilgrims of today whose roots lie in Latin America, Central America, the Caribbean, Africa, Asia, and the Middle East.

These pilgrims present a challenge to the churches of this country who live on the brink of a new millennium. They challenge the church in the United States to be ecumenical in the barrio, to be worldwide in their embrace of the poor and marginalized who live not across the ocean but across the street. The challenge is not one of defiance but one of great opportunity for the pursuance of a Christian unity that in word and deed will include "all the inhabited earth." To be ecumenical in the barrio is to confess that the veneer of Euro-American Protestantism is not required for entry to God's feast, that the declaration of someone's "illegality" is a human expression of fear. To be ecumenical in the barrio is to proclaim that God inhabits all the world and loves all its people. To be ecumenical in the barrio is to dare say that it is in keeping with God's plan that the church be disestablished so that it can become that authentic expression of God's redemption, of God's diversity, of God's inclusiveness—not at the center of power, not in a position of dominance, but in the margins, outside the gate, where Jesus came to serve, to redeem, and to empower.

Part VII

GLOBAL TRENDS

14

A New Christianity, but What Kind?

Peter C. Phan

Peter C. Phan, a native of Vietnam, emigrated as a refugee to the United States in 1975. He began his teaching career in philosophy at the age of eighteen at Don Bosco College, Hong Kong. He has taught at the University of Dallas, Texas; at the Catholic University of America, Washington, DC, where he held the Warren-Blanding Chair of Religion and Culture; at Union Theological Seminary, NY; at Elms College, Chicopee, MA; at St. Norbert College, De Pere, WI, and at Georgetown University, Washington, DC, where he is currently holding the Ignacio Ellacuría Chair of Catholic Social Thought. Also on the faculty of the East Asian Pastoral Institute, Manila, and Liverpool Hope University, England, he is the first non-Anglo to be elected President of Catholic Theological Society of America. His many writings have been translated into Italian, German, French, Spanish, Polish, Chinese, Japanese, and Vietnamese. One such writing is *In Our Own Tongues: Perspectives from Asia on Mission and Inculturation* (Maryknoll, NY: Orbis Books, 2004).

INTRODUCTION

The words "A New Christianity" in the title of my essay are deliberate. They mimic the title of Philip Jenkins's essay "The Next Christianity" in the *Atlantic Monthly* (2002b) but intentionally eschew the words "The Next Christendom" in the title of his earlier book (2002a). The difference between "A New Christianity" and "The Next Christendom" is not just semantics, a distinction without a difference, but, as I hope to show, the choice of the former expression bespeaks a fundamentally different interpretation of the face of Christianity of the next fifty years. I begin with brief historical reflections on the concept of Christendom, then present Jenkins's basic theses on Southern Christianity as a "new Christendom" and a "new Counter-Reformation," and finally offer an alternative interpretation of Southern Christianity on the basis of Asian Christianity.

First published in *Mission Studies* 22, no. 1 (2005): 59-83. Permission bought from, and full credit given to, Koninklijke Brill.

"CHRISTENDOM" VS "CHRISTIANITY"

Even though Christendom, etymologically, can mean simply "Christians collectively" or "the Christian world" or "Christianity,"[1]—and this might well be the connotations intended by the title of Jenkins's book—nevertheless, historically and culturally, it is a heavily freighted term. It refers to the model of Christianity that has its distant roots in Augustine and was brought about by a series of medieval popes—most notable among whom are Gregory I or the Great, Gregory VII, and Innocent III—whose claim of supreme power over the church and the empire, greatly buttressed by forged documents (e.g., the "Donation of Constantine"), produced a kind of Christianity that is papal, Roman, legalistic, political, and military, in short, Christendom.

As is well known, by 1050, almost all of Western Europe was formally Christian. By then not only the older kingdoms had long been Christian but the rulers of newer ones such as Norway, Denmark, Poland, Hungary, and Russia had also accepted baptism and established ecclesiastical hierarchies in their lands. This Christian dominance would allow the church in the next two centuries to attempt a program of Christianization of society and culture, that is, to apply the principles of the gospel and of canon law to secular life.

Pope Gregory VII (1073-85) played a prominent role in this formation of Christendom, and his manifold activities are known under the sobriquet of "the Gregorian reform." With his famous twenty-seven *Dictatus Papae*, Gregory attempted to found a Christian world in which the pope would exercise the *plenitudo potestatis* [fullness of power], in virtue of which he would be the supreme authority in the church as well as the supreme lord of the world. The pope alone, it was asserted, may, among other things, have the title of universal bishop, depose or reinstate bishops, wear imperial insignia, depose emperors. It was also claimed that all rulers have to kiss the pope's feet, that the Roman Church has never erred and will never err, that he can release subjects from their oath of loyalty to evildoers, and that no one who is not in accord with the Roman Church may be regarded as a Catholic (for a full list of these *dictatus papae*, see Küng 1995: 383-84).

This formation of Christendom was facilitated by the social changes caused by the demographic expansion in the countryside, the growth of urban centers, the institution of cathedral schools and universities, the foundation of new monasteries, the increase in international trade and the circulation of money, and the shift of church authority from East to West. The sense of a unified Christendom and of a common cultural and religious identity as "Westerners" or "Christians" was later fortified by the crusades, which united several western Mediterranean kingdoms together in military campaigns against Islam. Indeed, it was after the First Crusade (1095-1100) that the word *Christianitas* came into common use to refer to

---

1. *The American Heritage Dictionary,* 2nd College ed. (Boston, MA: Houghton Mifflin, 1985).

both Christianity and Christendom (on the building of Christendom, see McManners 1990: 199-232; Bredero 1994; Brown and Le Goff 1997).

This building of Christendom, which Hans Küng calls the "mediaeval Roman Catholic paradigm" (1995: 379), reached its climax at the end of the twelfth century with Pope Innocent III (1198-1216). It was under Innocent that Christendom was given an ecclesiastical, legal, political, and even military form. The pope now claimed to be the *vicarius Christi* [the vicar of Christ] and not simply "Peter's representative" (his successor, Innocent IV, outdid him by titling himself the *vicarius Dei*—the vicar of God!), and the Roman Church was declared the *mater omnium Christifidelium* [the mother of all Christian faithful]. Legally, thanks to the development of canon law by Gratian, the pope could assert his position as the highest ruler, absolute lawgiver, and supreme judge of the church. Politically, the pope claimed to have the right to intervene in secular affairs by reason of sin (*sub ratione peccati*) since as sinful men emperors and kings are subjected to the pope. Militarily, to strengthen their power, the popes of Christendom such as Gregory VIII, Urban II, and Innocent III did not hesitate to recruit armies and called for crusades and encouraged them with the granting of indulgences to crusaders and the status of martyr in the event of death.

But the Christendom that Gregory VIII and Innocent III built did not last long. Indeed, their successor, Boniface VIII (pope 1294-1303), continued with dogged determination their tradition of the absolute power of the papacy but tragically failed to understand that the foundations of Christendom were crumbling under his feet when he threatened Philip the Fair of France with excommunication. His pretension to papal supremacy over princes and kingdoms and to absolute jurisdiction over every human creature in his famous bull *Unam Sanctam* (1302) sounded pathetically hollow. Boniface was made a prisoner at Agnani by the French troops, and though released by the Italian troops after three days, he died in Rome a month later, a pitifully impotent man.

The idea of Christendom did not, of course, die with Boniface VIII. It surfaced again and again in the Roman Catholic Church. In the late fifteenth century, with the so-called discovery of the "New World," it appeared under the guise of worldwide evangelization; in the second half of the sixteenth century, following the Council of Trent (1545-1563), it took the form of the so-called anti-Protestant Counter-Reformation or Catholic Reformation; in the second half of the nineteenth century, after the French Revolution and the revolutions of 1830 and 1848, it emerged with an explicitly restorationist social and political agenda; in the first part of the twentieth century, following the pontificate of Pius IX (pope 1846-78) and the First Vatican Council (1869-70), it appeared in a wholesale condemnation of modernity, especially the doctrine of separation of church and state (e.g., Pius IX's 1864 *Syllabus errorum modernorum*), and in the fortification of papal power through the definition of papal primacy and infallibility. In the post-Vatican II era, there has been a systematic and sustained effort on the part of the Roman Curia to roll back what it considers the excesses of

Vatican II's reform and to reestablish its control over the whole church, though this time, of course, without pretension to power over political authorities.

In sum, Christendom is the politico-religious order—a sort of caesaropapism in reverse—promoted by medieval popes who championed a world in which Christian teachings and church law would imbue every aspect of human life, and in which they would exercise an absolute and supreme power over every human being, including political rulers. It was brought to an end by what Thomas Carlyle calls the three elements of modern civilization, namely, gunpowder, printing, and the Protestant Reformation. However, more important than cultural factors, the chief contributor to the demise of Christendom is, I submit, theological, namely, the gradual realization that Christendom is not Christianity and has nothing to do with Jesus and his gospel.

"A NEW CHRISTIANITY": A "NEW CHRISTENDOM" AND A "NEW COUNTER-REFORMATION"?

Anyone even slightly familiar with recent missiological literature would be alert to the current demographic shift of the general population as well as of Christian membership from the North to the South, that is, from Europe and North America to Africa, Asia, and Latin America, though Jenkins righty laments that this fact is still unknown to or at least not taken into serious account by the wider public and church policy makers in the North. His book *The Next Christendom* (2002a) is an informative *tour d'horizon* of contemporary global Christianity. Chock-full of statistics, it hammers home the fact that "over the last century . . . the center of gravity in the Christian world has shifted inexorably, toward Africa, Asia, and Latin America" (2002a: 2) and that, if his predictions prove correct, "by 2050, only about one-fifth of the world's 3 billion Christians will be non-Hispanic whites" (2002a: 3).

Of course, statistics and projections, especially in matters of religious membership and beliefs, are notoriously unreliable, as Jenkins himself has acknowledged (2002a: 85-89). Even so, from the major trends in the development of Southern Christianity, one may confidently predict that it will enjoy a "surging growth" (2002a: 89) in the next fifty years. But the most difficult task is not gathering numbers but what to make of them, since there is a very thin line between, to use Jenkins's expression, "damned lies and statistics" (2002a: 85). But before coming to the interpretation of data, it would be helpful to give a summary of the basic features of Southern Christianity as Jenkins sees it.

1. Economically and socially, "the great majority of Southern Christians (and increasingly, of all Christians) really are the poor, the hungry, the persecuted, even the dehumanized" (2002a: 216).

2. Politically, because of their geographical concentration, Southern Christians are liable to come into conflict with the followers of other religions, in particular Islam and Hinduism (2002a: 168-85), especially if certain countries declare Christianity, or Islam, or Hinduism the state religion.

3. Biblically, Southern Christians favor a literalist reading of the Scriptures and make abundant use of prophetic and apocalyptic books of both the Old and New Testaments (2002a: 217-20).

4. Theologically, Southern Christians, whether Catholic, Protestant, or Evangelical, are "far more conservative in terms of both beliefs and moral teaching. The denominations that are triumphing across the global South are stalwartly traditional or even reactionary by the standards of the economically advanced nations" (2002a: 7).

5. Religiously, Southern Christians are "traditional, orthodox, and supernatural" (2002a: 8). They favor prophecy, faith-healing, exorcism, and dream-visions (2002a: 8).

6. Devotionally, Southern Christianity (particularly Roman Catholicism) promotes the cult of the saints, especially of Mary, processions, pilgrimages, and other practices of popular religion (2002a: 117-19).

To paint a sharper image of Southern Christianity, Jenkins contrasts it with Northern Christianity which is, in his account, progressive in theology (e.g., advocating married clergy and the ordination of women), liberal in morality (e.g., accepting divorce, contraception, abortion, homosexuality), dismissive of such biblical practices as faith-healing and exorcism, and discrediting popular devotions. Indeed, the difference between Northern and Southern Christianity is such that, Jenkins warns, "if . . . Church officials in North America or Europe proclaimed a moral stance more in keeping with progressive secular values, they would be divided from the growing Catholic churches of the South by a de facto schism, if not a formal breach" (2002b).

There can no gainsaying the fact that both the general world population and the Christian population have been shifting toward the Southern Hemisphere and will continue to do so at a significant rate in the next fifty years, and that this demographic shift presents enormous challenges as well as opportunities for Christianity. What is controversial about Jenkins's reading of this "New Christianity" is his use of the historical realities of Christendom and Counter-Reformation as interpretative tropes to understand the nature of Southern Christianity.

As far as Christendom is concerned, Jenkins suggests that "today across the global South a rising religious fervor is coinciding with declining autonomy for nation-states, making useful an analogy with the medieval concept of Christendom—the *Res Publica Christiana*—as an overarching source of unity and a focus of loyalty transcending mere kingdoms and empires. . . . Christendom was a primary cultural reference, and it may well re-emerge as such in the Christian South—as a new transnational order in which political, social, and personal identities are defined chiefly by religious loyalties" ("The New Christendom"). In this account, a new sociopolitical regime, similar to the Christendom envisaged by popes from the sixth to the sixteenth century, would emerge when (not if!) Christians in Africa and South America begin to form alliances with each other: "Once that axis is established, we really would be speaking of a new Christendom, based on the Southern Hemisphere" (Jenkins 2002a: 12). Jenkins even asks us to contemplate the horrifying but not unlikely scenario in which this new Christendom comes into conflict with the Muslim world, bringing about "a new age of Christian crusades and Muslim jihads" but now with "nuclear warheads and anthrax" (2002a: 13).

With regard to the Counter-Reformation analogy, Jenkins argues that the next demographic explosion of Christianity in the Southern Hemisphere recalls that of the post-Tridentine or Counter-Reformation period in which Catholic missionaries, with the help of Spain, Portugal, and France, created a transoceanic church structure in Africa, Asia, and North and South America. Due to the current population shift to the Southern Hemisphere, notes Jenkins, "the likely map of twenty-first-century Catholicism represents an unmistakable legacy of the Counter-Reformation and its global missionary ventures" (2002b). Furthermore, given its more conservative theology and morality as well as its promotion of devotional practices, says Jenkins, "the Catholic faith that is rising rapidly in Africa and Asia looks very much like a pre-Vatican II faith, being more traditional in its respect for the power of bishops and priests and in its preference for older devotions" (2002b). Again, Jenkins asks Catholics to savor the bitter irony that the next ecumenical council, which Northern liberals have been calling for to complete John XXIII's revolution, may very well turn out to be not one "that would usher in a new age of ecclesiastical democracy and lay empowerment," not "a new Reformation but a new Counter-Reformation" (2002b).

WHITHER ASIAN CHRISTIANITY?

Readers of *The Next Christendom* are reassured to learn that for Jenkins, "in the case of the southward movement of Christianity, we can be quite sure that the event will occur, but interpreting it or preparing for it is quite a different matter" (2002a: 211). Earlier Jenkins has also noted that "time and again, when European and American Christians look South, they see what they want to see" (2002a: 209). The question then is whether the historical analogies of Christendom and Counter-Reformation are the most illuminating tropes to understand Southern Christianity or whether they lead to the pitfall of, in Jenkins's words, seeing what one wants to see. In other words, the question is whether there is not some other, more plausible and fruitful way of understanding Southern Christianity and its relationship to Northern Christianity.

To begin with, those who disagree with Jenkins's prognosis of the future of Christianity in the first half of the twenty-first century may want to contest his very diagnosis of Southern Christianity which I have summarized above. It may be pointed out that for each of the six features Jenkins notes in Southern Christianity, it is not difficult to cite numerous credible counter-examples, and I will do so when I discuss Asian Christianity. Suffice here one colorful example: for every Moses Tay, the Singapore-based Anglican archbishop of Southeast Asia, who tried to exorcise Canada's totem poles, there are hundreds if not thousands of Catholic bishops who would see in them, to use the language of Vatican II's Dogmatic Constitution on the Church (*Lumen Gentium*), attempts, albeit possibly contaminated by sin, of "those who in shadows and images seek the unknown God, since God gives to all life and breath and all things (see Acts 17:25-28) and since the Savior wills all to be saved (1 Tim 2:4)" (no. 16). These bishops would recall Vatican II's affirmation that "the Catholic Church rejects nothing of what is true and holy in these [non-Christian] religions. With sincere respect the church looks on those ways of conduct and life, those precepts and teachings which, though differing on many points from what it itself holds and teaches, yet not rarely reflect a ray of the Truth which enlightens all" (*Nostra Aetate*, 2).

Furthermore, it may be argued that all of the six features that Jenkins attributes to Southern Christianity are found—and abundantly—in Northern Christianity as well. Again, to give just a few examples: Literalist interpretation of the Bible enjoys widespread popularity in North America. Appeals to Daniel and Revelation and other prophetic and apocalyptic books are plentiful among televangelists and their armies of followers. Healing, ecstatic utterances, visions, and exorcisms are frequent even among North American white charismatic Catholics. Pilgrimages, the cult of Mary and the saints, processions, and other forms of popular devotion are alive and well even in the heart of Europe, and any doubt about this will be quickly dispelled by a trip to the numerous Marian shrines and holy places in France, Ireland, Poland, Portugal, Italy, Spain, and Bosnia-Herzegovina.

Rather than offering a full evaluation of Jenkins's characterization of the whole of Southern Christianity, here I will focus only on Asian Christianity, and more narrowly, Asian Catholicism, partly because it is less well known than Latin American and African Christianity, and partly because a recent but highly significant event—the Asian Synod—offers a concentrated look at what has been going on in Asian Catholic Christianity and is intended to be a blueprint for the Catholic Church's future in Asia in the twenty-first century. The picture that emerges is quite different from Jenkins's portraiture of Southern Christianity.[2]

---

2. An excellent resource on the Catholic Church is Bryan T. Froehle and Mary L. Gauthier, *Global Catholicism: Portrait of a World Church* (Maryknoll, NY: Orbis Books, 2003). On Asian Catholicism, see pp. 85-99. All the statistics are taken from this book.

Asian Catholicism

By Asia is meant here the land containing the regions referred to as Western Asia (i.e., 25 nations of the Middle East and Central Asia), South Asia (7 nations), Southeast Asia (11 nations), and Northeast Asia (7 nations)—comprising a total of 50 countries. Though covering only 30 percent of the world's land mass, Asia is the home of 60 percent of the world's population in 2000, that is, about 3.7 billion people. This number represents a tremendous rate of growth: from 1950 to 2000, the Asian population grew 104 percent.

The Vatican's latest *Annuario Pontificio*, published at the end of 2002, reports more than 1.07 billion Catholics worldwide, an increase of 11 million over the previous year (17.2 percent of the world population of 6.2 billion). Of the world Catholic population, 10.3 percent live in Asia, that is, about 107 million, about 28 percent of the total number of Asian Christians (313 million). This Catholic population, however, represents only 3 percent of the Asian population. Seven in ten Asian Catholics live in Southeast Asia, and most of them are in the Philippines and East Timor. In terms of the Catholic population by regions, only 0.40 percent of Asian Catholics live in Northeast Asia, 1 percent in South Asia, 15 percent in Southeast Asia, and 1 percent in Western Asia, which incidentally is the cradle of Christianity.

Beyond numbers, what is the nature of Asian Catholicism and whither is it going? Perhaps the two best sources from which to paint an accurate portrait of the Asian Catholic Church and to project its future are the documents of the Federation of Asian Bishops' Conferences (FABC) and the Asian Synod (for a popular and helpful presentation of Asian Catholicism, see Fox 2000).

The FABC was founded in 1970, on the occasion of Pope Paul VI's visit to Manila, Philippines. Its statutes, approved by the Holy See *ad experimentum* in 1972, were amended several times and were also approved again each time by the Holy See. The FABC is a voluntary association of episcopal conferences in South, Southeast, East, and Central Asia whose purpose is to foster solidarity and co-responsibility for the welfare of the church and society in Asia. Its decisions are without juridical binding force; their acceptance is an expression of collegial responsibility. Structurally, the supreme body of the FABC is the plenary assembly, which meets in ordinary session every four years. So far there have been eight plenary assemblies (the latest being in 2004), at the end of which a final statement is issued. These statements constitute the FABC's official theological and pastoral orientations. Besides the plenary assembly, there are also Regional Assemblies to take into account the special needs of each geographical region. The FABC is governed by a central committee, the standing committee, the central secretariat, and its offices and commissions.[3] Currently there are

---

3. A copy of the "Statutes of the Federation of Asian Bishops' Conferences (FABC)" is available at FABC Central Secretariat, 16 Caine Road, Hong Kong.

nine offices dealing with various facets of church activities. From time to time these offices organize conferences and issue documents which, though not enjoying the authority of the final statements, do indicate the theological orientation of the FABC.[4]

The second source is the Special Assembly of the Synod of Bishops for Asia, the Asian Synod for short, and Pope John Paul II's apostolic exhortation *Ecclesia in Asia*. Convened by Pope John Paul II as part of the celebration of the Jubilee Year 2000, the Asian Synod met in Rome from April 19 to May 13, 1998. The theme chosen by the pope for it was "Jesus Christ the Savior and His Mission of Love and Service in Asia: 'That They May Have Life, and Have It Abundantly' (John 10: 10)."

In preparation for the synod, the general secretariat of the Synod of Bishops sent out to all the bishops of Asia an outline of the themes to be discussed called the *Lineamenta*, and solicited their comments and suggestions. On the basis of these, the secretariat prepared an *Instrumentum laboris* presenting the issues to be discussed by the synod. This working document was later summarized in a text called the *Relatio ante disceptationem*. The synod began with 191 eight-minute "interventions" by synod participants. A summary of these interventions, called the *Relatio post disceptationem*, together with a list of questions, was used as the basis for group discussions. At the end of these discussions, fifty-nine "propositions," expressing the consensus of the synod participants, were compiled and voted upon. They were then submitted to the pope for his use in writing the postsynodal Apostolic Exhortation. On November 6, 1999, John Paul II promulgated *Ecclesia in Asia* in New Delhi, India, in which the pope said he wished "to share with the church in Asia and throughout the world the fruits of the special assembly" (*Ecclesia in Asia,* no. 4; see Phan 2002).

A Kingdom-Centered Church

In terms of theology, the fifty-nine "propositions" of the Asian Synod did not introduce anything novel, beyond what has been said again and again by the various plenary assemblies and documents of the FABC. What was new is not what the Asian bishops said but *that* they said it and *how* and *where* they said it. In front of the pope and the Roman Curia, with surprising boldness and candor, humbly but forcefully, the Asian bishops affirmed that the churches of Asia not only learn from but also have something to teach

---

4. For the documents of the FABC and its various institutes, see Gaudencio Rosales and C. G. Arévalo, eds., *For All the Peoples of Asia: Federation of Asian Bishops' Conferences. Documents from 1970 to 1991* (Maryknoll, NY: Orbis Books; Quezon City: Claretian Publications, 1992); Franz-Josef Eilers, ed., *For All the Peoples of Asia: Federation of Asian Bishops' Conferences. Documents from 1992 to 1996* (Quezon City: Claretian Publications, 1997); and Franz-Josef Eilers, ed., *For All the Peoples of Asia: Federation of Asian Bishops' Conferences. Documents from 1997 to 2001* (Quezon City: Claretian Publications, 2002). These works are cited as *For All Peoples,* followed by their year of publication and pages.

the Church of Rome as well as the universal church, precisely from their experiences as churches not simply in but of Asia. What was being proposed is not a new doctrine but a new way of being church.

In what does this new way of being church in Asia consist? To put it succinctly, it consists in making the kingdom of God and not the church the center of the church's life and activities, and to promote the kingdom of God through dialogue. There are two operative words here: kingdom of God and dialogue. First, the Asian Catholic Church espouses a kingdom-centered ecclesiology in which no longer is the church considered the pinnacle or the center of the Christian life. Rather it is moved from the center to the periphery and from the top to the bottom. Like the sun around which the earth and the other planets move, the reign of God is the center around which everything in the church revolves and to which everything is subordinated. In the place of the church, the reign of God is now installed as the ultimate goal of all the activities within and without the church. Now both what the church is and what it does are defined by the reign of God and not the other way round. The only reason for the church to exist is to serve the reign of God, that is, to help bring about what have been commonly referred to as the "kingdom values." It is these values that the church must promote and not its self-aggrandizement or reputation or institutional survival. Every law and policy of the church must pass the litmus test of whether they promote the reign of God. In the church, the supreme law is the "salvation of souls" (*salus animarum, suprema lex*).

The point of all this is by no means to devalue the role of the church but to determine it correctly with regard to the kingdom of God. Needless to say, there is an intrinsic connection between the reign of God and the church, as is well expressed by Pope John Paul II in his apostolic exhortation *Ecclesia in Asia,* promulgated after the Asian Synod:

> Empowered by the Spirit to accomplish Christ's salvation on earth, the Church is the seed of the Kingdom of God and she looks eagerly for its final coming. Her identity and mission are inseparable from the Kingdom of God which Jesus announced and inaugurated in all that he said and did, above all in his death and resurrection. The Spirit reminds the Church that she is not an end unto herself: in all that she is and all that she does, she exists to serve Christ and the salvation of the world. (*Ecclesia in Asia,* no. 17)

Clearly, the church is not identical with the kingdom of God, nor is the kingdom of God confined to the church. The church is only, as Vatican II puts it, "the seed and the beginning of that kingdom" (*Lumen Gentium,* no. 5). Its constitution is defined by the kingdom of God, which acts as its goal and future, and not the other way round. The church is not an end unto itself; its raison d'être is to serve the kingdom of God. It is a means to an end. When this relationship is reversed, with the church turned into the goal of one's ministry, the possibility of moral corruption, especially by means of power, is enormous. Worse, one is tempted to protect one's personal advantages and interests under the pretext of defending the church! The roots of Christendom, I submit, are sunk deep in this church-centered ecclesiology. And in rejecting ecclesiocentric ecclesiology and in espousing a regnocentric ecclesiology, the Asian Catholic Church removes the very humus in which Christendom can grow.

An ecclesiology that is kingdom-centered must then seek and promote the "kingdom values." But what are these? Or, more concisely, what does the kingdom of God stand for? Despite Jesus' frequent use of the symbol of the reign of God, he did not give it a clear definition. What is meant by the reign of God and the values that it proclaims are implicit in Jesus' parables, miracles, and above all in his death and resurrection. After all, the kingdom of God has come in and with Jesus who himself is the *auto-basileia*. In a nutshell, the reign of God is nothing less than God's saving presence in Jesus by the power of the Holy Spirit, a presence that brings about gratuitous forgiveness and reconciliation and restores universal justice and peace between God and humanity, among humans themselves, and between humanity and the cosmos. These gifts of forgiveness and reconciliation, of justice and peace are extended to all without any distinction but preferentially to the poor, that is, to those who lack the minimum conditions required for a decent human life, whose dignity and rights have been denied, who have been oppressed and abused in any way by authorities, secular and religious. The church, which is a community of those who have accepted the gospel of the kingdom of God in faith, in whose life the kingdom has taken visible form, who are the light of the world and the salt of the earth, must dedicate itself to these values, to this preferential "option for the poor," and not to its membership expansion, its institutional prosperity, its survival, its good reputation, or what has been euphemistically called "church growth."

A Church as a Local Community of Equal Disciples

To be a kingdom-centered church, that is, an efficacious sign of the reign of God anywhere, the church must be a truly local church built on communion and equality everywhere. And to achieve this goal, the church, according to the FABC, must be characterized by the following features.

1. First, the church, both at the local and universal levels, is seen primarily as "a *communion of communities,* where laity, Religious and clergy recognize and accept each other as sisters and brothers" (Eilers 1997: 287). At the heart of the mystery of the church is the bond of communion uniting God with humanity and humans with one another, of which the Eucharist is the sign and instrument par excellence.

2. Moreover, in this ecclesiology there is an explicit and effective recognition of the *fundamental equality* among all the members of the

local church as disciples of Jesus and among all the local churches insofar as they are communities of Jesus' disciples and whose communion constitutes the universal church. The communion (*koinonia*) which constitutes the church, both at the local and universal levels, and from which flows the fundamental equality of all Christians, is rooted at its deepest level in the life of the Trinity in whom there is a perfect communion of equals. This fundamental equality among all Christians, which is affirmed by Vatican II,[5] annuls neither the existence of the hierarchy in the church nor the papal primacy. Rather it indicates the modality in which papal primacy and hierarchical authority should be exercised in the church, that is, in collegiality, co-responsibility, and accountability to all the members of the church. Unless this fundamental equality of all Christians with its implications for church governance is acknowledged and put into practice through concrete policies and actions, the church will not become a communion of communities. This vision of church as communion of communities and its corollary of fundamental equality are the sine qua non condition for the fulfillment of the church's mission. Without being a communion, the church cannot fulfill its mission, since the Church is nothing more than the bond of communion between God and humanity and among humans themselves. As *Ecclesia in Asia* puts it tersely, "communion and mission go hand in hand" (*Ecclesia in Asia*, no. 24; see Phan 2002).

3. This pastoral "discipleship of equals" leads to the third characteristic of the new way of being church in Asia, that is, the participatory and collaborative nature of all the ministries in the Church: "It is a *participatory* Church where the gifts that the Holy Spirit gives to all the faithful—lay, Religious, and cleric alike—are recognized and activated, so that the Church may be built up and its mission realized" (Eilers 1997: 287).[6] This participatory nature of the church must be lived out not only in the local church but also among all the local churches, including the Church of Rome, of course, with due recognition of the papal primacy. In this context it is encouraging to read in *Ecclesia in Asia* the following affirmation: "It is in fact within the perspective of ecclesial communion that the universal authority

---

5. See *Lumen Gentium*, no. 32: "All the faithful enjoy a true equality with regard to the dignity and the activity which they share in the building up of the body of Christ."

6. See also ibid., 56: "It [the church] is a community of authentic *participation and co-responsibility*, where genuine sharing of gifts and responsibilities obtains, where the talents and charisms of each one are accepted and exercised in diverse ministries, and where all are schooled to the attitudes and practices of mutual listening and dialogue, common discernment of the Spirit, common witness and collaborative action." The Exhortation also recognizes this participatory character of the church but emphasizes the fact that each person must live his or her "proper vocation" and perform his or her "proper role" (*Ecclesia in Asia*, 25). There is here a concern to maintain a clear distinction of roles in ministry, whereas the FABC is concerned that all people with their varied gifts have the opportunity to participate in the ministry of the church.

of the successor of Peter shines forth more clearly, not primarily as juridical power over the local churches, but above all as a pastoral primacy at the service of the unity of faith and life of the whole people of God" (*Ecclesia in Asia*, no. 25). A "pastoral primacy" must do everything possible to foster co-responsibility and participation of all the local churches in the triple ministry of teaching, sanctification, and service in the church and must be held accountable to this task so that these words do not remain at the level of pious rhetoric but are productive of concrete structures and actions.

4. The fourth feature of the new way of being church in Asia is *prophecy*: The church is "a leaven of transformation in this world and serves as a *prophetic sign* daring to point beyond this world to the ineffable Kingdom that is yet fully to come" (Eilers 1997: 288). As far as Asia is concerned, in being "a leaven of transformation in this world," the church must now understand its mission of "making disciples of all nations" not in terms of converting as many Asians as possible to the church (which is a very unlikely possibility) and in the process increasing its influence as a social institution (*plantatio ecclesiae*).

It is in this context that numerical growth in Asian Christianity must be viewed. Despite a dramatic increase in the last century, Christians in Asia constitute no more than 9 percent of the Asian population. After several centuries of evangelization, Christianity is still a "small remnant" in Asia, and contrary to Christianity in Africa and Latin America, Asian Christianity is likely to remain so for the foreseeable future. One of the fundamental reasons for this state of affairs is the presence of other religions in Asia which will continue to play an irreplaceable role in the religious life of Asians. The prospect of Asian Christians forming political and ecclesiastical alliances with their counterparts in Africa and Latin America to build a Christendom is nothing more than a pious wish. Consequently, in Asia Christians must journey with the followers of other Asian religions and together with them—not instead of, or worse, against them—work for the coming of the kingdom of God. That is why the Asian churches insist that in Asia there should be not only Basic Christian Communities, as in Latin America, but also Basic Human Communities in which Christians and followers of other religions and even persons of no religious affiliation at all can work together for justice, peace, and the integrity of creation.

The Church's Mission as Dialogue

The new way of being church in Asia is characterized by the *dialogical* spirit: "Built in the hearts of people, it is a Church that faithfully and lovingly witnesses to the Risen Lord and reaches out to people of other faiths and persuasions in a dialogue of life towards the integral liberation of all" (Eilers 1997: 287-8). Ever since its First Plenary Assembly in Taipei, Taiwan, 1974,

214   *Peter C. Phan*

the FABC has repeatedly insisted that the primary task of the Asian churches is the proclamation of the gospel. But it has also maintained no less frequently that the most effective way to be church in Asia is through dialogue, indeed a triple dialogue, that is, with Asian cultures, Asian religions, and the Asians themselves, especially the poor (see Eilers 1997: 13-16). In other words, the new way of being church in Asia is by means of liberation, interreligious dialogue, and inculturation. These three activities, to be truly effective, must be carried out together. Liberation without interreligious dialogue and inculturation is not much more than political and economic activism; interreligious dialogue without liberation and inculturation runs the risk of religious escapism; and inculturation without liberation and interreligious dialogue leads to cultural elitism and is but skin-deep. It is this insight of the Asian Catholic Church into the intrinsic connection—or to use a term of Trinitarian theology, the *perichoresis* or *circuminsession*—of these three dialogues that will vastly enrich the theology of liberation as this has been developed in Latin America and Africa. Furthermore, this triple dialogue is carried out, the Asian bishops insist, in four interrelated ways: by common sharing of life, by common action, by theological exchange, and by sharing religious experiences. A threefold dialogue in a quadruple way, that is in a nutshell the way of being church in Asia.[7]

An Asian Ecclesiology for a "Renewed Church"

This necessity to be local churches living in communion with each other was reiterated by the FABC's Seventh Plenary Assembly (Samphran, Thailand, January 3-12, 2000). Coming right after the Asian Synod and the promulgation of the Apostolic Exhortation *Ecclesia in Asia* and celebrating the Great Jubilee, with the general theme of "A Renewed Church in Asia: A Mission of Love and Service," this assembly is of particular significance because it highlights the kind of ecclesiology operative in the Asian churches. In the first place, the FABC takes a retrospective glance over a quarter of a century of its life and activities and summarizes its "Asian vision of a renewed church." It sees it as composed of eight movements which constitute a summary of Asian ecclesiology. This eightfold movement describes in a nutshell the new way of being church in Asia. Given its central importance, the text deserves to be quoted in full:

1. A movement toward a church of the poor and a church of the young. "If we are to place ourselves at the side of the multitudes in our continent, we must in our way of life share something of their poverty," "speak out for the rights of the disadvantaged and powerless, against all forms of injustice." In this continent of the

---

7. For a presentation of Asian theologies on liberation, inculturation, and interreligious dialogue, see Peter C. Phan's trilogy: Phan 2003a, 2003b, 2004).

young, we must become "in them and for them, the church of the young" (Meeting of Asian Bishops, Manila, Philippines, 1970).

2. A movement toward a "truly local church," toward a church "incarnate in a people, a church indigenous and inculturated" (Second FABC Plenary Assembly, Calcutta, 1978).

3. A movement toward deep interiority so that the church becomes a "deeply praying community whose contemplation is inserted in the context of our time and the cultures of our peoples today." Integrated into everyday life, "authentic prayer has to engender in Christians a clear witness of service and love" (Second FABC Plenary Assembly, Calcutta, 1978).

4. A movement toward an authentic community of faith. Fully rooted in the life of the Trinity, the church in Asia has to be a communion of communities of authentic participation and co-responsibility, one with its pastors, and linked "to other communities of faith and to the one and universal communion" of the holy church of the Lord. The movement in Asia toward Basic Ecclesial Communities expresses the deep desire to be such a community of faith, love and service and to be truly a "community of communities" and open to building up Basic Human Communities (Third FABC Plenary Assembly, Bangkok, 1982).

5. A movement toward active integral evangelization, toward a new sense of mission (Fifth FABC Plenary Assembly, Bandung, Indonesia, 1990). We evangelize because we believe Jesus is the Lord and Savior, "the goal of human history, . . . the joy of all hearts, and the fulfillment of all aspirations" (Gaudium et Spes, no. 45). In this mission, the church has to be a compassionate companion and partner of all Asians, a servant of the Lord and of all Asian peoples in the journey toward full life in God's kingdom.

6. A movement toward empowerment of men and women. We must evolve participative church structures in order to use the personal talents and skills of laywomen and men. Empowered by the Spirit and through the sacraments, laymen and women should be involved in the life and mission of the church by bringing the Good News of Jesus to bear upon the fields of business and politics, of education and health, of mass media and the world of work. This requires a spirituality of discipleship enabling both the clergy and laity to work together in their own specific roles in the common mission of the church (Fourth FABC Plenary Assembly, Tokyo, 1986). The church cannot be a sign of the kingdom and of the eschatological community if the fruits of the Spirit to women are not given due recognition, and if women do not share in the "freedom of the children of God" (Fourth FABC Plenary Assembly, Tokyo, 1986).

7. A movement toward active involvement in generating and serving life. The church has to respond to the death-dealing forces in Asia. By authentic discipleship, it has to share its vision of full

life as promised by Jesus. It is a vision of life with integrity and
dignity, with compassion and sensitive care of the earth; a vision of
participation and mutuality, with a reverential sense of the sacred,
of peace, harmony, and solidarity (Sixth FABC Plenary Assembly,
Manila, Philippines, 1995).

8. A movement toward the triple dialogue with other faiths, with the
poor, and with the cultures, a church "in dialogue with the great
religious traditions of our peoples," in fact, a dialogue with all
people, especially the poor (Eilers 2002: 3-4).

A Different Analogy: Solidarity in Communion

In the light of the FABC's kingdom-centered ecclesiology and deep
commitment to the triple dialogue, the inadequacy of the historical tropes of
Christendom and Counter-Reformation to understand Southern Christianity,
at least in Asia, becomes apparent. I have already alluded to the fact that
kingdom-centered ecclesiology undercuts the possibility of a renascence of
Christendom as this politico-religious arrangement was envisioned in the
Middle Ages. Indeed, far from seeking to establish a new "Christendom,"
the Asian bishops demand the formation of authentically local churches. Far
from promoting "respect for the power of bishops and priests," the Asian
bishops vigorously and repeatedly urge an expansion of the role of the laity,
especially women, in the decision-making process in the church. Far from
denigrating the sacred objects and rituals of non-Christian religions, the
Asian bishops promote respect for and even adopt them as far as possible
into Christian worship. And, of course, no Asian Catholic bishop would
ever imagine that he could ordain conservative foreign priests so that they
can go back home to propagate a Christendom version of Christianity.

Furthermore, the Counter-Reformation paradigm is equally unhelpful
to understand Asian Catholicism. While it is true that there is in Asian
Catholicism a renewed (though, to the best of my knowledge, not very
extensive) interest in popular devotions and other forms of Christian
spirituality such as healing, exorcism, and prophetic utterance, nevertheless
the context in which these phenomena occur is not that of the privatistic
and individualistic piety of the Counter-Reformation or the pre–Vatican
II era. Rather, they are heavily invested with a communitarian and even
political significance, that is, they are promoted for their potential not
only for personal edification but also for social transformation. Because
the similarities between the current forms of piety and those of the former
eras are only superficial, a return to a "pre-Vatican faith" among Asian
Catholics is extremely unlikely. Moreover, the likelihood that Vatican III,
if and when it occurs, will turn out to be "a new Counter-Reformation"
is, on the basis of the FABC's official theology, next to nil. In this regard,
it is interesting to note that none of the better-known traditionalist or even
anti-Vatican II movements such as Archbishop Lefevbre's schismatic group

or the Comunione e Liberazione or the Opus Dei originated in Southern Christianity. Rather these and hundreds of other reactionary movements were born in Northern Christianity, allegedly the hotbed of liberalism!

It would seem then that a paradigm other than Christendom and Counter-Reformation is called for to portray Southern Christianity and its relationship to Northern Christianity. Rather than contrasting the two Christianities, the former conservative and the latter liberal, and seeing them as moving along on a collision course, resulting perhaps in a de facto if not formal schism, I suggest that, while recognizing the severe challenges posed by the demographic shift toward the South, we view the two Christianities more realistically as communities in solidarity and communion, at least for two reasons. First, Southern and Northern Christianities should be viewed as communities in communion because theologically this is the most fruitful and the most widely accepted ecclesiology, at least among Roman Catholics, with which to explicate the relationship among the various local churches of both Northern and Southern Christianity. To use the language of Vatican II, the universal church does not exist apart from nor is simply a collection of local churches; rather it is constituted by the reciprocal communion among the local churches.[8] This communion is no mere sentimental bonding nor legal association; rather it is rooted in the interpersonal communion of the Triune God and is embodied in the one faith, hope, and love. Furthermore, this communion, at least in the Roman Catholic Church, is protected and nurtured by canonical structures that would prevent serious disagreements from degenerating into a large-scale rupture.

Second, Northern Christianity and Southern Christianity are communities in solidarity because both need each other to be fully church and to liberate themselves from possible excesses.[9] Thus, for example, while Northern Christianity will have to learn a lot from Southern Christianity's serious (which is not the same as "literal") engagement with the Bible and its practices of healing, prophetic utterance, and exorcism, Southern Christianity will find it profitable to take seriously (which is not the same as slavishly) Northern Christianity's more scholarly interpretation of the Bible and more sober approach to supernatural phenomena. A tragic case in point: One of the greatest challenges Africa faces over the next decades is AIDS. So far it has created thirteen million orphans and will reduce life expectancy and population in many countries. Eight in ten AIDS-related deaths in the world occur in Africa. Whatever one's belief in the biblical teaching on faith healing and exorcism, it would be highly irresponsible of Christians of both Northern and Southern Christianities to appeal to it as a means to combat this epidemic. While a cure of AIDS through faith healing and exorcism is

---

8. See Vatican II, *Lumen Gentium*, no. 23: "Individual bishops are the visible source and foundation of unity in their particular churches, which are modeled on the universal church; it is in and from these *(in quibus et ex quibus)* that the one and unique catholic church exists."

9. This solidarity is beautifully expressed by the common practice of "twinning" parishes and dioceses of Northern Christianity with those of Southern Christianity.

not a priori impossible, it would be a sacred duty for Southern and Northern Christians to provide modern medicine as part of health care.

All available data tend to indicate a southern shift in the Christian population. As a result, for the first time in its history Christianity is becoming a truly global or world church. This phenomenon presents tremendous challenges to its unity but also provides numerous opportunities for its growth into catholicity. The way to meet these challenges and to become truly global does not seem to lie in a return to Christendom or the Counter-Reformation but in forging communities of communion and solidarity.

15

Mission Studies—Past, Present, and Future

J. Samuel Escobar

J. Samuel Escobar, a leading Latin American theologian, was born in Peru
and has been a missionary among university students in Argentina, Brazil,
Spain, and Canada. He is the Thornley B. Wood Professor of Missiology
at Eastern Baptist Theological Seminary, Wynnewood, Pennsylvania,
and President Emeritus of the Latin American Theological Fraternity. A
theological consultant for the Board of International Ministries in Valencia,
Spain, he is also president of the United Bible Societies and past president
of the International Fellowship of Evangelical Students. He was one of the
key participants in the International Congress on World Evangelization
at Lausanne, Switzerland, in 1974. His most recent books are *Changing
Tides: Mission in Latin America* (Maryknoll, NY: Orbis Books, 2002), and
A Time for Mission (Downers Grove, IL: InterVarsity, 2003).

The title assigned to my presentation implies such a vast field to cover that
I am painfully aware of my inadequacy. However, within the rich dynamism
of the program for which this paper was a starting point, I dared to present
a working document in an effort to outline an agenda for collegial dialogue
and reflection.

Mission studies have developed significantly in both quantity and
quality during the most recent decades. Such a growth has accompanied
developments in mission history so we can say that at its best it has been
a good case of reflection on praxis. An overview of mission studies allows
us also to see the results of a great variety of experiences in ecumenical
dialogue that have marked this second half of our century. Mission studies
register also the widening and deepening of their agenda, which is required
by the slow but irreversible process of globalization of the Christian mission.
Within our own American Society of Missiology (ASM) and Association of
Professors of Mission (APM) communities in North America, as well as
within the International Association for Mission Studies (IAMS) on a global
scale, there has been an ongoing dialogue registered in publications, but also

First published in *Missiology: An International Review* 24, no. 1 (January 1996): 3-29.
Reprinted here with permission.

operative in our memories, as we carry on our daily tasks in missionary life, in missiological research, and in teaching about mission.

MISSIONARY DEVELOPMENTS AND MISSIOLOGICAL UNDERSTANDING IN OUR CENTURY

The close relationship between mission studies and missionary practice and the fact that on the North American scene missiology has not attained yet the status of a highly theoretical discipline (Scherer 1987b) account for both the divergences and the convergences of the most recent years. The very existence of the ASM and the IAMS is proof that the different sectors of Christendom active in mission studies—Catholic, conciliar, Orthodox, and evangelical (including Pentecostal)—-have found enough common ground to keep their friendly and collegial conversation going, asking the same fundamental questions and hearing one another at the time answers are given. Moreover, it can safely be said now that there has been a movement of convergence in mission studies, and in this overview I would like to move within those points of convergence. I agree with the analysis offered by Efiong S. Utuk, whose review of developments in evangelical missiology between 1966 and 1974 brought him to the conclusion that "the new fact of our time" in missiology is not "the widening gulf between evangelicals and conciliarists," but rather "an emerging consensus on many missiological questions . . . as well as the fact that 'evangelicals' are becoming more 'ecumenical' than ever, while 'ecumenicals' are becoming more 'evangelical'" (1986: 218). On the other hand, we should not underestimate the realities uncovered by a more detached historical analysis, such as the one offered by Hutchison:

> The notion of a new consensus was plausible if one were using it to contrast the agreements affected by 1985 with the hostility evangelicals and ecumenicals had felt toward each other in 1965. But it was more helpful, perhaps, to speak of a "new mainstream" that embodied as much consensus and as much dissensus, as that of about 1920. (1987: 199)

These references to intra-Protestant dialogue and consensus should not obscure the fact that there has been also Protestant dialogue ad extra. This is evidenced for instance in the World Council of Churchess statement on *Mission and Evangelism: An Ecumenical Affirmation* (Stromberg 1983) and in the irenic spirit as well as in the many convergences mentioned in the report of the *Evangelical-Roman Catholic Dialogue on Mission* (ERCDOM 1986). The very existence of those conversations and that report in themselves point to a new spirit and to new patterns of relationships.

I approach this overview considering that there are some basic questions that have guided mission studies during our century. Several of those questions that seem characteristic of the most recent decades after World War II were already posed in the missiological dialogues of the decades that preceded the war. Some of them were first formulated in a forceful way right after World War I. That was a most critical period for mission practice and mission theology, and it is evident today that in some way or another the events of that period were announcing historical trends that became more acute and generalized at a global level after 1945. Those questions are simple but profound, and from each one of them a host of other questions may be derived. Let me mention briefly some of them.

1. The recent forceful question posed by Lesslie Newbigin, "Can the West Be Converted?" (1987) with its references to pre- and post-Enlightenment realities was already posed in a different way in the Jerusalem meeting of the International Missionary Council (IMC) in 1928. "Need the West be converted?" was the question that involved an appraisal of mission, taking into account the state of Christianity and secularism in the West. Posing the question involved an openness to "relentless and exacting self-criticism" that would be healthy for the missionary enterprise.[1] Multiple questions were derived from this one.

2. Another question is one that Andrew Walls keeps before us. It refers to the fact that "the most obvious method" used to explore basic questions about the Christian faith in our time is "by studying Christianity as expressed in the experience of the southern churches" (1991: 147). The IMC at Tambaram in 1938 had already noted this need when attention started to be paid to the distinct voices of the younger churches. Today Western missions have to face the questions posed not only by the voices of non-Western Christians but by the growing missionary activity of their churches in the territory that used to be Christendom.

3. A new question has come to the fore that relates to the wider frame in which question (2) is being posed today. It points to the fact that "Christian expansion has characteristically come from the margins more than from the center" (Walls 1991: 147). Bühlmann (1977) centered his vision and description of contemporary Christianity around that fact in *The Coming of the Third Church*. This renewed awareness about the masses and their challenge was also an important factor in McGavran's missiology (1980: 269-94). The vast pentecostal missionary movement will be better understood within this frame (Hollenweger 1972: 986; Martin 1990).

4. Inevitably, the previous questions bring to light the need to define approaches to other religions. This was one of the most controversial points in the North American debates of the 1930s and the 1940s, and its urgency today relates to the development of pluralism in Western societies. During the Lausanne II conference in Manila, in 1989, Colin Chapman reminded evangelicals of the urgency of this question of the relation of Christianity to other religions and the fact that they had not yet done their basic homework

---

1. The expression belongs to William Temple and is quoted and commented on by Scherer (1968: 32).

in relation to it. Today this question is not posed in reference to missionary activity in distant frontiers, but in reference to the growth of other religions in the heart of North American and European cities.

5. By 1912 Roland Allen was proposing a drastic revision of existing missionary methodologies and asking the question about the relevance and validity of New Testament patterns for mission. That basic concern was later taken on with passion and thoroughness by people coming from a variety of missionary situations as diverse as Donald McGavran (1955), Kenneth Strachan (1968), Michael Green (1970), and some of the founders of the Catholic Base Communities (Cook 1985). The question is alive today, and there is a world of new suggestions coming from the great amount of recent research about the social and religious transformation of the Roman Empire.[2]

6. The search for New Testament missionary patterns took Allen to serious consideration about the Holy Spirit and mission. The growth of the Pentecostal movement, which was missionary from its inception, eventually forced the issue of the Holy Spirit and mission into the academic level. The Pentecostal movement in itself became a vast field for research (Dempster, Klaus, and Petersen 1991). In the study of the Holy Spirit in relation to mission a succession of names comes to mind that are milestones in the more recent search for answers: Harry R. Boer (1961), John V. Taylor (1972), James D. G. Dunn (1970, 1975, 1977) and more recently Gordon Fee (1994) and Howard Snyder (1989).

7. The question about the nature of the missionary presence was a logical outcome of question (1) in this list. Criticism of the West, and of a Christian church totally identified with it, brought also criticism of a form of missionary presence too closely linked to a Western colonial presence. The missionary practice and the spirituality of Charles de Foucauld (1858-1916) proposed a silent, patient, and tenacious expression of the love of Christ among Muslims. A missionary presence in the world was posed forcefully in the influential reflection of Jacques Ellul (1951), and later on radicalized in the proposals of the World Student Christian Federation in 1963. It was also posed in a different key by the evangelical missiological reflection before and after Lausanne 1974, especially by the rediscovery of the Johannine version of the Great Commission (Stott 1975).

8. The nature of the missionary presence points in the final analysis to ecclesiology, Christology, and spirituality. The missiology of Vatican II in *Ad Gentes* was preceded by the definitions about the nature of the church in *Lumen Gentium*. Within evangelicalism there was a reverse course, and the missiology of the Lausanne Movement required an ecclesiological follow-up. This was developed positively by Howard Snyder (1975, 1977) and polemically in the debates about the church-growth school (Shenk 1983).

---

2. See the impressive bibliography on this subject in Duhaime (1992). This literature is a veritable gold mine of sources for missiologists which has not been tapped yet. A very promising effort in that direction is the work of Alan Kreider (1994).

If one accepts the fact that the key questions posed by liberation theologies have to do with the way the church is to accomplish its mission in the world, ecclesiological keys will help us to appreciate the valuable missiological contributions of Gustavo Gutiérrez and Juan Luis Segundo at this point.

9. In the final analysis, Christology is the source to which missiological exploration must turn in its search for new patterns for mission. The most lively exploration into christological questions has been coming from the missionary frontiers, from the places where two-thirds of humankind now live, and from the marginalized segments of populations in North America. Theologians from the Two Thirds World (Samuel and Sugden 1983; Dyrness 1994) and especially from Latin America and the Hispanic world have made important contributions to the missiological dialogue (Costas 1982; Míguez Bonino 1984; González 1990).

The importance of these persistent questions becomes evident as we pay attention to the outline of a recent book that is a masterful piece of historical synthesis. I refer to the work of Timothy Yates, *Christian Mission in the Twentieth Century* (1994). The different periods in which he has divided the vast amount of material he covers are constructed around key words and ideas. In their simplicity, these key words and ideas elicit significant characteristics of each period, and a comparative exercise would show that they relate to the persistent questions I have mentioned. Thus, we have mission as expansion (1900-1910); mission as the church of a people (1910-1920); mission appraised (1920-1940); mission as presence and dialogue (1950-1960); mission as proclamation, dialogue, and liberation (1960-1970); mission as proclamation and church growth (1970-1980); and finally, mission in the context of pluralism and enlightenment (1980-1990).

A consideration of the questions I have sketched and the work of authors I have mentioned would show that the different missionary experiences in a variety of mission frontiers, and the different theological and ecclesiological convictions of the missiologists, have configured different approaches and ways to pose the questions and search for answers. However, the persistence of the questions proves in some cases the weight of tradition and routine, the difficulty of moving from critical theoretical formulations into the reformation of practices and structures. In other cases, new generations of missionaries without an adequate historical awareness were condemned to repeat the mistakes of the past and to reinvent a missiological reflection in what Hutchison calls "familiar debates in an unfamiliar world" (1987: 176).

I find comfort in the fact that the explosion of evangelical missionary activity after 1945 provided a bulk of new practice on the basis of which it was possible to reflect and to find new theories. Dana Robert has described the situation in North America in which from the missionary activity of conservative evangelicals a renewed effort has come at the level of scholarship: "The 'sectarian' evangelicals that Beaver had excoriated in 1964 reached such a level of institutional maturity and ecclesiastical dominance that critical historical analysis became possible and necessary"

(1994: 146). By contrast I also find sobering the remark of Joel Carpenter pointing to the evangelical isolation from previous missionary practice and experience: "when a post-fundamentalist, 'neo-evangelical' theological movement appeared in the 1950s and 1960s, it virtually had to reinvent evangelical missions theology" (Carpenter and Shenk 1990: 131).

On the other hand, the persistence of the basic questions and the convergent march toward a certain degree of consensus have also allowed us to have now a wider and continuous dialogue that does not always seem to be possible in other disciplines. I find especially valuable the fact that *Missiology, International Bulletin of Missionary Research, Missionalia,* and *International Review of Mission* are all open platforms, ecumenical in the most pristine sense of the term. Maybe a situation has developed at this point in which the discipline we call *mission studies* is that unique academic and scholarly *locus* in which a wide diversity of scholars from biblical studies, history, the social sciences, and systematic theology, which have no other point of real encounter, may come together for creative reflection. If that is the case, I propose that we should not despair if we cannot create neat satisfactory definitions of what is missiology. We should nevertheless keep practicing it.

Precisely in some of these missiological publications we have had excellent overviews of the vast range of mission studies that have been taking place in recent years. We are in debt to Gerald H. Anderson (1991) for his general overview, "Mission Research, Writing and Publishing," that covers the years 1971 to 1991, and for other specialized bibliographies (1990); to Dana Robert (1994) for her overview, "From Missions to Mission to Beyond Missions: The Historiography of American Protestant Foreign Missions Since World War II"; and to Andrew Walls (1991) for mapping the vast field that is ahead of us in "Structural Problems in Mission Studies." The bibliographies in *Missiology* and the abstracts in *Missionalia* are invaluable tools for which we have to give thanks to a host of colleagues and institutions around the world. We are also in debt to other colleagues for longer and more elaborate overviews in book form. I am thinking of the work of Rodger Bassham, *Mission Theology, 1948-1975: Years of Worldwide Creative Tension—Ecumenical, Evangelical, and Roman Catholic* (1979); of James A. Scherer, *Gospel Church and Kingdom: Comparative Studies in World Mission Theology* (1987a); and of Arthur F. Glasser and the late Donald A. McGavran, *Contemporary Theologies of Mission* (1983).

These overviews do not limit themselves to theology, but they offer us good historical background because they ground theological reflection in the processes of missionary activity, organization, consultation, and dialogue that have been taking place in a variety of missiological foci. In the field of history, I have already mentioned Timothy Yates. In relation to North American mission, I must add the solid critical work of Hutchison (1987) and the ground-breaking symposium put together by Joel Carpenter and Wilbert Shenk (1990). From the deluge of publications about the fifth centennial of

Columbus's coming to the Americas, the perspective of mission studies is well served by an excellent volume edited by Enrique Dussel (1992).

Special mention needs also to be made of a different kind of interpretative overview when the panoramic picture is accompanied by a new and original missiological proposal. The best example of this is provided by David Bosch in *Transforming Mission: Paradigm Shifts in Theology of Mission* (1991), who processed a massive amount of information in the different disciplines that relate to mission studies, and in each case has offered also his own choice and a foundation to explain it. A similar methodology in a more synthetic way is offered by Lesslie Newbigin in *The Open Secret*, of which a revised edition has just been published (1995).

Within this truly ecumenical spirit, another valuable type of instrument for mission study and teaching has been provided by compilations of missiological sources and biographies. James A. Scherer and Stephen B. Bevans have started to publish a series of sourcebooks or anthologies with an ecumenical sweep, under the general title *New Directions in Mission and Evangelization*. Volume 1 (1992) deals with basic statements from conferences, congresses, and study groups between 1974 and 1991, and volume 2 (1994) has a collection of fifteen essays organized in sections about the nature of mission, historical background, missionary praxis, the study of mission, and documentation.

Two other books that have appeared this year promise to be a great help in years to come. *Mission Legacies* (1995), edited by Gerald H. Anderson, Robert T. Coote, Norman A. Horner, and James M. Phillips, offers seventy-five "biographical studies of leaders of the modern missionary movement." Promoters, interpreters, theologians, historians, theorists, strategists, and administrators are included, as well as missionaries who worked in Africa, China, and southern Asia. The editors mention the possibility of a future additional volume that will include mission leaders associated with North Africa, the Middle East, Northeast Asia, the Pacific, and Latin America. Norman E. Thomas has compiled a sourcebook of *Classic Texts in Mission and World Christianity* (1995) which he intends to become a reader's companion to the book *Transforming Mission* by David Bosch. Following a chronological approach, one-fourth of the book is dedicated to the first 1,800 years of Christian history and three-fourths to the more recent two hundred years. Another tool that has to be mentioned is the statistical work of David B. Barrett (1982), which is updated in each January issue of the *International Bulletin of Missionary Research*. The information that Barrett offers is incorporated in a wide variety of publications at every level of mission studies, including the promotion of prayer for missionary work (Johnstone 1993).

In order to fulfill my assignment, I have decided to try an approach that I call a bio-bibliographical synthesis. Instead of proceeding to trace an outline of the great general lines of mission studies, past, present, and future, I am going to use a short narrative approach about some writers of mission study material, combined with reflection about their books. As I move along each case, I will try to show how each particular author and book summarizes some of the great lines that have developed in recent decades and also how in some way or other they point to what needs to be done in the future.

Without exception, the authors I have selected are practitioners of mission and also productive scholars. However, most of the books I consider were not written only or mainly for a scholarly public, but for a wider readership. I am trying this narrative approach in order to explore the way in which the matrix for missiological reflection may be located in the frontiers where praxis takes place. It is true, as Andrew Walls has reminded us, that we need top quality scholarship in the field of mission studies, but there is also an urgent need to put the results of top quality scholarship in the hands of the average Christian public. I must admit that my selection is arbitrary and that others could put together a different set of books and authors, following their own experience and preferences. I hope, however, that in spite of great differences of choice, we would find many points of convergence in the general lines of analysis.

BIBLE AND MISSION: THE SEARCH FOR SOURCES

I start with the book *Unity and Plurality: Mission in the Bible* (1990) written by Lucien Legrand, a Frenchman who has been a missionary in India under the Paris Mission Society since 1953. Before going to India, Legrand had completed the standard curriculum for an advanced degree in biblical studies at Paris, Rome, and Jerusalem. His missionary assignment included tasks of teaching Scripture, translation, and dialogue, and he went with a vision about the importance of Asia for the future of Christianity. His immersion in India, learning a language and experiencing a culture in which religion impregnates the whole of life, was a dramatic experience that he has described vividly:

> One cannot live in India without feeling its spell. But the experience of this seduction was both ravishing and disquieting. Was I not betraying my vocation in allowing myself to be fascinated by the world I should be converting? Furthermore, even to go out into the street was to feel swallowed up by its enormous throngs, to become an infinitesimal drop in an ocean of humanity. Did the church I represented really have the capacity to gather up all of these masses' suffering and anguish, vitality and hope, yes, spiritual wealth? (1990: x)

Legrand has brought to his reading of the Bible the authenticity of these vital questions that missionaries face daily, especially in the Asian frontiers. In the foreword of his book, he explains in great detail the pilgrimage that his biblical work reflects, "a number of different journeys, distinct but intertwined" (ix). He places his own journey as a European missionary in India within other journeys, in an interplay of concentric and eccentric circles: the journey of his church, the Roman Catholic, especially during this century; the journey of India, the country that received him at the beginning of its independent life; and the journey of twentieth-century humanity, "sovereign [with] new techniques that have opened unsuspected horizons, but helpless to solve its conflicts, close its economic and social gaps and surmount its racial and cultural divisions" (1990: ix).

Legrand's purpose in this book is to "situate this theme of mission in the context of the divine plan for human beings as manifested to us in the Bible" (1990: xv) or in other words, to "search the Bible for a clarification on the nature of mission" (1990: xiii). As a Bible scholar, he is aware of the special difficulties involved in his task. He knows that from a European perspective in our time there are many ambiguities in the use of the terms *missionary* and *mission,* and he writes, "There are milieus in which the word missionary calls forth an instant smile, ironic or tender, depending on the cultural context" (1990: xiv). He argues however that we do not forgo the use of words such as *freedom, youth, wine, bread,* and *father* because they are fraught with ambiguity in modern discourse. And then he goes on to remind us that the word *mission* "can boast a respectable biblical pedigree" (1990: xiv).

Legrand's treatment of his material is made especially helpful by his willingness to include in his research the totality of the biblical message. For instance, in relation to the Old Testament, he pays equal attention to each one of what he calls the "twin poles of Israel's mission," the particularism of "election," and the universality of "the nations." In relation to Paul, he treats with equal seriousness the writings of Luke and the Pauline writings, making room for the tension involved in correlating them. This treatment of the text is part of an approach in which he acknowledges the possibility of several "points of departure" in the reading of the biblical material, which will allow us to sketch "various types of missiology." He finds such variety also detectable in his reading of mission history and in his observation of contemporary models of mission. His book is a good example of the pattern that Bosch presented as the most desirable: "The validity of mission should not be deduced from isolated sayings but from the thrust of the central message of Scripture" (Bosch 1993: 177). In the book *Transforming Mission,* Bosch makes good use of Legrand's work. I find especially valuable his comments when the French edition of the book appeared:

> In his exposition Legrand makes ample use of critical Old and New Testament scholarship but he does this in a circumspect way. He does not really break any new ground but prefers to weigh the evidence cautiously and to adopt positions which are widely held. Because of this he becomes a dependable guide through the maze of contemporary critical scholarship on the biblical foundation for mission. (1989: 64)

Legrand's book reflects the theological quest in which he has accompanied the church in India. He is aware that this effort has not yet forged a coherent

synthesis comparable, for instance, to liberation theology. The reason is
the vastness of the task: "perhaps never in the history of the church has
the Christian faith encountered a culture so solid and so comprehensive,
a religion so living and as profoundly mystical as it has in today's India"
(1990: x). In reference to that, he makes an observation that points to one
of the difficulties of mission studies:

> This theological quest would be a vain one unless it sought its roots
> in the toils, the trials and the hopes of daily life. I have been fortunate
> enough to share the life of poor peasants of a village of the Dekkan, to
> be accepted into the fabric of their community, to live their problems,
> their prayer and their struggle with poverty, drought, ignorance and
> disease. I have found far more enculturation here than I have found
> in books. Cultural authenticity has not emerged from an academic
> effort to connect faith with culture. Cultural authenticity has been the
> visceral fidelity of the inmost Indian soul. It has been no veneer; it is
> life. (1990: xi)

What provisions could be taken, what methodological rules should be
followed, what disciplines of life are needed to ensure a close and permanent
connection between the missionary frontier and the laboratory of biblical
scholarship?

As a Latin American evangelical, I have found especially significant the
fact that Catholic scholars have produced books about the biblical basis
of mission that are becoming standard works in the field. The Spanish
translation of Senior and Stuhlmueller (1983) is now a textbook in many
evangelical seminaries across Latin America. Bosch also refers to this fact
and adds an eloquent comment: "One might even say that by and large,
Catholic biblical scholars are currently taking the missionary dimension of
Scripture more seriously than their Protestant counterparts" (1993: 178). At
this point Bosch places Legrand side by side with Senior and Stuhlmueller.

Legrand also offers us his own summary of the way in which the life
of his church has been challenged by God and by history during his own
lifetime. For him, "to have experienced mission in the latter half of the
twentieth century is to have taken part in the great forward march of the
church during and after Vatican II" (1990: xi). The elements of this long
process that he mentions are a good outline of factors that have also affected
mission studies in our time. He mentions (1) a return to the word of God,
(2) a view of the church as a presence of Christ among human beings, (3) the
theology of liberation, (4) the reintegration of mission into ecclesiology,
(5) the changing political and religious situation, and (6) the dialogue with
non-Christians. Mission studies have accompanied that process and have
been enriched by it in at least two ways. First, they have been enriched by
the process of rediscovery of the Bible that culminated in Vatican II and
then was fostered by it. When one reads the documents of the Catholic
magisterium about mission after Vatican II, it is immediately evident that

biblical categories have become a ferment of change in the most creative points of missiological renewal. There is a wealth of biblical material in those documents, from *Lumen Gentium* and *Ad Gentes* to *Redemptoris Missio*, and that means that any Protestant commentator must stop and read twice before coming to conclusions. In spite of my divergences, I have found this an enriching exercise. Second, Vatican II made possible an interconfessional or ecumenical dialogue of biblical scholars. Legrand's endnotes are a valuable testimony to this dialogue. His book is a conversation with interlocutors that include a wide range of scholars, Catholic and Protestant, conservative and liberal, young and old.

The great test of the value of Legrand's book—or any other book on the biblical basis for missions, for that matter—would be if we, the missiologists, can get our colleagues who teach Old Testament and New Testament to adopt the book as one of their textbooks in basic courses that are not specifically dedicated to mission. This rediscovery of the centrality of mission in Scripture still has to be assumed by biblical scholarship as a sine qua non of their own way of understanding and clarifying the meaning of Scripture. Because this book is not just a series of proof texts and because it reflects familiarity with ongoing scholarship without hiding an intelligent enthusiasm for its subject matter, I think it would be a good candidate for missiological infiltration into that other field.

MISSION HISTORY AS AN INSTRUMENT FOR LIBERATION

Eduardo Hoornaert was born in Belgium in 1930, and in 1958 he went as a missionary to Brazil, where he has remained and now lives permanently. He had studied classical philology and ancient history at Louvain, and theology at Bruges. Most of his missionary work was carried on in the poor and explosive region of the Northeast, where the Roman Catholic Church experimented with some of the most creative and courageous pastoral reforms. Hoornaert was active in the development of what is known as the "popular church" and the Christian Base Communities. He is an untiring researcher, and his writings have been controversial and influential. He has held professorships of history of the church in several theological institutions in Brazil and was one of the founders of CEHILA (Comisión de Estudios de Historia de la Iglesia en América Latina [Commission for the Study of the History of the Church in Latin America]). Among the books he has written about the history of the Catholic Church in Brazil, the best known are *Formaçao do Catolicismo no Brasil* (1974) and *Historia da Igreja no Brasil: Primeira Epoca* (1977). He has paid special attention to the history of the church among the Indians and the blacks, and in his books he tries to present the perspective of the poor and the marginalized.

The book by Hoornaert that I want to consider is *The Memory of the Christian People* (1989). This book is a historical study about the first three centuries of the Christian church from a missiological perspective. By this

I mean that in his research Hoornaert asks questions that come from his missionary practice among the Base Communities. At several points in the book, he establishes parallels between the life of the Christian communities among the poor of Brazil and the life of the church before Constantine, because as he says in his preface,

> There is actually a surprising parallel between the current experience of the Base Communities and the life of the first Christian communities. The pastoral ministers of today's Base Communities who so enthusiastically exclaim, "Why, this is the way the Christians lived" are far from mistaken. The following pages have been prepared, most painstakingly, in the hope of etching this historical memory still more profoundly into the minds and hearts of the Christian people of Latin America. (1989: xii)

Hoornaert starts with the conviction that Judaism and Christianity are "memory religions." The Exodus event had enabled the Jewish people "to fashion a collective memory unrivaled by any other people, and Israel based its religion on this memory." Christianity has inherited this memorial character, "but it has centered its memory on the incarnation, life, passion, death and resurrection of Jesus Christ, liberator of his people not from Egypt merely, like Moses, but from domination in all its forms" (1989: 4). However, keeping the memory of Jesus has been a continuous struggle with heretical views that differed from the apostolic tradition, or efforts to manipulate that memory. Because of that, "church history will always have its role to perform in the mission of reanimating the memory of the Christian communities" (1989: 9). Hoornaert accepts for church historians the saying of Jacques Le Goff, "The historian's task is to transform memory into science." Hoornaert proposes that,

> The science of church history is at the service of the memory of the Christian people. It is at the service of this memory not only in the sense that it gathers their recollections but also in the sense that it transforms their memory into a coherent intelligible discourse, based on objective documents. (1989: 9)

The recovery of the memory that Hoornaert proposes is refreshing and controversial. Because it starts from questions that come from the daily life of the people among whom he serves, at several points he challenges the accepted wisdom of respected scholars who have left aside important segments of the Christian experience. Because his effort is to put history as "a science at the service of the people," he does not pretend to be "objective." He rather uses his own ideological assumptions to uncover ideological biases of certain historians who have lost part of the memory of the people. One of those who comes under attack is Eusebius, whose *Ecclesiastical History* has been so influential through the centuries. Hoornaert first commends Eusebius as a true historian in contrast with his predecessors. He is "the first Christian historian to cite his sources faithfully and credit them correctly. His work evinces patience, scruple and an excellent organization of material" (1989: 13). But Eusebius had an axe to grind, an ideology that derived from "the stark dichotomy he draws between Christianity's victory under Constantine and its afflictions under earlier emperors" (1989: 13). The conclusion is as follows:

> For, indeed, Eusebius' theology, altogether novel for the time, can only be characterized as an "imperial theology," a theology of empire. It is difficult to imagine, however, that all strata of Christianity could have shared his view of the church. Withal the fact remains that, through his historiographical effort, Eusebius founded a new Christian literary genre, one which sees no problem in equating Christian memory with an "apostolic succession" in the sense of a simple succession of bishops in local churches. (1989: 13-14)

As practiced by Hoornaert, the reading of history with a new key brings to light some aspects of the life of the church in mission that have special significance for those who work among the marginalized in the world today. Reading mission history from Hoornaert's perspective speaks to the issues of the role of lay people, women, children, and elderly people; the place of money and the community of goods; and the social dimension of theological controversies. This kind of reading provides new theological insights about the New Testament epistles taking into account the category of marginalization, what he calls "the theology of the marginalized as 'chosen.'" For Hoornaert, "the theology of the election of the marginalized was deeply rooted in the practice of Jesus. . . . Jesus' insistence on God's predilection for the 'last' was categorical" (1989: 41-42). The practice of Jesus was opposed by the leadership of the official religion of his day, and as time went on, the day came when an established church lost the memory of that practice and also forgot the marginalized.

Hoornaert came to Brazil as part of a wave of North American and European priests and nuns after World War II. A church in crisis called them, and they immersed themselves in the thick of the crisis. Hoornaert's name may be placed among those of other missionary colleagues who became very influential in the renewal of the Catholic Church in Latin America: Vekemans, Comblin, Houtart, Rosier, Lepargneur, and Pin. They were conversant with the theological trends and pastoral movements that had been developing in Europe during the war and after it. The key for their action was the nature of their missionary presence, an immersion among the poorest segments of the population in Latin America. While Americans and Canadians shocked by the poverty and oppression organized rural leagues, credit unions, and neighborhood clubs, the Europeans sharpened their tools of social analysis in order to understand the pastoral and theological dimension of the situation.

The concreteness of this missionary action made possible the formulation of theologies of liberation which are conceived as "reflection on praxis." For instance, Gustavo Gutiérrez and Juan Luis Segundo, two of the most articulate liberation theologians, studied in Louvain, Belgium, in the late 1950s, like Hoornaert before them, and came back to work and reflect. After Vatican II, the bishops in Medellín (1968) moved from the *immersion* among the poor, pioneered by the missionaries, to an *option* for the poor, that is, a proposal to identify with the cause of the poor. This was nothing but a political and social realignment for a church that had occupied such a significant position in the history of Latin America. The Medellín documents represent a notable reformulation of the mission of the church, which involves a new reading of the Latin American situation and of many biblical texts, reflection about some of the missionary experiences that North Americans and Europeans had gone through, and approval of bold new pastoral practices (Escobar 1987; Cleary 1990).

The theology that had shaped the type of Catholic missionary represented by Hoornaert was the result of a long process. Yates refers to it, commenting on the importance of the book *La France: pays de mission?* [France, a mission field?], in which abbés Godin and Daniel "reflected on religionless paganism in France . . . and the need for the church to find new ways of identifying with and being present among the alienated masses" (Yates 1994: 136). This book was the result of careful social analysis, including a study of church attendance and lay participation in the life of the church. It was a devastating analysis. The basic thesis is that although France considered itself a Christian nation sending missionaries to pagan lands, facts demonstrated that France was herself a missionary land that should be evangelized. The book was really an urgent cry to acknowledge that there was a serious pastoral and missionary crisis in French Catholicism. The phenomenon came to be described as the "absence of God," a process of "dechristianization," affecting especially the nominally Christian nations of Europe.

Several efforts to renew the pastoral methodology of the church were the direct result of this new awareness. Probably the one that attracted more public attention was the experiment with the worker-priest movement. The priests who immersed themselves among the workers in France were attracted to communism, and some of them left the church after going through the agonizing experience of discovering the close links between bourgeois mentality and Catholicism (Arnal 1986). They came to the conviction that the church could not really respond to the pastoral needs of the workers unless there was a radical change in its outlook and methods.

One important aspect of the pastoral renewal was the change from a mentality of *conquest* to one of *presence*. The vocabulary of the missionary and pastoral literature, especially that of the lay movements such as Catholic Action, had used the language and the imagery of "conquest." The workers, the intellectuals, and the students had to be "conquered" for the church. A new theological outlook brought the notion and the imagery of "presence."

These two words connote a totally different set of presuppositions and methodologies. It is interesting to notice that the idea of presence had been championed by the mystic Charles de Foucauld, who was a missionary in the Arab world of North Africa at the time in which the imperial grip of France was being contested in the wake of deep ideological and political confrontations.

In Vatican II the old mentality of confrontation and war against modernity and against other foes of the church was to be replaced by a living and costly "presence" in the midst of the world, even if that world was hostile. The Christian was to convey the qualities of presence of Jesus and to be like the yeast in the dough. There is no doubt here of an implicit departure from the Constantinian mentality that had nourished the Counter-Reformation. The decree *Ad Gentes* has been considered a clear expression of the concern of the church for evangelization, and it was influential in several national or regional episcopal conferences. Together with *Nostra Aetate*, the "Declaration on the Relation of the Church to Non-Christian Religions," this document stated for the first time in a comprehensive and systematic way the Catholic theory and practice of mission.

Hoornaert is aware of the ideological dangers implicit in the use of social analysis as part of the research and interpretation of history. He writes:

A church history at the service of the collective memory of the Christian people must know how to avoid the pitfalls of a totalitarian historicism provoked by the deviations of an excessively dogmatic and mechanistic Marxist interpretation of history: everything must now start again from nothing, we are told, church tradition contains nothing good or constructive; the church has always been on the wrong side. Generalizations of this sort are scarcely likely to assist the Christian people in the reconstruction of their memory. (1989: 10)

Unfortunately, not all liberation historians and theologians worked with these caveats, as a cursory analysis of the rhetoric of 1992 may prove. The need for continued monitoring of the use of social sciences is important in mission studies.

Other missiological approaches have also adopted a sophisticated use of the social sciences in order to develop the type of mission studies that will facilitate missionary action. While Europeans in the French-speaking world made special use of sociology, Americans have given their preference to anthropological studies. In a varied and colorful collection of essays by Jacob Loewen (1975), I have found a subtle but sometimes powerful critique of missionary myths and methodologies, truly a self-critical exercise similar to the one we described above, but not so far-reaching in its results. A different approach is the one taken by the church-growth school. Writing about Donald McGavran's contribution to it, Hunter (1992) mentions this specifically as one of eight distinctive themes and claims of this school: "The Christian movement can be advanced by employing the insights and research tools of the behavioral sciences, including the gathering and graphing of relevant statistical data for mission analysis, planning, control and critique" (1992: 158). My impression however is that while the use of social sciences in liberation theologies adopts a militant stance and does not refrain from a missionary action that creates conflict and confrontation, church growth has been more inclined to use the social sciences in order to carry on a missionary strategy that will convert people spiritually with the least possible social disruption.

THE MEMORY OF WOMEN IN MISSION STUDIES

We have seen some of the painful reforming effects that a recovery of memory can bring to Christian mission. In my next case, what produces the loss of memory seems to be in the heart of the communities that send missionaries to other lands. It is the existence of a "male-dominated institutionalized church [that] has deeply entrenched concepts of power, authority, and office—and women have not fit into the scheme" (Tucker 1988: 9). Paradoxically, this fact could well explain equally two other facts: on the one hand, the lessening of restrictions for women if they went to distant lands, which allowed them to participate massively in the missionary enterprise, and on the other hand, the strange loss of memory about that massive involvement of women in missions.

The first step that is necessary then is to work at the level of historical research in order to help Christians to recover the memory of the role of women in the missionary enterprise. This does not seem an easy task, because it means breaking new ground against entrenched attitudes in the opposite direction. Ruth Tucker, a historian, a professor of missions, and the author of a popular book about mission history (1983), was surprised by what she found in the case of some classic books in the field of mission studies. Her research in the history of missions showed the massive participation of women both overseas and at the home front. But when she went to the standard manuals of history of missions there seemed to be a loss of memory:

> In light of the magnitude and influence of this female missionary movement, it is unexplainable that the foremost missions historians have neglected to even mention it. "As so frequently happens in the writing of history," writes Patricia Hill, "the women have simply disappeared." This is true of the mission texts written by Stephen Neill and J. Herbert Kane. Neither author even mentions the women's missionary movement . . . yet the women's missionary movement not only sponsored thousands of missionaries and Bible women and built schools and hospitals, but it also produced some of the greatest mission strategists and missiologists of the late nineteenth and early twentieth centuries. (1987: 76)

Entrenched habits have a way of persisting. Six years after Tucker wrote this paragraph, the editor of the *International Bulletin of Missionary Research,* in the October 1993 issue, lamented the fact that from the near seventy articles he had published for the "Mission Legacies" series, only six were about women. This context helps us to appreciate Tucker's effort at recovering the memory of women in missions in her book *Guardians of the Great Commission* (1988). This book is a call to recover a memory that has remained hidden or lost. It reflects the sensitivity about discrimination against women that has grown in North American society in our time and that has also provoked intense polemics within the Christian churches. Tucker finds in the women she studies a painful awareness about discrimination. Sometimes it is explained away by women themselves with the tenets of traditional theology. Other times, however, women missionaries had long battles for justice and liberation that are well documented. One chapter in this book deals with women who excelled in missionary writing and became influential through it. Tucker presents the stories of Elisabeth Elliot, Amy Carmichael, Mildred Cable, and others, and makes an important point from the perspective of the historian:

Many of the most insightful and honest books about the realities of missionary work have been written by women. . . . Without the woman's perspective, missionary literature would be sorely deficient. The trials of family life and the inner spiritual struggles are often dealt with in greater depth by women, and women are often more open in admitting their own personal conflicts than men are. (1988: 195).[3]

On the other hand, writing elsewhere, Tucker takes issue with Elisabeth Elliot and others like her who suggest "that missionary women had no right to protest unequal treatment because their very numbers indicated they were not being discriminated against" (1987: 73). Elliot had argued that position in emphatic terms:

Today strident female voices are raised, shrilly and ad nauseam, to remind us that women are equal with men. But such a question has never even arisen in connection with the history of Christian mission. In fact, for many years, far from being excluded, women constituted the majority of foreign missionaries. (Tucker 1987: 73)

Tucker comments that Elliot's assumption that because women were in the majority they never fought for equality is logically faulty and leads to a false conclusion. In two chapters of her book, Tucker documents the many

3. From the viewpoint of historical work in mission studies, it is important to keep in mind what Dana Robert says, "The bias toward intellectual history also kept the contributions of missionary women hidden from view because women tended to produce popular writing" (1994: 152).

cases of women who carried a long struggle for justice within the missionary structures at home and abroad. In other writings she also refers to women missionaries whose struggles against the oppression of women in mission lands could well be described as "an early version of today's liberation theology" (1987: 79).

Other scholars are helping us in this process of recovering the memory of women's work in mission. Dana Robert gave us not long ago a fascinating piece of scholarly research about mission strategies and the role of missionary wives in Burma and Hawaii (1993). Her rigorous and detailed analysis of documents goes hand in hand with her understanding of the context within which missionaries live their lives both in North America and abroad. That allows us to see how changing societal factors in North America shape the worldview and the mission policies of the missionary societies. At the same time, it illuminates the dissonance between these factors and the condition of the missionaries in distant countries which will demand accommodation or conflict. In this way it is possible to see the dynamic interaction between missionary action abroad and the life of the church at home. Theologically, this can help us to understand better the relationship between "church and world," one of the key issues when we pose the question about the nature of the missionary presence and the nature of mission itself. Missiologically, this can help us in the search for more contextual patterns of mission.

EVANGELICAL MISSIONARY FERVOR
AND CRITICAL THEOLOGY

My fourth case is the book *Mission Between the Times* (1985a) by C. René Padilla, and it comes from evangelical missionary experience in Latin America.[4] Padilla was born in Ecuador in the home of an evangelical lay preacher within the tiny Protestant minority of that country. He studied philosophy and theology at Wheaton College in Illinois, and then obtained his Ph.D. in New Testament under F. F. Bruce in Manchester, England. From 1959 to 1982, he and his American wife, Catharine, and their family were active in student evangelism, teaching, and writing, mostly in Argentina, under the International Fellowship of Evangelical Students. During those years the universities were among the most secularized institutions in Latin America, and the task of evangelism was carried on among young people who had openly rejected their Christian background, some of them having embraced Marxism with almost religious fervor. Some of the chapters of this book were first produced in Spanish at the request of university student leaders who were demanding a deeper and contextual exposition of the gospel that would allow them to live as Christians in an ideologically hostile milieu.

---

4. I am thankful to Padilla for providing data and precise details after reading an earlier draft of this paper.

As a Baptist minister, pastor of a local church, and editor of two evangelical magazines, Padilla also taught and carried on editorial work among evangelical leaders of the growing Protestant communities in Latin America. His teaching ministry needed to forge a critical side that would make leaders aware of the lack of an adequate evangelical theology and of the need to ground missionary and evangelistic patterns in solid biblical truth and not in a shallow fundamentalist's literalism. Like many other Christian leaders who had a clear awareness of the critical social conditions and the Christian responsibility, he lived with the tensions and the harassments of the years of "dirty war" in Argentina (1976-1983).

In the late 1960s and the 1970s, Padilla became part of a generation of evangelical theologians in Latin America that entered into an active and fruitful dialogue within Protestantism at a global level. The main context of that dialogue was the Lausanne Movement, to which Padilla made a key contribution that is incorporated in this book. He was also active in the Theological Commission of the World Evangelical Fellowship and the International Fellowship of Evangelical Mission Theologians (INFEMIT) and a member of the board of IAMS (1974-1982). In the case of Latin America, most of the contributors to this dialogue have come from the Latin American Theological Fraternity that was founded in 1970.[5] Within those circles, the conversation with Asian and African theologians led to identifying common concerns with Latin Americans, and all were able to establish some agreement with evangelical theologians from North America and Europe. The Willowbank Report expressed that conviction:

> We should seek with equal care to avoid theological imperialism or theological provincialism. A church's theology should be developed by the community of faith out of the Scripture in interaction with other theologies of the past and present, and with the local culture and its needs. (Stott and Coote 1980: 334)

Like other evangelical missiologists in Latin America, Padilla worked in a two-pronged theological approach. On the one hand was a *critical task,* which included an ongoing debate with the liberation theologies that have dominated the theological scenario for the last two decades. Such a critical task in some ways was a continuation of the debate with the Protestant predecessors of these theologies. What is distinctive of the evangelicals' stance is their emphasis on the primacy of biblical authority in their theological method and the insistence to keep the Evangel and evangelistic activity at the center of the mission of the church. However, their critical task has also developed a consistent debate against the theological assumptions— not always explicit—of church-growth mission theories and research methodologies (Shenk 1983). On the basis of biblical exegesis of the New

---

5. For a history of the Latin American Theological Fraternity, see A. Christopher Smith's Ph.D. dissertation (1983), which focuses on the Fraternity's missiology.

Testament material, Padilla opposed strongly some tenets of the church-growth missiology. "Its advocates," he says, "have taken as the starting point a sociological observation and developed a missionary strategy; only then, a posteriori, have they made the attempt to find biblical support" (1985a: 168). What he envisages is a different missiology: "The missiology that the church needs today ought to be perceiving the people of God not as a quotation that simply reflects the society of which it is a part but as 'an embodied question mark' that challenges the values of the world" (1985a: 169).

On the other hand, Padilla has worked also in the *constructive task* of developing a theology of mission that would express the dynamic missionary thrust of the evangelical churches in Latin America. From his practice as an evangelist and teacher of university students, he knows that millions of Latin Americans ignore the basic message of the gospel. Consequently, in many places basic evangelism and church planting are not an expression of religious piracy, but rather the response of sensitive Christians to the deeply felt spiritual needs of the people. At the same time, there is a growing participation of Latin Americans in the mission of the church at a global level, and this demands a contextual missionary formation. His response as a New Testament scholar is an effort to provide a solid biblical basis for new patterns of mission, evangelism, and discipleship in continuity with the best of the evangelical missionary tradition with its holistic commitment to spiritual and social transformation. Padilla has worked on the assumption that commitment to biblical authority requires continually a fresh exploration into the depths of the biblical text, with the questions raised by the Latin American context. The context of this reflection has been the Latin American reality, and at the global level he has worked within the Lausanne Movement.

The Lausanne Movement was the result of three vigorous evangelical movements following World War II. First was the renewal of mass evangelism that reached public notice with Billy Graham in Los Angeles in 1949. Some classic elements of revivalist Protestantism combined with the use of mass media shook the dormant religious routine of people, especially in the big cities, first in North America and then in Europe. Second was the renewal of serious evangelical scholarship in biblical studies and theological reflection, following renewal of evangelical university life in Europe and especially in England. Third, around the world, the effects of a new stream of missionary fervor and activity from North America and Europe became visible. It was mostly of the "faith mission" type, a new generation that threw itself with great vigor into the task of planting churches, translating Scripture, and reaching the restless masses of the so-called Third World. These three movements converged in the Berlin 1966 World Congress on Evangelism, under the leadership of journalist-theologian Carl F. H. Henry, to celebrate the tenth anniversary of the magazine *Christianity Today*. In contrast to other revival preachers, Billy Graham connected his evangelistic activity with the kind of theological education through the press that Carl Henry practiced. The vision of the Berlin congress, summarized in the motto "One Race, One Gospel, One Task," was communicated in a series of follow-up national and regional congresses around the world. The message from Berlin said: "Our goal is nothing short of the evangelization of the human race in this generation, by every means God has given to the mind of the will of men" (Henry and Mooneyham 1967).

The follow-up congresses after Berlin were platforms of convergence not only for reaffirming evangelical truth, but also for sober consideration of the spiritual needs of the world. The pragmatic concerns of evangelicals from North America and the theological and missiological acumen of European evangelicals were matched by the restless sense of mission of evangelicals in the young churches of the Third World or among the oppressed minorities. The agenda of the ongoing reflection had to make room for the burning questions of those who were serving God in situations where the ferment of nationalism, social upheaval, and ideological conflict was testing the theological depth of both evangelical and non-evangelical missionaries and churches. Thus, Lausanne 1974 was preceded by the gatherings of Singapore in 1968 for Asia, Minneapolis in 1969 for the United States, Bogotá in 1969 for Latin America, Ottawa in 1970 for Canada, Amsterdam in 1971 for Europe, and Madrid in 1974 for Spain and Portugal. Because of that, Lausanne was not the missiological and theological monologue of white, middle-class Anglo-Saxon evangelicals, but a fraternal dialogue, and at some points with an acute controversy, of a community that had grown beyond expectations all over the world—a dialogue in search of ways of obedience to the missionary imperatives of Jesus the Lord.

In a recent article about Lausanne, John Stott (1995) has outlined the spirit and history of the movement. He refers to the consultations that followed Lausanne, which in my opinion were missiological laboratories on a global dimension. Stott mentions four of them: Pasadena in 1977 about the homogeneous unit principle, Willowbank in 1978 about gospel and culture, High Leigh in 1980 about simple lifestyle, and Grand Rapids in 1982 about evangelism and social responsibility. A reading of Padilla's introduction to *Mission Between the Times* brings the realization that the chapters of his book are the papers he presented to those consultations. They are, therefore, an interesting index of a Latin American contribution to the kind of mission studies that have been taking place within the frame of the Lausanne Movement. They reflect on the one hand the commitment to evangelism and church planting, understood in classical evangelical terms, and on the other hand the exploration into the maze of cultural, social, and political realities that evangelists or missionaries cannot avoid if they take seriously their contexts and the people among whom they minister. Within this frame it is possible to detect the convergences with some of the questions that liberation theologies and Catholic missiologies have been posing: the nature of the Christian presence in the world, the impossibility of separating mission from church, the need to revise ecclesiology, the cry of the poor and the authenticity of forms of Christian faith that grow among the poor, the need to detach the gospel from the ideology of the West, and the inevitability of the social and political questions that demand decision, alignment, and options.

TURNING TO THE FUTURE

As my fifth case I have chosen Lamin Sanneh, an African scholar from Gambia who has secured an important place for a missionary agenda in the world of Ivy League scholarship in the United States.[6] I am inclined to say that Sanneh has given a certain missionary thrust to the serious scholarship that he practices. His book *Translating the Message* (1989) is a well-written and well-researched study about the missionary impact on culture. Sanneh's life story points to some of the issues that mission studies will have to explore in the future. A convert from Islam, he is familiar with Islamic theology and life, with the interaction of theological developments and historical events within the Islamic communities, especially in Africa. His writings evoke sometimes the depth of the spiritual experience within the Islamic religion. We follow him not so much as a polemicist engaged in superficial apologetics, but as one who wants the reader to understand what goes on in the soul of the believer. Reading his personal testimony (Sanneh 1984) brought to my own memory the writings of the Spanish mystics of the sixteenth century that were so influenced by the form and content of Arab spiritual poetry.

Sanneh is also a historian of religion by trade, and he is familiar with the history of missions in Africa. As a man who has crossed from culture to culture in his training and teaching career, he has first-hand knowledge about cultural identities, processes of translation, and processes of learning the Christian faith within the context of cultural transition. From the perception of missionary history he represents a moment of maturity from the side of the receivers of missionary action. His proposal is clear:

> The subject of Western missions needs to be unhinged from the narrow colonial context and placed in the much wider setting of African culture, including the religious background of African societies. This would not deny that missions played an active political role, but it would analyze that role as one strand of missionary history, not its warp and woof. It would not still concede that missionaries occupied the most prominent stage in the dissemination of Christianity, for in most instances they did not. (1983a: 165)

---

6. I am thankful to Sanneh for his clarification of some points in this paper through personal correspondence.

There is no iconoclastic intention here, but an honest effort to see the larger picture and to see it from an African perspective. He is very aware that the exaggeration of the role of the missionary has been alternatively used either as "a propaganda value for home committees" or as "an easy target for patriotic denunciation." The result will be a better assessment of mission than the ones that predominate when either superficial Marxism or managerial missiology is applied to the reading of history.

> Western missions have to be assessed against the background of the African societies with which they were involved. By shifting our attention in this way we also renounce statistical measures for judging missionary effectiveness, applying instead the much more relevant criteria of local significance. (1983a: 165)

Thus, Sanneh provides a reading of missionary history that I would describe as "mature." It has gone beyond the naïveté of hagiography that looked at missionaries as angels and saints. But it has not remained at the demythologizing level with its simplistic equation of mission and imperialistic advance. By moving beyond that simplistic criticism and the defensiveness that it evoked, he is able to look at the totality of mission history and its impact with all the grey zones, where there is no room for white legends or black legends, but an effort to take a sober and mature reading of the past. All these elements of his formation are brought to his reading of Scripture, history, and theology in *Translating the Message* (1989). In this book there is a careful, comparative exercise of the missionary impulse and the missionary approaches of both Christianity and Islam, trying to find what is at the core of both impulses shaping the different methodologies. One important methodological issue that Sanneh develops is the relationship between history and theology which in my opinion is key in order to understand the process of mission studies in the immediate past and the course it could take in the future. Sanneh deals with mission history, paying attention to the internal forces as well as to the external circumstances that shape the religious phenomenon.

> One way of describing what I have done here is to say that I treat Christianity as a religious movement, or as a vernacular translation movement, in contradistinction to Christianity either as Scripture or as a dogmatic, creedal system, without, of course, denying the validity of those views. (1989: 7)

From the clarification he offers about his methodology, I like the conciseness and the precision of this crisp sentence from Sanneh: "The 'normative' issues with which theology concerns itself are important for illuminating the human factor in the shaping of values, while the 'descriptive' preciseness of historical investigation gives solidity to the promptings of the Spirit"

(1989: 7). The sentence connects naturally with an observation of Yates in the introduction to his history of missions in our century:

> In the view of the writer, missiology is at its best when history and theology are held in tension and there is a continuing oscillation between historical context and Christian input, so that the analysis of the form in which the Gospel is expressed, the theory of the mission, is related firmly to the setting. (1994: 5)

By placing translation at the center of the Christian mission, Sanneh has developed an interpretative principle that helps us read mission history with new keys, thus finding the significance of old facts and helping us to identify new facts that are to be taken into account. As he has moved with this approach into the earliest documents about the Christian mission, the writings of Luke and Paul, he has also brought a new ferment into theological reflection. Looking at the result of the missionary impulse at that early stage, Sanneh can say that "Paul formulated pluralism as the necessary outworking of the religion he believed Jesus preached. That pluralism was rooted for Paul in the Gentile breakthrough, which in turn justified cross-cultural tolerance in Christian mission" (1989: 47). With this conclusion Sanneh places in the Pauline agenda issues that are burning in our time and that sometimes we tend to think are unique to our end-of-the-century milieu. At this point he helps us to see how biblical accounts as well as mission history may provide us with understanding for some of the most crucial concerns of our time.

Sanneh himself applies this as he looks, for instance, to the contemporary encounter of Islam and the West. He reminds us, "The Muslim challenge in asserting a religious interest in government and education may be considered a challenge also to the prevailing Western attitude of secular accommodation or even abdication" (1993: 164). Relationships between Islam and the West must not be handled on the basis of political expedience within the frame of a secularized society. Sanneh thinks that we as Christians must rediscover the basic belief which is at the heart of a notion of pluralism, and that we should take moral responsibility for the heritage of the West, including tolerance for religion. "Such tolerance for religion cannot rest on the arguments of public utility but rather on the firm religious rock of the absolute moral law with which our Creator and Judge has fashioned us" (1993: 168). Interestingly enough, Sanneh's call at this point evokes the voice of the most recent Newbigin:

> Westerners must recover responsibility for the Gospel as public truth and must reconstitute by it the original foundations on which the modern West has built its ample view of the world. The continuing disregard of the spiritual heritage is damaging to the tolerance and open-mindedness that have been the safety net averting the penalty of

suppression from religious differences and allowing for the preservation of minorities in our midst. (Sanneh 1993: 168)

From the theological perspective, the principle of translatability points to the central fact of our faith and our message—Jesus Christ, the incarnate Son of God. This principle places God at the center and cultures at the periphery. This translatability also reminds us of the essential missionary nature of the Christian faith. The missionary expansion of the faith has created a dynamic plurality of cultures sustained by one faith in the God and Father of Jesus Christ. Plurality is possible because all cultures are equal in terms of access to God. At the same time, no culture in itself is totally adequate in terms of transcendent truth. The gospel does not find expression outside of a cultural form; however, the gospel cannot be restricted to any given cultural form—it transcends all of them.

In one of his autobiographical reflections, Sanneh conveys the powerful conviction that came to him from the consideration of the truth that "the Word became flesh and dwelt among us." He was impacted also by the way in which the passion of Jesus makes him, the prophet, the supreme subject and victim of human disobedience. Sanneh evokes Isaiah, "It pleased the Lord to bruise him," and comments, "No proximity to the human condition is more poignant than that." Sanneh's conclusion is challenging:

Our perception of this truth is indispensable to our obtaining a right and fulfilling relationship with God. Redemptive suffering is at the very core of moral truth, and the prophets were all touched by its fearsome power. But only One embodied it as a historical experience, although all, including the Prophet of Islam, walked in its shadow. Those who consult their hearts will hear for themselves the persistent ordinance proclaiming God's ineffable grace. (1984: 174)

I find that many of the questions that have shaped mission studies in our time can be related to this conviction about Jesus Christ, the incarnate and crucified Son of God who is himself the gospel that Christian mission offers. This conviction will continue to give us clues for mission in the future. Let me explain this statement with a conclusion that I take from Newbigin:

The real triumphs of the gospel have not been won when the church is strong in a worldly sense; they have been won when the church is faithful in the midst of weakness, contempt and rejection. And I would simply add my own testimony, which could be illustrated by many examples, that it has been in situations where faithfulness to the Gospel placed the church in a position of total weakness and rejection that the advocate has himself risen up and, often through the words and deeds of very "insignificant" people, spoken the word that confronted and shamed the wisdom and power of the world. (1995: 62)

References Cited

Ajayi, Ade, and E. A. Ayandele. 1969. "Writing African Church History." In Peter Beyerhaus and Carl Hallencreutz, eds., *The Church Crossing Frontiers: Essays on the Nature of Mission*, 90-108. Studia Missionalia Uppsaliensa 11. Lund: Gleerup.

Allen, Roland. 1930. *Missionary Methods: St. Paul's or Ours?* London: World Dominion Press.

Allmen, Daniel von. 1975. "The Birth of Theology: Contextualization as the Dynamic Element in the Formation of New Testament Theology." *International Review of Mission* 64/1: 37-52.

Anderson, Allan. 1992a. *Moya: The Holy Spirit in an African Context*. Pretoria: University of South Africa Press.

————. 1992b. *Bazalwane: African Pentecostals in South Africa*. Pretoria: University of South Africa Press.

————. 1993. "African Pentecostalism and the Ancestor Cult: Confrontation or Compromise?" *Missionalia* 21/1: 38-39.

Anderson, Gerald H. 1988. "American Protestants in Pursuit of Mission: 1886-1986." *International Bulletin of Mission Research* 12/3: 98-118.

————. 1989. "The Truth of Christian Uniqueness." *International Bulletin of Mission Research* 13/2: 49.

————. 1990. "Christian Mission and Religious Pluralism: A Selected Bibliography of 175 Books in English, 1970-1990." *International Bulletin of Missionary Research* 14/4: 172-76.

————. 1991. "Mission Research, Writing, and Publishing: 1971-1991." *International Bulletin of Missionary Research* 15/4: 165-72.

————. 1993. "Theology of Religions and Missiology: A Time of Testing." In Charles Van Engen et al., eds., *The Good News of the Kingdom*, 200-210. Maryknoll, NY: Orbis Books.

———— et al., eds. 1995. *Mission Legacies: Biographical Studies of Leaders of the Modern Missionary Movement*. Maryknoll, NY: Orbis Books.

Anderson, G. H., and T. F. Stransky, eds. 1981a. *Christ's Lordship and Religious Pluralism*, Maryknoll, NY: Orbis Books.

————. 1981b. *Mission Trends No. 5: Faith Meets Faith*. Grand Rapids: Eerdmans; New York: Paulist.

Anderson, Norman, ed. 1950. *The World Religions*. Grand Rapids: Eerdmans.

Anglican Communion News Service LC014. 1998. "Background Briefing, Lambeth Conference at a Glance" (July 18).

Appiah-Kubi, Kofi. 1979. "Indigenous African Christian Churches: Signs of Authenticity." In Kofi Appiah-Kubi, ed., *African Theology Enroute*, 117-18. Maryknoll, NY: Orbis Books.

Ariarajah, Wesley. 1988a. "The Religions and Tambaram." *International Review of Mission* 78/307: 419-20.

———. 1988b. "Religious Pluralism and Its Challenge to Christian Theology." *World Faiths Insight* 19 n.s.: 2-15.

Arnal, Oscar L. 1986. *Priests in Working-Class Blue: The History of the Worker Priests.* New York: Paulist Press.

Asamoah-Gyadu, Kwabena. 1998. "Fireballs in Our Midst: West Africa's Burgeoning Charismatic Churches and the Pastoral Role of Women." *Mission Studies* 15/1: 27.

Ayegboyin, Deji, and A. Ademola Ishola. 1997. *African Independent Churches: An Historical Perspective.* Lagos, Nigeria: Greater Heights Publications.

Baëta, Christian G., ed. 1968. *Christianity in Tropical Africa.* London: Oxford University Press.

Bakker, R., R. Fernhout, J. D. Gort, and A. Wessels, eds. 1985. *Religies in Nieuw Perspective.* Kampen: Kok.

Barrett, C. K. 1971. *A Commentary on the First Epistle to the Corinthians.* London: Adam & Charles Black.

Barrett, David B. 1970. "AD 2000: 350 Million Christians in Africa." *International Review of Mission* 59: 39-54.

———. 1982. *World Christian Encyclopedia.* Nairobi, Kenya: Oxford University Press.

———, and M. Todd Johnson. 2000. "Annual Statistical Table on Global Mission 2001." *International Bulletin of Missionary Research* 24/1: 24-25.

———. 2001. "Annual Statistical Table on Global Mission 2001." *International Bulletin of Missionary Research* 25/1: 25.

Bartchy, S. Scott. 1973. *First Century Slavery and 1 Corinthians 7:21.* Missoula, MT: University of Montana Press.

Barth, Karl. 1962a. *Theology and Church: Shorter Writings, 1920-1928.* New York: Harper & Row.

———. 1962b. "Church and Cultures." In *Theology and Church: Shorter Writings, 1920-1928,* 334-354. New York: Harper & Row.

———. 1980. "The Revelation of God as the Abolition of Religion." In John Hick and Brian Hebblethwaite, eds., *Christianity and Other Religions: Selected Readings,* 32-51. Glasgow: Fount Paperbacks.

Bassham, Rodger C. 1979. *Mission Theology, 1948-1975: Years of Worldwide Creative Tension—Ecumenical, Evangelical, and Roman Catholic.* Pasadena, CA: William Carey Library.

Bauckham, Richard. 1979. "Universalism—A Historical Survey." *Themelios* 4/2: 48-53.

Bays, Daniel H. 1996. "The Growth of Independent Christianity in China, 1900-1937." In *Christianity in China: From the Eighteenth Century to the Present.* Edited by Daniel H. Bays. Stanford: Sanford University Press.

Bediako, Kwame. 1984. "Biblical Christologies in the Context of African Traditional Religions." In Vinay Samuel and Chris Sugden, eds., *Sharing Jesus in the Two-Thirds World,* 81-121. Grand Rapids: Eerdmans.

———. 1985. "The Missionary Inheritance." In Robin Keeley, ed., *Christianity: A World Faith,* 303-11. Tring: Lion Publishing.

———. 1989. "World Evangelization, Institutional Evangelicalism and the Future of the Christian World Mission." In V. Samuel and A. Hauser, eds., *Proclaiming Christ in Christ's Way: Studies in Integral Evangelism,* 52-68. Oxford: Regnum Books.

————. 1990. *Jesus in African Culture: A Ghanaian Perspective.* Accra, Ghana: Asempa Publishers.

————. 1993. "Cry Jesus! Christian Theology and Presence in Modern Africa." *Vox Evangelica* 23/2: 7-25.

————. 1994. "The Impact of the Bible in Africa." In Ype Shaaf, ed., *On Their Way Rejoicing: The History and Role of the Bible in Africa,* 243-54. Carlisle: Paternoster.

————. 1994-1995. "Christ Is Lord: How Is Jesus Unique in the Midst of Other Religious Faiths?" *Trinity Journal of Church and Theology* 14/2: 50-61.

Berg, Mike, and Paul Pretiz. 1994. *The Gospel People.* Monrovia, Calif.: MARC and Latin American Mission.

Berger, Peter L., Brigitte Berger, and Hansfried Kellner. 1973. *The Homeless Mind: Modernization and Consciousness.* New York: Random House.

Berkhof, Hendrikus. 1964. *The Doctrine of the Holy Spirit.* Richmond, VA: John Knox.

————. 1979. *Christian Faith: An Introduction to the Study of the Faith.* Grand Rapids: Eerdmans.

————. 1988. "The Double Image of the Future." *Perspectives* 3/1: 8-9.

————. 1994. "The Impact of the Bible in Africa." In Ype Shaaf, ed., *On Their Way Rejoicing: The History and Role of the Bible in Africa,* 243-54. Carlisle: Paternoster.

Blough, Neal. 1993. "Messianic Mission and Ethics: Discipleship and the Good News." In Wilbert R. Shenk, ed., *The Transfiguration of Mission: Biblical, Theological and Historical Foundations,* 178-98. Scottdale, PA: Herald.

Blum, E. A. 1979. "Shall You Not Surely Die?" *Themelios* 4/2: 58-61.

Blyden, Edward W. 1967 [1887]. "Ethiopia Stretching Out Her Hands unto God, or Africa's Service to the World." In Edward W. Blyden, ed., *Christianity, Islam and the Negro Race.* Edinburgh: Edinburgh University Press.

Boer, Harry R. 1961. *Pentecost and Missions.* Grand Rapids: Eerdmans.

Boff, Leonardo. 1984. *Jesus Christ Liberator: A Critical Christology for Our Time.* Maryknoll, NY: Orbis Books.

————. 1986. *Ecclesiogenesis: The Base Communities Reinvent the Church.* Maryknoll, NY: Orbis Books.

Bosch, David J. 1972. "Systematic Theology and Missions: The Voice of an Early Pioneer." *Theologia Evangelica* 5/3: 165-89.

————. 1979. *A Spirituality of the Road.* Scottdale, PA: Herald.

————. 1980. *Witness to the World.* Atlanta: John Knox.

————. 1982. "Theological Education in Missionary Perspective." *Missiology* 10/1: 13-34.

————. 1983a. "The Structure of Mission: An Exposition of Matthew 28:16-20." In Wilbert R. Shenk, ed., *Exploring Church Growth,* 218-48. Grand Rapids: Eerdmans.

————. 1983b. "An Emerging Paradigm for Mission." *Missiology* 11/4: 485-510.

————. 1983c. "Missionary Theology in Africa." *Indian Missiological Review* 6/2: 105-39.

————. 1984. "Missionary Theology in Africa." *Journal of Theology for Southern Africa* 49/4: 14-37.

————. 1988. "The Church in Dialogue: From Self-Delusion to Vulnerability." *Missiology* 16: 131-47.

————. 1989. Review of *Le Dieu qui vient: La mission dans la Bible,* by Lucien Legrand. *Missionalia* 17/1: 64.

————. 1991. *Transforming Mission: Paradigm Shifts in Theology of Mission.* Maryknoll, NY: Orbis Books.

————. 1993. "Reflections on Biblical Models of Mission." In James M. Phillips and Robert T. Coote, eds., *Toward the 21st Century in Christian Mission: Essays in Honor of Gerald H. Anderson,* 175-92. Grand Rapids: Eerdmans.

————. 1995. *Believing in the Future: Toward a Missiology of Western Culture.* Valley Forge, PA: Trinity Press International.

Braaten, Carl. 1981. "The Uniqueness and Universality of Jesus Christ." In Gerald Anderson and Thomas Stransky, eds., *Mission Trends No. 5,* 69-92. Grand Rapids: Eerdmans. (Originally published in the January 1980 issue of *Occasional Bulletin of Missionary Research.*)

————. 1987. "Christocentric Trinitarianism vs. Unitarian Theocentrism: A Response to Mark Heim." *Journal of Ecumenical Studies* 24/1: 17-21.

————. 1990. "The Triune God: The Source and Model of Christian Unity and Mission." *Missiology* 18/4: 415-28.

Bradley, James E. 1993. "Logos Christology and Religious Pluralism: A New Evangelical Proposal." Unpublished paper. Fuller Theological Seminary, Pasadena.

Bredero, Adriann H. 1994. *Christendom and Christianity in the Middle Ages.* Grand Rapids: Eerdmans.

Brown, Peter, and Jacques Le Goff, eds. 1997. *The Rise of Western Christendom.* Oxford: Blackwell.

Bruce, Frederick F. 1957. *Commentary on the Epistle to the Colossians.* London: Marshall, Morgan & Scott.

————. 1961. *The Epistle to the Ephesians.* London: Pickering & Inglis.

————. 1969. *New Testament History.* Garden City, NY: Doubleday.

Brueggemann, Walter. 1982. "The Bible and Mission: Some Interdisciplinary Implications for Teaching." *Missiology* 10/4: 397-411.

Bufford, Rodger K. 1981. *The Human Reflex: Behavioral Psychology in Biblical Perspective.* San Francisco: Harper & Row.

Bühlmann, Walbert. 1977. *The Coming of the Third Church.* Maryknoll, NY: Orbis Books.

Bujo, Bénézet. 1992. *African Theology in Its Social Context.* Maryknoll, NY: Orbis Books.

Burrows, William R. 1998. "Reconciling All in Christ: The Oldest New Paradigm for Mission." *Mission Studies* 15-1/29: 86-87.

Cantwell Smith, Wilfred. 1980. "The Christian in a Religiously Plural World." In John Hick and Brian Hebblethwaite, eds., *Christianity and Other Religions: Selected Readings,* 87-107. Glasgow: Fount Paperbacks.

Carey, William. 1891. *An Enquiry into the Obligation of Christians to Use Means for the Conversion of the Heathen.* London: Baptist Missionary Society. Facsimile of 1792 edition.

Carpenter, Joel A., and Wilbert R. Shenk, eds. 1990. *Earthen Vessels: American Evangelicals and Foreign Mission, 1880-1980.* Grand Rapids: Eerdmans.

Chapman, Colin. 1990. "The Riddle of Religions." *Christianity Today* 34/8: 16-22.

Clark, Donald N. 1986. *Christianity in Modern Korea.* Lanham, MD: University Press of America.

Cleary, Edward L. 1985. *Crisis and Change: The Church in Latin America Today.* Maryknoll, NY: Orbis Books.

———. 1990. *Born of the Poor: The Latin American Church Since Medellín.* Notre Dame, IN: University of Notre Dame Press.

Clowney, Edmund P. 1976. "The Missionary Flame of Reformed Theology." In Harvie M. Conn, ed., *Theological Perspectives on Church Growth.* Nutley, NJ: Presbyterian and Reformed Publishing Company.

Cobb, John. 1975. *Christ in a Pluralistic Age.* Philadelphia: Westminster.

Coleman, Richard J. 1980. *Issues in Theological Conflict.* Grand Rapids: Eerdmans.

Comblin, Joseph. 1979. *Sent from the Father.* Maryknoll, NY: Orbis Books.

Congregation for the Evangelization of Peoples and the Pontifical Council for Interreligious Dialogue. 1992. "Dialogue and Proclamation (Excerpts)." *International Bulletin of Mission Research* 16/3:82-86.

Conn, Harvie, ed. 1990. *Practical Theology and the Ministry of the Church, 1952-1984: Essays in Honor of Edmund P. Clowney.* Phillipsburg, NJ: Presbyterian & Reformed.

Connelly, Matthew, and Paul Kennedy. 1994. "Must It Be the Rest Against the West?" *The Atlantic Monthly* (December).

Cook, Guillermo. 1985. *The Expectation of the Poor.* Maryknoll, NY: Orbis Books.

———, ed. 1994. *New Face of the Church in Latin America.* Maryknoll, NY: Orbis Books.

Coote, Robert T. 1990. "Lausanne II and World Evangelization." *International Bulletin of Mission Research* 14/1: 10-17.

Costas, Orlando E. 1981. "Church Growth as a Multidimensional Phenomenon: Some Lessons from Chile." *International Bulletin of Missionary Research* 5/1: 2ff.

———. 1982. *Christ Outside the Gate.* Maryknoll, NY: Orbis Books.

———. 1989. *Liberating News: A Theology of Contextual Evangelization.* Grand Rapids: Eerdmans.

Cottrell, Jack, and Stephen Burris. 1993. "The Fate of the Unreached: Implications for Frontier Missions." *International Journal of Frontier Missions* 10/2: 1-6.

Covell, Ralph. 1993. "Jesus Christ and World Religions: Current Evangelical Viewpoints." In Charles Van Engen et al., eds., *The Good News of the Kingdom,* 162-80. Maryknoll, NY: Orbis Books.

Cox, Harvey. 1994. *Fire from Heaven: The Rise of Pentecostal Spirituality and the Reshaping of Religion in the Twenty-First Century.* Reading, MA: Addison-Wesley.

Cragg, Kenneth. 1968. *Christianity in World Perspective.* New York: Oxford University Press.

———. 1977. *The Christian and Other Religions: The Measure of Christ.* London and Oxford: Mowbrays.

———. 1986. *The Christ and the Faiths: Theology in Cross Reference.* London: SPCK.

Crockett, William V., and James G. Sigountos, eds. 1991. *Through No Fault of Their Own? The Fate of Those Who Have Never Heard.* Grand Rapids: Baker.

Cullmann, Oscar. 1963. *The Christology of the New Testament.* Philadelphia: Westminster.

Daneel, Mathinus L. 1987. *Quest for Belonging: An Introduction to a Study of African Independent Churches*. Gweru, Zimbabwe: Mambo Press.

———. 1991. "The Liberation of Creation: African Traditional Religion and Independent Church Perspectives." *Missionalia* 19/2: 99-121.

———. 1993. "African Independent Churches Face the Challenge of Environmental Ethics." *Missionalia* 21/3: 311-32.

———. 1996. "Earthkeeping in Missiological Perspective: An African Challenge." *Mission Studies* 13/1, 2: 130-88.

———. 1998. *African Earthkeepers*, vol. 1. *Interfaith Mission in Earth-Care*. Pretoria: University of South Africa Press.

———. 1999a. *African Earthkeepers*, vol. 2. *Environmental Mission and Liberation in Christian Perspective*. Pretoria: University of South Africa Press.

———. 1999b. "African Initiated Churches in Southern Africa: Protest Movements or Missionary Churches?" Paper presented at Currents in World Christianity Conference. Cambridge University. July 15.

Danker, William J. 1971. *Profit for the Lord*. Grand Rapids: Eerdmans.

Dawe, Donald, and John Carman, eds. 1978. *Christian Faith in a Religiously Plural World*. Maryknoll, NY: Orbis Books.

Dayton, Donald W. 1976. *Discovering an Evangelical Heritage*. New York: Harper & Row.

Dempster, Murray A., Byron D. Klaus, and Douglas Petersen, eds. 1991. *Called and Empowered: Global Mission in Pentecostal Perspective*. Peabody, MA: Hendrickson.

Desroche, Henri. 1979. *The Sociology of Hope*. London: Routledge & Kegan Paul.

Douglas, James D., ed. 1975. *Let the Earth Hear His Voice*. Minneapolis: Worldwide Publications.

Driver, John. 1983. "Mission: Salt, Light, and Covenant Law." *Mission Focus* 11/3: 33-36.

———. 1993. "The Kingdom of God: Goal of Messianic Mission." In Wilbert R. Shenk, ed., *The Transfiguration of Mission: Biblical, Theological and Historical Foundations*, 83-105. Scottdale, PA: Herald.

Duhaime, Jean. 1992. "Early Christianity and the Social Sciences: A Bibliography." *Social Compass* 39/2: 275-90.

Dunn, James D. G. 1970. *Baptism in the Holy Spirit*. London: SCM.

———. 1975. *Jesus and the Spirit*. London: SCM.

———. 1977. *Unity and Diversity in the New Testament*. London: SCM.

———. 1980. *Christology in the Making: A New Testament Inquiry into the Origins of the Doctrines of the Incarnation*. Philadelphia: Westminster.

Dussel, Enrique D. 1981. *A History of the Church in Latin America: Colonialism to Liberation (1492-1979)*. Translation and revision by Alan Neely. Grand Rapids: Eerdmans.

———, ed. 1992. *The Church in Latin America 1492-1992*. Maryknoll, NY: Orbis Books.

Dyrness, William A. 1994. *Emerging Voices in Global Christian Theology*. Grand Rapids: Zondervan.

Echegaray, Hugo. 1984. *The Practice of Jesus*. Maryknoll, NY: Orbis Books.

Eilers, Franz-Josef., ed. 1997. *For All the Peoples of Asia: Federation of Asia Bishops' Conferences. Documents from 1992 to 1996*. Quezon City, Philippines: Claretian Publications.

————, ed. 2002. *Church and Social Communication in Asia—Documents, Analysis, Experiences.* Manila: Logos.

Ellul, Jacques. 1951. *The Presence of the Kingdom.* London: SCM.

ERCDOM. 1986. *The Evangelical-Roman Catholic Dialogue on Mission, 1977-1984.* Edited by B. Meeking and J. Stott. Grand Rapids: Eerdmans; Exeter, UK: Paternoster.

Erickson, Millard. 1991. "The State of the Question." In William Crockett and James Sigountos, eds., *Through No Fault of Their Own? The Fate of Those Who Have Never Heard,* 23-34. Grand Rapids: Baker.

Escobar, J. Samuel. 1987. "Missions and Renewal in Latin American Catholicism." *Missiology* 15/2: 33-46.

————. 1991. "Evangelical Theology in Latin America: The Development of a Missiological Christology." *Missiology* 19/3: 315-32.

————. 1996a. "Evangelical Theology in Latin America." *Evangelical Review of Theology* 20: 315-32.

————. 1996b. "Mañana: Discerning the Spirit in Latin America." *Evangelical Review of Theology* 20: 312-26.

————. 1999. "Missionary Dynamism in Search of Missiological Discernment." *One in Christ* 35/1: 69-91.

Fasholé-Luke, Edward W. 1975. "The Quest for an African Christian Theology." *Ecumenical Review* 27/3: 267-68.

Fee, Gordon D. 1994. *God's Empowering Presence: The Holy Spirit in the Letters of Paul.* Peabody, MA: Hendrickson.

Fernando, Ajith. 1987. *The Christian's Attitude toward World Religions.* Wheaton, IL: Tyndale.

Filson, Floyd V. 1963. *Three Crucial Decades.* Richmond, VA: John Knox.

————. 1965. *A New Testament History.* London: SCM.

Forman, Charles. 1993. "Christian Dialogues with Other Faiths." In James Phillips and Robert Coote, eds., *Toward the 21st Century in Christian Mission,* 338-47. Grand Rapids: Eerdmans.

Fox, Tom. 2000. *Pentecost in Asia: A New Way of Being Church.* Maryknoll, NY: Orbis Books.

Frazier, William M. 1987. "Where Mission Begins: A Foundational Probe." *Maryknoll Formation Journal* (Summer): 13-52.

Froehle, Bryan T., and Mary L. Gauthier. 2003. *Global Catholicism: Portrait of a World Church.* Maryknoll, NY: Orbis Books.

Gilliland, Dean, ed. 1989. *The Word among Us: Contextualizing Theology for Mission Today.* Waco, TX: Word.

Glasser, Arthur F. 1989. "Mission in the 1990s: Two Views." *International Bulletin of Mission Research* 13/1: 2-8.

————, and Donald A. McGavran. 1983. *Contemporary Theologies of Mission.* Grand Rapids: Baker.

Gnanakan, Ken R. 1992. *The Pluralist Predicament.* Bangalore: Theological Book Trust.

González, Justo L. 1970. *Historia de las misiones.* Trans. O. E. C. Buenos Aires: La Aurora.

————. 1990. *Mañana: Christian Theology from a Hispanic Perspective.* Nashville, TN: Abingdon.

Gorostiaga, Xabier. 1978. "Notas sobre metodologia para un diagnostico economico del capitalismo latinoamericano." In Elsa Tamez and Saul Trinidad, eds., *Capitalismo: violencia y antivida*, 1:40-48. Coleccion DEI. San José, Costa Rica: EDUCA.

Gort, Jerald D., Hendrik M. Vroom, Rein Fernhout, and Anton Wessels, eds. 1992. *On Sharing Religious Experience: Possibilities of Interfaith Mutuality*. Grand Rapids: Eerdmans.

Green, Michael. 1970. *Evangelism in the Early Church*. London: Hodder & Stoughton.

——. 1977. "Jesus in the New Testament." In Michael Green, ed. *The Truth of God Incarnate*, 18-50. London: Hodder & Stoughton.

——, ed. 1977. *The Truth of God Incarnate*. London: Hodder & Stoughton.

Guelich, Robert A. 1989. *"What Is the Gospel?"* Inaugural address (May 9, 1989), Fuller Theological Seminary, Pasadena, CA.

Gundry, Robert H. 1994. "Diversity and Multiculturalism in New Testament Christology." Unpublished paper. Westmont College, Santa Barbara, CA.

Gutiérrez, Gustavo. 1988 [1973]. *A Theology of Liberation: History, Politics, and Salvation*. Fifteenth anniversary edition with new introduction. Translated and edited by Sister Caridad Inda and John Eagleson. Maryknoll, NY: Orbis Books.

Guthrie, Donald. 1969. *Galatians*. London: Thomas Nelson.

Hall, Douglas John. 1975. *The Reality of the Gospel and the Unreality of the Churches*. Philadelphia: Westminster.

Hallencreutz, Carl. 1969. *New Approaches to Men of Other Faiths*. Geneva: World Council of Churches.

Hardman, Keith J. 1990. *Charles Grandison Finney: Revivalist and Reformer*. Grand Rapids: Baker.

Harris, Mary G. 1994. "Cholas, Mexican-American Girls, and Gangs." *Sex Roles* 30/3: 289.

Hastings, Adrian. 1976. *African Christianity: An Essay in Interpretation*. London; Geoffrey Chapman.

——. 1989. *African Catholicism*. London: SCM.

Heim, Mark. 1985. *Is Christ the Only Way? Christian Faith in a Pluralistic World*. Valley Forge, PA: Judson.

——. 1987. "Thinking about Theocentric Christology." *Journal of Ecumenical Studies* 24 /1: 1-16.

Hengel, Martin. 1983. "The Origins of the Christian Mission." In Martin Hengel, ed., *Between Jesus and Paul: Studies in the Earliest History of Christianity*, 48-64, 166-79. London: SCM.

Henry, Carl F. H. 1947. *The Uneasy Conscience of Modern Fundamentalism*. Grand Rapids: Eerdmans.

——. 1991. "Is It Fair?" In William V. Crockett and James G. Sigountos, eds. *Through No Fault of Their Own? The Fate of Those Who Have Never Heard*, 245-56. Grand Rapids: Baker.

——, and W. S. Mooneyham, eds. 1967. *One Race, One Gospel, One Task: World Congress on Evangelism, Berlin, 1966*. 2 vols. Minneapolis: World Wide Publications.

Herrera, Marina. 1992. *A Strategic Plan to Prepare Ministries for the Multicultural Church*, Research Monograph. Washington, DC: Washington Theological Union.

Hesselgrave, David J. 1981. "Evangelicals and Interrelegious Dialogue." In Gerald Anderson and Thomas Stransky, eds., *Mission Trends No. 5: Faith Meets Faith*, 123-27. Grand Rapids: Eerdmans; New York: Paulist.

————. 1988. *Today's Choices for Tomorrow's Mission: An Evangelical Perspective on Trends and Issues in Missions.* Grand Rapids: Zondervan.

————. 1990. "Christian Communication and Religious Pluralism: Capitalizing on Differences·" *Missiology* 18/2:131-38.

————, ed. 1979. *New Horizons in World Mission.* Grand Rapids: Baker.

Hick, John. 1982. *God Has Many Names.* Philadelphia: Westminster.

————, and Brian Hebblethwaite, eds. 1980. *Christianity and Other Religions: Selected Readings.* Glasgow: Fount Paperbacks.

————, and Paul Knitter, eds. 1988. *The Myth of Christian Uniqueness: Toward a Pluralistic Theology of Religions.* Maryknoll, NY: Orbis Books.

Hiebert, Paul G. 1978. "Conversion, Culture and Cognitive Categories." *Gospel in Context* 1/ 3: 24-29.

————. 1979. "Sets and Structures: A Study of Church Patterns." In David J. Hesselgrave, ed., *New Horizons in World Mission,* 217-27. Grand Rapids: Baker.

————. 1982. "The Flaw of the Excluded Middle." *Missiology* 10/1: 35-47.

————. 1983. "The Category 'Christian' in the Mission Task." *International Review of Mission* 72/3: 421-27.

————. 1985. *Anthropological Insights for Missionaries.* Grand Rapids: Baker.

————. 1987. "Critical Contextualization." *International Bulletin of Missionary Research* 11/3: 104-12.

————. 1991. "Beyond Anti-Colonialism to Globalism." *Missiology* 19/3: 263-82.

————. 1994. *Anthropological Reflections on Missiological Issues.* Grand Rapids: Baker.

Hillman, Eugene. 1968. *The Wider Ecumenism: Anonymous Christianity and the Church.* London: Burns & Oates.

Hocking, William. 1932. *Re-Thinking Missions: A Layman's Inquiry after One Hundred Years.* New York: Harper.

Hollenweger, Walter J. 1972. *The Pentecostals.* London: SCM.

————. 1986. "After Twenty Years' Research on Pentecostalism." *International Review of Mission* 75/297: 3-12.

————. 1997. *Pentecostalism: Origins and Developments Worldwide.* Peabody, MA: Hendrickson.

Hoornaert, Eduardo. 1974. *Formaçao do Catolicismo no Brasil.* Petrópolis, Brazil: Ed. Vozes.

————. 1977. *Historia da Igreja no Brasil: Primeira Epoca.* Petrópolis, Brazil: Ed. Vozes.

————. 1989. *The Memory of the Christian People.* Maryknoll, NY: Orbis Books.

Houtondji, Paulin J. 1980. *Sur la "philosophie africaine: critique de l'ethnophiloso- phie."* Yaoundé: Editions Clé.

Howard, David M. 1983. "From Wheaton '66 to Wheaton '83." Manuscript.

Hunter, George G., III. 1992. "The Legacy of Donald A. McGavran." *International Bulletin of Missionary Research* 16/4: 158-62.

Hutchinson, Mark. 1998. "It's a Small Church After All." *Christianity Today* (November 16): 46-49.

Hutchison, William R. 1987. *Errand to the World: American Protestant Thought and Foreign Missions.* Chicago: University of Chicago Press.

Idowu, Bolaji. 1962. *Olódùmarè: God in Yoruba Belief.* New York: Praeger.

————. 1965. *Towards an Indigenous Church.* London: Oxford University Press.

————. 1973. *African Traditional Religion: A Definition.* London: SCM.

International Missionary Council. 1938. *The World Mission of the Church: Findings and Recommendations of the Meeting of the International Missionary Council.* London: International Missionary Council.

Jeal, Tim. 1973. *Livingstone.* London: Heinemann.

Jenkins, Paul. 1986. "The Roots of African Church History: Some Polemic Thoughts." *International Bulletin of Missionary Research* 10/2: 67-71.

Jenkins, Philip. 2002a. *The Next Christendom: The Coming of Global Christianity.* New York: Oxford University Press.

———. 2002b. "The Next Christianity." *The Atlantic Monthly* 290/3: 53-68.

Jeremias, Joachim. 1955. *Jesus' Promise to the Nations.* London: SCM.

———. 1971. *New Testament Theology: The Proclamation of Jesus.* London: SCM.

Johnston, Arthur. 1978. *The Battle for World Evangelism.* Wheaton, IL: Tyndale House.

Johnston, James. 1886. *A Century of Protestant Missions.* London: James Nisbet; Edinburgh: Oliver & Boyd.

Johnstone, Patrick. 1993. *Operation World.* Grand Rapids: Zondervan.

Jongeneel, Jan A. B., ed. 1992. *Pentecost, Mission and Ecumenism: Essays in Intercultural Theology.* Berlin: Peter Lang.

Judge, Edwin A. 1960. *The Social Pattern of Christian Groups in the First Century.* London: Tyndale.

Kähler, Martin. 1971 [1908]. *Schriften zur Christologie und Mission.* Munich: Christian Kaiser Verlag.

Kalu, Ogbu. 2000. "The Estranged Bedfellows: Demonization of the Aladura in African Pentecostalism." In Mathinus L. Daneel, ed., *African Christian Outreach: The AIC Contribution.* Pretoria: University of South Africa Press.

Kantzer, Kenneth. 1991. "Preface." In William Crockett and James Sigountos, eds., *Through No Fault of Their Own? The Fate of Those Who Have Never Heard,* 11-15. Grand Rapids: Baker.

Kärkkäinen, Veli-Matti. 1999. "Mission, Spirit, and Eschatology: An Outline of Pentecostal-Charismatic Theology of Mission." *Mission Studies* 16/1: 75, 87.

Kasting, Heinrich. 1967. *Die Anfänge der urchristlichen Mission.* Munich: Christian Kaiser Verlag.

Kertelge, Karl., ed. 1982. *Mission im Neuen Testament.* Freiburg: Herder & Herder.

Kiernan, Jim P. 1990. "The Canticles of Zion: Song as Word and Action in Zulu Zion Discourse." *Journal of Religion in Africa* 20/2: 188-204.

Kinney, John. 1979. "The Theology of John Mbiti: His Sources, Norms and Method." *Occasional Bulletin of Missionary Research* 3/2: 65-67.

Kirk, J. Andrew. 1992. *Loosing the Chains: Religion as Opium and Liberation.* London: Hodder & Stoughton.

———. 1997. *The Mission of Theology and Theology as Mission.* Harrisburg, PA: Trinity Press International.

———. 2000. *What Is Mission? Theological Explorations.* Minneapolis: Fortress.

Knitter, Paul. 1974. *Towards a Protestant Theology of Religions: A Case Study of Paul Althaus and Contemporary Attitudes.* Marburg: N. G. Etwert Verlag.

———. 1985. *No Other Name? A Critical Survey of Christian Attitudes toward the World Religions.* Maryknoll NY: Orbis Books.

Koyama, Kosuke. 1984. *Mount Fuji and Mount Sinai: A Critique of Idols.* Maryknoll, N.Y.: Orbis Books.

Krabill, James R. 1990. "Dida Harrist Hymnody (1913-1990)." *Journal of Religion in Africa* 20/2: 118-52.

———. 1995. *The Hymnody of the Harrist Church Among the Dida of South-Central Ivory Coast (1913-1949): A Historico-Religious Study.* Frankfurt: Peter Lang.

Kraemer, Hendrik. 1938. *The Christian Message in a Non-Christian World.* London: Edinburgh House.

Kraft, Charles H. 1979. *Christianity in Culture: A Study in Dynamic Biblical Theologizing in Cross-Cultural Perspective.* Maryknoll, NY: Orbis Books.

———. 1991a. *Communication Theory for Christian Witness.* Maryknoll, NY: Orbis Books.

———. 1991b. "Allegiance, Truth and Power Encounters in Christian Witness." *Evangelical Missions Quarterly* 27:258-265.

———. 1992. "Allegiance, Truth and Power Encounters in Christian Witness." In Jan A. B. Jongeneel, ed., *Pentecost, Mission and Ecumenism: Essays in Intercultural Theology,* 215-30. Berlin: Peter Lang.

Kreider, Alan. 1994. "Worship and Evangelism in Pre-Christendom." The Laing Lecture 1994. *Vox Evangelica* 24: 7-38.

Kuitse, Roelf S. 1993. "Holy Spirit: Source of Messianic Mission: Biblical Theological and Historical Foundations." In Wilbert R. Shenk, ed., *Holy Spirit: Source of Mission: Goal of Messianic Mission,* 106-29. Scottdale, PA: Herald.

Küng, Hans. 1976. *On Being a Christian.* New York: Doubleday.

———. 1987. *The Incarnation of God.* New York: Crossroad.

———. 1995. *Christianity: Essence, History, and Future.* New York: Continuum.

Lash, Nicholas. 1985. "What Might Martyrdom Mean?" *Ex Auditu* 1:14-24.

Lee, Robert. 1981. "Service to Christ and Country." In Ray A. Moore, ed., *Culture and Religion in Japanese-American Relations: Essays on Uchimura Kanzo, 1861-1930.* Ann Arbor: University of Michigan, Center for Japanese Studies.

Legrand, Lucien. 1990. *Unity and Plurality: Mission in the Bible.* Maryknoll, NY: Orbis Books.

Levision, John R., and Priscilla Pope-Levision. 1994. "Toward an Ecumenical Christology for Asia." *Missiology* 22/1: 3-18.

Libby, Bob. 1998. "How Many Anglicans Are There?" *Lambeth Daily* 8: 4.

Listowel, Judith. 1974. *The Other Livingstone.* Sussex, England: Julien E Friedman.

Loewen, Jacob A. 1975. *Culture and Human Values: Christian Intervention in Anthropological Perspective.* Pasadena, CA: William Carey Library.

Lohfink, Gerhard. 1984. *Jesus and Community.* Philadelphia: Fortress; New York: Paulist.

MacInnis, Donald, ed. 1972. *Religious Policy and Practice in Communist China.* New York: Macmillan.

Mackay, John A. 1933. *The Other Spanish Christ: A Study in the Spiritual History of Spain and South America.* New York: Macmillan.

———. 1953. *God's Order: The Ephesian Letter and the Present Time.* London: Nisbet.

Manikam, Rajah B., ed. 1954. *Christianity and the Asian Revolution.* Madras: Joint East Asia Secretariat of the International Missionary Council and the World Council of Churches.

Manson, Thomas W. 1962. In Matthew Black, ed., *Studies in the Gospels and the Epistles.* Manchester: University Press.

Manson, T. W. 1955. *Jesus and the "Non-Jews."* London: Athlone.

Mariz, Cecilia. 1994. *Coping with Poverty.* Temple University Press.

Marsden, George M. 1972. "Evangelical Social Concern—Dusting off the Heritage." *Christianity Today* 16/16: 8-11.

———. 1980. *Fundamentalism and American Culture.* New York: Oxford University Press.

Marshall, Paul. 1997. *Their Blood Cries Out: The Worldwide Tragedy of Modern Christians Who Are Dying for Their Faith.* Introduction by Michael Horowitz. Dallas: World Publishing.

Martin, David. 1990. *Tongues of Fire: The Explosion of Protestantism in Latin America.* Oxford: Basil Blackwell.

Marty, Martin. 1986. *A Short History of Christianity.* Philadelphia: Fortress.

Mazrui, Ali. 1980. *The African Condition: A Political Diagnosis.* London: Heinemann.

Mbiti, John S. 1969. *African Religions and Philosophy.* London: Heinemann.

———. 1970a. "The Future of Christianity in Africa 1970-2000." *Communio Viatorum* 13/1-2: 34f.

———. 1970b. "Christianity and Traditional Religions in Africa." *International Review of Mission* 59/236: 438.

———. 1970c. *Concepts of God in Africa.* London: SPCK.

———. 1971. *New Testament Eschatology in an African Background.* Oxford: Oxford University Press.

———. 1972. "Some African Concepts of Christology." In Georg F. Vicedom, ed., *Christ and the Younger Churches,* 51-62. London: SPCK.

———. 1979. "Response to the Article by John Kinney." *Occasional Bulletin of Missionary Research* 3/2: 68.

———. 1986. *Bible and Theology in African Christianity.* Nairobi: Oxford University Press.

McGavran, Donald. 1955. *The Bridges of God: A Study in the Strategy of Missions.* London: World Dominion Press.

———. 1970. *Understanding Church Growth.* Grand Rapids: Eerdmans.

———. 1974. *The Clash between Christianity and Culture.* Washington, D.C.: Canon.

———. 1980. *Understanding Church Growth.* Rev. ed. Grand Rapids: Eerdmans.

McInnis, Donald, ed. 1972. "The Christian Manifesto: Direction of Endeavor for Chinese Christianity in the Construction of New China." *Religious Policy and Practice in Communist China.* New York: Macmillan, 158-60.

McKinney, William. 1989. "Of Centers and Margins." *Cutting Edge* 18/1: 1, 3, 4.

McManners, John, ed. 1990. *The Oxford Illustrated History of Christianity.* Oxford: Oxford University Press.

McQuilkin, J. Robertson. 1973. *How Biblical Is the Church Growth Movement?* Chicago: Moody.

Meyer, Ben F. 1986. *The Early Christians: Their World Mission and Self-Discovery.* Wilmington, DE: Michael Glazier.

Middleton, John. 1983. "150 Years of Christianity in a Ghanaian Town." *Africa* 1-8.

Míguez Bonino, José. 1997. *Faces of Protestantism in Latin America.* Grand Rapids: Eerdmans.

———, ed. 1984. *Faces of Jesus.* Maryknoll, NY: Orbis Books.

Miles, Jack. 1992. "Blacks vs. Browns, the Struggle for the Bottom Rung." *The Atlantic Monthly* (October).

Miller, Larry. 1993. "The Church as Messianic Society: Creation and Instrument of Transfigured Mission." In Wilbert Shenk, ed., *The Transfiguration of Mission: Biblical, Theological and Historical Foundations,* 130-52. Scottdale, PA: Herald.

Minear, Paul S. 1971. *The Obedience of Faith: The Purpose of Paul in the Epistle to the Romans.* London: SCM.

Moltmann, Jürgen. 1967. *Theology of Hope.* London: SCM.

———. 1974. *The Crucified God.* New York: Harper & Row.

———. 1990. *The Way of Jesus Christ: Christology in Messianic Dimensions.* San Francisco: Harper.

Molyneux, K. Gordon. 1990. "The Place and Function of Hymns in the EJCSK." *Journal of Religion in Africa* 20/2: 153-87.

Mulago, Vincent. 1968. "Christianisme et culture africaine." In C. G. Baëta, ed., *Christianity in Tropical Africa.* London: International African Institute and Oxford University Press.

Mulder, Dirk C. 1985. "Alle geloven op éen kussen?" In R. Bakker, R. Fernhout, J. D. Gort, and A. Wessels, eds., *Religies in Nieuw Perspective,* 137-151. Kampen: Kok.

Munck, Johannes. 1959. *Paul and the Salvation of Mankind.* London: SCM; Atlanta: John Knox [1977].

Murray, Gilbert. 1935. *Five Stages of Greek Religion.* Republication, Mineola: NY: Dover, 2002.

Neely, Alan. 1989. "Mission as Kenosis: Implications for Our Times." *The Princeton Seminary Bulletin* 10: 202-23.

Neill, Stephen. 1957. *The Unfinished Task.* London: Edinburgh House.

———. 1968. *The Church and Christian Union: Bampton Lectures for 1964.* London: Oxford University Press.

———. 1970. *Christian Faith and Other Faiths.* New York: Oxford University.

Netland, Harold. 1988. "Toward Contextualized Apologetics." *Missiology* 16/3:289-303.

———. 1991. *Dissonant Voices: Religious Pluralism and the Question of Truth.* Grand Rapids: Eerdmans.

———. 1994. "Response to 'The Uniqueness of Christ: Shaping Faith and Mission' by Charles Van Engen." Unpublished paper presented at the ETS/EMS Midwestern Conference, March 17-19, Chicago, IL.

Newbigin, Lesslie. 1966. *Honest Religion for Secular Man.* Philadelphia: Westminster.

———. 1969. *The Finality of Christ.* Richmond, VA: John Knox.

———. 1977. "What Is 'A Local Church Truly United'?" *The Ecumenical Review* 29/2: 124.

———. 1978. *The Open Secret: Sketches for a Missionary Theology.* Grand Rapids: Eerdmans.

———. 1981. "The Gospel among the Religions." In Gerald Anderson and Thomas Stransky eds., *Mission Trends No. 5: Faith Meets Faith,* 3-19. Grand Rapids: Eerdmans; New York: Paulist.

———. 1986. *Foolishness to the Greeks: The Gospel and Western Culture.* Grand Rapids: Eerdmans.

———. 1987. "Can the West Be Converted?" *International Bulletin of Missionary Research* 11/1: 2-7.

———. 1989a. *The Gospel in a Pluralist Society.* Grand Rapids: Eerdmans.

————. 1989b. "Religious Pluralism and the Uniqueness of Jesus Christ." *International Bulletin of Mission Research* 13/2: 50-54.

————. 1990. "Religous Pluralism and the Uniqueness of Jesus Christ." In J. I. Packer, ed., *The Best in Theology*, 4:267-274. Carol Stream, IL: Christianity Today.

————. 1991. *Truth to Tell: The Gospel as Public Truth*. Grand Rapids: Eerdmans.

————. 1992. "The Legacy of W.A. Visser 't Hooft." *International Bulletin of Mission Research* 16/2: 78-82.

————. 1994. "Ecumenical Amnesia." *International Bulletin of Mission Research* 18/1: 2-5.

————. 1995. *The Open Secret*. Revised edition. Grand Rapids: Eerdmans.

Nicholls, Bruce. 1979. "The Exclusiveness and Inclusiveness of the Gospel." *Themelios* 4/2: 62-69.

————. 1984. "A Living Theology for Asian Churches." In Bong Rin Ro and Ruth Eshenaur, eds., *The Bible and Theology in Asian Contexts: An Evangelical Perspective on Asian Theology*, 119-38. Taichung: Asia Theological Association.

————. 1990. "The Church and Authentic Dialogue." In Harvie Conn, ed., *Practical Theology and the Ministry of the Church, 1952-1984: Essays in Honor of Edmund P. Clowney*, 255-72. Phillipsburg, NJ: Presbyterian & Reformed.

Nicholls, B., ed. 1985. *In Word and Deed—Evangelism and Social Responsibility*. Grand Rapids: Eerdmans.

Niebuhr, H. Richard. 1937. *The Kingdom of God in America*. New York: Harper & Row.

1991 U.S. Hispanic Market. 1991. Strategy Research Corporation, 172-378.

Nolan, Albert. 1976. *Jesus before Christianity*. Cape Town, South Africa: David Philip.

Nyamiti, Charles. 1984. *Christ as Our Ancestor: Christology from an African Perspective*. Gweru: Mambo.

————. 1991. "African Christologies Today." In Robert J. Schreiter, ed., *Faces of Jesus in Africa*. Maryknoll, NY: Orbis Books.

Odagaki, Masaya. 1997. "Theology after 1970." In Y. Furuya, ed., *A History of Japanese Theology*, 113-40. Grand Rapids: Eerdmans.

Ohm, Thomas. 1962. *Machet zu Jüngern alle Völker: Theorie der Mission*. Freiburg: Erich Wevel Verlag.

Oosterwal, Gottfried. 1973. *Modern Messianic Movements as a Theological and Missionary Challenge*. Elkhart, IN: Institute of Mennonite Studies.

Packer, J. I. 1986. "'Good Pagans' and God's Kingdom." *Christianity Today* 30/1: 22-25.

Padilla, C. René, ed. 1976. *The New Face of Evangelicalism*. London: Hodder & Stoughton.

————. 1982. "Bible Studies." *Missiology* 10/3: 319-38.

————. 1985a. *Mission Between the Times: Essays on the Kingdom*. Grand Rapids: Eerdmans.

————. 1985b. "Evangelism and Social Responsibility: From Wheaton '66 to Wheaton '83." *Transformation* 2/3: 27-33.

————. 1986. "Toward a Contextual Christology from Latin America." In C. René Padilla, ed., *Conflict and Context: Hermeneutics in the Americas*, 83-84, 89. Grand Rapids: Eerdmans.

———. 1987. "The New Ecclesiologies in Latin America." *Evangelical Review of Theology* 11/4: 342.

Pannikar, Raimundo. 1978. *Intra-Religious Dialogue*. New York: Paulist.

Pauck, Wilhelm. 1959. "Theology in the Life of Contemporary American Protestantism." In Walter Leibrecht, ed., *Religion and Culture*, 270-83. New York: Harper & Brothers.

p'Bitek, Okot. 1971. *African Religions in Western Scholarship*. Kampala: East African Literature Bureau.

Pelikan, Jaroslav. 1985. *Jesus Through the Centuries*. New Haven: Yale University Press.

Pesch, Rudolf. 1976. *Das Markusevangelium*. Freiburg i. B.: Herder & Herder.

Phan, Peter C. 2003a. *Christianity with an Asian Face: Asian American Theology in the Making*. Maryknoll, NY: Orbis Books.

———. 2003b. *In Our Tongues: Perspectives from Asia on Mission and Inculturation*. Maryknoll, NY: Orbis Books.

———. 2004. *Being Religious Interreligiously: Asian Perspectives on Interfaith Dialogue*. Maryknoll, NY: Orbis Books.

———, ed. 2002. *The Asian Synod: Text and Commentaries*. Maryknoll, NY: Orbis Books.

Phillips, James M., and Robert T. Coote, eds. 1993. *Toward the 21st Century in Christian Mission: Essays in Honor of Gerald H. Anderson*. Grand Rapids: Eerdmans.

Pickard, William M. 1991. "A Universal Theology of Religion?" *Missiology* 19/2: 143-51.

Pinnock, Clark H. 1991. "Acts 4:12—No Other Name under Heaven." In William V. Crockett and James G. Sigountos, eds., *Through No Fault of Their Own? The Fate of Those Who Have Never Heard*, 107-16. Grand Rapids: Baker.

———. 1992. *A Wideness in God's Mercy: The Finality of Jesus Christ in World Religions*. Grand Rapids: Zondervan.

Pobee, John S. 1979. *Toward an African Theology*. Nashville: Abingdon.

———, and Gabriel Ositelu II. 1998. *African Initiatives in Christianity*. Geneva: WAA Publications.

"Poorest of the Americans." 1991. *Catholic Ministry*, a publication of the Diocese of Brownsville (February).

Poulton, John. 1973. *People Under Pressure*. London: Lutterworth.

Quigley, Thomas. 1999. "Anti-Christian Violence in India." *America*, April 3, 10.

Rahner, Karl. 1966. *Theological Investigations*. Vol. V. *Later Writings*. Translated by Karl Kruger. London: Darton, Longman & Todd.

———. 1974. *The Shape of the Church to Come*. Translated with introduction by Edward Quinn. London: SPCK.

———. 1980. "Christianity and the Non-Christian Religions." In John Hick and Brian Hebblethwaite, eds., *Christianity and Other Religions: Selected Readings*, 52-79. Glasgow: Fount Paperbacks.

Ramachandra, Vinoth. 1996. *The Recovery of Mission: Beyond the Pluralist Paradigm*. Grand Rapids: Eerdmans.

Ramsay, William M. 1949. *St. Paul the Traveller and the Roman Citizen*. Grand Rapids: Baker Book House.

Ranger, Terence. 1987. "Religion, Development and African Christian Identity." In Kristen Holst Petersen, ed., *Religion Development and African Identity*, 29-57. Uppsala: Scandinavian Institute of African Studies.

Rhem, Richard A. 1988. "The Habit of God's Heart." *Perspectives* 3/7: 8-11.

Rin Ro, Bong, and Ruth Eshenaureds. 1984. *The Bible & Theology in Asian Contexts: An Evangelical Perspective on Asian Theology.* Taichung: Asia Theological Association.

Robert, Dana L. 1993. "Evangelist or Homemaker? Mission Strategies of Early Nineteenth-Century Missionary Wives in Burma and Hawaii." *International Bulletin of Missionary Research* 17/1: 4-12.

———. 1994. "From Missions to Mission to Beyond Missions: The Historiography of American Protestant Foreign Missions since World War II." *International Bulletin of Missionary Research* 18/4: 146-62.

———. 1998. "Christianity in the Wider World." In Howard Kee et al., *Christianity: A Social and Cultural History*, 563-70. Second edition. Upper Saddle River, NJ: Prentice-Hall.

Roof, Clark Wade, and William McKinney. 1988. *American Mainline Religion.* New Brunswick, NJ: Rutgers University Press.

Roukanen, Mikka. 1990. "Catholic Teaching on Non-Christian Religions at the Second Vatican Council." *International Bulletin of Missionary Research* 14/2: 56-61.

Rouner, Leroy S., ed. 1983. *Foundations of Ethics.* Notre Dame, IN: University of Notre Dame Press.

Runia, Klaas. 1984. *The Present-Day Christological Debate.* Downers Grove, IL: InterVarsity.

Samartha, Stanley. 1981. "The Lordship of Jesus Christ and Religious Pluralism." In G. H. Anderson and T. F. Stransky, eds., *Christ's Lordship and Religious Pluralism*, 19-36. Maryknoll, NY: Orbis Books.

———, ed. 1977. *Faith in the Midst of Faiths: Reflections on Dialogue in Community.* Geneva: World Council of Churches.

Samuel, Vinay, and Chris Sugden, eds. 1983. *Sharing Jesus in the Two Thirds World.* Grand Rapids: Eerdmans.

Sanders, John. 1992. *No Other Name: An Investigation into the Destiny of the Unevangelized.* Grand Rapids: Eerdmans.

Sanneh, Lamin. 1983a. "The Horizontal and the Vertical in Mission: An African Perspective." *International Bulletin of Missionary Research* 7/4: 166.

———. 1983b. *West African Christianity: The Religious Impact.* Maryknoll, NY: Orbis Books.

———. 1984. "Muhammed, Prophet of Islam, and Jesus Christ, Image of God: A Personal Testimony." *International Bulletin of Missionary Research* 8/4: 169-74.

———. 1989. *Translating the Message: The Missionary Impact on Culture.* Maryknoll, NY: Orbis Books.

———. 1993. "Can a House Divided Stand? Reflections on Christian-Muslim Encounter in the West." *International Bulletin of Missionary Research* 17/4: 164-68.

Sanon, Anselme T., and René Luneau. 1982. *Enraciner l'Evangile: Initiations africaines et pédagogie de la foi.* Paris: Les Editions du Cerf.

Sawyerr, Harry. 1970. *God-Ancestor or Creator?* London: Longman.

Scherer, James A. 1968. "Ecumenical Mandates for Mission." In Norman A. Horner, ed., *Protestant Crosscurrents in Mission*, 19-49. Nashville, TN: Abingdon.

———. 1987a. *Gospel Church and Kingdom: Comparative Studies in World Mission Theology.* Minneapolis: Augsburg.

————. 1987b. "Missiology as a Discipline and What It Includes." *Missiology* 15/4: 507-22.

————, and Stephen B. Bevans, eds. 1992. *New Directions in Mission and Evangelization 1: Basic Statements, 1974-1991.* Maryknoll, NY: Orbis Books.

————. 1994. *New Directions in Mission and Evangelization 2: Theological Foundations.* Maryknoll, NY: Orbis Books.

Schlatter, Adolf. 1961. *The Church in the New Testament Period.* Translated by Paul P. Levertoff. London: SPCK.

Schreiter, Robert. J. 1982. "The Bible and Mission: A Response to Walter Brueggemann and Beverly Gaventa." *Missiology* 10: 427-34.

————. 1985. *Constructing Local Theologies.* Maryknoll, NY: Orbis Books.

————. 1990. "Jesus Christ and Mission: The Cruciality of Christology" *Missiology* 18/4: 429-38.

————. 1997. *The New Catholicity.* Maryknoll, NY: Orbis Books.

————, ed. 1991. *Faces of Jesus in Africa.* Maryknoll, NY: Orbis Books.

Scott, Waldron. 1981. "'No Other Name'—An Evangelical Conviction." In G. H. Anderson and T. F. Stransky, eds., *Christ's Lordship and Religious Pluralism,* 58-74. Maryknoll, NY: Orbis Books.

Sebastian, J. Jayakiran. 1998. "Sensitivity and Proclamation: Perspectives on Mission from the Writings of Cyprian." *Mission Studies* 15/2: 40-50.

Semmel, Bernard. 1973. *The Methodist Revolution.* New York: Basic Books.

Senior, Donald. 1984. "The Struggle to Be Universal: Mission as the Vantage Point for New Testament Investigation." *Catholic Biblical Quarterly* 46: 63-81.

————, and Carroll Stuhlmueller. 1983. *The Biblical Foundations for Mission.* Maryknoll, NY: Orbis Books.

Shank, David A. 1973. "The Shape of Mission Strategy." *Mission Focus* 1/3: 1-7. Republished in W. R. Shenk, ed., *Mission Focus: Current Issues,* 118-28. Scottdale, PA: Herald, 1980.

Shenk, Wilbert. R. 1980. *Mission Focus—Current Issues.* Scottdale, PA: Herald.

————. 1983. *Exploring Church Growth.* Grand Rapids: Eerdmans.

————. 1990. "The Origins and Evolution of the Three-Selfs in Relation to China." *International Bulletin of Missionary Research* 14/1: 28-35.

————. 1995. *Write the Vision: The Church Renewed.* Valley Forge, PA: Trinity Press International.

————. 1996. "Toward a Global Church History." *International Bulletin of Missionary Research* 20/2: 51.

Smith, A. Christopher. 1983. "The Essentials of Missiology from the Evangelical Perspective of the Fraternidad Teológica Latinoamericana." Ph.D. dissertation, Southern Baptist Theological Seminary, Louisville, KY.

Smith, Timothy L. 1957. *Revivalism and Social Concern.* New York and Nashville, TN: Abingdon.

Snyder, Howard A. 1975. *The Problem of Wineskins.* Downers Grove, IL: InterVarsity.

————. 1977. *The Community of the King.* Downers Grove, IL: InterVarsity.

————. 1989. *Signs of the Spirit.* Grand Rapids: Zondervan.

————. 1995. *Earthcurrents: The Struggle for the World's Soul.* New York and Nashville, TN: Abingdon.

Song, C. S. 1975. *Christian Mission in Reconstruction: An Asian Analysis.* Maryknoll, NY: Orbis Books.

————. 1984. *Tell Us Our Names: Story Theology from an Asian Perspective.* Maryknoll, NY: Orbis Books.

————. 1987. "God's Grace in the World of Religions." *Perspectives* 2/1: 4-7.

Spindler, Marc. 1988. "Bijbelse fundering en oriëntatie van zending." In Arnulf Camps, L. A. Hoedemaker, M. R. Spindler, and F. J. Verstraelen, eds., *Oecumenische inleiding in de Missiologie,* 137-54. Kampen: Kok.

Stadler, Anton P. 1977. "Dialogue: Does It Complement, Modify or Replace Mission?" *Occasional Bulletin of Missionary Research* 1/3: 2ff.

Stafford, Tim. 1999. "The Criminologist Who Discovered Churches." *Christianity Today* (June 14): 35-39.

Stanton, Graham N. 1985. "Interpreting the New Testament Today." *Ex Auditu* 1: 63-73.

Stine, Philip., ed. 1990. *Bible Translation and the Spread of the Church: The Last Two Hundred Years.* Leiden: Brill.

Stott, John R. W. 1970. *Christ the Controversialist.* Downers Grove, IL: InterVarsity.

————. 1975. *Christian Mission in the Modern World.* Downers Grove, IL: InterVarsity.

————. 1981. "Dialogue, Encounter, Even Confrontation." In G. H. Anderson and T. F. Stransky, eds., *Mission Trends No. 5: Faith Meets Faith,* 156-72. Grand Rapids: Eerdmans; New York: Paulist.

————. 1989. "Taking a Closer Look at Eternal Torture." *World Christian* 8/5: 31-37.

————. 1995. "Twenty Years after Lausanne: Some Personal Reflections." *International Bulletin of Missionary Research* 19/2: 50-55.

————, and Robert T. Coote, eds. 1980. *Down to Earth: Studies in Christianity and Culture.* Grand Rapids: Eerdmans.

Strachan, R. Kenneth. 1968. *The Inescapable Calling.* Grand Rapids: Eerdmans.

Stromberg, Jean, comp. 1983. *Mission and Evangelism: An Ecumenical Affirmation.* Geneva: World Council of Churches.

Synan, Vinson. 1998. "Current News Summary." Religion Today.com.

Taber, Charles R. 1991. *The World Is Too Much with Us.* Macon, GA: Mercer University Press.

————, and Betty J. Taber. 1992. "A Christian Understanding of 'Religion' and 'Religions.'" *Missiology* 20/1: 69-78.

Taylor, John V. 1963. *Primal Vision.* London: Student Christian Movement.

————. 1972. *The Go-Between God: The Holy Spirit and the Christian Mission.* London: SCM.

————. 1981. "The Theological Basis of Interfaith Dialogue." In Gerald Anderson and Thomas Stransky, eds., *Mission Trends No. 5: Faith Meets Faith,* 93-110. Grand Rapids: Eerdmans; New York: Paulist.

Thomas, Norman E., ed. 1995. *Classic Texts in Mission and World Christianity.* Maryknoll, NY: Orbis Books.

Thomsen, Mark. 1990. "Confessing Jesus Christ within the World of Religious Pluralism." *International Bulletin of Mission Research* 14/3: 115-18.

Tillich, Paul. 1980. "Christianity Judging Itself in the Light of Its Encounter with the World of Religions." In John Hick and Brian Hebblethwaite eds., *Christianity and Other Religions: Selected Readings,* 108-21. Glasgow: Fount Paperbacks.

Tippett, Alan R. 1970. *Church Growth and the Word of God.* Grand Rapids: Eerdmans.

Triebel, Johannes. 1988. "Leiden als Thema der Missionstheologie." *Jahrbuch Mission* 20: 1-20.

Trinidad, Saul, and Juan Stam. 1984. "Christ in Latin American Protestant Preaching." In J. Míguez Bonino, ed., *Faces of Jesus: Latin American Christologies.* Maryknoll, NY: Orbis Books.

Troeltsch, Ernst. 1971. *The Absoluteness of Christianity.* Richmond, VA: John Knox.

———. 1980. "The Place of Christianity among the World Religions." In John Hick and Brian Hebblethwaite, eds., *Christianity and Other Religions: Selected Readings,* 11-31. Glasgow: Fount Paperbacks.

Troutman, Charles. 1976. "On Missions as Corporations." Unpublished paper, San Jose, Costa Rica.

Tucker, Ruth A. 1983. *From Jerusalem to Irian Jaya: A Biographical History of Christian Missions.* Grand Rapids: Zondervan.

———. 1987. "Female Mission Strategists: A Historical and Contemporary Perspective." *Missiology* 15/l: 73-89.

———. 1988. *Guardians of the Great Commission.* Grand Rapids: Zondervan.

Turner, Harold W. 1974. "The Contribution of Studies on Religion in Africa to Western Religious Studies." In Mark E. Glasswell and Edward W. Fasholé-Luke, eds., *New Testament Christianity for Africa and the World: Essays in Honour of Harry Sawyerr,* 169-78. London: SPCK.

———. 1977. "The Primal Religions of the World and Their Study." In Victor Hayes, ed., *Australian Essays in World Religions,* 27-37. Bedford Park: Australian Association for the Study of Religions.

Turner, Philip. 1971. "The Wisdom of the Fathers and the Gospel of Christ: Some Notes on Christian Adaptation in Africa." *Journal of Religion in Africa* 4/1: 45-68.

Tutu, Desmond. 1978. "Whither African Theology?" In E. W. Fasholé-Luke et al., eds., *Christianity in Independent Africa.* London: Rex Collings.

Utuk, Efiong S. 1986. "From Wheaton to Lausanne: The Road to Modification of Contemporary Evangelical Mission Theology." *Missiology* 14/2: 205-20.

Van Engen, Charles. 1981. *The Growth of the True Church.* Amsterdam: Rodopi.

———. 1989. "The New Covenant: Knowing God in Context." In Dean Gilliland ed., *The Word among Us: Contextualizing Theology for Mission Today,* 74-100. Waco, TX: Word.

———. 1991a. "The Effect of Universalism on Mission Effort." In William V. Crockett and James G. Sigountos, eds., *Through No Fault of Their Own? The Fate of Those Who Have Never Heard,* 183-94. Grand Rapids: Baker.

———. 1991b. *God's Missionary People: Rethinking the Purpose of the Local Church.* Grand Rapids: Baker.

———, Dean S. Gilliland, and Paul Pierson, eds. 1993. *The Good News of the Kingdom: Mission Theology for the Third Millennium.* Maryknoll, NY: Orbis Books.

———. 1996. *Mission on the Way.* Grand Rapids: Baker.

Verkuyl, Johannes. 1978. *Contemporary Missiology: An Introduction.* Grand Rapids: Eerdmans.

———. 1986. "Contra de twee kernthesen van Knitter's theologia religionum." *Wereld en Zending* 2: 113-20.

———. 1989. "Mission in the 1990s. *International Bulletin of Mission Research* 13/2: 55-58.

_____. 1993. "The Biblical Notion of Kingdom: Test of Validity for Theology of Religion." In Charles Van Engen et al., eds., *The Good News of the Kingdom*. Maryknoll, NY: Orbis Books.

Vidler, Alec. 1985. *The Church in an Age of Revolution: 1789 to the Present Day*. New York: Penguin.

Visser 't Hooft, W. A. 1963. *No Other Name: The Choice between Syncretism and Christian Universalism*. Philadelphia: Westminster.

Viviano, Benedict T. 1988. *The Kingdom of God in History*. Wilmington, DE: Michael Glazier.

Von Campenhausen, Hans. 1974. "Das Martyrium in der Mission." In H. Frohnes and U. W. Knorr, eds., *Kirchengeschichte als Missionsgeschichte. Bd. I: Die Alte Kirche*, 71-85. Munich: Christian Kaiser.

Vroom, Hendrik M. 1989. *Religions and the Truth: Philosophical Reflections and Perspectives*. Grand Rapids: Eerdmans.

Wagner, C. Peter. 1979. *Our Kind of People: The Ethical Dimensions of Church Growth in America*. Atlanta: John Knox.

Walls, Andrew F. 1976. "Towards Understanding Africa's Place in Christian History." In J. S. Pobee, ed., *Religion in a Pluralistic Society: Essays Presented to C. G. Baëta*. Leiden: Brill.

_____. 1978. "Africa and Christian Identity." *Mission Focus* 6/7: 11-13.

_____. 1980. "A Bag of Needments for the Road: Geoffrey Parrinder and the Study of Religion in Britain." *Religion* 10/2: 141-50.

_____. 1981. "The Gospel as Prisoner and Liberator of Culture." *Faith and Thought* 108/1-2: 39-52.

_____. 1991. "Structural Problems in Mission Studies." *International Bulletin of Missionary Research* 15/4: 146-55.

_____. 1996a. *The Missionary Movement in Christian History: Studies in the Transmission of Faith*. Maryknoll, NY: Orbis Books.

_____. 1996b. "Origins of Old Northern and New Southern Christianity." In Andrew Walls, *The Missionary Movement in Christian History*, 68-75. Maryknoll, NY: Orbis Books.

_____. 1998. "Africa in Christian History—Retrospect and Prospect." *Journal of African Christian Thought* 1/1: 8-14.

_____. 1999. "In Quest of the Father of Mission Studies." *International Bulletin of Missionary Research* 23/3: 98-105.

Watson, David Lowes. 1990. *God Does Not Foreclose: The Universal Promise of Salvation*. Nashville: Abingdon.

Wessels, Anton. 1992. "The Experience of the Prophet Mohammed." In Jerald D. Gort, Hendrik M. Vroom, Rein Fernhout, and Anton Wessels, eds. *On Sharing Religious Experience: Possibilities of Interfaith Mutuality*, 228-44. Grand Rapids: Eerdmans.

Westermann, Diedrich. 1937. *Africa and Christianity*. London: Oxford University Press.

Wilson, Samuel, ed. 1980. *Mission Handbook: North American Protestant Ministries Overseas*. Twelfth edition. Monrovia, Calif.: MARC.

The World Mission of the Church: Findings and Recommendations of the Meeting of the International Missionary Council, Tambaram, Madras, India, Dec. 12-29, 1938. London: International Missionary Council, 7.

"World Missionary Conference" (Edinburgh). 1910a. *Report of Commission I: Carrying the Gospel to All the Non-Christian World*. New York.

"World Missionary Conference" (Edinburgh). 1910b. *Report of Commission IV: The Missionary Message in Relation to Non-Christian Religions.* Edinburgh and London: Oliphant, Anderson & Ferrier.

Wright, G. Ernest. 1952. *God Who Acts: Biblical Theology as Recital.* London: SCM.

Wright, N. T. 1975. "Universalism and the World-Wide Community." *The Churchman* 89/3: 197-212.

———. 1979. "Towards a Biblical View of Universalism." *Themelios* 4/2: 54-58.

Yamauchi, Edwin. M. 1972. "How the Early Church Responded to Social Problems." *Christianity Today.* November 24.

Yates, Timothy. 1994. *Christian Mission in the Twentieth Century.* Cambridge, UK: Cambridge University Press.

Yinger, J. Milton. 1957. *Religion, Society and the Individual.* New York: Macmillan.

Yoder, John Howard. 1983. "'But We Do See Jesus': The Particularity of Incarnation and the Universality of Truth." In Leroy Rouner, ed. *Foundations of Ethics,* 57-75. Notre Dame, IN: University of Notre Dame Press.

ZIRRCON Trust. 1997. *Annual Report.* Masvingo, Zimbabwe: n.p.

Index

accompaniment: as model of mission, 67

action: and theology, 141

Adveniat, 38

African Christianity, 95-115
 affinity with early Gentile Christianity, 143, 144
 and African theological literature, 97-100
 as example to the church, 112-15
 and scholarship, 100-103
 and the West, 109-12

African Independent/Initiated Churches (AICs), 54, 55
 and restoration of the environment, 126
 Idowu and Mbiti on, 107, 108

African life: as object of study for African Christianity, 103-9

Allen, Roland
 and New Testament patterns for mission, 222
 on Judaizing viewpoint of missionary movement, 122

amulets, 181

anakephalaiōsis, 74

ancestors: and Asian and African mission studies, 123, 124

Anderson, Allan: on ancestor cult and confrontation with the Spirit, 125, 126

anticolonialism: in China and Africa, 51, 52

Antioch, church at: and unity, 79-80

Appiah-Kubi, Kofi: on AICS, 125

Ariarajah, Wesley: and salvation of non-Christians, 154

Asian Christianity, 206-18
 revival of, 53, 54
 and solidarity in communion, 216-18

Asian Synod (Special Assembly of the Synod of Bishops for Asia), 209

Banda, Hastings, 50

baptism, 27, 28

Barth, Karl: and exegesis of Great Commission, 17-30

Base Christian Communities, 56, 129, 229, 230

Bediako, Kwame: missionary theology of culture, 123

Bible: and mission, 226-29

Billy Graham: and mass evangelism, 238, 239

Boff, Leonardo: and priesthood of all believers, 130

Boniface VIII: and Christendom, 203

Bosch, David: and paradigms of mission, 66

Bread for the World, 38

British Baptist Mission Society, 37

Bruce, F. F.
 on "God-fearers," 85
 on Jewish and Gentile Christianity, 83

Bujo, Bénézet: and ancestor theology, 123, 124

Campenhausen, Hans von: on martyrdom and mission, 10

capitalism
 global, 63, 64; and migration, 64, 65
 and missions, 42

Carey, William
 on Great Commission, 4
 missionary work of, 36, 38, 45

Caritas, 38

Catholic Church: and mutuality in mission, 41

Catholic Patriotic Association, 51

265

Catholicism
  Asian, 208-9
  in Latin America, 56
Catholics: and biblical foundations of
  mission, 5, 6, 228
China: and missions, 51
China Christian Council, 54
Cho, David Yonggi, 60
Christendom
  versus Christianity, 202-204
  new, 204-6
  post-fifteenth-century manifestations
    of, 203, 204
Christian Aid, 38
Christianity
  continuity of, 137
  cultural diversity in, 57, 58
  and dialogue with world religions,
    158, 159
  European dominance of, 202, 203
  Gentile: as model for theology of
    mission, 143, 144
  global: and local churches, 57-60
  historical variety of, 133-37
  indigenous forms, in Africa, 53, 54,
    55
  influence of local cultures on, 57
  Japanese: and identity, 120
  and nationalism, 48-52
  new, 204-6
  Northern, 205, 217
  and renewal of Vatican II, 55
  shift from Europe to Southern
    Hemisphere, 47-60, 140, 204,
    205, 206
  Southern, 204, 205, 206, 217
  as translation movement, 241, 242
  and world religions, 149, 150, 151,
    157, 158, 221, 222
Christology
  African, 104
  Docetic, 127
  and missiology, 223
  missional, 126-29; and *missio Dei*,
    128, 129
  and soteriology, 170
church
  Antiochene: and unity, 79-80
  as communion of communities,
    211

early Corinthian, 86-88
early Roman, 88-89
Gentile, 81-84
house: and mixed community, 78
  of Jews and Gentiles, 76-89
kingdom-centered, 209, 211
as local community of equals, 211-
  13
mission as dialogue, 213-14
participatory nature of, 212, 213
as prophetic sign, 213
unity in Jesus Christ, 74-76
Church Growth movement, 91
Church World Service, 38
circumcision party, 81-84
colonialism, revolt against, 49, 50, 52,
  53, 57, 67
communalism, missional, 36
Community of Latin American
  Evangelical Ministries, 41
compassion: as missionary motif, 7-9,
  14
congresses, missionary, 41
connection: and community of memory,
  70, 71
consciousness, continuity of, 137
continuity/discontinuity model, 122
conversion: and identity, 119, 120
Costas, Orlando
  and missional ecclesiology, 129
  and theology of contextual
    evangelization, 129
Council for World Mission, 41
Counter-Reformation, new, 206
Cox, Harvey: on fundamentalism and
  experientialism, 124, 125
Cragg, Kenneth: on engagement with
  culture, 122
creation, liberation of, 126
Crowther, Samuel Ajayi: on book of
  Leviticus, 142
cultural conditioning, 140-45
cultural pluralism: and lordship of Jesus
  Christ, 172, 173
cultural relativity, 169
culture
  and encounter with the gospel, 117,
    118, 119
  and faith, 167-69
  local: and Christianity, 57

Previously Published in
The American Society of Missiology Series

The American Society of Missiology Series, published in collaboration with Orbis Books, seeks to publish scholarly work of high merit and wide interest on numerous aspects of missiology—the study of Christian mission in its historical, social, and theological dimensions. Able proposals on new and creative approaches to the practice and understanding of mission will receive close attention from the ASM Series Committee.